Praise for *Investment Biker*

"[Written with] charm and incisive financial commentaries."
—*Entertainment Weekly*

"A great book about a motorcycle adventure . . . This Indiana Jones of finance made his bundle in exotic foreign stock. His book is especially timely now that country funds are all the rage. Unlike the rest of us, he actually visits these places before he invests."
—*Time*

"Rogers's advice is sage: Stick with nations where hardnosed bureaucrats push fiscal reforms, maintain sound currencies, advocate free trade, and stay out of areas best left to the private sector. And Rogers also dishes up ample adventure."
—*Business Week*

ABOUT THE AUTHOR

JIM ROGERS co-founded the Quantum Fund and retired at age thirty-seven. Since retirement, he has served as a professor of finance at Columbia's Business School, and as a commentator in electronic and print media worldwide. Rogers is also the author of *Adventure Capitalist* and *Hot Commodities*.

He lives in New York City.

ALSO BY JIM ROGERS

Adventure Capitalist

Hot Commodities

Investment Biker

Visas

Entries/Entrées   Departures/Sorties

IMMIGRATION & ETHNIC AFFAIRS

5 JUN 1991
DEPARTED
AUSTRALIA

-04-02
BLOEMFONTEIN
AIRPORT CONTROL

REPÚBLICA ARGENTINA

12 JUN 1991

IMMIGRATION
ARRIVED
23 APR 1991
PERTH AIRPORT
024 V
AUSTRALIA

J

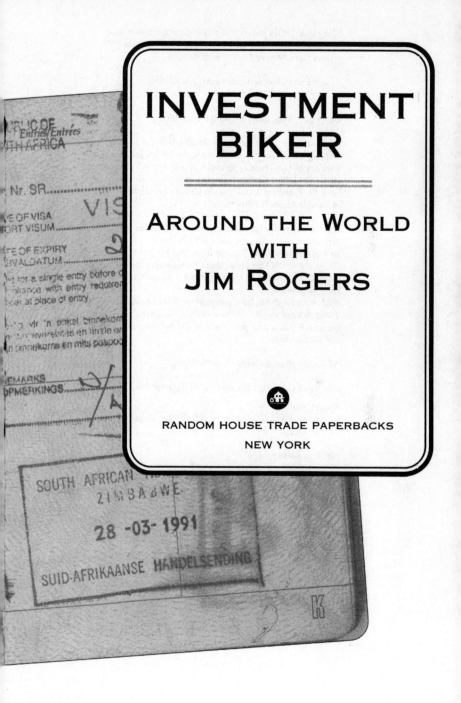

INVESTMENT BIKER

AROUND THE WORLD WITH JIM ROGERS

RANDOM HOUSE TRADE PAPERBACKS

NEW YORK

2003 Random House Trade Paperback Edition

Grateful acknowledgment is made to the following for
permission to reprint previously published material:
MCA MUSIC PUBLISHING: Excerpt from "See See Rider" by "Ma" Rainey.
Copyright © 1943 by MCA Music Publishing, a division of MCA, Inc.
Copyright renewed. All rights reserved. International copyright secured.
Used by permission.
TIMES BOOKS AND BARTHOLOMEW: Maps from *The New York
Times Atlas of the World, New Family Edition,* to illustrate
the text. Reprinted by permission of Times Books
and Bartholomew.

All photos from the author's collection.

Library of Congress Cataloging-in-Publication Data

Rogers, Jim
Investment biker: around the world with Jim Rogers
by Jim Rogers.
p.   cm.
ISBN 0-8129-6871-9
1. Investment.   2. Adventure.   3. Travel.   4. Political
Analysis.   5. Political Philosophy.   I. Title.
[B]

Printed in the United States of America

Random House website address: www.atrandom.com

9 8 7 6 5 4

Book design by Carole Lowenstein

For those of you
consumed by the passion
to see it all and
fathom the world
as it really is.
And for C. Rider,
of course.

I would like to thank Donald Porter,
without whose insight and editorial guidance
this book could not have been written.
Thanks also to Marshall Loeb
at *Fortune*.

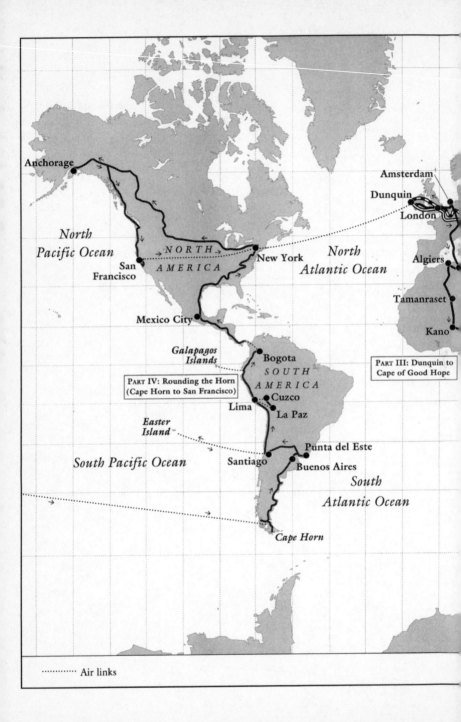

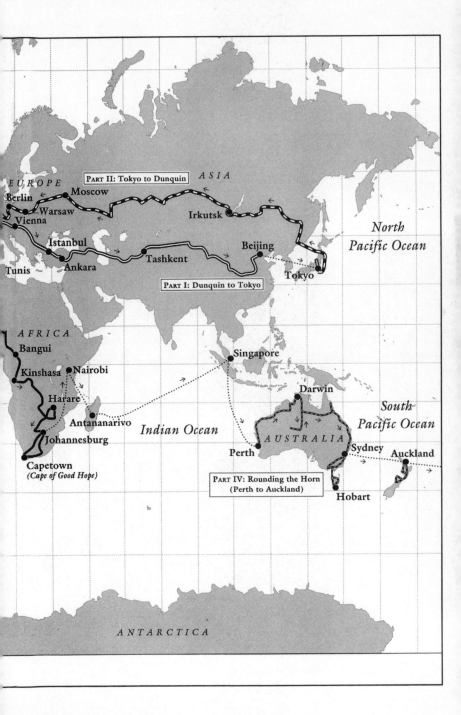

CONTENTS

PART I: DUNQUIN TO TOKYO

PART II: TOKYO TO DUNQUIN

PART III: DUNQUIN TO THE CAPE OF GOOD HOPE

PART IV: ROUNDING THE HORN

Contents

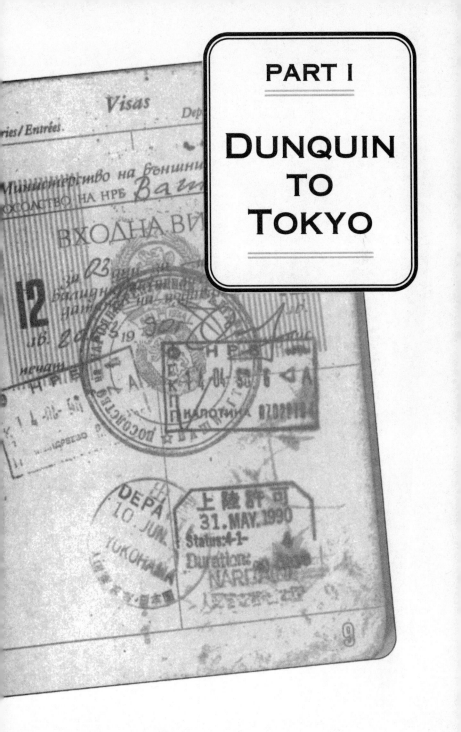

PART I

DUNQUIN
TO
TOKYO

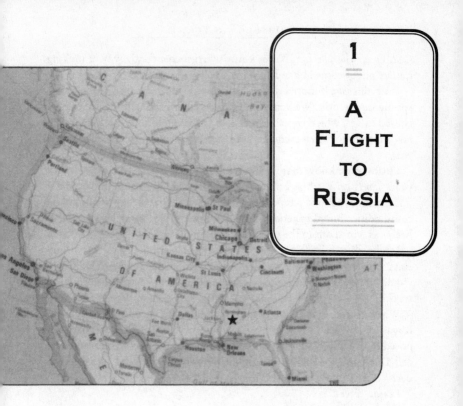

1

A
FLIGHT
TO
RUSSIA

I WAS BORN IN 1942, the eldest of five brothers. My parents met in the thirties at the University of Oklahoma, where both belonged to academic honor societies. During the war, my father served as an artillery officer in Germany. After the war, he joined his brother in running a factory in Demopolis, Alabama, a state in which my people had lived since the early nineteenth century.

With the birth of so many boys, my mother, an only child, was rapidly in over her head. She made us competitive and full of high jinks. The five of us learned drive from our father, who taught us to push to make happen whatever it was we wanted to do. From him we learned how to work hard.

My entrepreneurial efforts started early. I had my first job at the age of five, picking up bottles at baseball games. In 1948 I won the concession to sell soft drinks and peanuts at Little League games. At a time when it was a lot of money, my father gravely loaned his six-year-old son one hundred dollars to buy a peanut parcher, a start-up loan that put me in business. Five years later, after taking out profits along the way, I paid off my start-up loan and had one hundred dollars in the bank. I felt rich.

(I still have the parcher. Never know when such a dandy way of making money might come in handy.)

With this one hundred dollars, the investment team of Rogers & Son sprang into action. We ventured into the countryside and together purchased calves, which were increasing in value at a furious rate. We would pay a farmer to fatten them, and sell them for a huge profit the following year.

Little did we know that we were buying at the top. In fact, only twenty years later, on reading one of my first commodity chart books, did I understand what had happened. My father and I had been swept into the commodities boom engendered by the Korean War. Our investment in beef was wiped out in the postwar price collapse.

I did well in our isolated little high school, finishing at the top of my class. I won a scholarship to Yale, which thrilled and terrified me. How would I ever compete with students from fancy Northeastern prep schools?

When I went to Yale, my parents couldn't take me up to New Haven. It was too far. So on that first Sunday, when all college students are supposed to call home, I got on the phone and told the operator I wanted to call Demopolis, Alabama. She said, "Okay, what's your phone number?"

I said, "Five."

She said, "Five what?"

"Just five."

She said, "You mean 555-5555?"

"No," I said politely, "just five."

She said, "Boy, are you in college?"

"Yes, ma'am."

She blazed, "I don't have to take this from you, college boy!"

Finally, persuaded I meant no disrespect, she gave it a try. This was back in the days when the Connecticut operator had to get the Atlanta operator who had to get the Birmingham operator who finally got the Demopolis operator on the phone.

My Connecticut operator spoke first. "I've got a boy on the line who says he's trying to reach phone number five in Demopolis, Alabama."

Without missing a beat, the Demopolis operator said, "Oh, they're not home now. They're at church." The New Haven operator was stunned speechless.

As my college years sped by, I considered medical school, law school, and business school. I loved learning things, always have, and I certainly wanted to continue to do so. In the summer of 1964 I happened to go to work for Dominick & Dominick, where I fell in love with Wall Street. I had always wanted to know as much about current affairs as I could, and I was astounded that on the Street someone would pay me for figuring out that a revolution in Chile would drive up the price of copper. Besides, I was poor and wanted money in a hurry and it was clear there was plenty of money there.

At Yale I was a coxswain on the crew, and toward the end of my four years I was lucky enough to win an academic scholarship to Oxford, where I attended Balliol College and studied politics, philosophy, and economics. I became the first person from Demopolis, Alabama, to ever cox the Oxford-Cambridge Boat Race on the Thames.

I began to use some of what I had learned in my summer job on Wall Street, investing my scholarship dollars before I had to turn them in to the Balliol bursar.

After Oxford I went into the army for a couple of years, where I invested the post commander's money for him. Because of the bull market, I made him a tidy return. I came back to New York and went to work on Wall Street.

I eventually became the junior partner in a two-man offshore hedge fund, which is a sophisticated fund for foreign investors that both buys and sells short stocks, commodities, currencies, and bonds located anywhere in the world. I worked ceaselessly, making myself master as much as possible of the worldwide flow of capital, goods, raw materials, and information. I came into the market with six hundred dollars in 1968 and left it in 1980 with millions. There had been costs, however. I had had two short marriages to women who couldn't understand my passion for hard work, something my brothers and I had inherited from our father. I couldn't see the need for a new sofa when I could put the money to work for us in the market. I was convinced, and I still am, that every dollar a young man saves, properly invested, will return him twenty over the course of his life.

In 1980 I retired at the ripe old age of thirty-seven to pursue another career and to have some time to think. Working on Wall Street was too demanding to allow reflection. Besides, I had a dream. In addition to wanting another career in a different field, I wanted to ride my motorcycle around the entire planet.

I'd always wanted to see the world once I realized Demopolis, Alabama, really wasn't the center of the Western World. My longtime lust for adventure probably came from the same source. But I saw such a trip not only as an adventure but also as a way of continuing the education I had been engaged in all throughout my life—truly understanding the world, coming to know it as it really is. I would see it from the ground up so that I would really know the planet on which I walked.

When I take a big trip, like a three-month drive across China, Pakistan, and India, the best way to go is by motorcycle. You see sights and smell the countryside in a way you can't from inside the box of a car. You're right out there in it, a part of it. You feel it, see it, taste it, hear it, and smell it all. It's total freedom. For most travelers the journey is a means to an end. When you go by bike, the travel is an end in itself. You ride through places you've never been, experience it all, meet new people, have an *adventure*. Things don't get much better than this.

I wanted a long, long trip, one that would wipe the slate clean for me. I still read *The Wall Street Journal* and the *Financial Times,* and I wanted to wean myself away from the investment business. I wanted a change of life, a watershed, something that would mark a new beginning for the rest of my life. I didn't know what I would do when I got back, but I wanted it to be different. I figured a 65,000-mile ride around the world ought to be watershed enough.

In 1980 it was difficult to circle the planet—you couldn't get anywhere. There were twenty-five to thirty wars going on, and the Communists wouldn't let you pass through Russia or China. If I were going to go around the world, it was going to be like everything I do: I was going to do it to excess or not at all. My dream was to cross six continents completely—west to east across China, east to west across Siberia, from the top of Africa to the horn, across Australia's vast desert, and from the bottom tip of Argentina right up to Alaska.

In 1984 and 1986 I went to China to approach officials about crossing the country. I even rented a motorcycle, a little 250-cc Honda, and drove around Fujian province to see what I could learn. Fujian wasn't all that big, maybe the size of Louisiana, but with 26 million inhabitants it had almost seven times Louisiana's population. I drove and flew to several provincial capitals, and put two thousand miles on that bike as research. Then, at last, in 1988, I drove clear across China on my own bike.

Back in New York, I went to see the Russians, as I'd often done before. Russia was still the big stumbling block to a drive around the world. I wrote letters and got others to write testimonials on my behalf. I hit an absolute stone wall. I'd go down to Intourist, and Ivan Kalinin, the director, would tell me it wasn't even conceivable. There's nothing out there in Siberia, he'd say, except bears and tigers and jungle and forest. Nobody goes there, nobody *wants* to go there, and in fact, all the people the Russians sent there had wanted to come back.

To my astonishment, no Russian I'd met had ever been to Siberia or knew anyone who had. No Soviet citizen seemed to have a clue as to what was in his equivalent of our nineteenth-century Wild West, just as most New Yorkers today know nothing about Alaska. Take the train, the Russians told me—the Trans-Siberian Railroad—or fly. Only a fool or a madman would drive.

I finagled a proper introduction to the Russian ambassador in Washington, but even he was no help.

I was slowly getting the point. Siberia wasn't like driving across the United States, one boring freeway after another. It would be different. Maybe they were right. Maybe there wasn't much in the way of roads. But you couldn't drive around the world without going through Siberia, and if I were to fulfill my dream, I'd have to find a way across.

The maps told me that Siberia was seven thousand miles wide, about twice the width of the United States. As far as anybody knew, it had fewer than 20 million people, about the size of New York State's population, but nobody knew for sure because no one had ever gone there and counted noses. I figured it was no wilder than northern Canada and Alaska, which would be fine with me.

In a desperate moment, I took a videotape of my trip to China to Ivan, the Intourist official, hoping it would show him that I was serious. He smiled wearily as he took it, but he actually watched it. The next time I came, he said, "There is one group you could write." He didn't know the English name of it, but he looked up the group in his official handbook. He found that he couldn't translate the group's name, so he just wrote it down in Russian, along with the address and everything else. It seemed to be an esoteric group called Sovintersport. I took the paper home, Xeroxed it, and pasted it on an envelope containing a letter in English stating that I wanted to drive my motorcycle from the Pacific Ocean to Moscow and on to Poland.

I said I'd meet any conditions the group wanted to impose—stay wherever they wanted, take any escort they needed to send along, even soldiers—I didn't care. I had to go. Whenever I looked at a globe, Russia's huge landmass jumped out at me. If I didn't go across Russia I couldn't tell myself I had actually gone around the world, and if I didn't go around the world, it wasn't the trip I wanted to take. I didn't have much hope. Over the years I'd sent out twenty letters like this one.

Months later—after I'd forgotten about sending the letter—an answer arrived. It said, "Dear Mr. Rogers: Yes, you can drive across Russia. When would you like to go?" Three or four lines, two paragraphs, and a Mr. Valeri Sungurov was saying yes.

I couldn't believe it. It was as if I'd been sitting outside a door, knocking on it every day for nine years, and it never opened, and then one day the damn door did open and a guy said, "Oh, come on in." How could he have known I'd been standing there for nine years?

I promptly flew over to Russia to meet the people who'd said yes. I kept asking Oksána, the translator, "Do these guys mean this?" and she would reply, "Yes, what's the matter with you?"

"Is this really gonna happen?"

"Yes, it's going to happen. Why are you so perplexed and curious and disbelieving and questioning?"

Sovintersport was a Russian sports group that sponsored one-of-a-kind international sporting events. I'd been beating up on the diplomatic and tourist channels, and here were these Russians who considered long-distance motorcycle riding a sport. Lesson number one in going around the world: Know enough about the culture you're entering so you can maneuver in it; otherwise you'll get locked out.

I was elated, still a little disbelieving—could you really trust the Russians? Would one hand know what the other had agreed to? I might arrive at the border and be turned away.

But this might be my only chance. This trip was something I desperately wanted to do. I was going around the world! Full of excitement, I flew back to New York in December of 1989, planning to set off the following March.

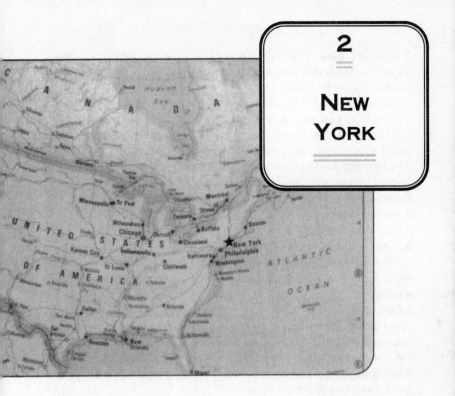

"HOW'D YOU LIKE to go around the world?" I asked Tabitha, my companion over the past few years.

"They said yes?" she asked. She'd traveled with me across Pakistan and India the year before, two saddlebags and one bike, five thousand miles, and she'd loved it.

"I want to leave in March; that's four months," I said. "Are you game? Africa, the Sahara, Siberia, across the Andes, and this time you can go to China, too."

"What about my job?" she said. It was a job she loved, administering the grants for a small foundation, a great job for someone not long out of college.

"Quit it," I said. "This is a once-in-a-lifetime trip."

I loved the way she ran her hand through her long blond hair, scrunched up her face, and cocked her head to think.

"How can we carry enough stuff?" she asked. "Some of these places—we'd need parts, gas, extra tires."

She was right. I'd driven BMW motorcycles for the past twenty years. Being hopeless mechanically, I wanted the bike that needed the fewest repairs. Still, when I looked at the worldwide list of BMW repair shops, it didn't include Zaire or Siberia or China, stretches of thousands of miles along the world's worst roads.

"The ideal would be to take two bikes," I said.

"But I don't know how to drive a bike," she said.

"Maybe you could learn. There's a motorcycle school in Queens."

She winced, not answering. She loved riding with me as a passenger. The motorcycle associations said 90 percent of their riders were men, but that was changing. There were even a couple of magazines now devoted to women's motorcycle riding. At twenty-three, Tabitha was as adventuresome as any woman I'd known. Now in my mid-forties, I would have twenty years of motorcycle driving experience to draw on; Tabitha would have her youth.

"If something happens to one bike," I went on, "the trip won't be over. You take the driving lessons, and we'll both sign up for the BMW mechanics course so if we break down in the middle of the jungle, we can fix the bikes."

While I had sometimes spied her in the background as she was growing up, I first really met Tabitha Estabrook when her mother, Biffie, an old friend, dragged her over to my house so I, who taught finance at the business school at Columbia University, could tell her it was in her best interest to go to business school.

She was a tall, leggy blonde who had grown up on the Upper West Side of Manhattan where, at the all-female Nightingale-Bamford School on the East Side, she had absorbed the fashionable political ideas of her time and place: that in an enlightened society the state would fix almost all of society's problems. The Republican Party was an enemy of decency, a temple to greed, possibly the Great Satan Himself. Her father had been a Navy pilot after college, and now he was practicing law. As a schoolgirl, caught in the middle of her parents' bitter and nasty divorce, she found Nightingale-Bamford to be a surrogate parent at an important time, and she continued to have great affection for her alma mater. At Amherst she fashioned her own major, an interdisciplinary course featuring Islamic studies.

At that first meeting we were attracted to each other. Even though I taught at the business school, I told her what I tell all my students, that she shouldn't go to business school, that it was a waste of time. Including opportunity costs, it would cost her or her parents more than a hundred thousand dollars, money better spent starting a business, which would succeed or fail, either of which would teach her more about business than would sitting in a classroom for two or three years listening to "learned professors" who had never run a business prate on about doing so.

I asked her out, one thing led to another, and we began to see a lot of each other.

We kept discussing the trip over the next few days, and she began to plan as if she were going. It was natural for me to take her along. I'd made many long-distance trips—across Europe, the United States, India, China, and to Alaska along the Alcan Highway—and often I'd taken my current woman friend.

However, while she continued to be enthusiastic, as the week wore on I began to wonder about her driving her own bike. Yes, she once traveled on the back of my motorcycle from San Francisco to New York, but five hundred miles a day on a superhighway was no preparation for what we were planning. Sure, the roads in Pakistan had been bad, but there too she'd been merely a passenger.

"I've changed my mind," I announced one night at dinner. "I don't think it's a good idea for you to drive your own bike. It's too difficult for a beginner. Remember how bad the roads were in India and Pakistan? The ones in China, Siberia, and Africa are going to be even rougher."

She shot me a hard glance. "You don't think I'm tough enough?"

"No, I didn't say that. This is just a long, long trip. This is the longest and toughest ride of all."

"I can do it."

I sighed. What had I started? "A rider needs several thousand miles—several tens of thousands of miles—under her belt for something like this. The pace we'll have to keep up, the terrible roads, the weeks—*months*—of driving day after day will wear you out. You need experience. I remember how I was as a beginner. One time I came off an interstate, for God's sake, and shot off into a cornfield because I was green and wasn't paying enough attention. The first time I was on a gravel road the wheel skidded out from under me. I had bruises and raspberries everywhere. Well, in many of these places, we're going to *wish* we had something as good as a gravel road."

"We're not leaving for three months. I'll practice before we go."

I took a deep breath and launched in. "Look, I'm not explaining this well enough. On the China trip I set out from Turpan to Hami with a film crew in a bus behind me. This was to be two hundred fifty miles, a quick day. We didn't take much food or water because we were assured the road was fine and we'd arrive in Hami before dark. Well, that day turned out to be seventeen hours across roads that were a nightmare. We couldn't stop because there was nowhere *to* stop—no place to buy anything to eat. We were in the desert, so there was no water. It was like being halfway across a sea—you are in trouble no matter what you decide to do. Once we were out there, we had to push on. I think we'd all have died if we'd stopped. Two thirds of the way there, the film crew was ready to give up, and they were riding in the bus."

She stared at me so fixedly, I wasn't sure what she was thinking.

I continued. "There're going to be times on this trip when we'll have to bust a gut to keep going, and it's going to be hard, the hardest thing you've ever done. Half the world—more than half the world—is still rough, wild, unpaved, savage."

Her eyes seemed to stare through me as she thought this over. "You don't think I'm tough enough."

"I think you're plenty tough, but you might not have enough experience, even by the time we set out, for such a long, hard trip."

"I'll work and make myself ready, Jim. We've traveled thousands of miles on your bike. I have a pretty good idea of what I'm getting into."

"But the pace. I run six miles a day to keep fit. You know enough to know this will wear you out as well as beat you up. There's no way you can build up enough stamina in just three months."

"I think I can."

"You also know I'm a real pusher sometimes. I have to be. Like on that Hami drive, when I had to make sure we made it. As a matter of fact, the same damn thing happened the next day. A simple two-hundred-fifty-mile drive from Hami to Turpan took another seventeen hours."

"Jim, I'll keep up."

I was still not sure she knew what she was getting into, not sure I knew what *I* was getting into. "We can't go around the world driving three or four hours a day."

Now she gave me a direct look. "Jim, if you don't want me to come, say so. Go alone."

"No, I didn't say that. I'd love you to come. It'll be wonderful having you along. But we're going over the world's worst roads, through some of its harshest weather, across the Sahara and the Andes, through epidemics in places where there aren't hospitals, telephones, airports, or even telegrams, where there are bandits, terrorists—who knows what."

Over the next few days we looked on the darker side of the trip.

We discussed the possibility that we might get killed. Tabitha's reaction was that she could get killed in New York, too. As for me, I expected to make it or otherwise I wouldn't have planned to set out.

I had to figure out what to do with my investments while I was gone. Investment markets are volatile beasts, and you have to keep an eye on your positions. They've always fascinated me. One of the first things I noticed about them was that they went down as well as up, and I remembered how excited I was when I learned you could sell them short—sell what you don't own, and profit from their fall as well as from their rise. Where we were going there wouldn't be phones, telexes, or faxes, much less daily newspapers. Most of my investments had always been long term, so I didn't need to make any major moves. I cut back on my shorts, and I kept no futures positions at all.

Then, early in 1990, most of my money was in utility stocks, U.S. government bonds, and foreign currencies, and I pretty much left it where it was. I owned utility stocks, mainly distressed ones with nuclear plants such as Illinois Power and Niagara Mohawk, because I was convinced they'd hit bottom and would solve their problems. I thought U.S. interest rates were headed south, so I was bullish—optimistic—on bonds and bearish—pessimistic—on the dollar, that is, I expected the price of bonds to rise and that of the dollar to fall. I figured the politicians would do everything they could to keep the economy going. Since they're not very smart, all they really know how to do is cut interest rates. I bought foreign currencies, mainly certificates of deposit denominated in guilders or deutsche marks, reasoning that the dollar would go down as the politicians cut interest rates.

As an American, I hated to see this happen. But as an investor about to set off around the world, I had chanced upon the perfect investment scenario, because these were holdings I wouldn't have to watch on a daily basis. I would make money if I were right, and I wouldn't get wiped out if I were wrong, because government bonds and utility stocks might go down, but basically they were secure instruments over time, as were the currencies of sound countries.

Whenever I travel, because of who I am, I notice promising investment opportunities. While this wasn't an investment trip by any means, I suspected I would visit promising stock exchanges. In addition to experiencing the world and its people firsthand in the vivid and close way you can on a motorcycle, I knew I would learn about the markets in Africa, China, and South America, which I felt might explode in the nineties. I was also curious about the markets in Australia and New Zealand. I'd made a lot of money for myself and others by investing in sleepy markets that exploded upward. In fact, one of my first stops on this trip was to be Austria, where I was to give a speech to the investment clients of Oberbank. A few years before, my investment in the Austrian stock market had quintupled in three years. I wondered if I would find more such places to invest. With the world throwing off the shackles of socialism and Communism, I figured not only was the time right, but the opportunity might not be repeated for decades, if ever again in my life.

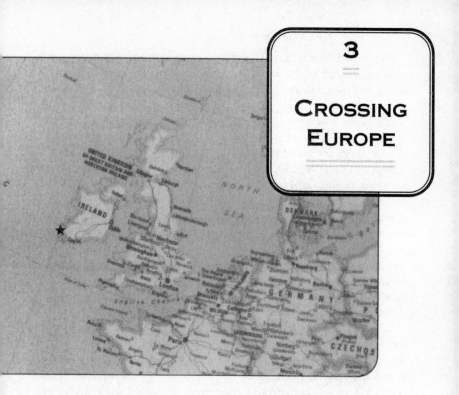

As THE WEEKS SPED BY Tabitha stuck with it. She was going to go. I still worried that the trip was wrong for her and that she would change her mind at the last minute, but March got closer and we kept moving forward as if we were going to do it.

We bought spare cables, mirrors, a carburetor, and extra Michelin tires. We packed rolls of 3M's magic construction tape, two inches wide, clear, and seemingly indestructible, my favorite item for emergency repairs. We got sleeping bags, rain suits, and an extra helmet. Tabitha hunted up the wedding band she'd used on our previous adventures. We'd learned it made traveling a lot simpler if she wore one. We bought maps and plotted routes, as AAA had no trip tickets for getting through the Central Asian Republics, Siberia, and the Sahara. We doped out ways to get money into places without American Express offices and where the sight of a traveler's check would produce suspicious stares. I battened down my office, and I made sure someone would look after my house while I was away. There were vaccinations to take and visas to obtain.

However, I wasn't going to get any letters of introduction, nor did I pack my address book. We made the choice to make this trip serendipitously and spontaneously. We wouldn't depend on old friends, personal or business, to put us up and pull us into gatherings of their friends. It would be more of an adventure to meet our own new friends, friends of the road. In this way we would have a different adventure, maybe better, maybe worse. We would play the trip as we found it.

And still I was holding my breath, hoping Tabitha wouldn't change her mind, hoping she'd come.

Finally the big day arrived. I couldn't believe it. March 25, 1990, was a bright spring day, and I was about to set out around the world. The way we planned the first leg, we'd leave from the west coast of Ireland and drive across Europe and China to Japan, becoming the first ground travelers ever to ride from the Atlantic to the Pacific. The second leg would be to return to Ireland across Siberia, Russia, and Central Europe, another first—the Pacific to the Atlantic. Back to back, the trip would be twenty thousand miles.

Tabitha crated the bikes and took them out to the Aer Lingus freight terminal. I wondered if we'd taken care of everything. Had I given enough instructions about the boiler for next winter? What would the housesitter do if the roof leaked? Too late now. We were in the air. For a few minutes a sense of unreality and strangeness struck me, and I mused on who I was and how I happened to be hurtling over the Atlantic on what might prove to be a fool's errand.

We had pored over our maps and decided that the westernmost point in Ireland was Dunquin, population less than one hundred. It would be our starting point. In Ireland, after uncrating the bikes, we drove from Shannon Airport through the lush countryside to Dunquin, where we looked for the post office.

It was Saturday afternoon when we arrived in the tiny village of thatch-roofed stone cottages and haystacks, its lush green slopes topping slate-gray cliffs. The post office was closed. We knocked on the door anyway. It turned out that the postmistress lived there—just as post-office officials sometimes did back in Alabama when I was a child—and we told her we were traveling around the world and wanted to prove we had been here in Dunquin at the start. Ruddy faced, sixty, and plump, Mrs. Campion reminded me of dozens of Alabama churchwomen, pillars of their communities, who had clucked approvingly as I'd served as an acolyte in the Episcopal church. Would she sell us some postcards, then postmark and date them?

She laughed with Irish delight at the whole absurd idea and invited us in for a cup of tea. She signed the cards, then a Gaelic student who was there signed them, and then we signed them, and then she stamped them. It was like a party. The official start!

Riding through this part of Ireland was wonderful, great for motorcycles, the roads curvy and small and convoluted, green and beautiful. All my life, from my history courses at Yale to my work at Oxford and later on Wall Street, I've studied geography, politics, economics, and history intensely, believing they are interrelated, and I've used what I've learned to invest in world markets. I was on the lookout for investment opportunities, for some country—and its investment market—about to take off, where I could jump in and make five, ten, fifteen times what I put in.

Ireland wouldn't be one of those countries. In fact, the lush countryside made me sad. For centuries Ireland has been in a state of war or rebellion or depression. It seemed such a shame that despite all this beauty, despite the ebullient, warmhearted Irish temperament, there should be for so long this raging instability. All the country had was tourism and pastureland, although I figured with its pool of semiskilled labor, it might make it as the back office for English or German banks, insurance companies, and brokerages.

Ireland is a victim of statism, which my dictionary defines as the concentration of economic controls and planning in the hands of a highly centralized government, and which I further define as the belief that the state is the mechanism best suited for solving most if not all of society's ills, be they health related, natural disasters, poverty, job training, or injured feelings. Statism is *the* great political disease of the twentieth century, with Communist, socialist, and many democratic nations infected to a greater or lesser degree. When the political history of our century is written, its greatest story will be how a hundred variants of statism failed.

When a country is run by the government, when the government not only owns the post office, the telephone system, the railroads, and the utilities but also the service sector and light and heavy industry, the country begins to have the air of the U.S. postal service in the nineties compared with what it was in the fifties. A couple of generations later, all vigor is drained out of that society.

Across the Irish Sea, Margaret Thatcher was the first major example of a leader who reversed this trend. When she was elected in 1979,

Britain was bankrupt from its government's efforts to solve every social problem. She began to sell off the assets and businesses that had been nationalized by the Labour Party, invigorating the country's economy. Ireland was late in beginning this process.

I had last been in Ireland in 1964, while a student at Oxford, and it now shocked me how empty the countryside was. What hit me was that the talented genes kept leaving Ireland, and that they had been leaving for generations. That didn't mean there weren't some smart, delightful, wonderful people here, but there had been a great migration out of the gene pool.

On our second day out, near Cork, Tabitha's bike broke down. I had no idea what was wrong, and for all her mechanic's training, neither did Tabitha.

Back in New York we had both signed up for the BMW mechanics course, but with even the best intentions, I had never made a single class. Other things were always more pressing. Besides, we both knew she was far more mechanically oriented than I was. I can't operate venetian blinds without getting tangled in the cord. Tabitha not only had time and a mechanical bent, but her father had taught her a lot about machinery, how machines worked. This was one more aspect that had attracted me to her.

Before we left, we had hired her BMW instructor, Scott Johnson, who had a passion for these motorcycles, to come over and give her extra lessons, private tutorials. Over several winter weeks Tabitha worked with him in the side yard of the house. Late in the frigid days, sometimes at night under a lamp's yellow glare, they'd take a bike apart, put it back together, and then take it apart again.

While he showed her what each mysterious part did and how it worked, I was doing a million other things. I was the host of a TV show about economic affairs in addition to teaching finance at Columbia. But most of my attention had gone into organizing my investments and devising ways to put my New York life in the deep freezer while we were gone.

Unfortunately, all Tabitha's training had been in the classroom and not on the road. She could strip down an engine and put it back together, but she couldn't diagnose what was wrong when it broke down. In this case, we needed practical street smarts, not theoretical expertise.

Along came a local motorcycle gang, dressed the way they are everywhere in the world. Barry O'Keefe and Kevin Sullivan, the leaders, turned out to be wonderful folks, just good old motorcycle trash like us. They loaded Tabitha's bike into a truck and fixed it in five minutes at their shop. The bike looked good, black with white racing stripes on the fairing, chrome exhaust pipe gleaming. They invited us to a dive called the Mojo Pub, where we had a party.

We crossed Ireland and headed for England, exultant.

After a week in England, I was antsy to leave for Europe. I needed to get to Linz to speak to Oberbank's clients about developments in Central Europe.

As we had been to Europe many times, we zipped across its familiar face, a thousand miles in a few days. During the 527 miles from Paris to Munich we were pummeled by cold spring rains, no fun on a motorcycle but a real-world consequence of being close to the road. I led, and Tabitha complained about doing such a long distance in one day, but I was sure she would get used to the pace.

I had fond, fond memories of Austria and its stock market, where I'd made one of my best coups.

Six years before, believing the time was right to invest in Vienna, the sleepy former capital of the Austro-Hungarian Empire, I had put out feelers by calling the New York office of Creditanstalt, its largest bank. I asked the manager how I could go about investing in his country's stock market.

"We don't have a stock market," he said.

I laughed. This was music to my ears. The largest bank in the country—and the New York rep didn't even know he had a stock market!

I knew there was one and that big changes were taking place in Austria. The bank manager's ignorance showed me how wonderfully obscure the stock market was, just what I like as an investor.

I assured him that his country had a stock market and asked if he could find out how I could buy shares. It was hopeless dealing with him. But that just whetted my appetite. The largest bank in Austria and no one knew how to buy shares on its stock market!

I knew what was going on in Germany—that it was becoming an industrial powerhouse—and how Austria, like Germany, was loosening its socialistic chains.

In November of 1984 I went to Austria. I went to the stock exchange. Nobody was there. It was dead, open only a few hours a week.

Finally I found the one guy in charge of the stock market at the Creditanstalt Bank's main office, Otto Breuer. One guy handling shares, without a secretary, in the country's largest bank. I felt as though I were in knee-high cotton.

The Austrian exchange had less than thirty stocks listed, and it had fewer than twenty members. Back before the First World War there had been four thousand members on the Austro-Hungarian stock exchange. Then it had been the largest stock market in Central Europe, dominant, as New York and Tokyo are today.

I got Otto to take me to see the government official in charge of the stock market, Werner Mehlberg, who assured me there would be changes made in the laws that would encourage people to invest in stocks. The government recognized that it had to have a capital market.

"What changes?" I asked, masking my excitement.

Lower taxes on dividends, said Herr Mehlberg. We're going to make the dividends tax-free if you reinvest them in stocks. Give tax credits for investing in stocks. Give special provisions in the laws for pension funds and insurance companies to invest in stocks, which they hadn't had before.

Other countries had done these things, and they had achieved dramatic results. These were copycat measures. The Austrians had seen the German stock market going up. But at the same time, I thought about the portfolio managers in Germany. They read German, while Americans might not, and these German portfolio managers knew where Austria was, practically a suburb of Germany. If this market started to move they would pile in and drive it up even higher.

But ever cautious—the first rule in investing is not to lose any capital—I went to the head of an Austrian labor union and asked him about the position of the socialist party—capitalism's loyal opposition, so to speak—on all of this. He told me the socialist crowd was in favor of these changes. They didn't like stock markets, but they knew they were necessary to make the country go. That was it—no opposition from the opposition. I decided to pile in.

My attitude is, if you believe in a country, you should buy shares of every decent stock on its exchange. If you've got the right concept going for you, they're all going to move up together. I bought shares in everything that had a solid balance sheet—a home-building construction company, finance and manufacturing companies, banks, other construction firms, and a big machinery company.

A few weeks later I was on the *Barron's* Roundtable, an annual forum for discussing investment ideas. I reminded the other members that the year before, I had invested in Germany, but this year the country to invest in was Austria. I laid out my reasons.

The paper comes out on Saturday morning. Saturday, Sunday went by, everything was quiet. On Monday morning Otto Breuer, the guy without the secretary at the Creditanstalt, came in late. His desk was covered with phone messages, and the market was going through the roof. Calls were pouring in from London, Munich, New York: "Buy me Austrian shares."

Otto had no idea what was going on. People just kept calling from everywhere—*Barron's* is read all over the world—wanting to buy shares on this dead stock exchange. Finally, somebody said to him, "Hey, don't you read *Barron's?*" Of course he didn't, because this was a backwater job. The market started to move up, which naturally attracted even more interest.

Now, I can't move a stock market. All I can do is point out the reality of a situation. It was one of those things, a simple idea, but once you looked at it, it was dead clear and everybody piled in.

To this day people say I kissed the sleeping beauty and woke her up. The smart ones say that, while the dumb ones think I actually did something magical. But everybody said what a beautiful thing it was when the princess woke up, because everybody made so much money. The stock market went up 125 percent that year, and then went up more and more.

Well, when the Austrians figured out that I was Prince Charming, the Creditanstalt invited me to speak at their quarterly forum, at which Kissinger had spoken not long before—a forum where I would definitely be heard.

So I went, and I said, "This ain't over yet, folks; hang on. You are all gonna make a whole lot more money in the Austrian market. This thing is big. You're going from a state of gross undervaluation to a normal valuation, and your economy's growing. Just because it's double up now doesn't mean more money's not going to be made."

The newspapers gave this lots of coverage. The Creditanstalt people rented me a motorcycle and I, the "eccentric Jim Rogers" according to the newspapers, drove up to Prague. I finally sold out of Austria in the spring of 1987—the market was up 400 percent or 500 percent by then—because I was worried about stock markets around the world. I was worried about a financial crisis, yet the Austrian market was one of the last ones I sold.

Now the Austrians had asked me back to make another speech. I was eager to get to Linz—I prefer to ride hard and arrive where I have to be and relax—but the closer I got the less keen I was on speaking.

The flattery of being called the father of the Austrian stock market was nice, but this time around I was terribly bearish on Austria and all of Central Europe.

The Austrian stock market was ripe for collapse, and like people everywhere, those involved weren't going to be happy to hear the bad news.

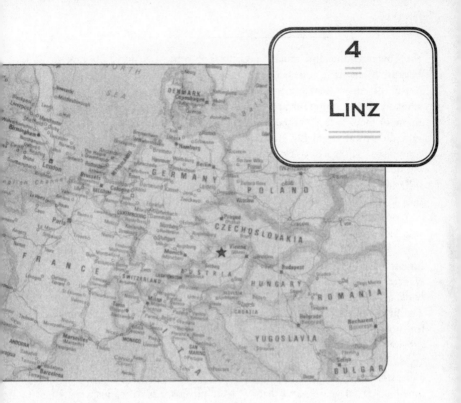

THE BERLIN WALL had just fallen, and everybody in the global market in early 1990 was certain that Central Europe—historically defined as that central part of Europe west of European Russia and the Ukraine—was going to be the next economic miracle, another Southeast Asia.

The consensus bullish argument went like this: The stock markets in Germany and Austria had historic ties to Central Europe, where their companies had owned businesses. The only neutral country between the eastern and western blocs of Europe, Austria was a natural crossroads. Vienna had been the economic and political gateway to Central Europe historically and geographically, and it would flourish as these new democracies grew. As late as the early twentieth century, Vienna was the capital of the Austro-Hungarian Empire, which over the centuries had dominated Central Europe. The Austrians had maintained closer ties to Central and Eastern Europe than had Germany, which had been the enemy. Plus, during the Cold War all the world's spies used to go through Vienna because it was a neutral city and it was right there.

I didn't see any of it this way. I thought anybody who put money into the Soviet Union and much of Central Europe was going to lose it because of the strife and chaos to come. There wasn't one legitimate border in the entire area. All its borders were settled in 1945 by victorious armies either granting rewards or extracting revenge, and I didn't expect many of them to last. As the Central Europeans discovered that democracy didn't automatically create prosperity, the politicians would print money to win votes. The resulting inflation and economic collapse would only heighten ethnic hostilities and lead to constant strife. Hyperinflation would turn Central Europe into a South American–type economy long before it could become the next Southeast Asia.

Word was leaking out about my ideas. An Austrian magazine article said Sleeping Beauty's prince thought Central Europe was going to collapse. Suddenly this little bank that had invited me to speak, the ninth largest bank in Austria, had a tiger by the tail: Everybody in Austria wanted to come to Linz for the speech. It had originally been for the bank's own customers, but now it had to hire the biggest hall in town. The bank sold it out and had to install video monitors outside the hall for those who couldn't get in to watch.

So we rolled into Linz, and I got up there in my black leather jacket and bow tie and told them how I saw it. Central Europe was going to be a disaster. I said the Austrian stock market had been going up for some time—seven fat years—and that we were now at a point of hysteria. I described the classic signs: All the university students wanted to do was go into the stock market. People were leaving their jobs to go into stock market work because it was such an easy and wonderful way to make a living. By every traditional measure—low dividend yields, high price-earnings ratios, staggering volume of trades—a top was near. This was a classic speculative bubble—only a pinprick would be needed to burst the balloon.

"This is coming to an end," I said, "and you'd better be selling, because it's gonna go down by at least fifty percent. I don't know if it's going to happen next week or next month, but it's gonna happen over the next few months."

Several questions from the audience: "Aren't you just saying this because you've sold short our market and want it to go down?"

I previously had said publicly that I was short the Austria Fund, which was the only way you could short the Austrian stock market. If the market fell, I would make a profit.

"I'm trying to explain to you that there is going to be a major change coming in your market that has nothing to do with whether I'm alive and well or have never been here," I explained.

There were more hostile questions from the audience, because nobody wanted this to happen. Why was I saying this? they muttered; this wasn't nice. "Why are you ruining our country?" they said. "We only invited you back because we thought you would say nice things."

They didn't want to look at the facts, but only at the idea that a big new market was opening up, that freedom was coming. They forgot that democracy doesn't equal prosperity, nor could they see that when the expected prosperity didn't arrive, the new democratic leaders would be blamed. All these countries—Hungary, Poland, Romania, Yugoslavia, Bulgaria, and Czechoslovakia—had huge foreign debts, among the highest in the world on a per-capita basis. None of these countries had a thing to sell. After all, their industries had produced only shoddy goods for almost forty years, which they had sold to captive markets in the COMECON. Except in the coming tourist boomlet, nobody in the West was going to buy anything—not a wristwatch, much less a car—from these countries.

Expectations would be aroused, and next time there wouldn't be Ceauşescu to shoot or Communists to throw out. One of history's lessons is that truly downtrodden peoples do not rise up, but hell hath no fury like suppressed peoples whose expectations have been aroused. And now that their expectations were piqued, this fury would have to find a target. The ethnic, national, and religious rivalries that had plagued the area for centuries would erupt again. None of the borders in Central Europe were rational—historically, linguistically, religiously, or ethnically. Could anyone explain why Moldavia was part of the USSR and not Romania? The Moldavians wanted to be part of Romania, while the Hungarians and Germans who were dumped into Romania desperately wanted out, and for good reason. Yugoslavia, an artificial conglomeration of six countries, had never been a nation except for a few forced decades in the twentieth century, and certainly wasn't one now.

History was on the march and nobody wanted to listen.

The next day Tabitha and I left. The Austrian stock market fell off a point or two as a result of my speech—nothing spectacular, or we might never have gotten out. However, there was a big controversy in the press. Because no one was allowed to short Austrian stocks, there were no bears in the Austrian market. Nobody wanted it to go down.

It was shoot the messenger all over again. People never want to hear bad news—never want to hear what upsets their view of life. Back in the oil boom days, guys on Wall Street would tell me oil was going to one hundred dollars a barrel, and I'd tell them it was impossible, that when the price got too high the same thing would happen that always happened with a high price: Somebody would find more of whatever it was, or somebody else would make a substitute. Consumption would go down. People would lower their thermostats and wear sweaters. The Wall Street types would get mad and call me crazy.

They will always tell you, "This time it's different." I hear that a lot, but it's *never* different. It's just a different situation. Trees don't grow to the sky, stock markets don't go up forever, and high prices cut back demand. With prices high, a million guys pile in to figure out how to take advantage of all that money, bringing in supply and eventually driving down the price. No one has ever repealed the law of supply and demand, and no one ever will—not Republicans, Democrats, Communists, or capitalists. It's a law of nature, a mechanism many governments can't seem to understand or trust to make things right. So in the United States we had to endure gas lines because the government thought it could legislate price. Well, it can't, or at least not for very long.

I T WAS CLEAR AND BRIGHT the day we pushed toward Hungary, a little cool because this was April and we were coming out of the mountains.

What struck me on nearing the border was what a vast, flat plain we were approaching—lots of farms, lots of farm buildings, broad, flat fields. Historically, all the way to the Ukraine this was the breadbasket of Europe, the Kansas and Nebraska for Vienna and Berlin.

I realized as we came down out of the mountains and onto the plains how often borders followed geographical features and changes such as rivers, mountains, lakes, deserts. Here the border ran along the edge between the mountains and the fertile plains.

Coming out of the first border checkpoint toward the second, I was leading. We slowly drove along a big S-curve covered with a long oil slick—all Communist cars leak oil. I checked Tabitha in my rearview mirror, and she was leaning to the right, accelerating, as you're supposed to coming out of a curve.

When I next checked my rearview, I saw her bike bouncing in the air from its right-side crash bars to its left, and then back onto its right—but no Tabitha!

I panicked, pulled to the side, and looked back. Her bike was in gear, now on its left side, but I couldn't see her. The bike bounced upright. With its throttle fixed and back wheel turning, the bike's gyroscopic tendency made it bounce back upright, then over again, up and down, up and down. Every time the back wheel touched the ground it gained new thrust.

Where was Tabitha? The bike was still moving on the other side of the two-lane road, into oncoming traffic, which scattered out of its way. She was gone and that damn bike was still flopping around.

I jumped off my bike and raced back. She was on the ground next to the road, struggling to get up.

I was terrified. I pictured her bloody, torn, ripped, this beautiful woman I loved. What had I done? I'd rarely traveled with another cyclist before, much less an inexperienced one. Had I put her through something she couldn't handle? Scarcely a week into the trip and here she was injured, possibly maimed.

But she sprang up and said she was okay. Relief flooded through me. As she pulled off her helmet I saw she wasn't bloody, not even scratched. Her leathers, boots, gloves, helmet, and the crash bar shielding the engine and her legs had all worked, protecting her as they were supposed to—plus, she'd been lucky.

Yards away, the bike was on its side, still in gear, its rear wheel still turning. She was so little hurt that she was able to run with me to it.

We flipped off the emergency switch and gas cocks and pulled it upright to stop any gas leaks. The Hungarians had left their cars and were gaping. When it was clear that we were okay, they waved and got back in their cars and drove on.

I was worried about Tabitha. She was more worried about the bike because she thought she was okay. But maybe she had a concussion and didn't know it. Sometimes these things didn't show up for a day or so. Maybe her parents had been right. Her mother had said this was madness; her father had put his foot down, even though at seventeen he had gone to Europe and, against his parents' specific instructions, bought a motorcycle and toured about for the summer. Maybe I should have found a soldier of fortune to come along, or should have done this alone.

After she assured me three or four times that she was okay, I had to buy it. We eyeballed the bike and it looked okay, too. We were delighted to find that it started up right away. I looked Tabitha over again to see if she had holes in her leathers and was hurt some place and didn't feel it. I figured we had been going twenty to thirty miles an hour, not at high speed, but she didn't know how to handle an oil slick because of her inexperience. No tears in her leathers, and on second inspection the bike again seemed to be fine.

Here near the border there was no place to stop for a cup of coffee or to rest, so there was little to do but press on to Budapest. If something was wrong with Tabitha internally, better to be closer to a large city than out here in the middle of farmland.

So we set out again. I had to hand it to her: I thought her driving might change or falter after the spill, but I noticed nothing in my mirror. Same steady course as before. We did have a recovery period because we were in a queue at the border shortly thereafter, but then we barreled along to Budapest. Such courage told me she was the right person to take with me. After all, at the beginning of any trip like this, there were bound to be problems. Still, the crash gnawed at me. These weren't bad roads, not compared with what was coming up in the Central Asian Republics and China. Maybe a thousand miles of practice before starting out to motorcycle around the world wasn't enough. Had my bullheadedness and optimism pushed Tabitha into a trip for which she wasn't ready? I pushed the thought aside. I had no choice.

More farmland, more plains. It didn't take a genius to see that despite Hungary's glorious past as the center of an empire, agriculture was its future. With a market of only 10 million people, it wouldn't be easy to set up a manufacturing base, and it would be even harder to train Hungarians, used to the commercial standards of Communism, to produce high-quality manufactured goods, the hallmark of the nearby Germans.

On the other hand, it made no sense for some of the advanced countries—Great Britain, France, and Germany—to compete with Hungary in agriculture, because they weren't able to. It was absurd that Europe kept trying to subsidize British farmers when so many nearby Hungarians had vast fertile plains.

As it grew dark we pulled into Budapest. Some time ago the city had been two cities, Buda and Pest, one on each side of the Danube, but now it was all one. It had been a major provincial capital of the Austro-Hungarian Empire, and back before World War I, it had been very rich. As I drove through the shadowy dusk, feeling like a Visigoth in battered leathers riding through Rome, I was awed by the beautiful nineteenth- and early-twentieth-century buildings with their classical stone architecture. I figured they would be here forever because the Hungarians didn't have enough money to tear them down and put up new ones. Budapest was going to be a museum. It was built when there had been lavish amounts of money, and then the country had suddenly become poor. By the time Hungary becomes wealthy enough again to afford to tear these buildings down and replace them, they will be too historic and the Hungarians won't allow themselves to destroy them. Prague, too, is in the same boat, a museum for decades to come, frozen in time.

The next day we were off to Belgrade. That morning I had hosted a special for Financial News Network concerning the opening of Hungary. It was supposed to finish up in the morning, but as is typical in Central Europe, we didn't finish till late in the day, and Tabitha and I got a late start. Both of us were unhappy over the delay, and we were hurrying to make up the lost time.

I was still in front. The road got much bumpier, pitted by potholes. It became more winding, with terrible grading, less shoulder, and it wasn't as smooth. I tore along, passing cars and trucks. Tabitha kept falling behind. At one point I passed another truck, accelerated, and looked in my mirror—*no Tabitha!* I kept looking for a few minutes—*nothing!* I pulled over and stopped. No cars, no traffic coming up behind me, and I had passed a slew of cars and trucks. I knew immediately something had happened back there.

Tabitha! I had pushed her and she was inexperienced, which had caused that first spill, and now I had been pushing to get to Belgrade—

I spun around and hightailed it back.

I saw her on the side of the road, off her bike, picking up things. Tools, maps, sweaters, shoes—everything she had been carrying in her saddlebags was scattered over the road. A few Yugoslavs were helping her.

But another miracle—she wasn't hurt! I followed the path of her strewn baggage and looked over into the ravine next to the road, which was ten to twelve feet deep. The bike was at the bottom, at the tail end of a trail of spare parts and jeans and shirts and sweaters.

I saw that Tabitha was all right, as she had been walking around for ten to twenty minutes before I got back. It hit me that she was only twenty-four and didn't know what she was doing. Maybe I didn't know what I was doing, bringing her. Should I call the whole trip off before I led her into a fatal accident?

I had worried about bringing Tabitha from the first day I'd broached the trip to her. Back then I had wanted to take my 1000-cc bike, on which I had mounted a custom seat, radio, extra gas tanks, and heated handlebars. Tabitha had wanted to take my classic 1967 boxer BMW R69US, a great bike but so classic it didn't sport an electric starter, just an old-fangled kick pedal.

It had been fine with me for her to take the bike, but it needed refurbishing, including a crash bar on each side of the motor to protect the rider. There was only one place in the country that could do that kind of work right, and it was in Ohio. So after the driving course and after practicing on the streets of New York, she had taken off alone for Ohio in the middle of winter to get this classic BMW in first-class shape for the mother of all motorcycle trips.

January—rain, snow, and cold. Bursts of wind on the freeway. Ice patches, inviting spills under the wheels of tractor-trailers. I was worried about her. Pretty gutsy, I thought, and dangerous, but as she had put it to me before she left, if she couldn't handle driving to Ohio on a smooth freeway in the middle of winter, she damn sure couldn't make it across the ruts that passed for roads in Zaire and Siberia. The hours passed slowly, and I was anxious to hear her voice every night. The most dangerous time for any motorcyclist is the first six months of driving because she thinks she knows what she's doing, but she doesn't.

She made it, proving to me she had what it took for such a tough trip. On the way back she stopped at her aunt's in Pittsburgh. The aunt and the neighbors were impressed with her young niece driving up on a motorcycle, making her way from Ohio to New York. She didn't tell them what she really had in mind, not wanting to deal with the flap that would have caused.

Now that bike lay in a ravine in Yugoslavia—smashed up! I took a deep breath and climbed down. The bike was a mess. The taillight was torn apart, the luggage rack was bent to hell, and it looked like this was it, this bike had had it. Even one of the spark plugs was bent.

There were a lot of guys standing around, so I commandeered them to come down and help me push it back up onto the road. The front wheel wouldn't turn because the fender was bent into it, so we had to lift and push the bike up the ravine's side.

Tabitha thought the trip was over, that the bike was gone. But when I looked specifically at each part I saw that the bike could be made to run, although it wasn't going to be a pretty sight. The fairing that had been lovingly crafted and pinstriped in Ohio was a mess, but I didn't see any major cracks in the motor or the frame.

Tabitha, however, appeared to be in shock. So much had happened since the spill yesterday that it seemed like an eternity had passed—a border crossing, Budapest, some sight-seeing, and then tearing off toward another border. She berated me for pushing the pace and I accepted it.

It was now six or seven o'clock, dusk. The police showed up and we explained that we had to get to Belgrade, did they know who could take us? They disappeared into a little town and came back with a guy and a trailer, a little trailer. I just said to them, "God Almighty." But I kept in mind that we were now in a Communist country—no parts, no mechanics, no BMW dealers, no nothing. What I did know was that in the past the Yugoslav police had ridden BMW motorcycles, so maybe we could find somebody who remembered how to fix one.

Tabitha climbed onto the back of my bike, and I followed the little trailer carrying her bike. What had happened, she said, resting her face against my shoulder, was that she had tried to pass a truck. After she was past it, another truck had come barreling down at her and she whipped back in as fast as she could, but the bike started fishtailing. She had lost control and went toward the ravine, but fortunately she'd been thrown to the side; otherwise she'd probably have been killed, five hundred pounds of bike on top of her. It was a very, very serious thing, and yet she was fine. If the bike had gone down into the path of traffic coming up behind her, she'd have been run over. She was sad and troubled, almost in shock; she questioned whether she should go home, but didn't know what to do. I was furious with myself for pushing the pace, for getting her into any of this. I vowed to change my behavior.

T HE NEXT DAY, down an old dirt road that could have come out of the Alabama of my boyhood, we found, as I had hoped, a mechanic who had worked on BMWs back when the Yugoslav police had used them. In the makeshift shed behind his house I pointed out to him what he needed to do to make Tabitha's bike run again. He even found an old Honda taillight in his junk box, which we agreed to take. We couldn't afford to be purists now. He would weld the luggage rack back together. We had packed extra spark plugs, but even though we looked through everything, we couldn't find them. Lost in the crack-up, we supposed. The worst part of the damage was done to the fairing, which was smashed.

"Come back at five," the mechanic told us.

After Tabitha was checked over by a doctor, we spent the rest of the day running errands, replacing lost items, and touring Belgrade. It was run-down, seedy, dreary, and gray. It had never had a period of great wealth, but there were some distinguished old buildings. Historically Belgrade had mainly been a provincial center under various empires, but it had been more like a Chattanooga, not an Atlanta or a Pittsburgh. The Communists had run it down further. Its few new buildings were Communist-style architecture—drab, square, gray boxes. No lines, no dazzle, no imagination, just the odd hammer and sickle tacked on.

We got a good night's sleep and were up at five for the drive to Turkey. A couple nights' rest and a day off and Tabitha was her old perky self, ready to ride. I vowed to take it easy.

Even though these Communist countries were drab and gray, the motorcycling itself was fun. Riding the bike, having the wind in our faces, seeing the countryside firsthand made it exciting. There wasn't much to stop and marvel over, but we saw, felt, experienced the fields and roads and the air in a way we wouldn't have by plane, train, or car.

This time I let Tabitha lead and set the pace, and we made great time. I was delighted that we had lost only a day, because I had been mentally mapping out the trip, figuring what would be our problems, trying to anticipate them.

We had a deadline imposed on us by the Chinese ferry system, the Siberian ferry system, and winter. I had conceived of the trip as a two-year summer trip. By moving constantly around the globe and by crossing back and forth from the northern to the southern hemispheres at the right time, I figured we could stay in summer throughout the trip, or at least in late spring and early autumn. However, if we missed the first ferry from China to Japan, we would then likely miss the Siberian ferry.

In the United States, ferries run every day, and if you miss one you wait a few hours for the next. The ferries from China to Japan and from Japan to Siberia go only once a month, and even then not on any regular schedule. If we missed one, it could throw us a month into the Russian winter, possibly two, which could prove fatal to the trip and to us. Napoleon and Hitler both blithely thought they could conquer the Russian winter. As history has shown, they found it was nothing to play around with. Plus, if we were delayed too much, it meant we'd wind up in Europe, Africa, and Australia in the winter. We'd go from a world-wide summer trip to a worldwide winter trip, which was madness. It was urgent that we meet the ferry deadlines.

We reached Bulgaria, our third Communist border. We had allowed hours to cross from one country to another—you never knew what you were going to run into—but the world was changing, and it was a fairly simple crossing.

Shortly after, Tabitha's engine began to run in a raggedy fashion, as if the fuel line were clogged. A drain plug from the engine's right carburetor had fallen out, and it wouldn't hold gas. We searched back along the road for it, but no luck. She rooted in the garbage by the side of the road for something makeshift.

I had visions of having to find another truck to haul us into God-knew-where. Nobody out here would have that damned particular carburetor plug. With this kind of luck we'd never make it to the ferry to Japan. Had I come off half-cocked, with an amateur for a mechanic and without thinking the real problems through?

As I saw it, the problem was that Tabitha had ignored my brilliant advice. I had wanted to buy her a BMW R100RT motorcycle like mine: a heavy 1,000-cc machine with electric starter, cassette deck, heated handlebars—all the comforts of home. More important, it would have been new and less likely to have problems, plus we'd have been using the same spare parts. She'd refused to ride a bike so big and cumbersome and ended up on a classic that wasn't bearing up well.

Tabitha held up something that looked like a muddy black snake.

"What's that?"

"Just what we need," she said. "An old inner tube."

"Come on, Tabitha. That'll never work."

"Get out that magic 3M tape you packed," she said. "I've got an idea."

She cut a piece of rubber and cleaned it. She used the tape to strap it to the bottom of the carburetor. We cranked up the bike. It sounded all right, and no gas was leaking.

She gave me a big smile of triumph, and I had to grin back even though I was worried. The next town was Sofia, but the book said there was no BMW dealer there. The next one was in Istanbul, four hundred miles away, and I saw us stopping every few miles to retape the rubber to the bottom of that carburetor. I made sure we packed the dirty inner tube.

"Let's push it," I said, "see if we can get to Istanbul tonight, get this fixed."

We did push it, and to my amazement we got to Istanbul without the jury-rigged plug coming loose. Tabitha was ecstatic we'd met this problem and conquered it.

At the dealer in Turkey we found the right carburetor plug and we bought spark plugs. Tabitha spent some time with the mechanics going over her bike. Between us and Tokyo, six thousand miles away, there was only one more BMW dealer, and he was in Ankara, only three hundred miles farther on.

We looked around. I had been in Istanbul before, Tabitha had not. She had been an Islamic studies major in college, so to her this was enthralling. She spent a day going from mosque to mosque. I spent the day bringing my log up to date, which is to say I wrote a string of post-cards covering our travels to my parents. Since they save all my post-cards, I have killed two birds with one stone. I did my daily six-mile run, and I got our laundry done, all of which served to pull me together. The trip had been on top of me up to this point, instead of my being on top of the trip.

In the back of my mind I'd had the idea that eventually I would invest in Turkey. Even though it's been the "sick man of Europe" over the past couple of centuries, historically it's been a political and economic cross-roads between Europe and the Middle East. Now that it was becoming reattached to Europe, I couldn't see why it wouldn't be as important as it had been in earlier centuries when trade between the East and West had flourished, especially with the opening of the European community. So I tried to find a reason to put some money here, but I couldn't. Not only was it still in the grip of statism, nothing seemed dramatically cheap, nor was the government on the verge of making some big economic change. True, the market was wildly overpriced and I could sell it short, hoping to profit on the downturn, but selling short requires more attention than being long. I was not in any position to be attentive for the next couple of years.

Tabitha and I assessed how we were doing. She blamed her accidents on the fast pace.

I agreed. We both realized that she needed more experience, so I suggested she stay in front. In fact, I'd wanted her in front from the beginning, but she'd wanted me to set the pace, find the right road, steer around the potholes. Also, I was worried about her getting rear-ended, because to me it seemed she never looked in her rearview mirror. As a truck passed her she would swerve to the right as if she hadn't seen him come up. I would keep muttering, "Look in your rearview mirror."

So, with Tabitha reveling in the Muslim culture, we pushed on. We drove into the Cappadocia region, passing breathtaking views much like those in Arizona and Utah and around the Grand Canyon.

We were now on the last leg of the old Silk Roads, the fabled east-west trade routes from China to Europe that for two thousand years carried Chinese silk, millet, anise, ginger, rosebushes, and mulberry trees west-ward. Through this network of trails and mountain passes the Persians exported dates, pistachio nuts, peaches, dyes, and the resins, frankin-cense and myrrh, into China and Europe. Through here India shipped spinach, the lotus, sandalwood, pepper, and most important, cotton.

Through this route in the thirteenth century Marco Polo, seventeen years old, made his first overland journey into China.

In my mind's eye I saw the early caravans, some of which were composed of a thousand camels and dozens of soldiers. For months at a time these living freight trains would move through some of the harshest landscapes on the planet, impeded by searing, waterless deserts and snow-locked mountain passes. Storms, filling the travelers' mouths, eyes, and ears with sand, would force them to pause for days. As they picked their way over rough, broken paths, they would be assaulted by mountain sickness and snow blindness. Of course bandits, attracted by the rich cargoes, were a danger, too.

We passed thousands of dwellings dug out of lava or sandstone, walls of man-made caves carved into cliffs.

The Christians had dug huge underground cities here, some more than a hundred feet deep, to avoid their enemies. When we examined a map of Turkey, we saw why. This was the only way through this part of the world, because the Black Sea was to the north and the Mediterranean was to the south. Over the centuries any army heading east or west would have pushed through this corridor. The Christian Turks, therefore, had built their cities underground and in the sides of mountains so they would be disguised. These cities had been discovered by travelers over the past five years, and now a tourist boom had started.

I hit a pothole and put a huge dent in my front wheel, which made me worry about the next ten thousand miles. In Ankara I had the dent pounded out and we hit the road again.

Now we would find out how well we'd planned. Not only was there no BMW dealer between here and Japan, there wasn't a single shop from which to buy so much as a spare tire or a spark plug for a Western vehicle—car or motorcycle. Six thousand miles to Tokyo, across mountains and deserts, with nothing more than what was strapped on our rear frames! We had four tires tied to our luggage racks, but once these were gone we'd be out of luck.

We made a dramatic drop to sea level, but the Black Sea, filthy and polluted, wasn't as romantic in reality as we had anticipated. The Communists had poured everything into it, all sorts of garbage and industrial wastes, and neither they nor the Turks cared about environmental protection.

Trabzon was lively and active. From the reactions we provoked—stares and excited talk about the bikes—it was clear that few foreigners had been through here recently. At night a cannon went off to signal *iftar*, the hour to break the Ramadan fast. The calls to prayer started at four in the morning, the cries clear and haunting in the thin early air.

On a trip like this it was impossible to take along much food. When we went into restaurants, naturally the menus were written in Turkish. As usual on these occasions, we used a combination of pidgin English and sign language to ask if we could go into the kitchen. They always said yes. These were big kitchens, as if built in more prosperous times. Usually there was only one stove working, a lot of space, and not much food. The kitchens weren't clean by my mother's standards, but they certainly looked hygienic enough to a hungry traveler. We peered into the pots and pointed. There would always be three or four things—chicken, mutton, maybe duck. We wouldn't eat anything raw. At the refrigerated drink-box we'd point to the bottled water, the soft drinks, or the cold beer.

Then we'd go back to the gray, dingy dining room to wait, where we were given slow and curious country stares. The two of us, in leather jackets and chaps to protect us from the wind, rain, and spills, were like a couple of Martians entering a provincial village.

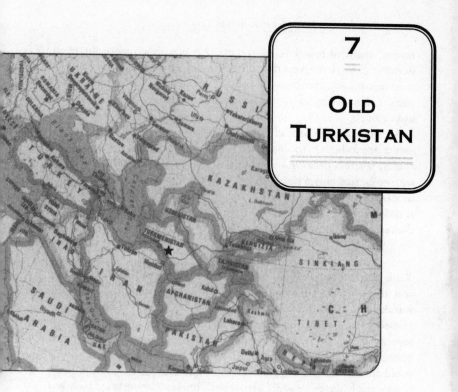

WITH ME LEADING, we headed for that part of the Soviet Union that used to be known as Turkistan.

More terrific driving along the Black Sea, then our first bad rain day since Europe.

As we approached the Georgian border, I decided that if I were a bright young man, I'd come here to the Turkish side and buy up all the land I could find. The map told the whole story: Now that the border was open, the traffic would return to this centuries-old route and there'd be a boom. Land here was selling for nothing, maybe twenty dollars an acre. Sooner or later this spot would be a major gateway to Europe for the Georgians, Armenians, and Azerbaijanis, who have always been the most prosperous people in the Soviet Union.

I didn't buy any land myself, because I invest only in what I believe I'll be able to sell quickly, whether I actually can or not. Besides, this would be work, and I didn't want to work anymore.

At the Georgian border, cars had to pass over a sunken viewing pit so they could be inspected from below, but we crossed without any trouble.

We headed straight for the black market. We rarely had to look far to find it; usually it found us. As you might expect, it is very profitable to deal in the black markets that existed in any country foolish enough to enforce currency exchange controls. The number of such countries was rapidly diminishing as governments came to realize that such controls didn't work.

At that time the official Soviet exchange rate for travelers was six rubles per dollar. On the black market I got between twelve and eighteen rubles, whereas today you might get 400 times that. This was one reason we carried only a small sum in traveler's checks but a healthy stock of cash in a variety of hard currencies: Black marketeers don't take traveler's checks. I preferred the slight risk of being robbed by a thief to the certainty of being ripped off by a state bank.

We headed across Georgia toward the Central Asian Republics, what I still think of as Turkistan—Turkmenistan, Uzbekistan, Kyrgyzstan, Kazakhstan—what romantic names they were!—on toward China.

Along here I could almost see the vast trains of two-humped Bactrian camels, chosen because they could carry four hundred to five hundred pounds of freight and keep up a killing pace across thousands of miles. I could almost hear the clopping of hooves and the jingle of pack bells.

The roads weren't good, narrow with broken pavement, gravel, and small shoulders, even worse than in Turkey, which was pretty damn bad. On a motorcycle you notice every inch of roadway, because any bad patch can cause a skid and a spill. You're closer to the road, physically and mentally, than in a car. Still, I'd driven through many countries without good roads, and out in front again because Tabitha was worried about accidents, I made a certain amount of speed.

As we approached Tbilisi, Tabitha again complained I was going too fast.

This bothered me; I'm always impatient with delays. I figured we were still in the breaking-in stage of the trip, and from my point of view things were getting better.

On all my trips I'd rarely had a companion on another bike. Of course, traveling with anybody means living in close quarters, and people rapidly get on each other's nerves. What is one traveler's essential rest stop is another's intolerable delay. From earlier trips I was used to a certain pace, a certain speed, and when there was no reason to tarry, to me it was normal to drive for eight to ten hours a day and make all the time I could. That way, when I got to an interesting stop, I'd have more time for it.

We talked it over and decided it would be better if she led, as then she could set the pace. If the going got rough, she would slow down.

Spring arrived. In Tbilisi, the capital of Georgia, we saw more evidence of the fall of Communism. Statues of Lenin lay toppled in the street, looking bizarre and out of place.

To my surprise, here at our first stop in the Soviet Union were state-run liquor stores fully stocked with vodka, wine, champagne, and brandy. Then I remembered the vineyards we had passed. It would be hard to deny the citizens of prosperous Georgia, Armenia, and Azerbaijan the fruits of their own vineyards. These were spirits of excellent quality, too. After all, Churchill himself drank Armenian brandy.

Intourist, the Soviet state tourism monopoly, was learning to overcharge wildly. A half-liter of Stolichnaya in the Intourist hotel was nine dollars, four times as much as in shops in the street.

There were lots of new monuments to Georgian heroes. We met some Georgian nationalists, local graduate students. Georgia had always been a hotbed of separatism, we learned. With great pride they told us their country had been a nation for over two thousand years. Historically there were fourteen alphabets in the world, they asserted, and the Georgian was one of them. Of course they had their own calendar. Georgia had always been a trading nation and a crossroads. There was a distinct Georgian form of Christianity that wasn't Russian Orthodox. Stalin had been a Georgian, to their embarrassment. They showed us Stalin's mother's grave. These Georgians felt their country had been stolen by the Russians and tacked onto the Soviet Union, which was true enough.

I saw similarities with the way the United States had tacked on Texas, New Mexico, and California, stealing the territories from Mexico. As those parts of the United States become more Latino, and as the United States begins to suffer its inevitable economic decline, I wonder if we won't see the same things: ethnic strife and a drive for separatism, either a desire to rejoin Mexico or to be independent.

The history of the world tells us that no borders have ever remained stable for long. The United States has been so isolated that we've forgotten this, but if history is any guide, in a hundred years the borders of the United States won't be what they are now.

The Georgians were grasping for their roots. Communism had been imposed on them, a religion, a faith, that had failed. They were forced into a melting pot they never wanted, and now these students were delirious with joy at the thought of liberation. Churches of all sorts were going up, Muslim and Christian. Becoming a man of the cloth was the area's fastest growing profession. I was seeing firsthand what I'd always thought, that most people build their identity on religion or nationalism.

Of course, I was curious as to whether capitalism was pushing up buds. Only small restaurants had opened and a few tiny tailor shops, but you could feel the beginning of change. Georgia had always been a merchant area and of a capitalist bent.

We decided to stay here for a few days. This was the rhythm we would develop on this trip, to drive till we found something interesting and then stop for some time. Meeting one Georgian led to meeting others—professors, writers, filmmakers, publishers, and minor government officials—who all wanted to talk about the massacre. A year before, in April 1989, there had been a street festival celebrating Georgia's nationhood—a lot of kids out dancing and playing the guitar and serenading, that sort of thing. It was spring, and it had been going on for a few nights. This was not a demonstration, because this crowd wasn't that far advanced politically; this was still a Communist, military-controlled state. But the damn local general sent in the tanks, at two o'clock in the morning. All these young people dancing in the square and he sent in the tanks. About fifty were killed.

We went home with a publisher, Alex Zaza, who showed us an underground film about the massacre. A Russian filmmaker had been in town and shot the entire thing. People had run every which way, panicked, and tanks rumbled by. We saw an interview with the father of a girl who had been killed by the Communist soldiers. He kept saying, "What'd they kill her for? My only child! She was a sixteen-year-old girl, down there dancing."

The filmmaker had even interviewed the general in charge, went to him as if he were a sympathetic interviewer. At the end he asked, "Don't you think this will arouse the people of the Soviet Union and they will get rid of people like you?"

The general looked stunned, as if he suddenly wondered, Wait a minute, what *have* I been doing here?

The students showed us the memorial in front of the town hall to those who had fallen in the massacre. Fresh flowers had been placed there. This was so risky, so courageous, that it made the hair on my neck rise, as if at any minute the Communists would sweep down with more tanks to punish the town for its uppity ways.

In an effort to keep up with world affairs, back home I read three papers, *The New York Times, The Wall Street Journal,* and the *Finan-*

cial Times of London, and yet I couldn't remember a line about this bloodbath.

Then it hit me. Few outside knew about it. A lot was going on in the Soviet Union that wasn't going to make the Western press, never would, because few from the West ever came to these places. The *Times* had one or two bureaus in the Soviet Union, in Moscow and maybe Leningrad. Even if it had wanted to send someone, it wasn't easy to travel here, and probably the reporter in Moscow wouldn't have wanted to come to Tbilisi. Besides, the spaces here were so vast, thousands and thousands of miles across, that there weren't enough reporters to cover it all. And of course the Russians weren't about to tell anybody they'd just had a massacre in Tbilisi.

The students gave us a copy of the video to smuggle out. Police states and dictators are going to have a hard time in the future. A hundred or even twenty-five years ago you would have printed your protest or plastered it on the wall with posters. Now an amateur with a video camera can make a wallop of a visual impact.

The next morning I was out jogging and puffed my way into the town square, over which rose the big statue of Lenin. I circled it on a look-see. Without warning the police came out of nowhere and stopped me, pointing guns.

I shook my head, not understanding Russian. They gestured at the statue and back at me, their eyes accusatory. They were afraid I was some rabid nationalist intent on destroying the last monument to Lenin in town. In sign language I gestured and said *hotel* in Russian, pointing in the direction I hoped it lay. I went jogging off.

Still under martial law, this was obviously a hot area. The Russian army told us not to take the main route to Baku, that it might not be safe, and suggested a more scenic way, which I was sure meant even worse roads. We talked it over and decided to ignore their directive and took the main route. We passed a column of twenty friendly tanks—friendly to us, anyway—heading east to help occupy Baku, their steel treads wrecking the road's already worn asphalt.

The next day, four hundred miles farther on, as we rode into Baku, a major center of oil production, all around the road lay rusted pipes and drill rigs, idle, unmaintained, a cluttered junk heap. No wonder Soviet oil production was down. Communism again. Nobody owned any of this, so nobody took care of it. As long as a manager met his quota, that was fine. If meeting his quota meant stripping a few drilling rigs to have six left instead of sixty, he'd do it, he didn't care. This oil field looked like a scrap yard. Under capitalism the eye of the owner is constantly on a building or a business or he loses it. Not the case here.

This was one of the reasons the Soviets never built their capital base, because they'd never built any capital. Riding along the Caspian Sea we saw hundreds of these discarded drilling rigs, all stripped. Nobody maintained the pressure in the wells. Back home you maintained them because you wanted the extra 50 percent from a well. Here, they took the oil off the top and left it. They were doing what they accused the capitalists of, skimming off the easy money and running. Capitalists would have maintained these wells till they ran dry, otherwise they'd be bankrupt capitalists.

We pulled into Baku, where there had been a gigantic massacre three months before in January. Three hundred to four hundred people had been killed, but this time it had been Christian Armenians slaughtered by Muslim Azerbaijanis. Baku was still under martial law—lots of Soviet personnel carriers, the army strongly in evidence—even though all the Armenians had left Baku since the killings. My thesis about ethnic strife in the Soviet Union was unfolding before my eyes.

Few Americans knew about the massacre, even though Baku is one of the largest cities in the Soviet Union, the heart of its major oil-producing region. It was down here on the Caspian Sea, where Western reporters didn't come much.

A large portion of Baku's population had been Armenian, but two months before we arrived they had returned to Armenia. They wouldn't sit here and be slaughtered anymore. The mobs had even ripped down the statue of the Armenians' best poet, their Shakespeare, from the outside wall of the main library, leaving a blank space. One ethnic group didn't want the heroes of another group to stand. When things go wrong on a macroeconomic level, it's almost always this way. People find someone to blame, whether it's the blacks, whites, Christians, Jews, Muslims—whoever—especially if there's a successful minority, like the German Jews in the 1930s.

Baku was under such tight martial law that we couldn't even find a restaurant open at night.

We crossed the Caspian by ferry to Krasnovodsk.

This put us on the eastern, desert side of the sea; in contrast, the western side had been wet and fertile.

Out here, too, the region was shifting, changing—Uzbeks against Meshedi Turks, Uzbeks and Kirghiz fighting in Osh. There had been clashes in Samarkand in 1988, and in Tashkent, Ashkhabad, and Novyy Uzen in 1989. Some of the skirmishes had been against the Russians, but much of this had been tribe against tribe, one ethnic group attacking another.

The usual reasons were all around us. Not only eco-catastrophe, but Islamic fundamentalism and plain old bigotry, plus all the usual economic reasons: a shortage of land, appalling living conditions, and a lack of jobs. Growing seasonal cotton meant that for much of the year the local men had no work.

What a fascinating part of the world! Back in the early days of Communism, this had been known as the Virgin Lands. The bright young men of that time had come down here to make their way in agriculture. They had to irrigate to grow crops in the deserts, so they'd used the Aral Sea for water. Khrushchev had been one of those bright young men, and he and his crew irrigated much of the Kara Kum Desert. Kazakhstan had become a gigantic farmland, a desert that had bloomed into vast arable tracts. The Russians had piled in here. The area became 40 percent Russian, whereas before it had been all Muslim and Turkic.

Khrushchev had come down here to make his fortune. Brezhnev had been here, too, under Khrushchev, which had given him his big chance. For them, this had been the California gold rush. If they could succeed, their fortunes under the Communist system would be made. In the same way that Ronald Reagan, from the Golden State of California, could become president of the United States, these fellows would hail from a golden part of their world, one they had transformed into the promised land. By the time they were done, Uzbekistan was producing 67 percent of the USSR's cotton. Kazakhstan was producing a huge proportion of its wheat.

This farming miracle, however, has required vast amounts of water as well as herbicides and insecticides, which are said to be used in this region at twenty-five times the national rate. The result, after all the years of draining, cultivation, and fertilizing, has been one of the world's largest environmental disasters. Khrushchev and his crew used two thirds of the water of the Aral Sea for irrigation, and much of the land has been poisoned by sea salt. Flowing north to the arctic, as do all rivers in Siberia, the Aral Sea used to provide 13 percent of all the fish in the Soviet Union; now not a fish in it is alive. The river water and groundwater were salty and contaminated. Rates of birth defects and infant mortality in the region were among the world's highest. Fishing villages, once at the edge of the Aral Sea, are now thirty miles away, surrounded by dry land.

Here was the result of bureaucracy and arrogance run amok. The Russians had thought they could use the water to turn the area into a cotton plantation. But they had treated the land the way they treated the oil fields we had passed: They stripped it and moved on. In the United States, if you were to go out and buy a hundred thousand square miles of farmland, and then go to the bank and get several billion dollars to cultivate it, sooner or later even a banker would say, "Whoa, this ain't working. We're not going to go on throwing money at this; it'll collapse." There would be some discipline. But not in Communism. You could ruin a resource by gutting it without anyone saying, "Halt."

China had the same problem back in the sixties and seventies, when after centuries of self-sufficiency it became a net importer of cotton. In the late seventies the Chinese government finally admitted its way wasn't working. It deregulated agriculture, turning it over to the peasants. It allowed farmers to lease land for a long time and, in some places, actually to buy it. Since direction from the top wasn't working, and communes weren't working, the people in the countryside were allowed to do whatever they wanted. Just as important, the government didn't insist that farmers sell their corn and cotton to the state at some artificially low price, but allowed them to sell it for what they could get on the world market.

The farmers went wild. That's one reason China is so capitalistic right now. Within five years these farmers began to export cotton. China also went from importing to being a major exporter of grain. When I rode through there in 1986 and 1988, I noticed that every field was planted and cultivated, every item reused, nothing wasted. The farmers didn't strip the land; it was theirs and they had to plant it next year and the year after that. In Russia, however, the land was nobody's, and it didn't matter. Next year we'll move on to the next acre, the thinking went, and we'll get some more water, and who cares? If I'm a commissioner, I'll make my grain quotas for ten years so I'll be promoted to Moscow.

Of course, many, many of these agriculture commissars were lying. The local Party chief, Sharaf Rashidov, was famous for inflating the cotton harvest in the seventies and eighties, but he wasn't the only one. None of the officials were producing their quotas, but they said they were. They were faking it, just lying—and there were no accountants, no checking, no bankers, no accountability. As long as the cotton factories got cotton, they didn't know or care; it was none of their business.

This is one of the primary things wrong with Communism—no accountability, no responsibility, no incentive.

As we drove through town after town and these scenes were repeated, it dawned on me that the Soviet Union had fallen apart. The idea was startling—this was mid-1990, and the coup wouldn't come for another year. The Soviet Union looked like nothing more than a Third World country with a big army and a space program. Nothing seemed to work here. Though much of what we saw was new, everything got old and seedy the minute it was built. Most of the hotels we stayed in, unlike the rare Intourist places for travelers, looked like bomb sites: busted elevators, broken plumbing, no soap, no towels, no toilet paper, not even toilet seats. Only for foreigners did the Soviets provide clean linens, but you always had to make your own bed, Comrade.

The other thing Tabitha and I noticed throughout the Central Asian Republics were the number of Muslims.

In America we tend to think Muslims are a people centered in the Middle East, not realizing that they run from Morocco to the Philippines, from the Atlantic to the Pacific. There are as many Muslims in the world as there are Christians. The fourth-largest country in the world is Indonesia, and it's Muslim. There's Pakistan, and then Bangladesh with more than 100 million people. India alone has something like 90 million Muslims, a population which, if spun off into an independent country, would be the eleventh largest in the world. In the USSR, 15 percent of the population was Muslim, and they weren't happy being dominated by Russians.

With Tabitha still leading, we moved on through the Kara Kum Desert, which was huge. It stretched hundreds of miles from the Caspian Sea across Turkmenistan and Uzbekistan to Samarkand. I'd been in other deserts, in the American Southwest and across the Taklamakan desert in China, but this one was plainer, simpler, scrubbier. Here, too, we ran into farmland, which I rarely did in other deserts.

Tabitha's bike had constant mechanical problems, which caused both of us to pay almost as much attention to it as to the countryside. I hoped this wouldn't take too much out of her, but she was becoming apprehensive about completing the trip.

In this region gas cost forty kopecks per liter. A gallon was about fifteen cents at black market rates, thirty cents at bank rates.

Every now and then we'd cross the Kara Kum Canal—fifty yards wide, full of muddy water—part of the irrigation system the Russians had set up. In a capitalist country there wouldn't have been all that dirt in the water, because it meant you were losing land, and no capitalist was going to let his land get eroded. We also ran into scores and scores of wild camels, as well as signs that warned BEWARE OF WILD CAMELS, just as in the States road signs warned of deer crossings.

Finally we reached Bukhara, where we were laid low and made wretched by food poisoning.

At the hospital the doctor asked if we had any medicine.

"No, that's why we came here," I told him.

"We don't have any medicine," he said. "Maybe you should call an ambulance."

I felt dizzy, confused. "But I'm already here at the hospital," I said. "Why would I need an ambulance?"

"Maybe they have some medicine," he said.

Dumbfounded, we left and treated ourselves with the patent remedies we'd brought with us.

A day later, we were better, well but tired. Tabitha was enthusiastic about Bukhara. Recalling her academic studies, she explained that it had been one of Central Asia's great early cities. Here there were lots of domes and minarets, the first signs of power and money we'd seen for a long time.

We went to the Soviet May Day parade, which involved long exhortations by political brass and a couple hours of paraders passing the reviewing stand. Red banners were everywhere, thousands and thousands of them. If the Soviets had put their banner facilities to work making cloth they could have exported clothes.

We drove on to Samarkand, one of the world's most ancient cities and the oldest of Central Asia. Although outside its graceful old-world center Samarkand was no more than the usual colorless Soviet city burdened by polluted air and traffic congestion, the ruins at its core dated back to between 3000 B.C. and 4000 B.C. After conquest by Alexander the Great, the city became a meeting point of Western and Chinese cultures. It reached its greatest splendor as the capital of Tamerlane's empire in the fourteenth century, when the Turkic conqueror also made it Central Asia's cultural epicenter. In the eighteenth century the city fell into decline, but it was later brought back to life by the Trans-Caspian Railway.

Despite its Communist yoke, Samarkand seemed to be the most prosperous city we had come across since Baku, a thousand miles back. In its bustling market we found good produce, including fresh cloves with an intoxicating fragrance that delighted Tabitha. We learned that few travelers came to Samarkand.

The centerpiece of the city's ancient splendor is the Registan, an ensemble of three madrasas, or Islamic schools. Majestic in their soaring lines and cobalt-blue mosaics, they made us gape at their beauty, for these magnificent schools are a sight as breathtaking as the Taj Mahal. There are a few things in the world that should never be photographed, because pictures cannot do them justice. The Taj Mahal and Samarkand are two that should be seen only in person.

Under the corner domes of the Ulug-bek Madrasa, completed in 1420, were lecture halls, and in its rear was a mosque. The Tiger Madrasa flouted the Islamic injunction against showing pictures of live animals by boldly displaying glorious tilework devoted to its namesake. Between these two was the Gold Madrasa, inside which lay an impressive broad courtyard.

Drinking in all this splendor, I remembered that as recently as a hundred years before, the Taj Mahal itself had just sat there, abandoned. Nobody went there, nobody cared. Some traveler stumbled upon it, started publicizing it, and now it's one of the great wonders of the world. But a hundred years before you could have bought it for five hundred dollars, the whole damn thing.

Samarkand was like the Taj Mahal in that way, if not even more extraordinary. I believed somebody was going to make a fortune opening a Hilton here, because once informed, people would stream to this city the way they stream to the Taj Mahal. Dusty Samarkand is a delicacy just sitting out there waiting to be discovered, a comely back-country-farmer's daughter not yet discovered by prosperous city suitors.

These resurgent Islamic schools around the square were part of a developing pattern. For decades there had been only one madrasa in all of the Soviet Union, and now they were opening everywhere. Every time we turned around in this part of the world, in Georgia, Azerbaijan, Turkmenistan, or Uzbekistan, a new school was opening up, an Islamic school. We discovered that forty mosques had opened in Uzbekistan alone in 1989, and at least one was being built in every town we passed through—Ashkhabad, Mary, Bukhara.

The culture was shifting, too. One night in Dzhambul we went out to a restaurant with a lot of outdoor tables. It didn't have a wine list, and we asked the owner if we could bring our own. He shrugged; why not? We went back to the hotel and bought a bottle of wine and came back to our table. We put the wine on the table and had dinner. About three quarters through our meal the manager came out screaming, "Get that goddamn wine out of here. You can't come in here and drink."

Putting it right on the table was a big faux pas. We really were in a center of Islam, which forbids alcohol—and this in the belly of the Soviet Union. Muslim people, Muslim monuments, Muslim schools, Muslim customs.

Tashkent, the capital of Uzbekistan, was more evidence of the vitality of these Muslim regions. A modern, glistening city, it had a major international airport and first-class hotels. Over the previous twenty years this regional capital had blossomed the way Los Angeles and Atlanta had in the United States, becoming the Soviet Union's fourth largest city.

The closer we got to Alma-Ata and the Chinese border, the more signs of ethnic unrest we saw.

Central Asia is a huge melting pot of Turkic and Persian ethnic groups. Many are Muslims with strong ties to Iran, Afghanistan, Pakistan, and Xinjiang, the Chinese province. At this point the newcomers, the Russians, outnumbered the Muslims in some areas, but the Muslims were multiplying at a furious rate, and to me the handwriting was on the wall.

We tend not to understand that a large part of Western history over the past thirteen hundred or fourteen hundred years has been Muslims against Christians—the Crusades, the gates of Constantinople, the Spanish Inquisition. The Muslims were always trying to come into Europe through Austria, through Hungary, through Spain. The Christians beat them back several times. During the centuries of the Dark Ages in Europe the Muslims were much more dynamic than the Christians. They expanded geographically, spreading their culture and religion from the Atlantic to the Pacific. In fact, if the Europeans hadn't come to the New World, hadn't brought Christianity to it long before anybody ever gave a hoot about the western hemisphere, the number of Christians today probably wouldn't come even close to the number of Muslims.

They're not over yet, these global battles. It may not be Communism versus capitalism next time: One of the thrusts of the future could well be the revival of Islam versus Christianity. All the Muslim areas are resurgent, not so much because they want to be Islamic, but because they need a vehicle to help them get more. If people are prosperous, they tend not to fight. What they're reaching out for is Islam, the only unifying thread they have, to help them achieve their own prosperity and identity.

As these Muslims move toward autonomy, clashes will occur, because the Muslims won't be able to blame their problems on the Communists anymore—they've all been swept out; they'll blame them on the Christians, for lack of a better scapegoat.

The Soviet Union, with its one hundred twenty-eight different ethnic, national, language, and religious groups, struck me as many civil wars waiting to happen. The economy would continue to collapse, and politicians always need somebody to blame. All these groups were going to be at each others' throats, and the Union would keep fragmenting into smaller and smaller pieces. There might be, say, fifty states, a hundred states, before it was done.

The USSR was one of the largest empires the world has ever seen or ever will see, both in terms of area and peoples. It was put together by force of arms and still contains many discontented people. When a political entity of such vastness comes apart, the process continues for years, even decades. Our journalists and bureaucrats thought the USSR would take only a year or two to dismantle, that after a little transition, things would be okay. This isn't the way history works. Witness the slow breakups of the Roman, Turkish, Ottoman, Chinese, Spanish, and British empires, and the aftershocks and reverberations that lingered for many decades after their demise.

Will these conflicts be dangerous to the United States, or to our trading partners in Western Europe? Do we need to continue to spend $150 billion to defend our allies against the threat from the former Soviet Union?

No. First, many of the previously much-feared Soviet weapons were junk from the start. We often saw broken-down missile launchers just sitting alongside the road. Vast numbers of trucks, tanks, and other mobile vehicles have been scavenged, and their parts have been used for myriad purposes in the private sector. Yes, there are still weapons, but large numbers of them do not work anymore.

Second, most of the remaining armaments will be used in the local civil and guerrilla wars that will be common in the former Soviet Union for years to come. The various warlords are going to have their hands full fending off encroachments and attacks from other warlords. There have been constant local wars in this area since before the days of Genghis Khan and nothing's changed, but this warfare will have little or no effect on us unless some meddling politician feels he has to make something of it.

Some of the remaining weapons will be sold in the international armaments market. This is not a big change; there has been a vast global trade in arms for decades—nay, centuries.

For a while there will also be the deterrent effects of Saddam Hussein's failure in Kuwait. None of these areas will provoke the combined interests of the developed world even if they had the military capacity—which they don't and won't.

The Soviet Union is actually headed toward a system that will resemble feudalism: the economic, political, and social system of medieval Europe after the breakup of the Roman Empire, in which there were innumerable and ever-changing fiefdoms.

V-E Day in Alma-Ata was still a major holiday, with parades, military displays, hundreds of banners, and lots of propaganda about World War II—all part of the effort to build up the image of the Communist Party and the state.

Lots of new buildings and heroic monuments, including of course the ubiquitous monument to the Soviet World War II dead. One sixth of the Russian population—about 25 million people—had died defending Mother Russia from Hitler. The battle for Stalingrad alone had cost the lives of a million Soviet troops. Awesome statistics. If the United States today were to suffer a similar loss, 45 million of us would perish defending our country. The war was the only thing the Communists had ever done right, and they never tired of celebrating it.

The Soviets had won the war, but they hadn't done anything since. Communism would have collapsed sooner if it hadn't been for the Second World War, and they knew it. As part of their ongoing propaganda movement, in every Soviet town stood a heroic monument to the war effort, often a single piece of granite twenty yards high and wide, along with an entire park of marble soldiers and workers battling fascists. Everywhere, an eternal flame. God knew what the Soviet Union was spending on eternal flames. When a bride got married, she would go to the eternal flame and honor the war-dead with flowers. Sure, you expected such monuments in Washington or Moscow, capital cities, but out here every little town had one. They were about the only things that were maintained. If the Communists had spent all the money on roads that they spent on monuments to Lenin and the Second World War, they would have had a hell of a road system by now.

It reminded me of the War Between the States here at home. Until 1914 the largest travelers' attraction in America was Grant's Tomb. Aging soldiers and their relatives kept visiting it, reliving their youth, their nostalgia, their glory, even though the war had been over for fifty years.

Tabitha and I had seen a few old guys wearing medals in many places in the USSR, but on the big day itself everybody came out in full regalia. We came across several people who were falling-down drunk. We tried to help some, even called the police, who came because it was the exotic Americans who wanted them, but they would say, "Oh, hell, it's just another drunk on V-E Day."

And everywhere there were babushkas—sweeping, doing laundry, selling little plates of onions, tomatoes, and meat in the market. They were widows from the war, left by an entire generation of lost husbands.

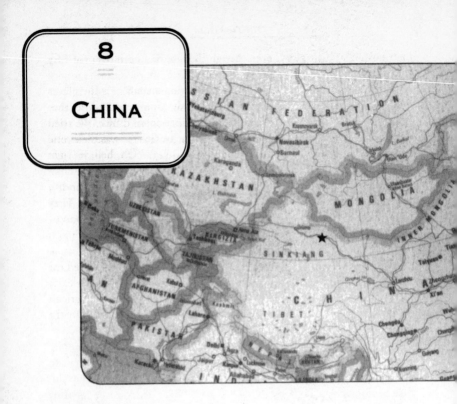

BY NOW we'd racked up six thousand miles and were making steady progress. From Alma-Ata in Kazakhstan we approached the Chinese border.

I had driven across China two years before, a year before Tiananmen Square, and I'd had a spectacularly delightful time. I wondered how much the country had changed. I had read the American press on the troubles, but I knew they wouldn't get it right. Describing the surface, usually with little training in history or economics and none in geography, journalists rarely understand what goes on inside foreign countries. From my previous trips I had a grounding in recent Chinese history that was at variance with the ideas parroted endlessly by the Western press. I also knew the Chinese were now understandably nervous about foreign opinion in general and foreign visitors in particular, so I wasn't sure how we'd be received.

Earlier in the eighties the Chinese had been happily becoming capitalists. Out in the countryside everybody was building houses. People in the cities were complaining because prices were going up. So the government gave bonuses to the city folk, which it paid for by printing money. Needless to say, this caused terrible inflation, a boom-bust bubble that soon got out of control. Finally the government cracked down on the money supply.

As I said earlier, revolutions don't come from oppressed people, they come from folks whose expectations have been aroused. By early 1989 China's harsh new monetary policy began to cause hard times. Several months later, people surged into Tiananmen Square to bitch about tight money. Then students, who didn't know any better, transformed a complaint about a slow-moving economy and monetary policy into a cry for democracy. Most Chinese weren't all that interested in democracy. They mainly wanted to get rich, like most people everywhere.

Marx was right about one thing: Money is the root of everything. If you figure out the money, you can figure out almost any political situation. (Most everything else Marx got wrong.) Look at what caused the Boston Massacre. The Boston economy had gone to hell in the early 1770s, with the unemployment rate at more than 30 percent. America's revolutionaries transformed a protest against unemployment into the higher moral ground of "no taxation without representation."

So the Chinese sent their troops into Tiananmen Square—a minor blip in the vast panorama of Chinese history, but a world-shaking event to foreign reporters. The outcry in the Western media so panicked the Chinese government that by 1990 this freewheeling country was a horribly stifling place to visit. The government didn't want travelers to come away with any negative impressions, so the best thing to do was keep them from seeing much. From the Chinese perspective, though, things were improving. Not only did I find some of my entrepreneur friends whom I had met while on previous rides still very much in business, but monetary and fiscal policies had gotten looser, and the economy was starting to pick up.

Everywhere on my trips through China I've seen signs that the sleeping dragon has awakened. It was a country in the grip of statism that was now throwing off its yoke. Few Chinese any longer believe that the government has the answers to their economic problems.

Like successful entrepreneurs in many parts of the world, Chinese entrepreneurs are bringing every scrap of energy, money, and technology they can marshall into their businesses. Two decades from now they are going to be among the best capitalists in the world. They may still call themselves Communists, but I promise you they will run circles around most of us. In the south they're already achieving great prosperity.

. . .

We had the usual confusion that results from crossing a border that sees few travelers. This border had only recently been opened. The officials here had never seen visas or carnets. No one wanted to change dollars into Chinese currency. Although we both had international driver's licenses, the Chinese weren't sure if they should accept them or even our international vaccination certificates. We got in. At once there were lots of people around, many more than I had expected. I concluded that the national government encouraged the Han, the country's major ethnic group, to move out west both to provide a buffer from the Soviet Union's military adventures and to dilute the predominant Muslim population.

We drove into Yining, the big border city. The so-called luxury hotel we stayed in had just been finished, and it seemed to be benefiting from transborder traffic. There was lots of beer but no more vodka.

Two years previously I had noticed that every Chinese town was building a tourist hotel, often spending lavishly on luxurious palaces that made me wonder who would ever rent them. These hotels were part of the wild inflationary boom of 1988 and 1989, which was a forerunner of Tiananmen Square.

Now the central government was telling the towns that they had to stop building these stupid hotels, that it wouldn't pay for them anymore. The local party cadre across China had built fancy hotels and office buildings the way the Soviet Communists had built monuments in the heroic style to the Second World War effort in every town—as status symbols, trophies, not on any economic basis.

I was worried about the road through the Taklamakan Desert, because it had been such a disaster when I had driven through in 1988. That was the five-hundred-mile stretch from Turpan east that I'd described to Tabitha, the worst motorcycle nightmare of my life, a constant struggle over sand dunes, rocks, hills—falling down, getting stuck, digging my way out. We had to go through Hami, a town right smack in the center of it all. I hoped Tabitha would be all right. Hell, I hoped *I* would be all right.

Picking our way along the mountainous road we saw strange dark objects—tents, or yurts, made from what appeared to be the skins of goats and bears. We pulled over and stared. Silence, except for the occasional bleat of a goat. A shy little girl with big eyes in a long skirt stared at us. The yurts made sense for these tribesmen, the Uygurs, because they could be dismantled in a hurry and packed on a camel.

The little girl was five or six and had an older sister, eight or so. We gave them some bread and they looked back over at their mother and the latest baby, mutely asking if they might take it. After she nodded, they took the bread and ran back to her.

We went over. In the usual combination of sign language and simple English we asked if we could look inside the yurt, which was fine with her.

At first glance the inside appeared bare, but that was only to a Western eye expecting the clutter of furniture. Along one wall a small cloth-covered table held clean pots and crockery, and hanging from the ceiling was an embroidered, flower-decorated white cloth that could be dropped to divide the inner space. A kettle stood on the bare ground beside a dark purple rug. Several pallets were turned against the wall to serve as backrests. There was a pile of skins, too. After all, this was a cold climate much of the year; they needed them.

I wondered why I had seen so few of the nomadic Uygurs on both trips, and then it hit me. Like the Eskimos, they were disappearing because of technology and the march of the twentieth century.

The Chinese were busily building a road from Ürümqi south to Pakistan and another from Ürümqi to the Soviet Union. Many of the Uygurs either worked on these roads or had regular jobs maintaining them. The new roads also allowed tribesmen to get regular work in the cities. Thus there were fewer nomads, and fewer Kashmir goats, and as a result cashmere has become almost prohibitively expensive in New York. An entire culture might be destroyed because of the roads.

This is how man's world is, constantly shifting, constantly changing everything around, opening opportunities for some and closing them for others, just like Mother Nature herself, and those who don't accept it will find themselves swimming against a powerful flood. I know all the arguments of how we must stop the boot heel of progress, how we must preserve the way things were in the good old days. I'm not convinced there ever were any good old days.

There are those—not me—who would look at this woman and say, "This is terrible, we shouldn't destroy these people, this culture, this way of life by tempting them with roadwork," just as we've been told we shouldn't destroy the Eskimos.

I wonder what the Eskimos and Uygurs would say. They certainly didn't have to stop being nomads because work in towns and cities opened up. I looked at this woman's life in these glorious yet windswept and desolate mountains and said to Tabitha, "Boy, I'd be glad the road came to town and I could go and do other things." I remembered how happy we'd been back in Demopolis when they finally paved the streets. Apparently most Uygurs agree with me.

That this road-building had driven up the price of cashmere intrigued me. Here was an example of how an investor has to think. If they're putting in a big road in Pakistan and China, it has to have an effect somewhere. Every time an investor sees a big change coming he has to start thinking, Okay, what does this mean? Where does it lead? What are going to be the economic, political, and social shifts because of it? And won't the new railroad to the USSR intensify these effects?

Well, in thirty years most of the yurts are going to be gone, with the owners of those left charging forty dollars a visit. They'll fix them up with a bed and indoor plumbing and charge you a fortune to have a genuine nomadic experience, plus you'll pay more for cashmere. (When I called my office, I had them stockpile two or three cashmere sweaters for my return.) But these would be only the beginning—only the superficial changes.

Spring was turning into summer. We drove from Yining over the mountains to the city of Shihezi in Xinjiang province, a pretty drive but with patches of bad road. This western province was a sixth of the size of the continental United States, but it had only 15 million people. Compared with China's population of 1.2 billion, this was nothing.

The next day we reached Ürümqi, still a big, growing, modern city. The railroad to the USSR was just about finished, which would help the region prosper.

Out here we feasted on roasted sheep, mutton shashlik, pilafs, and steamed mutton dumplings. Street vendors offered us *kao baozi,* packets of baked bread dough stuffed with mutton and onions, as well as steaming mutton soups, dumplings stuffed with mutton and herbs, and rice pilafs with apricots, mutton, onions, and carrots. Boiled noodles with a side of sautéed mutton, onions, tomatoes, and green peppers was a popular dish. Delicious!

Of course I learned to say *beer* in Chinese. In fact, after this trip, I can say *beer* in forty languages.

To my delight, I learned that the Dunhuang-Ürümqi Highway was completed; that old northern route that had given me such nightmarish trouble on my last trip was a thing of the past.

As I traced out on my map the recent development of highways and railroads through this desolate part of the world, which I still thought of as Turkistan, I saw it was going to be transformed by its new infrastructure. The ancient Silk Roads, once mountain trails fit only for camels, were being replaced by those suitable for long-haul trucks and the iron horse.

This vast area, bounded east and west by the Caspian Sea and the Taklamakan Desert, by the Himalayas to the south and the Kirghiz steppes to the north, would become prosperous. Trade, tourism, and their resulting opportunities would create dozens of ways for sharp-eyed entrepreneurs to become rich.

Why hadn't it happened before? Back in the fifties the Chinese and the Russians had been pals, and spying the opportunities here, part of their military, political, and economic alliance had been to develop an infrastructure to link the two countries. They'd set out to extend the Chinese railroad through Xinjiang province to connect up with the Soviet presence in Turkistan and onward to Europe. Then they'd had a spat, and the railroad was never finished beyond Ürümqi.

When India went to war with China in the early sixties, it had become allies with the USSR against their new common enemy. To maintain the balance of power, China had aligned itself with Pakistan. Naturally, China and Pakistan needed road transportation in the event that either would have to rush in troops and materials to prevent an invasion from the other axis. The Karakoram Highway, linking Ürümqi, Kashgar, and Islamabad, this seven-hundred-mile joint project of Pakistan and China that also had been interrupted by political tiffs, was finally finished.

Not only had these projects given local workers jobs, but they would now bring in tourism and commerce. Tribesmen were romantic nomads before because they had little else to do. Now they would have a choice.

Before this southern route was finished it had been one of the worst driving experiences in the world, less a road than a river of broken boulders tumbling across the mountains. Its completion was a tribute to man's courage and ingenuity. Part of the route was blasted out of sheer rock faces over deep canyons of the Indus River. In many places workers had to hang suspended by ropes to drill holes for dynamite. More than four hundred men had lost their lives building it, and now small cairns marked their graves.

It had been dangerous to build and was still dangerous to drive on, for rock slides and flash floods were a constant threat. On their side of the border the Pakistanis deployed ten thousand soldiers just for road maintenance and emergency clearance.

Now the railroad was being completed from both sides of its northern route by the Chinese and Russians, which would link this area to Alma-Ata and Kazakhstan, and from there to anywhere west—Istanbul, Moscow, London. Turkistan would be open to the outside world in every direction—north, east, south, and west—after centuries of isolation brought on by primitive communication and transportation. I knew that as apparently simple as this railroad and these two new Chinese roads were, they would have major ramifications for the political, economic, social, and historical future of not only Asia, but the entire world beyond.

Now we drove through real desert, dunes and distant mountains, into Turpan and the Turpan Depression, the lowest dry land in the world. Turpan was a Uygur town with Muslim mosques and domes, non-Chinese in many ways.

While it was hot and dry, thankfully it was May and not August. In this desert the winds were more ferocious than I'd experienced in any setting, especially on a motorcycle. Last time through I'd had to constantly fight to keep my motorcycle upright. Once I'd parked on the asphalt, and a gust had knocked over my five-hundred-pound machine. I remember watching a woman in a passenger car unlock her door over and over in her struggle to open it, unaware that the powerful wind had kept the door jammed shut.

What amazed me on both trips through several thousand miles after leaving the border region of western China was the lack of people. Nowhere can you go a hundred yards in eastern China without seeing someone. But out here, eighty or ninety miles inside the western border and on the other side of the hills, we drove scores of miles without seeing anybody.

It was startling, too, that the cultivated portion of the desert here was greener than on the Russian side, and we soon discovered why. Not only were the Chinese better organized, they had devised a clever system of irrigation tunnels beneath the desert that drew water from the mountains to augment the natural oases they'd built their cities around. Hundreds of years old, these tunnels kept the loss from evaporation to a minimum. I was stupefied, stunned, that the Chinese had not only run them for hundreds of miles but had done so for centuries. In the towns, sluice gates, irrigation ditches, and intricate valve systems sent water when and where they wanted it. They even watered down the roads every morning to reduce dust. With a system that survives to this day, the ancient Chinese had cleverly turned straggly desert oases into prosperous towns surrounded by fertile fields.

This Chinese ingenuity and conservation contrasted sharply with the Russian use of the Aral Sea over the past few decades. The Chinese had turned the same countryside into a garden that the Russians had turned into an eco-catastrophe. I wasn't surprised to learn that the Chinese were the first to increase crop productivity by planting in rows instead of scattering seed around.

A lot of the Chinese success had to do with economic and political organization. The Russians had set into action a system without accountability, and were quickly reaping what they had sown. The Chinese had nowhere to go—no frontier, no Siberia, no Virgin Lands, no conquered territory—so they made do with what they had. They reminded me of societies of hunters, such as the Eskimos and other Native Americans, who lived in harmony with nature because they knew if they killed off the animals, that was it. Some Chinese farmers were so skillful they got three crops a year. They planted right to the edge of the road, using every square inch of land. They fertilized their soil, they rotated crops, they did everything that had to be done to make the land work well for them.

In Turpan, while we were having a new head gasket made for Tabitha's bike, I went to the market, an outdoor bazaar. It had beautiful melons, not at all what you'd expect in the middle of the desert, another tribute to the Chinese skill with water management.

We needed local cash, so I hunted up the black market in currency. Wherever there are exchange controls, as there are in China, there's a currency black market. I find such markets, capitalism in the raw, fascinating, because if there's one quick and sure way for an investor or a traveler to find out what's going on in a country, this is it. The price of the currency is to the prudent investor what an X ray is to an experienced radiologist.

The premium over the bank, or official, rate gives me my most important clue as to what the government is up to. If I can buy five zlotys for a dollar at the bank, but I can get eight on the black market, it tells me the government is trying to foist its currency on its own people, that it's afraid to let it float on the world market.

Even without asking I know if a country has currency controls, import taxes, and probably export restrictions. Governments think exchange controls keep money in their country, but they keep it out. If the currency is freely convertible, outsiders will bring money in and insiders won't be in a desperate struggle to smuggle it out, which they always are if the currency isn't convertible. Certainly the last place you or I want to put our money is someplace where we can't get it out. So many other investors feel the same way that no one will come in with or behind us to bull up the market. This simple test often tells me whether to bother exploring a country further for investment.

If the rate on the black market is five-and-a-half zlotys to the dollar, compared with the state bank's rate of five, then things might not be so bad. But if it is ten or fifteen to the dollar, then I know the country is in terrible shape, with maybe the collapse of the government or hyperinflation on the horizon. It spells trouble for everybody, massive instability.

Most travelers have a vague understanding that the ups and downs of a currency are an indication of the health of a country, much the way the rise and fall of a stock price discloses the problems and strengths of a company. What they don't realize is that in the same way company presidents and treasurers try to bull up the price of a stock, a country's treasury secretary and finance ministers stay up nights doing the same thing. Smart finance ministers know that gimmicks, restrictions, and regulations won't attract foreign capital to be invested in their country over the long run. They strive to inspire confidence by creating sound value. The dumb ones put on endless restrictions and can't understand why no one wants their currencies.

"I want to trade dollars," I said to the runner, who was about sixteen, just a trainee.

His limit was ten dollars, so I asked him to take me to his boss.

Now I was on my guard. As you travel you hear stories of hustles by currency traders on the black market. But as usual, I felt better taking my chances with them than with the state bank, which I knew would rob me with its artificial exchange rates. If I kept my wits about me, at least with the black marketeers I had a chance for a fair deal.

One favorite trick is the slight-of-hand shift. One traveler told me he had carefully counted the bills he was given, never allowed his new stash to leave his hand, and yet he had found he possessed a stack of carefully cut newspaper on his return to his hotel.

Another trick is the engineered danger. "The police!" they cry as they disappear into the crowd with your side of the transaction, or you're hurriedly handed a wad of bills that are mostly blank paper. Always agree on a price first, count what you are given next, make sure it doesn't leave your hand, and only then fork over what's due. After all, you're buying merchandise, even if it is money, and you should examine your purchase before accepting it, a sensible custom that holds true worldwide. In fact, to prevent having counterfeit bills foisted on us, we often bought a few dollars' worth of currency as samples from the state bank before we hiked over to the black market for the bulk of our purchases.

If someone mutters, "police," either hand back what you're holding or coolly walk away with it. The black market is guaranteed to find you again.

The yard boss was at the market's entrance, keeping an eye on his runners. He was Turkic, about twenty-four. The black market is a young man's game, to judge by the guys I've met on the front lines. But for all I knew, there was a middle-aged guy upstairs with an account in Switzerland. The pockets of the Turkic yard boss's jacket were stuffed with big wads of Japanese yen, Chinese renminbi, and U.S. greenbacks. He pulled them out in a circumspect manner, as this was illegal. All this furtiveness reminded me of buying moonshine back in Alabama, another transaction in which vendors had to dodge the federals' efforts to skim a share of the proceeds.

"How many renminbi for a dollar?" I asked in sign language and primitive English. The demographers tell us half the world's people speak some English, and from the evidence we accumulated on this trip, I'd say they're right. He had no trouble understanding me.

He offered me five, and I said no, because I'd heard I could get eight. The rate wasn't as good as when I'd come through two years before, back when they had had all that inflation. Then I had received six for a dollar, when the official rate was four, a 50 percent premium. It told me that back then, the Chinese people were paying up for foreign currencies, wanting out of their own money because it was falling fast in value, as distrusted by the natives as the pound sterling and the lira were later in England and Italy. This time I got only a 35 percent premium.

The only currencies the yard boss was interested in buying were dollars and yen. He wouldn't take sterling or deutsche marks. After all, this was the middle of the Taklamakan Desert, thousands of miles from any trading center. I guessed he wanted these two because the dollar had been a reserve currency for a long time and Japan did a huge trade business with China.

After horsing around we settled on seven to the dollar.

He actually gave me too much for the dollar compared with the yen, so I was tempted to swap my dollars for yen. With my more up-to-date knowledge of the international currency markets, I could have made a nice little arbitrage profit because I knew what the market was and he didn't. The Dow Jones ticker hadn't arrived in Turpan.

Give it another couple of years.

On the road to Hami Tabitha developed a hole in her piston. This bike had done everything to us but lie down and die, and I had the feeling that that was near. It was a hole the size of a dime, and here we were in a country as large as the United States without a single dealer who sold BMW parts.

We threw her bike into the back of a truck we flagged down, hauled it into Hami, and began asking endless questions. Finally we were lucky enough to find a mechanic, who stayed up till four-thirty in the morning welding the hole. It had to be done carefully, with Tabitha supervising the work, built up thin layer by thin layer so it wouldn't blow out at a critical time. Here was where it really paid to have brought along a trained mechanic, someone who understood what she was doing. We didn't know if it would work, but there was no way to get a spare BMW part into the middle of the Taklamakan Desert. This is the kind of repair you make in the backwoods of China, Africa, and South America. It would cause a factory-certified mechanic to shudder. God knew what it would do to the long-term health of the engine, but there was no way to get out of here but to try it.

We poked around a little. Hami itself was still the isolated desert town I remembered, although it looked a bit more prosperous. I still dreaded the drive to Dunhuang, since last time it had taken me seventeen hours to cover the two hundred fifty miles.

We set out, worried about the jury-rigged piston. Still leading, Tabitha had to watch for potholes and traffic and yet we couldn't help but keep our ears tuned to every thump and rattle coming from her engine.

We kept moving, one mile, five, twenty, forty. It was working! Maybe it would hold till we got to Japan.

As we edged across the desert, afraid to strain the engine, what struck me was the vastness of western China, how strange it looked, how un-Chinese. Here was China, with more people than any other country in the world, and where were they?

Imagine that the United States had five times its present population and that we all lived east of the Mississippi. China is that dramatic.

Imagine what the eastern half of the United States would be like if it were eight times as populated as it is now. Imagine the living conditions, the social conditions, the markets, and the scramble for money, food, and space.

That's China. The crowded east, the deserted west.

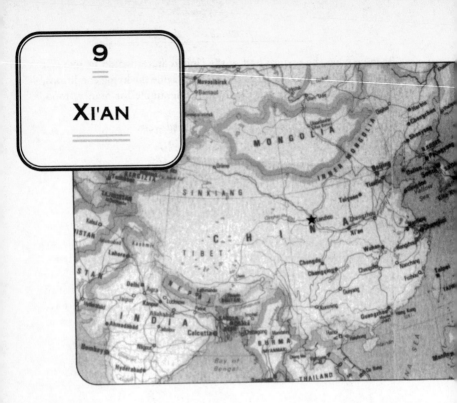

THERE ARE a thousand manmade underground rooms in the Buddhist caves in Dunhuang, and they are packed with extraordinary wall art, documents, carvings, and statues devoted to Buddha. Discovered by accident, by a guy chasing a sheep into a hole, they had been sealed for nine hundred years, till 1900, so they weren't ravaged like older finds.

On my last trip through here I had eaten at a restaurant owned by Mr. Ji. He treated me so well, I wanted to look him up again. We'd hit it off. Mr. Ji was a sunny forty-five-year-old with the Chinese air of agelessness. He was a man who knew his business because he had built it up from nothing. He had been a farmer who started out by selling food to the other farmers in a little breakfast shop. He expanded it into a fullfledged restaurant with an inn attached. He loved what he did, and despite the long hours, his workers liked working for him, where they could make more money than they could by working for the state.

His place reminded me of an inn out of the American Old West or England three hundred years ago. He had six rooms, four beds to each, basically cots. Toilets were down the hall. This was the standard Chinese hotel, and it was everywhere. We tended not to stay in hotels like it, preferring the newer, more comfortable Friendship Hotels, which catered to foreign travelers.

I wanted to see how the economy had affected him, because here we were a year on the other side of the Tiananmen Square troubles. Before I had visited him in the crescendo of boom times, back when everyone had been buying everything they could, getting rid of their paper money, back before the government was forced to devalue the currency and tighten money.

He remembered me and greeted me warmly, pleased I'd come back. Tabitha and I were the only foreigners who'd ever been in his place. We were welcome, exotic visitors, just as in the fifties back in Alabama we had regarded Chinese or Pakistani people as visitors from another planet.

Seating us at a big table, he insisted that we eat as his guest. We were treated to a feast of chicken, goat, and wonderful cold noodles garnished with onions, garlic, scallions, and a host of vegetables that don't have English names because they aren't grown in English-speaking parts of the world. Here in the middle of the desert he even managed to serve us fish. Since the Chinese didn't send meats and produce for any distance, this fish must have been raised locally, a tribute to Chinese ingenuity.

Yes, he had noticed there had been a falling off in business a year or so before, but now things were picking up again. The economy was reviving.

Like entrepreneurs the world over, Mr. Ji worked overtime—twelve hours a day, seven days a week—at building up his restaurant and getting rich. To him this was no burden, because he was having fun, as such people often do. He was living proof of what it took to make the real world work. Despite what Americans might think about what's happened to the Chinese since Tiananmen Square, twelve hundred miles from Beijing Mr. Ji, left alone by meddling central planners to build up his own business, appeared to be one of the world's happy men.

As soon as we hit Jiayuguan, the historical dividing line between the deserted west and the crowded east, we had another accident.

As she had for weeks, Tabitha led, maneuvering along the two-lane blacktop at thirty-five to forty miles an hour. Both sides of the road were packed with people. It was maddening in China the way trucks, bicycles, pedestrians, everyone pulled into the street without looking.

I was somewhat used to it, but not Tabitha. An old man on a bicycle swerved in front of her, and she was suddenly boxed in—she had to hit someone, there were so many people on both sides and this bicycle was in front of her. She slammed on her brakes and blew her horn, but the old guy was deaf or ignored her, because in China the larger vehicle always has to move out of the way of the smaller. Having slowed but unable to stop, she hit him and his bike at five to ten miles an hour.

A mob surrounded us. The police arrived. Tabitha was shattered and had a hard time talking. I took over. The old man didn't seem badly hurt, but he had fainted. Under local law, Tabitha was automatically the guilty party even though I had seen that the accident wasn't her fault. The old man was carted off to the hospital.

The crowd muttered and shot us nasty looks. Afraid we would become the center of another disturbance, the head policeman insisted we move on out of town. In the States he might have taken us to the police station so he could find us when he wanted us, but he wasn't worried about losing us. Out here we were rare birds. Two foreigners on foreign bikes on the region's only road were ridiculously easy to run down.

Upset, we cranked up and headed out as he instructed, awaiting his report.

The policeman caught up with us later at the westernmost end of the Great Wall, crumbling here in the desert.

"Well, you know," he said, "we've really got to do something about this man and his family."

Relieved that he wasn't arresting us, I said, "Okay, how much?"

"Two hundred dollars."

Dollars! On the black market here in the wilds of China, two hundred dollars was the equivalent of a year's pay or more.

Whenever I figure I'm being held up by an official, I ask for a receipt. Half the time it makes him back down, because he doesn't know to whom I'm liable to show it. He starts to think, Suppose he shows it to my boss and I've kept the money....

But this policeman was happy to give me one.

I forked over the money and asked him to convey our concern to the injured man's family. I would bet my net worth the poor old guy never saw a penny, that the policeman kept the entire amount.

I've still got that receipt, in Chinese, of course, scrawled on a ragged scrap of paper. For all I know it says, "Stick it in your ear."

Gas was a constant worry, as it was hundreds of miles between public pumps. We always drove with one eye on our odometer, calculating when we might be able to fill up again.

On one occasion our tanks were so low and we were so far from a town that we'd taken to coasting down inclines, striving to conserve every drop.

We came across a fenced-in military outpost and drove up to the guardhouse. By using sign language—pointing at our gas tanks and pantomiming how empty they were—we persuaded the guards to escort us to a pump on the base. The attendant didn't have the authority to sell us gas, so we were bumped up to the base commandant.

In his bare office we showed Commander Lu our passports, maps, and permission papers. He frowned. In our usual pidgin of the local language, basic English, and sign language, with which we seemed to get along in any culture, we explained that we had run out of gas.

Commander Lu was not only mystified that two Western motorcyclists were in the middle of his country, but astonished that we had penetrated his military security.

Finally we told him he had "to arrest us as spies or sell us some gas."

Laughing, he instructed his people to give us gas, and nobody would take any money for it.

A few hundred miles past Jiayuguan, we were again close to running out of gas when we saw dozens of guys in hillside dugouts and shacks by the side of the road with ten, fifteen, twenty liters of gasoline in plastic and tin containers. Once again the black market had come to our rescue.

We learned many things in going around the world, and one of them is you don't have to worry too much about running out of gas. In many places the black market will figure out where travelers are likely to run out and be there to sell it to you. In this case, hundreds of miles between Chinese cities these enterprising spirits had figured out how to get gas to the middle of nowhere and were delighted to sell it to us.

We drove over the mountains, the highest pass at 10,500 feet, into Lanzhou—beautiful scenery, sculpted terraces, with coal-burning locomotives chugging in the distance.

We visited the local market. It had expanded since I'd last been there, with better quality produce but higher prices. As it was early in the season and nobody trucked produce great distances in China, a small watermelon cost $2.70.

I hunted up a teahouse, never easy for a foreigner to find. Ask the Chinese where to find one, and you won't get a straight answer, as these places aren't approved of. I suppose if a Russian or Chinese visitor to Chicago in 1926 had asked to be guided to a speakeasy, he'd have had a hard time, too.

At the Culture Palace Tea House, rumpled old men dappled by the sunlight filtering through the thatched roof lounged around playing cards, dominoes, and mah-jongg. A sign said that no drunkenness, no fighting, and no bad language were allowed. A painfully thin middle-aged male singer, backed by a three-piece string combo, wailed a lament of the cruelties of love and life while being ignored by the crowd. These sprawling ne'er-do-wells, wreathed in cigarette smoke, had a lethargic, vegetative manner, laid-back and contemplative, as if they had seen life outside the teahouse and found it wanting.

Glad to see us, they pushed tiny glasses of mao-tai on us, which I couldn't get out of drinking. The Chinese speak of mao-tai with reverence, the way Southerners smack their lips over bourbon or the Scots revere Scotch. It's a highly potent liquor, made in Guizhou province from sorghum and wheat yeast and aged five or six years, but it tastes so foul that nobody but the Chinese can stand to drink it. I begged off after one glass.

From the waitress I bought a deck of Chinese cards as well as two jackets made fashionable with embroidered English words that no one here realized were nonsense syllables. Even though the place housed a couple of drunks, I was struck by its serenity. It reminded me of men sitting around a store, barbershop, or pool hall back in Alabama, gossiping, drinking, gambling, having some place to go to get away from the women, just as many primitive tribes have a men's lodge for the same purpose. Here there were constant cups of tea, some beer, a drop of mao-tai, a little gambling, and a lot of gossip and camaraderie. No signs said, WOMEN NOT ALLOWED, but you never saw women. This was a place my grandfather Brewer in Oklahoma would have appreciated. Late in the afternoon my grandmother would go looking for him, and she'd storm into all the domino parlors. It just infuriated her. When she'd find him at last, she'd always say, "Damn it, I told you not to play dominoes!" Back then Oklahoma was dry, but bottles in paper bags were behind the counter, snuck in by the bootleggers. And after all, Dutch Brewer was somebody in town. He not only owned its radio station, he also owned shares in the bank, had roomed in law school with the state's future senator, and had been one of the most sought-after young lawyers of his class. I guess he was supposed to be helping at home or doing something, anything, productive, but like a lot of guys, he preferred to be with his cronies.

The Communists have been trying to shut down teahouses for forty years, just as our government back in Prohibition tried and failed to shut down speakeasies. Throughout history there have always been places for men to gather to do the things men like to do together. Places like this will always exist, no matter how politically incorrect. Men's clubs in England, men's lodges in African and Native American tribes, saloons out West, barber shops and pool halls in the South, and Chinese teahouses, all have an apparent universal appeal. Naturally, we also constantly found places where only women gathered together.

I noticed here in Lanzhou how the Chinese had polluted the air. No Third World country has pollution controls on its chimneys or smokestacks. However, the Chinese have done a better job on their rivers than most, probably because they need the fish, whereas the Russians, with fewer people to feed, have carelessly killed lots of their internal waterways.

The Chinese drink only boiled water. When we checked into Chinese hotels they gave us big, elaborate, wonderful thermoses filled with water that stayed hot for twenty-four to forty-eight hours, to use for tea or washing. Typically Chinese. Why waste all that fuel heating water and piping it around when a few thermoses will do the trick?

The drive from Lanzhou to Pingliang was spectacular. We climbed up to a seven-thousand-foot-high ridge and drove along the top. The Chinese had planted thousands of trees on top of this ridge to keep the winds from blowing everything away. All the way down on both sides were contoured terraces with saplings.

Without warning a dozen beekeepers and their hives appeared along both sides of the road—then hundreds of hives and scores of beekeepers. Worried about getting stung, we lowered our visors and pulled on our gloves, covering ourselves thoroughly.

These were nomadic, migrant beekeepers, we learned, with five to fifty hives each. Naturally, the worker bees went with the beekeepers to wherever they moved the queen bees. From spring to fall, the beekeepers followed the budding of flowers, spending a few days in a location till the bees had drunk all the area's nectar, then moved on.

Thousands, millions, billions of bees filled the air and buzzed everywhere! This extraordinary sight went on for fifteen miles, with hundreds of the beekeepers camped in tents along the side of the road, often with their families. The beekeepers for the most part wore no protection, living in perfect harmony with their bees.

This was yet another example of superb Chinese productivity. They took the bees to the blooming flowers, rather than allow the bees access only to what spring chanced to bud around them. Of course, like the Chinese themselves, the bees had to work six to seven times harder than their foreign counterparts, as their masters had extended their honey-gathering season from a few weeks to half a year.

We saw amazing sights in China, but little to match those miles of bees and migrant beekeepers. It's that kind of productivity, that kind of planning and industry, that convinces me the Chinese will do better than any other people in the next century.

Xi'an was called the glorious capital of the world two thousand or three thousand years ago. It flourished before Rome and was very likely even richer.

Long since fallen into decline, today Xi'an is a provincial capital—a common pattern. The success of a country, a culture, an enterprise, a people—particularly a very great success—also contains the seeds of its decline, possibly its destruction. It's one of the things the real world rubs your nose in as you move through it. The once-glorious civilizations of the Egyptians, the Mayans, the Aztecs, the Chinese, the Romans, the Greeks, the Persians, to name only a few—all are ruins now.

In a way Xi'an was lucky. It had found a new lease on life through its past. For years Beijing, site of the beginning of the Great Wall, had been the country's tourist center, but now Xi'an was suddenly its major attraction.

Several thousand years ago, whenever an emperor of China died he had been buried in an elaborate ritual with his entire court, his surviving wives, his children, courtiers, guards, cooks, everybody. Some prime minister had come along, knowing his fate, and had come up with an idea: Why not make statues of everybody, lifesize terra-cotta statues, bury them and not us? Somehow he'd sold the emperor on this, and so every single person in the court had been individually modeled and sculpted in terra-cotta. So far in Xi'an eight thousand of these buried life-sized statues—foot soldiers, chariots, horses, generals, weapons—had been found, entire armies facing every direction of the compass to ward off attacks on the dead emperor.

I'd seen pictures of the statues, but the first time you actually lay eyes on them is like first seeing the Taj Mahal or the Grand Canyon—it just knocks you out. It takes a few minutes to adjust to the fact that the army and court stretching in every direction are real, not a dream, that people actually molded so many statues, and did it so long ago, and then every few minutes it hits you again and you're amazed once more.

A few of these terra-cotta statues have been shown in museums around the world, but to really see them, to really feel their impact, you must go to Xi'an to the underground museum. All this was discovered only in 1974, and they're still digging. God knows what they're going to find before it's all over. So far, they've dug up one emperor's court. Who knows how many more there are?

As usual, we stayed at the best hotel in town—which in many towns was a five-flea instead of a five-star—the Golden Flower. We met the manager, a single Englishman named John Brown, a forty-two-year-old career hotel manager whose Midlands accent seemed wildly out of place. He supervised the five hundred Chinese employees, mainly teenage girls, who staffed the hotel and catered to all the foreigners flying in to see the terra-cotta statues. The hotel had its own beauty school, which taught the girls how to dress, make themselves up, and serve, taught them everything from the ground up. To them it was a glamorous job, like being an airline stewardess thirty-five years ago. It was here that we learned that the Chinese are taught it's dangerous to kiss a foreigner because the Chinese will get sick. Despite this, I must say I wondered about John's private life.

Tourism here was booming so much that even professors were giving up their positions to work in hotels as room clerks. They didn't see it as a step down, but as a move up to money and glamour. The lure of a more prosperous life has changed people's direction throughout history.

Here we saw a few beggars, but not as many in a week as you'd see in an hour in India. Some hung around restaurants waiting to move in on table scraps. They didn't seem to bother foreigners.

I'd always heard there was a fabulous bird market in Xi'an. Frequently going through a town we'd see fifteen to twenty old guys sitting in the park, each with a birdcage. In the U.S. we take our dogs to the park. In China you take your bird. A bird is the quintessential Chinese pet: It doesn't take up much room, nor does it eat much. In the same way, Ping-Pong and shooting pool are the quintessential Chinese sports. Cricket and baseball and football won't ever be as popular; they take up too much space.

Anyway, I wanted to see the bird market, but when I asked about it, I kept being told there was none. On two prior trips I had failed to find it. After making a nuisance of myself at the Golden Flower and with a dozen cab drivers, I finally found a driver who would take us.

He drove us to a tiny market about the size of an American living room, with a dozen cats and a few dogs. These aren't popular as pets in China; they, too, take up too much room, and the Communists discouraged them as capitalist-bourgeois. Knowing that governments rarely reveal their real reasons, I understood that they didn't want to have to feed millions of pets. So, Tabitha and I did our sign-language bit, going "tweet, tweet" and flapping our wings. After a couple more false stops, he finally let us out and pointed, indicating that we had to walk the rest of the way, that vehicles couldn't get any closer.

He was right. The road was too crowded, a sea of humanity. But when we turned the corner, there it was, a quarter of a mile of birds! Thousands of cages on both sides of the street, spilling beyond the road's edge, on the ground, dangling from bicycles, hung in trees, and along ropes stretched between poles. Every kind of bird was displayed—doves, parakeets, and ducks; parrots big and little; larks, canaries, swallows, thrushes, and titmice; exotic birds with brilliant headdresses, which we couldn't identify; hundreds of different kinds of birds, not to speak of the odd chicken destined for the pot, as well as snakes and goldfish meant for pets.

The area was packed with customers haggling with the sellers. As we were talking to a seller, a bird streaked over our heads, free of his cage, and headed for the hills, but the bird seller reached up and snatched it from the air with the nonchalance I would use to pick an apple. I couldn't decide who was more stunned—the bird or me.

Twice more we saw bird keepers pluck flying birds from the air. We didn't know whether to move forward or backward, afraid we'd miss something. We gathered that a bird was an inexpensive purchase, on a par with a cat back home. The Xi'an bird market was like so much in China—intense, packed, crowded. Between the crush and our curiosity, it took us forever to walk through it.

Since I've been back to the U.S. I've told friends, "If you go to Xi'an, yes, see the terra-cotta warriors, but also be sure to see the bird market." Every one has come back and said, "There is no bird market." I don't know why nobody will take them there. Usually there's a reason why natives don't want travelers to see places like the bird market or the tea-houses. Maybe the Chinese think Westerners will say rude things if they think some Chinese are layabouts and others eat parakeets. Well, it's true, the Chinese will eat any bird, so maybe that's what it is; perhaps they think the bird market is somehow not politically correct.

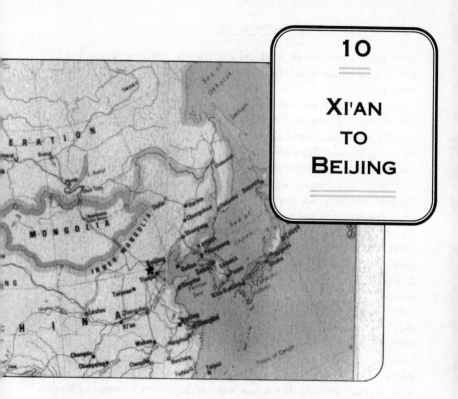

WE DROVE over the mountains to Luoyang, a day's drive of five hundred miles.

I had a flat on my rear tire, the second of what would be twenty or so between us over the entire trip. We both changed it, with me acting as Tabitha's assistant. With more than another thousand miles to Shanghai, we were now down to two spares, as with tubeless tires it's wise to discard them once they go flat, as per the manufacturer's instructions.

Mostly we drove on two-lane blacktop. In a few places the road was a mess, worse than on my last trip, although this time it wasn't washed away. Of course, there had been no signs saying, BEWARE, ROAD WASHED OUT, DETOUR. Imagine in the United States if a main road was out from New York to Boston; it would be all over the news. But the Chinese don't announce disasters.

We were about to leave Luoyang for Shanghai, where we had reservations on the monthly ferry to Japan, when some damn bureaucrat attached to the travel office panicked and threatened to call out the army if we drove there. We pleaded and showed Mr. Zhu our papers, but he was a local fellow who refused to understand that we already had permission.

I even tried to bribe him with my standard line, "I know this is out of the ordinary. There must be an extra fee that can be paid." Mr. Zhu wouldn't bite, and it was clear we couldn't go to Shanghai. As this was only a year after Tiananmen Square, he probably decided foreigners could be better controlled in Beijing.

This one functionary was screwing up our timing for the entire trip. By now, late May, we were on a tight schedule dictated by climate and ferry departures to and from Japan. We were desperate to avoid winter. Not just in Siberia, where winter began in September, only three months away, but also in South Africa and Australia and Argentina. We had only a thirteen-day window in Japan to catch the boat from Yokohama to Siberia. If we missed it, we'd have to wait an entire month for the next one.

So we were forced to alter our plans and drive north to Beijing. This didn't mean traveling more miles, but we didn't know what we would do after we arrived, how we would get to Japan. Of course this was often how we arrived in countries. A trip like this had so many variables, so many imponderables, such a changeable timetable, and was extended over so many months that it was impossible to obtain visas and book ourselves on every ferry and airline in advance. By necessity we had to make it up as we went along, discover our passage in the process of making our way.

Hurried inquiries told us the Beijing ferry to Japan was in dry dock for the summer. My next hope was to fly to Tokyo on the Chinese state airline, but airlines were often stuffy about bikes, disliking the idea of gas and batteries in their cargo holds. After all, they reasoned, even empty gas tanks held explosive vapor, and battery acids might wreak Godknew-what havoc on an airplane. Unless bikes were factory-new, Singapore Air refused to take them at all, no matter how well crated or prepped.

I was sure we'd have problems with the Chinese airline, but I didn't know whether they would be severe or mild.

Because the mania of Mao's Red Guards was long over and wall posters were rare, the fresh black-and-white posters caught my attention. Their bold ideograms on stark white paper made them look official and important.

Almost everywhere we stopped in China, within a few minutes a schoolteacher would appear to practice his English. As I collect political posters, and we were right under one of these fresh ones we'd seen so many of, I asked the thin schoolteacher with the nicotine-stained fingers about it. Mr. Li looked around furtively and edged closer to speak in a low tone.

This poster announced the pending execution of two criminals. What had they done? I asked.

Brandishing long pig knives, said Mr. Li, these men in their late twenties had broken into a widow's house and robbed and injured her. They had been caught, had been found guilty, and were sentenced to die.

Why the posters? I asked. Would there be a public execution?

No.

How would it be done?

With a pistol shot. Unless the robbers wanted a more brutal form of death, they or their families would buy the two bullets with which the police would execute them. The police assigned the task would drive them around until a suitable burial site was found, at which point the criminals would be given the task of digging their own graves. There would be no coffins. Once their graves were dug, the bullets they had purchased would make a swift end of them.

In contrast to the bold black ideograms on the white paper was a red check in the poster's bottom right-hand corner.

"What's that for?" I asked.

"It means the execution was carried out," whispered my informant.

Filled with unease, we pushed on.

From Lanzhou on we had begun to notice more people. Once we'd left Xi'an, once we'd crossed the mountains, we were right in it, smack in the fertile, populated part of China. From here to Beijing were constant masses of people. Everywhere, in the countryside, the cities, the towns, the villages, we were never out of sight of people. The roads were incredibly crowded, because everybody and everything was out using them—pigs, goats, people, bicycles, carts, trucks. The expression "teeming Asian masses" took on real meaning.

Slow traffic stayed to the side, and the few vehicles drove right down the road's middle. When we were lucky we made thirty to forty miles an hour.

Once along the road to Luoyang we came on a huge traffic tie-up. I rode up to see what the problem was. A wagon was sitting in the middle of the road, blocking everybody. The driver had disconnected it and left it there and had driven off with whatever was pulling that wagon to fetch a spare part. Whenever a vehicle broke down, the driver just went off and left it to get help. Nobody worried about his property being stolen. In this case, nobody got out of his car to move the damn wagon, either. I mean, eight guys could have pushed it to the side of the road if they had thought about it.

When I went back for Tabitha, I clocked it. The queue was three miles long.

From time to time we drove over a heap of grain in the road, put there to be threshed by traffic. We also rode across piles of nuts, placed in the road to be cracked.

We never saw any public displays of affection between the sexes. It must happen; people have been necking for thousands of years. We saw girls walking down the street holding hands with girls, boys with boys—not homosexual, which is against the law—just as friends, the way you see it in France or the Middle East.

On my last trip I had attended an outdoor dance, an afternoon disco. I noticed that the guys danced only with guys, the girls with other girls. Finally this guy came over and asked me to dance, taking me aback. I had never been asked to dance by a guy before. I protested, but when in China . . . still, I didn't particularly like it and I wasn't very good at it.

On the way to Shijiazhuang, a large industrial city that has sprung up over the past few decades, we stopped off at a big Buddhist temple with a martial arts school.

In China today there are many cities of 3 million and 4 million people, close to the size of Los Angeles, that forty years ago were no more than villages. If such growth happened in Kansas, it would be a much-remarked event; here in China the story has been lost to the outside world.

I noticed more gas stations than on previous trips, all state run, of course, except for the black marketeers'. Shijiazhuang, too, had one of the eighties' boom-time hotels, but as usual it was almost empty.

Approaching Beijing was very exciting to both of us. A sign said, BEIJING, 49 KILOMETERS—in Western letters, no less! Just seeing road signs was a shock. This was part of the new internationalism. We were moving back into the other world, the one we'd left behind in Istanbul, seven thousand miles ago.

Tabitha and I grinned at each other: We'd crossed the Eurasian mass on bikes. Ninety-four hundred miles of driving, Ireland to Beijing, mostly over two-lane blacktop pocked with treacherous potholes, often no better than a bad Southern dirt road, full of farm animals, ramshackle vehicles, and pedestrians careless about traffic. We'd done it in March, April, and May, and thankfully the weather hadn't been bad, only a few rainy days. We'd slept in five-flea and five-star hotels, we'd eaten off the best china in luxury hotels and fly-specked tin plates in outdoor bazaars, but we'd done it. At that moment I knew if we could do this, we could do anything together.

We hit the four-lane blacktop into Beijing, quite a luxury. We could now roar along at sixty or seventy miles an hour, unfettered.

We passed through Tiananmen Square, the heart of Beijing, a vast sea of cobblestones. In the old days, this had been the location of government offices, but Mao had changed its character. Wearing his Red Guard armband, he had reviewed parades of a million people here. In 1976 this had been the place where another million people had paid him their last respects.

On my 1988 visit the huge square had been a lazy place to fly one of those fancy Chinese kites or to sprawl around on a summer evening, a combination of Moscow's Red Square and New York's City Hall Park. History was on all sides of us here—Tiananmen Gate to the Forbidden City, the history museum and the Museum of the Revolution, the Great Hall of the People, Qianmen Gate, the Mao mausoleum, and the Monument to the People's Heroes. If you got out early in the morning you could watch a troop of PLA soldiers raise the flag in a precisely drilled ceremony of 108 paces to the minute.

But now, almost a year since Tiananmen Square, scores of police were everywhere, afraid of another demonstration on the anniversary of the first, not letting Westerners tarry. Under their suspicious eyes we took a few pictures and moved on.

With our plan to take the ferry from Shanghai thwarted by the army, I was in a sweat to make the jump to Japan. We had to stay inside the bubble of summer as we moved around the globe.

After checking into our hotel, we did a bit of sight-seeing, taking in the Forbidden City. While it would have been nice to see more of Beijing, the next day we rushed out to Beijing International Airport to see about getting ourselves and the bikes to Tokyo.

Although the passenger terminal was bustling, the freight terminal might have been in a sleepy Southern town, for all its inactivity. There was no traffic and not a lot of international trade, which I guessed went through the ports. Nothing was so urgent that it had to be rushed to China: That country hadn't had it for centuries, so why hurry now?

There is no guidebook that tells motorcyclists how to get from Istanbul to Beijing, much less from Beijing to Tokyo. I was dreading this, knowing what we had gone through to ship the bikes from New York to Shannon. Not only would we have to crate the bikes, but we would have to disconnect the batteries, drain the gas, and fill out God knew how many forms and deal with countless functionaries, each one impressed with the importance of his office or fearful of losing his job by allowing us to do what we wanted.

On May 29 we took the bikes to the airport, and we spent the whole day there, although we were the only people shipping out freight. We always allowed ourselves a full day to cross a border, and this time, in fact, it did take ten full hours to make the arrangements. The insurance office, the authorization office, the airline office, and naturally several cashiers' offices. We had to have the bikes weighed. To my astonishment nobody asked for a bribe or made any noises about draining the gas and disconnecting the batteries.

Actually, being the first motorcyclists to leave the Beijing airport for Japan worked in our favor. Had we been the tenth or the hundredth, they would have worked out a procedure that would have taken days instead of hours, but we took them by surprise.

I knew, too, from years of travel that once you start the process of crossing a border, you have to carry it through with all the speed you can muster. Don't ever stop, don't ever say I'll come back tomorrow or even in an hour. Keep it moving or it will never get done. While it might seem nice to lollygag your way around the world, it takes a kind of intensity to make a trip like this. Giving in to the desire to take it easy or to go off to sight-see, or allowing yourself to become discouraged by some bureaucrat's red tape during a border crossing—of which we would have more than a hundred—would probably mean not completing a trip as long as this, or that it would be extended by years.

Luckily, working your way across a border takes on a life of its own, and the last thing you want to do is to cripple that movement. One guy says, "Okay, now go see Joe." Or he shouts over, "Joe, take care of these guys, they're okay." If you stop the process it always runs into a snag. Any pause gives the clerks a chance to think, and what bureaucrats do when they stop to think is figure out a reason why you can't do what you want to do.

Pausing is dangerous even *after* you have crossed a border. For God's sake don't linger a few paces on the other side while the border guard mulls over what he's just done, what his boss is going to say when he gets back from lunch. You want to get the hell out of there, move on while the moving on is good. So, once we had made inquiries and the bureaucrats had committed themselves, the last thing we wanted to do was slow down the process of exiting by suspending it for a week to sight-see in town. I promise you, the next week that process would have been different, longer, more cumbersome—and maybe impossible. So we announced we were ready to leave on the weekly plane the next day, which helped push along the endless paperwork.

Worried that the job wouldn't be done right, we went with the bikes to see them strapped to pallets. Because that day no other freight was going to Tokyo, every freight handler at the airport showed up to attack this problem. Twelve husky Chinese handlers strapped this way and that, but nothing ever worked. Once they tied Tabitha's bike so tight that the metal pallet came up, buckled.

So finally Tabitha climbed on the pallet and said, "All right, guys, let me show you how to do this."

All these freight handlers stood back and watched this tall, long-haired blond woman strap the bikes down, which they had tried to do for two hours and failed. When she finished a little cheer went up, led as much by me as by anyone.

Tabitha wanted to see as much of the sights as we could squeeze in, so we taxied into town for the night.

In many ways Beijing is the stuffiest place in China and not at all characteristic of the country. While it has the best of everything—the best hotels, the best food, the best roads and streets—it's a city of straight-laced museums and pompous functionaries. Everywhere you turn there's a gray wall with a closed gate or door. The city's influence, however, is felt throughout China. Across all of China's three thousand miles, even as far away as Ürümqi, unbelievable as it may seem, the clocks are set on Beijing time. Thus we'd wake up at seven-thirty in the morning in the west and it was still dark, because in this geographic time zone it was really four-thirty. The capital's bureaucrats push their directives on to the far-flung countryside; but where for years they were obeyed, more and more they are not only resisted but ignored, especially in the south around Hong Kong, Guangzhou, and Shanghai, where the capitalist spirit is raging like a wildfire.

Tabitha wanted to go to the Summer Palace, but we were told it was closed for repairs. We found out later there had been a big incident there. The authorities had beaten someone to death.

For my part I was disappointed that we didn't have time to revisit either of the two main southern provinces, Fujian, right across from Taiwan, and Guangdong, which surrounds Hong Kong.

Both interest me enormously, because both have been strongly influenced by Taiwan's and Hong Kong's capitalistic prosperity, by their free-market, entrepreneurial fervor. Guangdong and Fujian are themselves major centers of capitalism, of entrepreneurship, of foreign investment. Most of the people who had fled to Taiwan came from Fujian province, for an obvious reason: It was right across the sea. Many of our own Chinese immigrants of the nineteenth and twentieth centuries came from those two provinces because they were near the ports, the easy way out. Plus, down there they get Hong Kong TV. *Dallas* is a powerful motivator throughout the world. People everywhere want to be rich.

These southern provinces have listened less and less to Beijing. The capital thinks it still controls the army, but it's beginning to have its doubts. When the Tiananmen Square troubles were at their height, Beijing considered bringing in the crackerjack army from Guangzhou to deal with the problem. Then it realized these guys probably wouldn't come. The southern army was intertwined with the capitalists and entrepreneurs down there, getting their share of the new profits, and they weren't going to waste their time putting down a bunch of kids in a square.

The Communist Party hasn't fallen in the eyes of the Chinese—yet. The Chinese down in the south and in the countryside still call themselves Communists even though they are as capitalist as they can be. The bureaucrats, the military, the generals—they are all in there trying to grab their piece of the action.

It's clear that over the most recent centuries China has been pretty corrupt, although we might not always agree on what that means. Once China was the richest, most powerful country in the world, but it's been in decline for a long, long time. Even in the eighteenth century China was still wealthy. The last sovereign, the empress dowager, wasn't corrupt so much as without dynamic, without the vision and enterprise needed to keep up with the world and the place of the Chinese in it. The ruling classes still sat around doing the mandarin things they'd been doing for the past five hundred years, totally isolated from the rest of the world.

Over a nearly forty-year period, from before the First World War until after the Second, China's empire was in turmoil and decline, just as the Soviet Union has been. What happened during that large empire's collapse is a model for what's likely to happen in the former Soviet Union: thirty to forty years of civil wars waged by warlords, i.e., military leaders exercising power over civilians by force. The collapse in the Soviet Union will be far more complicated, however, as China was more compact, with a billion people of a single ethnic group (the Han are 94 percent of the population and live mainly in the east) crowded into a space the size of the United States east of the Mississippi. The USSR not only sprawls across two continents, but is composed of more than a hundred different religious, language, ethnic, and national groups.

The nationalists, Chiang Kai-shek and his lads, got rid of all that mandarin decay, but they were replaced by Communists, who were even more corrosive to the native Chinese soul. Mao Tse-tung and his Communist cadres won the Chinese revolution and kept the Americans out of North Korea, but they lived as privileged elites and did not cleanse China's spiritual rot. Mao, who himself had begun his career as a warlord, was an extraordinary revolutionary and strategist who mobilized his guerrillas to wage an effective civil war. However, like other successful revolutionaries such as Castro, Lenin, Stalin, Cromwell, Bolívar, and Ghana's Nkrumah, after the revolution succeeded Mao didn't have the sharply different set of skills and understanding needed to run a country and an economy. His post-revolutionary Great Leap Forward, agricultural and industrial policies, and Cultural Revolution were all disasters.

Even thirty years later, the mainland Communists haven't undone the damage of Mao's Cultural Revolution. In addition to the devastating economic and social disruptions of that period, throughout China many monuments and historic sites were destroyed. They haven't been and probably never will be rebuilt.

Mao and his gang were lucky the Chinese infrastructure takes so little to operate; otherwise the country would have collapsed like some of the African countries after they'd used up what wealth the colonialists left. All the roads the Chinese seem to need are those for bicycles and pedestrians. The phones and railroads seem to work better than those in the Soviet Union and Africa, maybe because, relatively speaking, China is a more compact country.

What could happen is that China will split into three countries—the north, the south, and the west. The people from the south in Guangdong speak a different language from the people in Beijing, Cantonese versus Mandarin, as well as being in their hearts entrepreneurial and not Communist. Then there's the west, the desert, filled with Muslims, an area which no Chinese back east particularly wants but which might be valuable as a buffer against the forces from the west and might contain fabulous minerals, oil, gold, copper, or diamonds. As a buffer it struck me as an expensive anachronism. Sure, Genghis Khan or Tamerlane would have had to march across the desert to reach Beijing, but a modern army would fly over.

The western region may split off from China, not because of any ideological independence movement but because the region is still culturally, geographically, and spiritually part of the old Turkistan. As recently as the 1960s, there was armed resistance to Beijing in the west, although considering to whose tender mercies such independence would have laid them vulnerable—the Russians—I can't say the region's leaders had thought through their rebellion.

The mentality throughout the south and in the countryside in the north is different from that of the capital, and on my three prior trips—two of them close-to-the-ground motorcycle visits in 1986 and 1988—I had found its spirit being fed more and more.

To give you a sense of the economic entity coming into being, by the end of this decade China's economy will be the third largest in the world, although obviously this won't be on a per-capita basis. Sometime in the first half of the twenty-first century China will come to have the world's largest economy.

What will be the effect of China's one-child-per-couple policy on its future? After all, people in agricultural countries like China always have wanted lots of kids to help on the farm and as an insurance policy for their old age. In all of history such an unnatural policy has never been tried.

I ask myself if these only children will be so spoiled and self-centered as to shift the Chinese personality. Then, too, many studies document the success orientation of only and first-born children. Will an entire nation of them strive even harder than today's hardworking Chinese?

China could wind up as a nation of spoiled, driven achievers. Then I ask myself if parents and grandparents in such a country will send their only darlings to die in a war.

What I do know for sure is that the Chinese have a long history of trading, as far back as Roman times. It's a collective memory, a historic set of skills and attitudes. In the twenty-first century China is going to be the most capitalistic, most developed, and richest nation in the world. Forget Japan; our children should be learning Chinese. Here are more than a billion people being infected with the Taiwan miracle. Hong Kong is the site in the larger body where the growth has taken root, and its shoots are rapidly spreading northward. Sooner or later the southern provinces will influence those northward, and this fast-growing bamboo capitalism will spread across all of populous eastern China.

We forget, too, the overseas Chinese.

No one knows how many there are, but they are in every country—Taiwan, Thailand, Singapore, San Francisco and New York, Australia—many thriving, many rich. A third of the population of Malaysia is Chinese. They've been emigrating from China's southern provinces for more than a century, but especially since the Communists came, unwilling to be ground under the heels of self-righteous thugs.

Even if you're third-generation Chinese, a cheerleader living in Beverly Hills who doesn't know a chopstick from a baton and who has never heard a word of Cantonese, you're still Chinese to the Chinese. You're welcome back anytime, and they're happy to give you a passport.

Many of the overseas Chinese have expertise and capital and want to go back and help, or invest in China and make lots of money. The Chinese welcome them with open arms. There may be fifty to a hundred million overseas Chinese—seven to twenty times the population of Hong Kong—vast numbers around the globe with vast wealth. China goes so far as to set up three classes of hotels—one for the locals, one for foreign travelers, and one for the overseas Chinese.

Compare them with the overseas Russians. The Russians don't have a vast, successful overseas population to aid their stricken country. Why? First, there are not huge numbers of them overseas. Second, the overseas Russians haven't been as successful as the overseas Chinese. Third, they don't have the Chinese's historical capitalistic experience. The Russians weren't great capitalists even under the czars, whom the Communists threw out seventy-five years ago. The Communist takeover in China was only in 1949. Lots of Chinese alive today still remember capitalism. Fourth, few overseas Russians want to go back home, whereas the Chinese do. The Russians who left have been absorbed by other cultures.

Few Russians in Brooklyn think of returning to Russia. They want to move to a fancy suburb.

What Russia has in abundance are ethnic groups wanting to govern themselves. All that's going to lead to is chaos. If China disintegrates, it's going to be into three countries, the three reasonably coherent, rational parts I mentioned previously. Russia will disintegrate into, say, fifty or a hundred belligerent factions. Will this be dangerous to us, or even to Europe? No, because these factions will be too small to be of military importance, but more important, they have fought one another for hundreds of years, and what working weapons, including nuclear bombs, they have they will at worst use on one another.

Still, I'd be tempted to sell short almost any non-Chinese company with a massive investment in China, because the Chinese frame of reference won't allow outsiders to make the big money. Why? There is a centuries-old suspicion and contempt for foreigners first bred by the Middle Kingdom's certainty that it was the center of the universe. The rock-hard belief that persists until today that the Chinese way of doing things is best isn't going to be shaken anytime soon by the West.

Thus, because they're treated differently, the Americans, the Germans, and even the Japanese aren't going to make nearly as much money in China as the local and overseas Chinese will. Anyone else who invests in China, as the Japanese are doing, needs a strong stomach for risk and the patience to wait maybe twenty years for a proper return. The folks who do that probably will get rich, of course, because the market is so huge.

How, then, should a prudent Western investor play the Chinese economic explosion?

If you want to get involved, you should get a Chinese company to do business for you in China. For instance, if XYZ Corporation announced it was going to make a major effort to market directly in China, I'd be tempted to short it, but if instead it hooked up with an overseas Chinese health-and-beauty company already marketing successfully in China, perhaps one listed on the Thai or Singapore stock exchanges, I might be an eager buyer of XYZ Corporation or the overseas Chinese company itself.

At the airport the next morning we worried that the bikes hadn't made it onto the plane. We asked if we could see them in the cargo hold.

Sure, no problem.

I imagined what I would have gone through at Kennedy Airport to peer into a cargo hold. It would have taken seventeen bureaucrats seventeen hours to deal with such a simple request. There the bikes were, tucked away just as Tabitha had left them.

We took off, leaving China, the country with the most people, and heading for Japan, the country with the most money.

Visas

Entries/Entrées   Departures/Sorties

PERMITTED TO LAND IN
IRELAND FOR THREE MONTHS

30 MAR 1990

T.C. EDİRNE
GİRİŞ
14 IV 90
KAPIKULE KARA HUDUT KAPISI

TÜRKİYE
CUMHURİYETİ

10

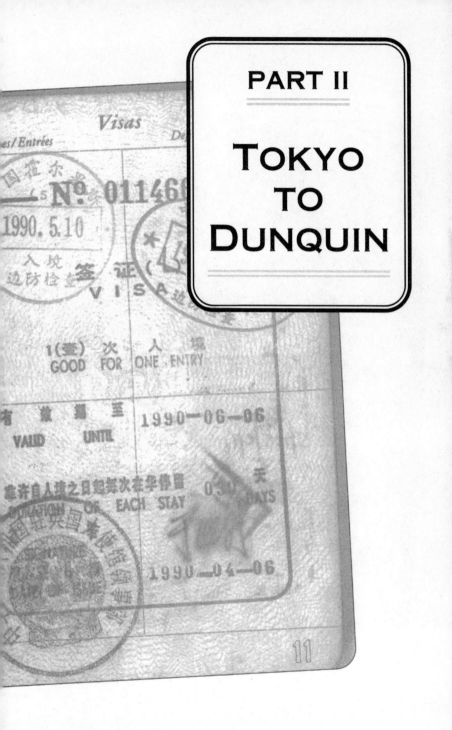

PART II

TOKYO TO DUNQUIN

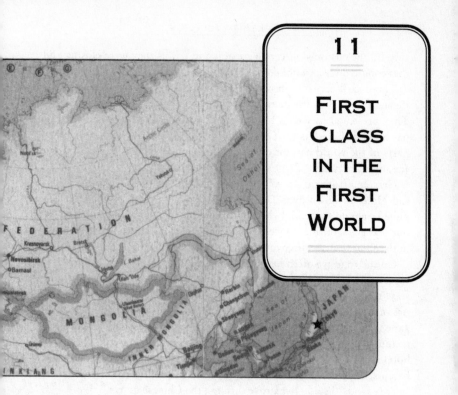

T NARITA AIRPORT we perplexed customs. Here we were, American citizens with German motorcycles flying into Tokyo from Beijing. It was a little too much for them.

Using less sign language and more English, we made our needs known, but the customs officers hadn't had much experience with carnets. These were bonds we'd bought from an English insurance company that guaranteed we wouldn't sell our bikes within the countries through which we passed. Fortunately, we'd prepared for this eventuality back in London by obtaining the name of an official at the Japanese Automobile Association who would be familiar with them. The customs official called him and was filled in.

What a difference from China, where most requests were met by *mei you,* "not have," which could mean "not available today," "not available for foreigners," "maybe later," "not possible because I'm on my break," or "I don't know anything about it, so I'm not taking any chances." The Japanese met every request, whether they could carry it out or not, with a vigorous *hai,* "yes."

At this point it was five o'clock in the evening. Any minute now, I was certain, the customs officers were going to tell us they were closing and that tomorrow was a holiday, come back Tuesday.

These civil servants, however, stuck with the job of processing us through till they finished, even though it took an hour or so of overtime. They presented us with a bill for the extra time, but I was delighted to pay and finish the hassle. If only border officials and bureaucrats in other parts of the world had the same can-do attitude! This is one reason the Japanese are rich.

Grinning from ear to ear like fools, Tabitha and I drove to the Imperial Hotel in downtown Tokyo, across from the Imperial Palace. We pulled right up to the lobby—motorcycles muddy, spare tires hanging off our rear ends, fairings busted—and nobody batted an eye. Once we were in the sumptuous room, we were beside ourselves with disbelief and joy.

On the road we often had been immersed in practical problems: how to get across the next border, what the road ahead was like, where to stay, would there be gas in the next town, could we buy tires, the logistics of it all. Although traveling through exotic locales had often made us gape with astonishment, we hadn't awoken every single day and thrilled to our new location. But now that we had an interlude in a first-class hotel room in a First World country, we sank back and realized what we had just done.

"My God," I said, "we drove through the Chinese desert."

"All of China," Tabitha said with a big smile, pleased with herself. "All the way from the Atlantic to the Pacific."

According to the folks at the *Guinness Book of Records,* no one before had ever done it by land.

"You're the first woman to do it," I said, which made us both beam with pride.

I was hoping the joy of accomplishment and the thrill of the exotic would rekindle her enthusiasm for the rest of the trip, because she had been making rumblings over the past few days of not being sure she wanted to go farther, that maybe she'd fly back to New York from Tokyo. Her bike was still giving her trouble, and she was weary of the road.

But I didn't say anything, figuring it best for her to rest a few days before we discussed it.

We both were amazed by the contrast of Japan, not just to China, but to nearly every other place in the world: how beautiful the roads were, in what good repair everything was, how clean the parks and buildings were. It wasn't like driving into New York, Rome, or London, which in areas made you think you were in the Third World. Japan was run like a very tight ship under the eye of a hard-boiled skipper.

We took our bikes to the local BMW dealer, where we told them to throw away our old tires and put on new ones. They would rebuild my carburetor and overhaul Tabitha's engine.

Back in January of 1990 I had predicted in *Barron's* that the Japanese stock market would fall by at least 50 percent. A local financial journalist caught up with me in Japan and wanted to know what I thought about the market now that it was down from near 40,000 to 29,000. Was this the bottom? Should investors be piling in?

A day or so before I had noticed that the front page of a local newspaper printed an index of the average price of membership in Tokyo golf clubs, the way back in the States newspapers published the Dow Jones stock index. It had hit a million dollars. A million dollars to belong to a golf club! This sounded like a speculative bubble to me, a financial feeding frenzy without intrinsic value, and the top of one at that.

When you see a value as out of whack as this, stand back and ask yourself if something is wrong. Stop and think about it. Perhaps everybody around you is losing his head. In 1929 you would have seen the same speculative hyperactivity in stocks. In the real world, golf memberships can't be worth a million dollars.

I said the stock and real estate market had a lot further down to go, as it was clear nobody in the market was suffering any pain from this drop. In addition to sky-high prices for golf memberships, Japan's real estate prices were still at cloudlike levels. The ground on which the Emperor's palace stood was said to be worth more than the entire state of Florida.

Moreover, I knew the Bank of Japan was tightening the money supply. It had announced that it wanted to get rid of the speculative bubble. When the Japanese central bank says something, it's like the German Bundesbank. It means it. It doesn't play around. But the guys in the Japanese market had never known anything but a bull market. They didn't know things could change. All they knew about stocks was that they went up. Well, the real world didn't work that way, but they weren't going to listen to me.

It all reminded me of how they'd gotten out on this limb in the first place. The Japanese have the largest foreign-currency reserves in the world, largely because they have had extremely large balance-of-trade surpluses over many past years. After the war, the way to get rich in many countries, Japan and Germany especially, was to get foreign—hard—currency, such as dollars, any currency that didn't lose its value. Just the way it is today in Russia or China. The more dollars, marks, or yen you have in those places, the better off you are in those economies.

So after the Second World War the Japanese said, "How do you get hard currency?" You export. You give the folks with hard currency something they want and they'll give some of it to you. They learned—taught themselves—that what foreigners want is quality. They pushed their workers to make quality goods because they were desperate for foreign currency. Their country was devastated. They couldn't buy anything with the local currency because it was basically worthless, or perceived as worthless outside their country because they didn't have any foreign-currency reserves.

What happened was the same thing that happens anytime an energetic people get an idea where the gold mine is. In California? Let's rush out there. It can be a real gold mine or a Wall Street boom or oil wells in Texas or tourism in Xi'an or a pile of hard currency, but once industrious people see where it is, they'll jump for it.

The Japanese export boom was born from that. It wasn't as though some evil Japanese minister said, "All right, guys, let's start exporting and put the Americans out of business, refight World War II." People say the Japanese copied everybody else. No, they just saw what the customers were buying. They saw that everybody wanted a TV, and they faced up to the hard truth that they had to make a cheaper, better TV or they wouldn't be able to sell the ones they made.

The results? Between 1957, when their pre-war economic benchmarks were regained, and 1970, their economy grew 10 percent annually, several times faster than ours. By 1980 their automobile production surpassed ours, and by 1986 they were supplying nearly a quarter of our imports.

What a difference between the Japanese attitude and that of the American government! We say, "Let's let the dollar depreciate and devalue. We'll be the low-cost producers and we'll sell more because our prices will be lower." Except for short periods, that policy has never, ever worked in the history of the world. You can sell only so far on price.

And why not? Say Chevrolet and Toyota sell more-or-less identical cars for ten thousand dollars. If the United States devalues the dollar by 30 percent, the Chevrolet will still sell for ten thousand dollars but the Toyota will now go for thirteen thousand dollars. At first blush, this looks good. Finally American automotive workers' jobs will be protected. How can it hurt us if we make it difficult for the Japanese to sell in our market?

However, in the real world what happens is that under the umbrella of the devalued currency, Chevrolet, Ford, and Plymouth will raise their price to, say, $11,500, as now it's easy to underprice the foreign competition.

Well, some say it's worth it if we keep our people employed, if we make America first. Unfortunately, it doesn't work that way. Because the dry cleaner on the corner has paid 15 percent more for his Chevrolet—as has every one of his suppliers—he must raise his prices to reflect the increase. He and his suppliers must also collectively pay 30 percent more for all the things we Americans import, be they palladium, titanium, cobalt, chrome, tin, coffee, cocoa—the list is endless. Add these to the domestic increases brought about by devaluation, and its seemingly no-cost benefits disappear in a year or so.

In addition, when you sell on price, you don't innovate and make your products better; they get shoddier in comparison with your competition's. You become fat and lazy and sloppy.

Now inflation starts. The Chevrolet creeps up in price till it sells at thirteen thousand dollars or even fourteen thousand dollars. Toyotas sell for less, and Chevrolet loses more market share. As this scenario is repeated, a powerful noose tightens around the country's financial jugular that it only rarely escapes. Your costs again catch up with you and you have to devalue again.

Devaluation creates a never-ending, vicious circle. If it worked, Italy would not have a stagnant economy, political and economic corruption, and constant inflation. Zaire, with an economy that is one of the world's basket cases, would be the world's most efficient producer. After all, on a purchasing-power basis, the Zaire currency is wildly underpriced because nobody wants it.

So, while our government today keeps saying, "Let's sell on price," no other country in the world will now even claim that devaluation is a good long-term strategy. The Brits excuse their devaluations by saying they need to buy some time, but they've been buying time now for decades. Thirty years ago the British pound sterling would buy eleven German marks; today it will buy less than two and a half. If the British don't change this, in thirty more years the pound will be that much less valuable.

Governments have only three choices in their fiscal management: be disciplined by spending no more than they take in from taxes, borrow to cover their deficits, or print new money. World markets made Zaire pay by depreciating its currency and refusing to lend it any more money, and so its currency has become worthless. The market will do the same to the United States if we don't shape up, if we keep running a budget deficit and borrowing our heads off. The longer we put off correcting the financial mess the federal government has produced, the worse the pain will be.

Right now we are the largest debtor nation in the world by a factor of seven times. Yes, if we did what it took now to set things right, it would be very painful. Lots of people who are feeding at the government trough would have to cut back. However, if we put off this housecleaning until we owe as much as all the other countries in the world put together—which may happen by 1999—it's going to be that much more painful, not a bad dream but a nightmare.

The only true cure is a rough, rough discipline that few countries' populations have the guts for, but those who do come to call the tune for the rest of the world.

The discipline? A country has to learn to compete and innovate. It must lower its costs. A manufacturer has to take another country's tape recorder and say, "Okay, let's put twelve new bells and whistles on it. Let's make it work as well as the German tape recorder at a better price."

How can a government aid this? Over the past thirty years, the British government might not have printed so much money and might have maintained a balanced budget. This would have held up the value of sterling and forced the country to be more competitive, to make better products and to innovate.

The government and the people should have taken the pain, borne it. Yes, the price would have been high: It would have cost them unemployment, even high unemployment. It would have caused some poverty, but it would have enabled the British people to come out on the other side, as have the French and the Chileans.

In the seventies the British government under Prime Minister Callaghan came to the conclusion that Britain badly needed a semiconductor industry if it were to compete in the world of the future. That same government turned down establishing a British Silicon Valley because it would have created too many millionaires, and it was philosophically opposed to people getting rich. As the English learned for a while in the 1970s and the Italians are learning now, eventually the worldwide market in currencies and bonds is going to say, "Okay, guys, it's over whether you like it or not." Someday the world markets will refuse to buy more U.S. dollars and bonds. Can you blame them? Would you buy overpriced bonds and currencies?

Unfortunately, it usually takes war, hyperinflation, depression, or some other grave calamity that impoverishes the populace to bring a people to the place where they'll follow such a tough economic necessity. After all, Germany and Japan were forced into it by the devastation of World War II. The South Americans were forced into it by seventy years of mismanagement. Usually politicians cannot, will not, stay the course.

Oddly enough, the French have maintained such a discipline. For thirty to thirty-five years after the war they continually devalued and inflated. They nationalized the banks and many large industrial companies. They imposed price controls to curb exorbitant profits and passed a large tax on millionaires, not only on their incomes, but also on their wealth. "We'll have easy money, too," they said, "which will bring prosperity and good times."

Of course it didn't work. French growth stagnated as the rest of the world recovered. Not only did unemployment rise, but French politicians constantly devalued the franc.

Of all people, the socialists under Mitterrand in 1983 said, "We gotta change this policy, it hasn't worked. Now what we're going to do is tie ourselves to the Bundesbank." This was the German central bank, renowned for its monetary discipline and constitutionally required to maintain a sound currency. "We're going to cut taxes, encourage investing, have low inflation, and make this country change into being an efficient producer of high-quality, competitive goods. We're going to develop our economy for the long term."

To my amazement the French government did what was necessary. It stayed the course despite the social pain. Maybe it was able to do this because it was socialist. The French people might not have put up with the hard road if the capitalists had done it, because they would have thought the capitalists were interested only in helping their rich friends. If only a right-winger like Nixon could go to China, perhaps only socialists could insist on social pain.

Keeping a rein on the money supply meant that the French businessman was hopping mad over the cost of capital. It meant high unemployment, which meant the French voters weren't all that happy, either. But it forced the French to be more competitive, to be willing to go in and work hard for reasonable wages, the essence of increased productivity and a more competitive product. Their economy became more efficient. The uncompetitive enterprises went out of business, merged, or adapted. The French figured out how to innovate and sell to the rest of the world.

Politically speaking, the socialists were able to bring this about because their people were fed up. From the fifties on, there had been a constant turnover in government. The people themselves finally realized that they had to bite the bullet, take their economic pain, clean their house—sober up—if they were to straighten out their country. To a government in economic trouble, printing money and inflation look as appealing as does a fifth of whiskey to a longtime drunk, but it never makes the long-term situation better. There's not a country or a people that has gone through what it takes to put its currency on a sound footing that has ever regretted it any more than an alcoholic who's hit bottom regrets being sober after he's been on the wagon for ten years.

Actually, now the French economy is in better shape than the German: lower inflation, better balance of trade, better everything. They've been off the bottle for a long time, yet ironically the market still doesn't believe them because it has a folk memory that runs, "Who're these guys trying to kid? We've known the French for a hundred years and they always give in. They're weak, they're pansies." Hitler thought that, and Kaiser Wilhelm thought that. The franc will come up against periodic pressure in the currency markets till the French convince them that they really and truly mean business, the way the Germans, Dutch, and Chileans have.

What about the gold standard as a way to enforce currency discipline? Can we, should we, return to the gold standard? Under it, by law, you can turn in a certain amount of your paper money for an ounce of gold. It's a way of making governments honest, of requiring them to keep a sound set of books.

There are several cogent arguments against the gold standard, one being that the world should not be held hostage to two of the largest gold producers, Russia and South Africa, both of which are potentially explosive. Even if they stabilize, why give them a huge advantage?

My problem with the gold standard is twofold: (1) It might work. A return to the gold standard would lead to strict discipline for our politicians and ultimately to hardship for our excess-ridden economy. When the pain became too great, the politicians would blame the problem on gold and abandon it, as they have always done. Back in 1973, Nixon took us off a modified gold standard when the pain of complying with its demands became more than the politicians would face up to. (2) It might not work. That is, the politicians would find ways to fudge, avoid, or reduce its discipline to save themselves. As a typical example, the gold coins from the latter days of the Roman Empire contained less gold than the coins of the early, dynamic period. Any gold-standard system our politicians put in place might well not be sound, yet all of us would be duped into thinking it was secure. By the time the fraud became clear, it would be too late for many.

There is a simple, low-cost way to solve the whole problem of the gold standard and its discipline on money—eliminate the capital-gains tax on gold. Today it's impossible to transact business in gold or to index transactions to it (or to anything else except paper money) because a huge capital-gains tax is imposed every time gold is used. Eliminate the tax and people will vote with their wallets, which is what the gold standard is all about anyway. That is, whenever the politicians debase a currency or an economy, more and more people will turn to gold. As the use of gold rises, the bankruptcy of a government's policies will be clear, even to the people in the street. They will insist that their transactions be carried out in gold rather than paper (fiat) money.

Needless to say, an even better solution would be to eliminate the capital-gains tax on all hard assets. Then, whenever politicians debased the currency the market would revert to gold, silver, diamonds, corn, lumber, or whatever else people saw fit to make their medium of commerce. We are now precluded from these choices because everything, except the governmental monopoly on paper money, is subject to a capital-gains tax.

The one thing the Japanese journalist didn't ask me was what local financial assets were undervalued.

The answer was—and still is—seats on the Japanese futures exchanges.

As everybody knows, for years the Japanese commodity markets have been closed to the outside world. As a result, their commodity exchanges are small and undeveloped. On a par with those in the States fifty years ago, they trade mostly local silk and rice.

I classify this government interference in markets as statism. That is, the politicians have protected the country's agricultural sector, causing its citizens to pay six times the world price for rice. The farmers' use of land for rice has driven up the per-acre price of all land to absurd heights. Since land values are overblown, no one can afford anything but cramped housing far from city centers.

Now, however, the Japanese are being forced to open their markets to foreign industrial products and commodities. They have copied some foreign trading operations, setting up an index futures contract for their stock market and one for the yen bond market. Part of opening up their financial markets is to let foreigners buy seats on their exchanges.

How can an investor profit? A clever person should buy a membership on the Japanese commodities exchanges. First, it's dirt cheap, and second, there will be an explosive price increase as more and more commodities trading takes place in Japan. Seats on the Japanese stock market hit $6 million, while those on the commodities exchanges are a fraction of this. Look at the comparables in the United States: Membership on the New York Stock Exchange sells for well over half-a-million dollars, and the price of a seat on a hot futures market is an equivalent amount.

Buying such a seat is a cheap way to enter these markets. Regional commodities markets will continue to develop and integrate further into worldwide markets. In a few years, every commodity will be traded at every hour around the globe, and at that point these seats will soar in price.

Buying one of these seats satisfies two basic principles of my investment approach.

First, we've found something that's cheap.

Second, a dynamic change in its favor is about to occur.

These principles may sound simple, but they are keys to successful investing and will repay the closest study.

Most investors don't have a problem knowing when an investment is cheap. The hard part is knowing that a change is about to occur in the near future. This is where studying markets and their history is so important. In my finance classes I insist that my students practice by studying everything that could have been known at a particular time in history and by making their own predictions. What would have told you in 1929 that the New York market was going to crash? How could you have known after the War Between the States that the Manhattan real estate market would soar? After World War II, Montgomery Ward predicted a recession and drew in its horns. Sears Roebuck correctly predicted a boom, expanded, and made a killing. What told an investor which company to bet on?

True, I may get the timing wrong. I'm usually early. As I've never been a particularly good trader, someone who runs in and out of positions and gets the timing right, I invest for the long haul.

A futures seat in Japan is an opportunity that an investor can hold for five, ten, fifteen years, making ten, twenty, or forty times his original stake.

This was such an attractive investment—and Tokyo was such an exciting, vibrant city with so many investment opportunities—that Tabitha and I strongly considered moving there after our trip was done.

Not that the Japanese don't have their problems.

Despite the hype in United States' newspapers, the kids don't work as hard as their parents. The children of the current generation of Japanese ant- or bee-like workers aren't going to make their parents' sacrifices. The second generation of wealth never does, and when wealth reaches the third and fourth generations, often little vitality is left.

Until recent years Japan's surging population growth was good for the country. By the mid-eighties it had fallen to an all-time low of .6 percent annually; today it's half that. In comparison, the population in the United States is increasing at a rate double this; in South Korea, triple. Japan's huge and aging workforce represents a bulge that will reach retirement age by the turn of the century. When it does, the proportion of workers to retirees will become unfavorable, producing economic and societal strains.

In addition, the Japanese don't have natural resources, a huge problem for a nation relying on industrial production. Somewhere along the line the Japanese must get a big natural-resource base. Unless they can find one to buy, they're either going to have to conquer one, as they tried to do in the thirties, which is unlikely, or eventually decline, somewhat more likely.

On the other hand, there is a strategic mix for the twenty-first century that might work for them. The Chinese, who also need resources for their massive population, have more labor than they have the capital to put to use. Siberia has more land and resources and no labor or money, while Japan has capital but nothing in resources and not enough labor. I can see Japanese capital combining with Chinese labor to develop Siberia's vast resources into fantastic wealth.

As we were riding about in Tokyo, we felt a tremor: an earthquake, we found out, 4.5 on the Richter scale. I was surprised. I thought any earthquake would be the end of Japan, but it turned out that it has them all the time. It's every fifty to a hundred years that a big one comes along and knocks down everything.

· · ·

The time to move on was approaching. Reluctantly, I had to face Tabitha's plans.

"Do you want to come?" I asked her.

"I've had enough," she said. "Siberia—it's going to be rougher than China."

I had to agree. No one had ever said a good word about driving across Siberia.

"But it won't be the same without you," I said. "I want you with me."

She smiled. "You don't need anybody, Jim."

"I need you," I said, and then softened the moment with some humor. "Who's going to fix my bike? Who's gonna keep me company? Who's going to get me by those huge border guards with her Nordic good looks? They're liable to put me in jail."

"I hate my bike," she said. "I spend all my time listening to its rattles and knocks, expecting it to conk out." I remembered those cold mornings when she had had to give it one or two dozen kicks to get it started.

"Your bike?" I said, a burst of hope rising in me. "Is that all? Come on, let's go to the BMW place. Let's get you a bike you like."

"A new bike?"

"Anything you want." Anything. It was true I would bull on without her, but I would miss her steadiness and mechanical ability. We made a good traveling team. Where I would throw myself around with border officials in an effort to break through their bureaucratic stupidity, she would sweet-talk our way past them.

But I might have hired all that. What I couldn't hire and would sorely miss was her wit, her excitement, our laughter together, and our teamwork, our partnership. More than any woman I'd ever known, she was game for adventure and held up under adversity. To top all this off, I was by no means easy to live with, and she understood me and put up with me. I realized that she was my ideal partner in every way.

She paused. She had come to love motorcycling, and the prospect of a new bike thrilled anybody who did. "I'll look," she said in a guarded voice, "but I'm not making any promises."

At the dealer where my bike was being overhauled she fell in love with a BMW R-80.

Astride its new seat, gripping the handlebars, breathing the heady aroma of new bike, and reveling in the bike's electric starter, she beamed at me and said, "God, you're persuasive."

I smiled back. I was halfway there; shortly after, she agreed to stay on. We shipped her old bike back to the States.

This new bike cheered her up immediately. With excitement we shopped for the dozens of travel items we had been unable to find in China and wouldn't be likely to find in Siberia: brake fluid, toothpaste, knit shirts, razor blades, cables, brake pads, and a collection of nuts, bolts, and screws. To travel so lightly through such primitive parts of the world you must think ahead. We bought new helmets and special tiny tents and sleeping bags for motorcyclists.

So, after this brief interlude in the First World, we set out again, this time toward one of the wildest parts of the world, Siberia.

Till now the Siberian cities across the Sea of Japan had been only names on the map—Nakhodka, Vladivostok, Khabarovsk. Both of us were excited, but of course we felt some apprehension. Where were we going to stay? Would we have to camp out a lot? Would the black market continue to see to it that we got gas? How would the Russians out there feel about Americans? And what about the danger the Russians back in New York had called *tayga*, "tigers"—would they attack us?

12

AT THE EDGE OF THE WORLD

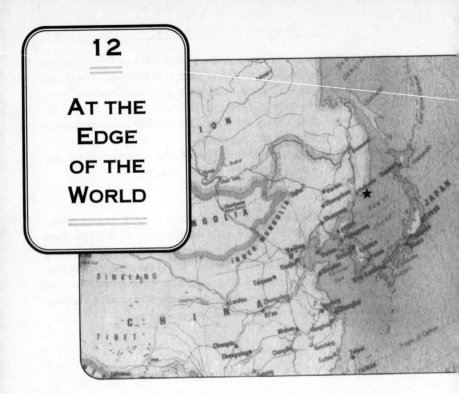

WE LANDED in the new city of Nakhodka, a few miles east of the larger port of Vladivostok, which was the home of the Soviet navy and thus closed to foreign visitors. A village before World War II, Nakhodka was now a major fishing port, a city of dull gray apartment houses spread high above and surrounding a sheltered bay. It was easy to believe that we were on the moon or on the edge of the world, a place where we could fall into some bottomless ravine we scarcely knew existed.

At customs in Siberia the officers didn't know what a carnet was and merely handed us a stamped piece of paper instead of marking our passports. I was amazed that they were so lax. This meant we could have sold our motorcycles and made a large duty-free profit, something we had no intention of doing but which most other borders were careful to prohibit. Of course, what this told me was how little vehicular traffic came through here.

At the hotel we asked where we could store our bikes, hoping for a parking garage or a sheltered courtyard. At the police station, we were told, right next door.

There we locked them behind a wooden fence and as usual chained the wheels and covered them with tarp. Covered bikes excite much less curiosity from bystanders than those standing brazenly ready to be tinkered with.

In addition to the two spare tires on our chained-up bikes, we had two extra spares and a rim. The hotel management suggested we protect them by storing them in a large foot locker in the lobby, which was padlocked.

Excited, we set out on foot to explore this new world.

Part of what gave Nakhodka its otherworldly impression was the lack of street life and stores. I'd seen backwater ports before, even back in Alabama. The port of Mobile was long past its prime, but compared with the rust and broken equipment here, it was a model of repair. There was no security around the docks; goods were piled up in such a fashion that anybody could walk off with anything.

Few people were in its drab streets, even downtown. To our surprise, in a port city of 170,000 there weren't more than twenty stores, each specialized, whereas most cities of this size would have boasted hundreds of small shops of one kind or another. There was a single children's clothing store, a single grocery store, a single auto-parts store, and a single hardware store. After all, this was Communism, and why would you need two, Comrade? Surely that was wasteful. Except for the bakeries—full of inexpensive, extraordinary bread, baked every day—the other stores shocked us. They were virtually empty of both goods and people.

The hardware store's shelves were bare except for a few nuts, bolts, and hinges. The grocery store sported a hundred four-liter jars of birch juice, a drink that tasted like a cross between apple juice and grape juice; a few cans of domestic condensed milk; some bags of flour; and little else. To call another an auto-parts store glorified it. It displayed a tire or two, a single motorcycle horn, and a couple of mirrors.

Where did people get what they needed? we asked ourselves.

We came across one small bank, but it seemed to be withering from a lack of business. Sticking to my usual methodology, I changed a few dollars to obtain sample rubles and a receipt to show officials that we had done the right thing, but we kept our eyes open for the currency black market—the real market.

As I kept in touch with my family and maintained my log by frequently sending postcards to my parents, I asked for the cards at the hotel and in the cavelike stores. Not only did they not exist, not only wasn't there a stationery store, but there wasn't even a place to buy a pencil or a pad of paper. After pushing, I was told maybe I could find something at the post office. Perplexed but glad I'd had the forethought to bring along extra ballpoint pens, I hunted it up.

The post office wasn't as inviting as Mrs. Campion's back in Ireland or the country post offices I had grown up with in Alabama. It looked like a government building anywhere—cement floor, horrible lighting, and three or four clerks sitting around doing nothing—its gray inner walls decorated with a couple of severe portraits of Lenin and Gorbachev. Fortunately, it displayed the few items it had for sale, and one of them was indeed a postcard. There was no picture on it, and the paper itself appeared to be flimsy oaktag, but at least it was a postcard.

Where were the customers? I wondered. Then it hit me. Not many people here would have a reason to go to the post office. You didn't get your bills through the mail, you didn't pay them through the mail, and you certainly didn't get any junk mail. The only reason to use the post office was to write to somebody or to receive a letter, but I came to learn there wasn't much paper and that the Russians often used telegrams, which were faster and more reliable. The telegraph system and the Trans-Siberian Railroad, both built under the czars by capitalists, were the only systems touching the ordinary Russian's life that worked.

About all that was on display besides the postcards were stamps and envelopes. I believe the only place in the Soviet Union you could buy an envelope was at the post office.

At the counter I smiled, pointed at the postcard display, and held up three fingers. The woman clerk looked at me blankly. I smiled again and laid a ten-ruble note on the counter. I held my three fingers up higher and with my other hand tapped the postcard in the display. "Three," I said slowly, hoping to force onto her the Platonic ideal of the number. She frowned and shook her head slightly. I went through my pantomime again, and this time she took a step back as if I were suggesting a shameful sexual act.

Even after I had gone through this charade ten times, the clerk didn't understand what I wanted. Perplexed by her incomprehension, I finally got the manager, Mrs. Fedorov, who smiled and nodded and told me I wanted to send mail to Australia.

"No, A-me-ri-ca," I said, enunciating the word syllable by syllable.

She understood me at last, but it had taken fifteen minutes to buy three postcards. I better get more, I thought. As the port through which all the foreigners passed, Nakhodka wasn't exactly the sticks. If it was this hard to get postcards here, what would it be like deeper in Siberia?

So I bought a dozen. On my way out I realized I was experiencing what we'd begun to understand all smart Soviet consumers do. When they have a chance to buy something, they buy all they can of it, because they never know when they're going to find it again. The Communists! They'd won the Second World War and put together a great space program, but making and distributing postcards and toothbrushes and hinges had beaten them.

Then I began to understand why all this had occurred.

These dozen postcards had cost me a total of about six cents, which included postage anywhere inside the Soviet Union, possibly a seven-thousand-mile journey. At the bakery there was plenty of bread and at such a low price, three kopecks—less than a tenth of a cent in our money—farmers fed it to their pigs and boys used loaves for soccer balls.

The Soviet Union hadn't raised its prices in fifty years!

It sounded good, even great for the consumer—low rent, postcards for kopecks, inexpensive bread, cheap birch juice, and low-cost hinges. But the flip side was that they had almost no consumer goods except bread, which of course was the one item not even the Communists dared allow to run out.

Even if they were Communists and noble, even though this was the largest empire the world had ever seen, state fiat could not overturn the laws of supply and demand. That is, by keeping these prices low the Communists had robbed everyone, including the state and the party, of any real-world incentive to produce and distribute every product. What possible incentive could there be to make hinges or socks when every pair lost money?

This was the society that legislated that it was a crime, one called "speculation," for an individual, organization, or the state to sell anything for more than it had paid for it. I didn't think even the most ardent Marxist professor at a Western university would believe that any economic unit could survive without tacking on something for its overhead, and possibly its profit.

No, the real crime here was the perversion of human nature, the original Communist notion that the natural way of trade and commerce that had existed throughout the world for thousands of years was somehow evil. The real crime was the misery—the shortages, the shoddy goods, and the lack of opportunity—perpetrated by the Communists on the Soviet people for decades.

Here was one of the twentieth century's largest experiments in statism—an experiment with 290 million lives—and what a failure it had been!

. . .

By now we had a small collection of maps in German, French, and Russian. When I sat down to plan our route to Moscow—six thousand miles away—I found that while the cities listed on our visas were represented with the mapmaker's usual little white circles, something was missing.

The roads between them.

Back west, around Moscow, were the mapmaker's red, brown, and yellow lines that marked roads. Over the four thousand miles from here to Omsk, however, there were no connecting roadways—not a red, yellow, white, or even broken road line. The crossties of the train line were clearly marked, but not the road.

"Maybe there aren't any roads," said Tabitha, giving me a fish eye, ever the realist.

"Come on," I answered. "They just haven't surveyed out here. You forget how huge Siberia is. It's cheaper to make the maps without running all over Siberia measuring the place. Besides, the German and French mapmakers probably couldn't get in."

"What about the Russian mapmakers?" she asked. "They couldn't get in, either?"

Ignoring her humor, I asked around. People stroked their chins, and a faraway look crept into their eyes. Some were sure there was a road to Khabarovsk, the next big town westward, but even they were uncertain about what lay beyond it toward Chita and Ulan-Ude.

"There have to be roads connecting these cities," I said to Tabitha.

Her fish eye had grown stronger. "How can you be so sure?"

I didn't have a particularly good answer, except whoever heard of a country's major cities, a few hundred miles apart, without connecting roads? It just didn't make sense. In all my travels I've found that locals know less about traveling in their country than do travelers. What New Yorker can tell you how to get to Kansas City, and what the roads are like to get there? Who in Montana can tell you how to get to Birmingham, Alabama? In Russia the locals knew less than usual, as Russians didn't travel. If your relatives never moved away and shopping was no better one or two hundred miles down the road, why go?

But if my informants were unclear about the route, they were quite sure about one thing: Whatever route did exist, it was not paved. That was all right. I'd grown up on unpaved roads in the backwoods of Alabama, and since then I'd traveled on my share of unpaved road, lots of it.

. . .

Here in Nakhodka we met some dockworkers who told us, through one of their number who spoke English, that they had learned only the year before that it was legal for foreigners to leave their countries and return without special permission. In the Soviet Union they'd always been told that if they left the country, they couldn't come back except under exceptional circumstances, and that this was true throughout the world.

Here was another way the Communists controlled their people, another way they'd brainwashed them.

These workers were furious at having been lied to, at finding out the world was different from the one they'd been told about.

Even though the Soviet Union was the largest country in the world, it was tormented by memories of prior invasions, from the Mongols seven hundred years before, down to those of Napoleon and Hitler. For many scores of years, their leaders had been consumed by the need to defend their long, vulnerable perimeter, which had pushed them to conquer more and more territories.

As generations of Russian novelists have described to us, the Russian soul *wants* to be different, to be Russian and Slavic, to be wild and free and moody. However, it also yearns to be a part of Europe, to embrace logic, order, and civilization. The Russian soul longs for freedom and originality, yet rightly is terrified that new ideas will stir up anarchy and chaos, for both Russia and the Soviet Union had been held together by fragile bonds.

With all this in mind, we went to visit the head of the docks, the boss of the whole shooting match here, a high Communist official sitting under a picture of Lenin. He spoke excellent English.

I asked why the dockworkers had been lied to, how their bitter anger affected their work.

"Why do you ask me these questions?" he shot back. "I'm as angry as everybody else. Don't think it's us against them. I'm fed up with Communism, too. From Gorbachev on down, we're all furious. I'm as angry as those guys on the docks. Life here is a nightmare."

This was a year before the coup in 1991. The army was fed up, too, even then uninterested in taking over a bankrupt state, one that, they saw clearly, they had no idea how to run.

"You Australia?" we were asked in a restaurant by a large, friendly Russian with a strong accent.

"No, American," I answered.

"No good beer, ya?"

"No, beer *is* good," I replied, wondering if something was being lost in the translation. We were drinking vodka.

"Yes, near no good. Australia better. Don't stay near."

He shuffled off, and I asked Tabitha what that was all about.

"Beer is good in Australia but not here," she said. "He'd like to be somewhere else."

"Was he drunk?"

"No, just practicing his English."

After the fifth person brought up Australia, it finally penetrated. We made inquiries and, to our surprise, learned that an Australian farmer and his family lived only a few miles from Nakhodka.

We drove out to visit, and indeed there was an Australian farmer. A day laborer on a farm back in Australia, Robert Sokob had left what sounded like tough conditions and had been here several months. He had become discouraged with his prospects back home and, like immigrants everywhere, came here to make more money.

Both his and his wife Lena's grandparents had emigrated out of Russia; they'd been White Russians. Both sets of grandparents moved south to China in the twenties or thirties to escape Stalin's takeover. When the Communists came yet again and took over China, they fled to Australia. Despite their Russian roots, Robert and Lena and their two sons, Peter and Paul, and their two daughters, Anna and Alexandra, sounded as Australian as could be.

Robert was about forty; Lena, a few years younger. Both declared that even after three generations they thought they might make it in Russia. They paid five-and-a-half rubles, about a dollar, as their monthly rent, and about half that for electricity. The couple said they missed the good roads, friends, and beer from back home.

The Russians had allocated Robert a hundred hectares, about two hundred and fifty acres, on which he proposed to raise cattle. He had acquired more assets to work with in one stroke than he would have been able to in a lifetime back in Australia. He said that the Russians at the embassy in Australia had tried to dissuade him, saying he didn't know what he was getting into, but he had insisted on coming. A chance to have his own place had to be better than the meager day wages he had been earning. He would take the chance, the immigrant's eternal gamble.

Several Russian magazines had come a long distance to interview him.

After all, he was probably the only nonideological person to immigrate to the Soviet Union in fifty years.

They gave him a house, but it was a house like all of them out here, no indoor plumbing, rudimentary electricity, and a primitive kitchen, not much more than running water and a wood-and-coal stove. Almost every Alabama sharecropper had more. Lena, a bit shy and reserved, seemed perplexed and still stunned by the move and the harshness of their new country.

Their nineteen-year-old son, Peter, wanted so little to do with this plan that he was enlisting in the Soviet navy. Their fourteen-year-old daughter, Anna, was even less enthusiastic. Of course, fourteen-year-olds aren't too pleased about anything, but this was life without music, no rock 'n' roll, no radio, no telephone, no pictures of pop stars, no soda fountain, no nothing.

The eight-year-old girl, Alexandra, was noncommittal, and five-year-old Paul was happy to have a bicycle. Other kids came over to play because they didn't have one. Every day Lena went to school with Anna and Alexandra to help them because the classes were in Russian and they didn't understand much yet.

Lena treated us to birch juice and vegetables, all she had. Robert said he wanted to build a proper house, but it was dawning on him that without a corner lumberyard, it was almost impossible.

"I go around all day trying to get things—lumber, cement, nails," he said. If the Russians had something, often they just gave it to him, wanting to be helpful to an immigrant.

"For weeks I've been trying to get gravel to put on the driveway to cover this damn mud," he said. "I put the word out, and every now and then a truck shows up and dumps a load of gravel. I can't pay for it. They don't want to be paid for it."

The Soviets had promised him a second hundred hectares, but they made it clear that no matter how hard he worked the land, they wouldn't allow him to sell either parcel. He could pass the farm on to his children. Of course, in thirty years who knew under what form of government he'd be living. I remembered that there had been a huge argument in the Soviet Union. "Yes, we want to privatize," they'd say, "but do we just give people land? Won't they then become speculators?"

Most farmers answered back, "I'm not interested in your thirty-year lease. I'll improve the land and you'll take it back? No thanks."

I thought raising cattle out here was a totally absurd concept, but maybe he would make it. If he had the staying power to last twenty or thirty years, maybe he would become a cattle baron in eastern Siberia. I hoped so, for his family's sake.

When we went to leave Nakhodka we opened the footlocker in the hotel lobby and found our rim and extra tires had been stolen. I insisted that Boris, the desk clerk, find them, but he only shrugged.

"Why would anybody want a BMW wheel and tires?" I asked Tabitha.

"You've been in the stores," she said. "Why wouldn't they?"

She was right. If I looked hard enough, I'd probably find a BMW tire and wheel on someone's homemade wheelbarrow or sitting in a living room as an exotic status symbol. Thank God we had put our bikes in the police compound. I resolved to continue doing this throughout the Soviet Union.

Luckily, I had set up an account with the BMW dealer back in Japan who overhauled my bike. It took a number of frantic phone calls that made buying postcards look like a snap, but I managed to order an extra rim and tires to be shipped to Khabarovsk, where we expected to be in a few days.

So we set out to drive the six thousand miles to Moscow across the *tayga*, which I had now learned was Russian for the Siberian wilds. Losing such important spare parts so early—before we'd even left the port city—brought home that if something went wrong in the middle of the *tayga*, we'd be in big trouble.

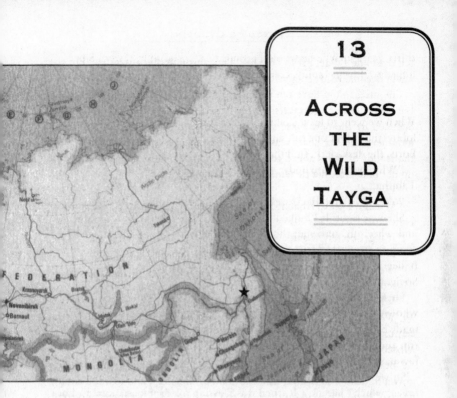

13

ACROSS
THE
WILD
TAYGA

YOU CAN SET DOWN the whole of the continental United States inside Siberia without touching its borders, and you can also put Alaska and all the countries of Europe, excluding Russia itself, into the remaining margin. After doing this, you'll still have enough room for a second state of Texas.

Foreigners were not allowed in certain strategic cities in the Soviet Union, except under extraordinary circumstances. The best road to Khabarovsk was via Vladivostok, which was one of these closed cities because it was the home of the Soviet navy. To our surprise, we weren't stopped by the military police but sped right through it. I figured we were too far from Moscow for the local gendarmes to be efficient.

True to what we'd been told, the paved road out to Khabarovsk quickly turned into gravel, big, baseball-sized stones on which it was almost impossible to ride. Afraid we'd go down, we couldn't drive fast. At such a slow speed, when our wheels hit a grapefruit-sized boulder, the bikes would try to spin out of our hands and push us over. Driving was a constant battle with the road. Every fifty or seventy-five miles Tabitha fell over and I'd get off to help her. I got through this unscathed, but she again became ready to give up.

She might now have ten thousand miles of motorcycling experience, but very few motorcyclists had experienced conditions like these. Seduced by the new bike, she had come from Japan against her better judgment and her heart wasn't in it. The road was just too terrible, the thousands of miles ahead too great. "Damn it," said Tabitha, cranking up her bike after her dozenth spill, "I'm going home."

"Home!"

"When we get to Khabarovsk I'm getting on a plane and going back to New York."

"It'll get better," I said.

"Now, how do you know that, Jim Rogers?" she asked, furious.

"Well, we'll get used to it. Surely it can't be like this all the way to Moscow."

"Why not?"

"Well, it just can't. This is like our Far West back in the nineteenth century. They haven't got around to putting in roads this far from Moscow."

"Bullshit," she said, flinging out her hands to take in the miles of gravel in front and behind us. "No road on the map, and lo and behold, no road here. No road on the map to Omsk, and I'll bet there's no road there, either."

I knew the driving was beating the hell out of her, but I wasn't happy about going on without her.

"Look, you said you'd come," I said. "I need you. We've learned so much together. Our partnership is stronger than this."

"You said there would be roads. This isn't a road, it's white-water rafting on a motorcycle. I want to go home."

"Okay, fine," I said, beaten. "I'll put you on a plane at the next airport." I hoped by the time we got to one, this would have passed.

We pressed on, slipping and sliding on that damn baseball-sized gravel.

It took us five long days to go from Nakhodka to Khabarovsk, five days of slipping and falling, five days of wrestling with our bikes. But it wasn't all bad, not by a long shot, and we didn't travel the entire day. This was open country with pure, clear air. The flowers were in bloom, and puff seedlings more than once swirled around us like warm snow on their journey to seed the earth. In one village Tabitha was taken for a traveling movie star, and the people stared at her blondness and touched her in wonderment. They had never seen foreigners. In Siberia we were as exotic as the first Europeans were to the Native Americans.

In Khabarovsk Tabitha hadn't changed her mind. The plane wouldn't leave for several days, so the question of what she was going to do hung fire. I argued with her, angry because I wanted her with me and she wanted to go back. Part of the excitement of a trip like this was having someone to share it with.

"No, these are hard roads and it's just a bitch," she said. "This isn't my dream, it's yours. Go around the world six times if you want. I'm going home."

She bedded down in a separate hotel room to show me she meant business.

Perturbed, I took a walk to reflect.

Khabarovsk was a city on a hill, sort of a cliff overlooking an enormously wide river, at least a mile or so across. I began to tramp about.

It was beginning to dawn on me what I had taken on in committing myself to this trip, and that it was more than I'd expected. Yes, I had known many of the roads would be rough, but even though I was an experienced rider and had been in many primitive countries, I hadn't realized how rough and for quite how long they would go on that way. Still, I was plenty game, but I could well understand that a novice might not be.

My feelings related back to my Wall Street days, as well as those I'd spent with students at Columbia University. I didn't teach the kind of finance usually taught at business schools, the kind dreamed up by professors whose only relation to real money was their monthly paycheck. I taught what I knew, how to invest the way I invested, how to think about markets and opportunities the way I thought. It wasn't orthodox in a time of computers and complicated mathematical models of the economy, the stock market, and index derivatives. However, I'd used my way of thinking not only to make some money, but to keep it.

If you ask a thousand people if they want to be rich, every one except the poet and the mystic will say yes. When you explain what is needed to become rich, maybe six hundred of that initial 998 will say, "No problem, I can do that." But when push comes to shove, when they have to sacrifice everything else in their lives—having a spouse and children, a social life, possibly a spiritual life, maybe every pleasure—to meet their goal, almost all of them, too, will fall away. Only about six of the original thousand will continue on the hard path.

Most of us don't have the discipline to stay focused on a single goal for five, ten, or twenty years, giving up everything to bring it off, but that's what's necessary to become an Olympic champion, a world-class surgeon, or a Kirov ballerina. Even then, of course, it may be all in vain. You may make a single mistake that wipes out all the work. It may ruin the sweet, lovable self you were at seventeen. That old adage is true: You can do anything in life, you just can't do everything. That's what Bacon meant when he said a wife and children were hostages to fortune. If you put them first, you probably won't run the three-and-a-half-minute mile, make your first $10 million, write the great American novel, or go around the world on a motorcycle. Such goals take complete dedication.

Of course, not all of us believe that the goals the obsessive among us take on are good things. Was it sane of Captain Ahab to chase Moby Dick? Was it necessary for Roger Bannister to break the four-minute mile? Was it essential for Edmund Hillary to be the first man to climb Everest? These were goals to which each man was willing to dedicate himself. Ahab drove his men with him to his goal, where all but one died. Even though he may be remembered with affection after he's won the war, during battle the colonel is hated for pushing his men into the enemy's jaws.

Well, corny as it may sound, I was totally absorbed and dedicated when I worked on Wall Street, and I was like that about this trip. I'd thrown myself into it, going to excess, the way I've done everything my whole life. I'd made up my mind to do it, and to do it in good time, not to take a decade. Nothing was going to stop me or slow me down.

However, there wasn't a lady friend I cared for more than Tabitha, and to have her along as a companion had come to be as important as the trip itself. Coming to this realization was a surprise to me in and of itself, as I'd never felt that way before about a traveling companion.

If she would continue, I would strive to accommodate her more, although I wasn't going to give up the trip because she was uncomfortable. If she couldn't handle it, I understood that. I would put her and the new bike on the plane back to New York and continue without her.

It wouldn't be as much fun—I would be terribly sad—but I'd get it done.

The black market again found me in the person of a burly mobster named Alex who wanted to sell me Russian-army belt buckles, hats, and trinkets for hard currency.

Alex was jovial and wary, open and guarded, the epitome of everything I'd always heard about the Russian soul. It turned out he had been in jail, a place that sounded even more dreadful than prisons back home. All the prisoners slept together in big barracks. They ate little but gruel and worked on the roads twelve hours a day, except when they worked on the railroad. His crime, he said, was that he kept telling the workers that capitalism was better and that Communism wasn't the way the world should be, which sounded to me like poppycock he used to flatter Western customers. On close questioning he said he had gone to jail for forging his work papers and his time card. I decided he had put down that he was at work while he was out hustling dollars on the black market.

He said he could get me anything, just name it—girls, booze, every sort of contraband—as long as I paid him in hard currency. Ever the intrepid traveler and always eager for an adventure, I bought a few dollars' worth of trinkets and got him to introduce me to the bootlegger, who made vodka, naturally.

As it happened, we bumped into Alex in the park the next day when he happened to have his girls-for-hire with him, a couple of plump, stolid eighteen-year-olds who despite their youth didn't look particularly attractive. Notwithstanding the fears of Western religions about Communism unleashing free love and rampant sex, the world's oldest profession seemed to have handily survived seventy years of scientific materialism.

His eyes gleaming, Alex drifted off with me to discuss my purchasing more Russian medals. His great goal, he now confided, was to buy a car in Japan for fifty thousand yen, or less than three hundred dollars. A used car. "In Japan they throw such cars away," he said. The Russians would let him bring it in duty-free, and he could turn his three-hundred-dollar car into maybe sixty thousand rubles, or thirty-five hundred dollars—a way to get rich.

He needed hard currency to start this process. Rubles were no good, as the Japanese didn't want them. In the real world the only money that counts is real money.

Alex declared that after he'd done it once he would do it again.

Tabitha stumbled on a woman's clinic and got to know the doctor there, Natasha Zollotorev, who talked about the more intimate details of Soviet life.

With none of the restraints imposed by religion, few movies, and the state TV yet more boring than that in the States, sex was a major pastime in the USSR. Dr. Zollotorev said abortion and IUDs were the country's only two means of birth control. Frequently the clinic didn't have IUDs, and even when it did the quality was poor. Abortion, which she detested, was the principal means of birth control. The average Russian woman had ten to fifteen abortions in her lifetime. As a result, 30 percent of the women wound up having emergency hysterectomies.

It was clear that if AIDS arrived in the Soviet Union, there was a strong chance of its devastating the population.

Back to sleeping in the same room, we were waiting for the tires from Japan and for Tabitha's outbound plane.

One day on the street we saw a huge, unruly mob outside a store, the sort that gathered wherever anything was for sale.

It was a jewelry store, and we went in. The mob was more ferocious, desperate, and frantic than usual. A shipment of gold jewelry had come in, and because gold was such an honest store of value, these Siberians were desperate to cash out of rubles and buy gold.

Intrigued by the importance of gold to the Soviet Union, we went to see the head of the local state gold-mining organization, Igor Sosnin. He was the bureaucrat in charge of all the Pacific far-eastern gold mines. I remembered how significant gold and oil were to the Soviet Union. In the States the head of a mere mining operation wouldn't be that important, but in the Soviet Union it was a different story. Igor was a big guy, the equivalent of the head of IBM or GM in the United States.

I especially wanted to speak to Igor about gold and other commodities because of what I understood had been happening to their raw materials and what would be happening in the future. The Soviet Union in the twentieth century is a fascinating study in national survival.

Back in the twenties, the Communist Party lived on the euphoria of surviving the First World War and the revolution, but by the thirties the country's economy had fallen apart. Millions starved, and Stalin hung on to power by executing tens of thousands of his enemies. Others he sent to the network of concentration camps called the Gulag, which grew in population from thirty thousand in 1928 to eight million in 1938. The country was on the verge of collapse.

Hitler, however, saved Stalin by giving him a menace against which to rally his people, staving off his overthrow and the country's economic ruin. We helped him, too, with our Lend-Lease Act Program in the Second World War. In the fifties and early sixties, the new colonies in Central Europe—Poland, East Germany, Bulgaria, etc.—began to produce new wealth. During the late sixties and seventies the country was helped by the worldwide commodities boom, as well as by the expansion into the Virgin Lands of the Central Asian Republics. Although the Soviets had no services and manufactured goods that the rest of the world wanted, vast increases in the production of copper, wheat, cotton, palladium, and aluminum gave them a new lease on life. For decades Russia was the world's largest producer of oil and its second-largest producer of gold. Naturally it put its best people in these important industrial and mining positions.

By the eighties, however, the Russians' luck had run out. No longer were they in the right place at the right time. Western central banks, including that of the United States, reined in inflation, bringing to a halt the commodities boom. This cut the economic ground out from under the Soviet Union, which had failed to develop a single industrial or consumer product that the rest of the world wanted. Not only was the commodities boom over, but Soviet managers were operating their lands and mines in precisely the fashion for which their political leaders condemned the West! They had stripped off the easy pickings without a consideration for what the next decade would need.

One of my theories was that the Russians would become more and more desperate to hold their ranch together, that is, to service their foreign loans and bring in Western necessities, whether computers or wheat. They would dump gold to earn hard Western currency, which would keep the price of gold low. After all, they didn't have much else to dump.

I asked Igor right out if they were dumping gold.

He wouldn't answer me directly, but we did have a long, general discussion.

"We're starting co-ops now," he said. "They're very efficient producers."

He even introduced us to some co-op owners at a big lunch out in the country, the best meal we had in this part of the world. Their chief, Georgy Abramov, put on the dog: soup, fish, good vegetables and salads, vodka, wine, and tea.

We learned that the co-op had been established for only a year, but that it was a rousing success. I gathered *co-op* was a Russian euphemism for a private enterprise devoted to profit. I asked what their territory was. Georgy pointed out on a map what looked to be thousands of square miles.

The term *co-op* dressed up the reality, made it politically more correct to engage in private enterprise, which in the old Soviet Union was on a par socially with belonging to the Mafia back in the States. A few guys in a partnership had obtained the franchise to mine gold, raised the money to finance the machinery, and hired a thousand workers to do the work. Of course they were forced to sell their newly mined gold to the state— the Russians weren't going to let them ship it to Japan without getting their slice—but if the co-op brought the gold in below the state price, it made a profit the partners could divvy up.

Georgy explained how they worked it. They paid their workers more, so they expected them to work harder. They didn't have the encumbrances and bureaucracy of the state's mining operations. They flew the workers for a month at a time into the middle of nowhere, and the workers were glad to go for the extra money.

I asked Igor why he hadn't joined with the co-op.

"Well," he said, "basically I'm a bureaucrat and I like my position. I'm very powerful, I've worked my way to the top. This is enough. I make enough money for me."

Gold has been one of the great mystical elements of finance for hundreds if not thousands of years.

Back in the seventies its price went through the roof. Investors were sure all paper money was going to lose its value. However, if they had done their homework and tracked the price of gold back through the centuries, they would have seen long periods when its price went down and stayed there, or didn't move up with other prices. Later on, gold would catch up, but then so would wheat, so would lumber.

For centuries gold's true believers have said that gold alone is a good store of value. On the other hand, over the centuries a lot of things have been a good store of value, including wheat, lumber, and iron ore.

Back in the 1930s, Franklin Roosevelt, in response to economic and currency crises, set the price of gold at thirty-five dollars an ounce, plucking that number out of the air. It had been twenty-one dollars an ounce.

Now, any government could convert the American dollars it held into gold at thirty-five dollars an ounce. Naturally, everybody who owned gold was happy to fall into line. They received a 67 percent premium in value. Everybody was delighted to hold dollars.

World War II came, which set external disciplines on all countries. In the thirties, of course, the external discipline had been worldwide economic collapse, which meant people didn't move gold around or exchange their currencies for it. There was little demand because economic trade had come to an end.

For thirty-seven years the price of gold was thirty-five dollars an ounce, which over time came to be a low price. Thus, the production of gold declined for many years, until 1970. This was yet another situation like the one here in Siberia, where the government underpriced an asset, thereby reducing its supply. Maintaining gold at thirty-five dollars an ounce had been similar to setting the price of gasoline in Russia at a nickel or a dime a gallon and keeping it there.

During this thirty-seven-year period, few had looked for gold, few gold mines opened, and all mining operations had run down their reserves. The marginal mines had closed. Most gold that had come on to the world market came from South Africa and Russia, where it was cheap to pull it out of the ground.

By the 1970s the price of gold had to go up. It was so cheap that its manufacturing uses had expanded, and demand was increasing partly because its price was so low. Gold was being used in teeth and electronics. Every time a new application came up, manufacturers said, "Let's use gold. That's the cheapest stuff around."

So the price had to go up. Not only did the supply keep going down, but the U.S. had currency crises because we were no longer running a sound economy. A lot of people, especially the French, came to us and said, "We want the gold you promised you would swap for dollars." There was a terrific run on Fort Knox.

Pressures for gold prices to rise grew in the fifties and sixties because the American government had begun to run an unsound economy: trade deficits, printing money, the whole works. The government then tried controls to prop up the value of the dollar artificially. In 1962, our government put on the interest-equalization tax to control Americans' investments abroad.

Instead of dealing with the problem of a badly valued currency, the government had applied a Band-Aid yet again. So the pressures only intensified, and in 1971 Nixon was forced to say, "Okay, guys, I'm not going to do it anymore. I'm changing the rules."

Of course, another reason we hadn't had a problem in the thirties, the forties, and the fifties was that the government had made it illegal for Americans to own gold, which made absolutely no sense. The French could own gold, the English could own gold, and the Japanese could own gold, but Americans couldn't. And why? "It's for your own good," the government said, although no one could explain why. We were being protected from ourselves, and yet other nations were taking advantage of us.

That's another thing about governments: They think little of changing the rules of the game. You and I would go straight to jail for a lot of things the government does. For instance, making an agreement with investors and then changing the rules. This would be called fraud.

Remember the savings and loan crisis? The S&Ls went to the government and said, "Look, we've got real problems here. Our earnings are collapsing. We are going to have serious capital problems. We can't raise money."

The government said, "Okay, we'll change the accounting rules just for you. You don't have to say what's really happening." Now, if you and I did that to a public company we ran, we'd flat go to jail for fraud.

But our government said it was okay for the S&L industry to change the rules so it could report its accounts fraudulently. As we know, the S&L mess blew up, and we're all paying the price. Did the government blame this on itself? Of course not. The government said, "This was caused by a few greedy guys who were doing fraudulent things."

Well, the government was part of it. It had said, "Change your accounting rules to report your books fraudulently, and we'll make it legal." Another Band-Aid that only delayed a crisis. The government didn't just say, "You're allowed to do it"; it directed the S&Ls to change their rules.

Prolonging the day of reckoning only makes things worse when the pressure finally breaks through. We're finding this out in Yugoslavia now, and we'll find this in the Soviet Union in the future. The coming crisis of the U.S. dollar will be all the worse because we aren't biting the bullet now.

So Nixon slammed the window down on the Europeans, the "horrible" Europeans, saying, "You can't come in here and take our gold, even though it's our own fault for ruining our currency."

Demand for gold kept going up. Governments tried to hold it at thirty-five dollars, but they couldn't hang on because everybody came in and cashed in his dollars for gold.

In all my years in investing, there's one rule I've prized beyond every other: Always bet against central banks and with the real world. In the seventies, the central banks were defending the United States' artificially low price of gold. Central banks and governments always try to maintain artificial levels, high or low, whether of a currency, a metal, wool, whatever. Usually these prices are absurd, and the market knows they're absurd. When a central bank is defending something—whether it's gold at thirty-five dollars or the lira at eight hundred to the dollar—the smart investor always goes the other way. It may take a while, but I promise you you'll come out ahead. It's a golden rule of investing. In its collective wisdom the market always knows that if some people are clinging to an artificially low price of thirty-five dollars, you should keep buying gold at that price.

When after thirty-five years the price of gold was finally released, it went up more than it should have because it had been kept low for so long. Such violent movement happens whenever a price has been kept high or low.

This is how markets work. Something, a stock, land, or some other store of value, will bump along at a stable price. Eventually something changes the supply-demand balance. The price starts going up because people realize, "Hey, they've got a new product," or "The railroad is coming through Smithtown." The price goes up for legitimate and sound reasons.

There comes a time, though, when people buy land in Smithtown only because its price is going up. At that point, my mother calls me and says, "I want to buy some acres," or "I want to buy this stock."

"Why, Mother?"

"Well, Jim, it's tripled over the past year," she says in a tone that reminds me of the one Tabitha reserves for calling me a dodo-head.

"That's not the way you're supposed to do it," I say. "You don't buy it *because* it's tripled. You buy it *before* it triples."

But this is what happens. People see the price going up and know that here is the gravy train that's going to make them rich. The newspaper will have stories about Joe and Sally, how they're now rich because they bought all this land or a few shares of stock in the coal mine. The price now goes up *because* the price is going up.

This stock or these acres become vastly overpriced. The smart guys who bought early, who bought because their family had lived in Smithtown for a hundred years, they start selling. They realize that this is becoming unsound. It turns out it's not economical to put yet another General Motors factory here, so new people don't buy land. The demand tapers off.

For sound economic reasons the price starts coming down. Now we have passed the peak. There are now sound economic reasons for manufacturers to put their factories in Taiwan instead of Smithtown. The price of land goes down and goes down—all for sound economic reasons.

Now comes the time when people start selling because the price is going down. People look back and say, "Everybody knows you shouldn't own land in Smithtown. It's been going down for five years."

Everybody now sells because it's the only thing to do. Before there was a buying panic; now there's a selling panic. People scream, "I don't care if land is cheap in Smithtown and I can have a mansion there for virtually nothing. Everybody knows it's a bad place to invest. Get me out!"

Prices collapse. Everybody knows the price is going to nothing. Panic, the crescendo—that's when you buy, because then it's all over. It'll be a while before things start to come back, but come back they will.

Well, this happened to gold—as well as to virtually every other commodity in the history of the world.

As I said earlier, back in 1980 learned scholars could show any fool why oil had to go to a hundred dollars a barrel. There was no way it couldn't. Mathematically, scientifically, historically, it just had to happen. They ignored one important thing, however. In 1978 and 1979, for the first time in years, the world production of oil exceeded its demand. For years, it had looked as if the world was running down oil reserves since we had been consuming more than we had been discovering. But in 1978 and the beginning of 1979, alert investors saw that production and reserves were coming up strongly—which was perfectly in accord with classical economic theory. Whenever you have a high price, you get supply. As supply came back into balance with demand and then exceeded demand, oil made its peak in 1981 rather than going to one hundred dollars a barrel.

To finish the gold story, if you get out your commodity chart book, you'll see that starting in 1980, for the first time in forty-five years, gold production started up worldwide. Every year since 1981, the world has produced more gold than in the year before. Remember, it takes a long time to bring a gold mine on stream. First, somebody's got to decide to look for gold. After he's found it, he has to rustle up the money to open his mine. It takes years to gear up. Now, look at the projections and you can see, with the number of mines coming on stream today, that the production of gold is going to continue to go up until at least 2000.

More supply.

Gold will have its day again, and that day is getting closer, but it'll be based on supply and demand—not hope or mysticism. Prices have been down for fourteen years. Ultimately the process will be reversed, and if given a kick by a currency or inflationary crisis, gold could soar.

Some people want to say, "No, it's supply, demand, and price." But they have to understand that price *is* supply and demand. Price describes where supply and demand hang out, the place they meet.

Forget the gold fanatics, forget everything else. Figure out supply and demand and you'll get extraordinarily rich. It's astonishing how many people cannot grasp this.

Finally the rim and tires came in. The moment of truth for Tabitha and me arrived, the moment I had been dreading.

"I wish you wouldn't go," I said.

"I want to go and I want to stay," she said.

"We'll take it easier," I said. "You want to rest more, we'll rest more."

"The roads, Jim. Riding over them is like wrestling with an alligator. It's not fun."

"They're bound to get better as we move west."

"West is a long way off—four thousand miles."

"Please," I said. "I'm going to miss you so much."

"Let me think about it," she said.

We went through the business of getting the tires and the rim. I was excited. I sensed I had a chance with her.

"Look, I'll go on some more," she said, "but this doesn't mean I'm going all the way. I may still fly back at some point. This whole trip is still more your dream than mine."

"Wonderful," I said. "But remember, if I read this map correctly, there's not an airport for the next two thousand miles."

That gave her pause and she nodded, but she had made up her mind. She was coming. I felt whole again, relieved, as we set out once more.

14

SIBERIA

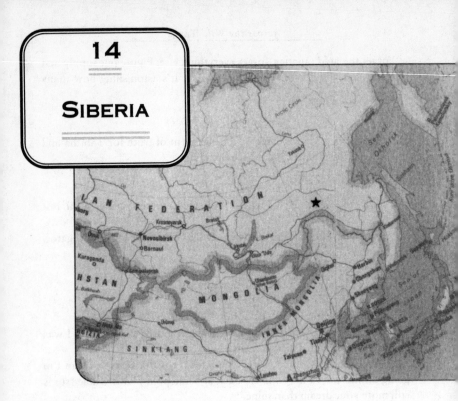

ON THE WAY TO Birobidzhan I dropped my bike three times, Tabitha none. She was getting much better now, navigating the mud, potholes, gravel, and boulders in these awful roads with the strength, endurance, and cunning of a pro. Maybe even better than me.

Hmmm, I wondered, was the strength and adaptability of youth trouncing experience and wisdom?

To our surprise, Birobidzhan turned out to be the capital of the Jewish Autonomous Region.

Back in the twenties, Jews in European Russia were faced with such severe poverty that many wanted to emigrate. To solve this and several other political problems, Stalin declared he would establish a "homeland" here for Jews, a region that would govern itself. Naturally, making real this age-old dream created worldwide euphoria in Jewish circles. This would be the first homeland for their people in nearly two thousand years.

For more than a hundred years the Russian leadership had wanted to develop Siberia. Stalin searched for a sparsely populated area for this homeland, so there wouldn't be much of a local protest. He chose this far-eastern portion of Siberia, thirty-six thousand square kilometers, on the Bira and Bidzhan rivers. Like the Chinese encouraging the Han to move west near the Central Asian Republics, moving the Jews here had the advantage of providing Stalin a human buffer against his traditional enemies, the Japanese.

News clips of that era show joyous Jews arriving from all over the world. The Communist Party and Stalin garnered immense goodwill, which they would sorely need when news of the purge trials hit the Western press.

We went to see a member of the national parliament from the region, Leonid Skolnik, the equivalent of a United States congressman, who was in fact Jewish.

Yes, Leonid confirmed, Jews had moved here from around the world, including France and Italy, but few had stayed. Unfortunately for the new arrivals, this part of Siberia had been full of swamps and bugs, the soil poor, and the winter temperatures would go down to -10 to -20 degrees Fahrenheit. Not only had building a life on this frontier been an agonizing experience, but the Communist system hadn't worked. He thought the region's eleven thousand remaining Jews accounted for about 5 percent of its population.

To my surprise, remembering how much anti-Semitism there was in the Soviet Union, everybody we ran into here with any power was Jewish, as if arriving all those years ago had enabled them to become well established.

Leonid said everybody in power was elected. He, too, was a member of the Communist Party, but as it happened he was resigning from the Party this very day. He explained, "The Party has lost its link with the people. We have to rebuild the Soviet Union on a new political, social, and economic basis."

There might be anti-Semitism in the Soviet Union, but Leonid certainly wasn't hiding the fact that he was Jewish, not with a flag displaying the Star of David hanging right there in his apartment.

Just as in the Muslim areas through which we passed, a religious revival was going on here. People were going to the synagogue more. They had started a pedagogical institute, a Hebrew language school, and a teaching school where the main language being taught was Hebrew. There were Hebrew summer camps.

To my amazement, in these hard times Moscow was budgeting a huge amount of money, millions of rubles, to build that teaching institute, to aid the revival of Jewish culture.

I figured the Soviets had several motives in spending so much: to stop the brain drain westward, to give themselves good press, and to build up the population here. In spite of this and a proposed increase in the housing stock, Leonid said many Jews were leaving for Israel.

We reached Obluch'ye at midnight, which wasn't as bad as it sounds because during the Southern Siberian summer, daylight lasts till eleven o'clock.

The hotel had a dozen rooms. We paid two dollars for ours, the foreign traveler's rate and ten times what the Russians paid. At the black-market exchange rate the cost to us was a dollar. I continued to be amazed that the Russians never changed a price.

We might have been in a slum. This building had been built twenty years before, but it had gone downhill so far it might have been built a hundred years before and never maintained. We had a sitting room, a small bedroom, and a bathroom with the standard Western appliances, but no water. As in the Central Asian Republics, in this and the other Siberian hotels, the beds were unmade, the bed linens folded at the foot of the bed.

Naturally, since there were no other travelers, there was no restaurant or food. Tonight we cooked our meal, the vegetables, bread, and cans of meat we carried with us, in the kitchen downstairs.

I love to sample the nightlife wherever I travel, but the nightlife here was watching the stars.

The next day the roads—gravel, dust, and loose dirt, immensely difficult to bike through—were so broken up and muddy it took us eight hours to travel 130 miles. While Tabitha still hated the roads, she was definitely getting better at handling her bike.

"I've gone from fear and dread to anger," she told me with a grim smile. "I take the mud wallows and gravel as a personal affront and attack them with a vengeance."

I was proud and a little in awe of her. This was on-the-job training in becoming a world-class motorcyclist. I was witnessing a true transformation of spirit, someone coming into her own through willpower and discipline.

The maps were certainly right: There were few paved roads in eastern Siberia. It reminded me of the Yukon, which when I passed through it years before contained only twenty-one thousand people in a territory the size of California and New York State combined. This was the Russian frontier, I decided, the wild land that had yet to be tamed.

Back in the Alabama of my youth, a familiar feature of the countryside was a county road scraper maintaining the gravel roads. If your stretch of road became too muddy or rut-riven, you called up the commissioner, whom you knew personally, and got him to send over a scraper.

Here, nobody took care of the public roads. In winter they put sand and gravel on the ice, and in the spring, after the ice melted, the sand and gravel fell onto the road, four and five inches thick. This loose sand and gravel slid out from under our wheels, tossing us into gentle yet still unsettling spills. We sometimes took the outside of the curve, but that threw us into the path of oncoming traffic. Fortunately there wasn't much traffic, maybe thirty short-haul trucks in a day, almost no cars.

The more towns through which we passed, the easier it was to see why no one traveled. Ussuriysk had no more goods than Spassk-Dal'niy, which had none at all; nor had Aunt Milly left Svobodny for a better job in Shimanovsk. In addition, people thought too much of their cars to drive them out here. Only knuckleheads like us went any distance on this road. When a sensible Russian wanted to go a thousand miles he took the Trans-Siberian Railway.

The sights around us, however, always lifted our spirits.

The skies and clouds were amazing, much like the Big Sky country of Montana and the Yukon, and yet in some strange way even larger. The enormous, billowing clouds were like none I'd ever seen in shape, color and texture. Why any one bowl of sky should seem larger than another was a mystery to us, but here the heavens felt vaster than any others under which I'd ever traveled.

Broad plains of flowers often stretched away from us, irises and lilies and daisies and phlox—purple, yellow, red, white, blue, every conceivable color—fields covered with them. Nobody owned any of it; it was all wild.

Ghostly mist rose as the sun set and the mountain streams meandered down to warmer levels. Hills ascended to our right and left, one thousand or two thousand feet high, covered with birch trees and flowers.

Sometimes we were treated to vast, jagged flashes of lightning, gorgeous, chaotic latticeworks of crisscrossing bolts filling entire regions of the sky with disorganized and frenzied electric webs, the power roaring and crackling overhead.

The few hotel restaurants out here—never more than one to a town; that would be competitive and wasteful—nearly always had a live band that played so loud no one could talk.

We were always hard-pressed to get a table because the locals reserved spaces weeks ahead to celebrate birthdays and anniversaries. Most of the people on the dance floor were women, and nobody seemed to be having any fun. This summer the lambada was two or three years out of fashion in the West, but in Siberia it was hot. In every hotel restaurant they played it along with the same three or four other songs—and that was all. Everywhere the same music, as if some central music committee in Moscow had decreed what had to be played this summer in hotel restaurants.

If there was alcohol, it was almost always vodka. To our astonishment, one night we were served dry Hungarian red wine. We still went into the kitchens to see what was available. Usually it was tomatoes, cucumbers, cabbage, potatoes, rice, and dumplings in a soup with a crust on the top, and one kind of meat.

Always such big kitchens and so few choices!

As we traveled along the Amur River, which separated China from Siberia, we often saw barbed wire on both sides and armed guards facing each other across a few hundred yards. Here we were next to the Trans-Siberian Railroad, which the czars foolishly had built too close to China, creating a security risk.

In Blagoveshchensk, an industrial city and a regional capital, we learned that every day a boat came across from China with Chinese merchants and traders, and the Russians went over there to sell goods to the Chinese. The Chinese brought over cosmetics, clothes, and textiles. All I could figure the Russians had of value to trade were timber and vodka, as there was a Stolichnaya vodka factory here. Certainly no sensible Chinese wanted the collapsing ruble.

This vodka was manufactured for export, we learned. Citizens could obtain vodka only from state stores, and they were allowed only two coupons a month with which to buy two bottles, which meant it was in severe shortage. We weren't allowed to buy alcohol in the state stores.

I found the story of Blagoveshchensk fascinating, as the city had belonged to both sides during its long history. Founded in 1644 as a military outpost by the Cossacks, it was taken by the Manchurians in 1689. In 1856 the Cossacks recaptured the city. Then, in 1900, to avenge the European deaths in the Chinese Boxer Rebellion, the Cossacks killed every Chinese in the city, thousands of them.

And yet despite this bloody history, trade flourished between the two peoples.

To our amazement, in the vodka factory we found North Korean workers, and on a state farm, Chinese laborers who lived in bunkhouses. In another factory Vietnamese girls in their late teens and early twenties spun cotton into cloth. When I thought about it, it made sense. The Soviets out here had little labor, so they imported it.

We met the head man of the textile factory, a Vietnamese called Mr. Trang. We dodged around the subject of our war with his country, but Mr. Trang dismissed the entire thing as of no importance. The women, he said, brought up big containers of goods from Vietnam—shirts, blouses, matches, cigarettes, and canned fruit—which they sold on the Soviet market, making their trip even more profitable.

At Muchino the transcontinental road became a couple of meager trails through grass. We drove along them gamely, but finally even they ended in a gigantic swamp. There was no road west, and the locals avowed there had never been one. The only way across the vast swamp was the Trans-Siberian Railroad. We had to backtrack fifty miles to the last station to ask the stationmaster for help.

For the equivalent of twenty-five dollars he sold us the right to ride a freight train westward, to have a nine-by-forty-four-foot flatcar to ourselves.

"What about food?" Tabitha asked. "Water?"

"He says we'll only be on it a few hours."

The yardmen helped us load and tie down the bikes. We had the last car on a seventy-car freight train. What a hoot! We were glad the road had ended. Hopping a flatcar is to railroading what motorcycling is to motoring: roughing it. The rail-yard crews in the scattered crossings through which we passed were stunned to see Westerners and motorcycles on a flatcar.

Tabitha was glad for the respite, and I, too, chuckled with delight. The wind blew in our hair, the breathtaking Siberian forests, fields, and hills sailed by, and the clouds presented their dazzling aerial stunts. This glorious ride could never happen at any price in the United States. Everybody connected with sanitation, food, unions, they'd all go berserk. The insurance company would have put us in jail. But there was no road in this part of Siberia, so here we were.

There was also no conductor to come through and say the next stop is Trenton, or that we'd be stopping here in Vostok for twenty minutes. We'd dash off at stops to relieve ourselves behind bushes, hoping to scramble aboard before the train pulled out. Usually we had to wait two hours for it to leave.

Freight trains passed every fifteen minutes carrying everything imaginable, often duplicating what was going the other way. Logs passed going east, yet we saw logs of the same type heading west.

We were on the flatcar longer than the stationmaster's "few hours." Night came. We were forced to buy potatoes, blueberries, onions, and bread from the babushkas who met the train to earn a few kopecks, the only vendors at stations. We had a bottle of vodka to wash down dinner. Occasionally it rained, but nothing our slickers couldn't handle. At night we rolled up in our tiny Japanese sleeping bags and went to sleep. Dawn arrived and we made tea on our butane stove.

Another day and another night.

We were told there was something of a road near Chernyschevsk, so at last we asked to be put off, having been on our personal flatcar for a little more than two days.

In this part of Siberia we often passed mobile missile launchers on the highways, Scuds, I suppose, and we saw hundreds of tanks. The launchers were fifty, sixty feet high, often broken down. This was due north of Beijing, so if war with the Chinese started, here was where there would be action.

At a big tank-training base a young soldier, to cement international Soviet-American relations, gave us a reproduction of a sketch, drawn in the heroic mode, of a youthful Brezhnev as a stalwart tank commander. The soldier had won it in a bicycle race. He didn't think much of it as a prize, but I was glad to have it. It now hangs over my pool table.

All those gigantic numbers about Soviet military hardware that the CIA and the Pentagon pumped out to justify their own spending—and here we passed missiles, launchers, and military equipment rusting by the side of the road and being fiddled with by half-assed mechanics. Much of these had been stripped for spare parts. A glance told you a lot of them wouldn't work.

Having seen both armies, the Chinese and the Soviet, I had the impression that neither side had very much, and that what it did have wasn't very useful. Granted, I hadn't seen as much on the Chinese side.

On every bridge out here—this was a war zone, remember—stood a guardhouse and a couple of armed soldiers. What the Chinese did have was all the soldiers in the world. In a war the Chinese would first take out the Trans-Siberian Railroad, cutting the vast Soviet Union into any number of helpless parts.

That afternoon we were on the road to Chita, a big city, where we hoped to stop and rest after the jolts of the flatcar.

A police car stopped to ask who the hell we were and what we were doing out here, just as the Alabama patrolmen might stop and check out strangers. After we showed them our papers, they pointed to the sky and said in pidgin English that we'd better find "skelter" because there was going to be a "sturm."

I thanked them and they left.

"What's a 'sturm'?" Tabitha asked.

"I guess a storm."

"Maybe we should pull over," said Tabitha. "Wait it out."

Although it had rained here for six days, today it was dry.

"I've seen storms before," I said. "We were on that flatcar too long. I want to spend the night in Chita, where we have the chance of a decent hotel room, not another night in a drafty barn."

At five o'clock we drove through a picturesque village where we saw no one, not a soul. It was so unusual and so eerie that the hairs on the back of my neck rose.

Outside the village it became ominously black and still. We kept moving. I thought about stopping, but I figured a little unpleasantness from a storm would be more than made up for by getting to Chita and some form of civilization. If you stopped in Siberia every time it rained, you'd never make it across.

Then a gust of wind hit the side of the bikes, and I thought it would knock me over.

The wind got wild quickly, rushing at us from all sides. No sooner had I figured out how to tack into it than it changed direction, whipping my bike around. In front of me Tabitha was having trouble, too.

It started to rain, buckets of lashing water, which turned into hail. Ice stones the size of mothballs and golf balls racketed against our helmets, face shields, and fenders. The protection of leather jackets, heavy sweaters, and shirts wasn't enough. Our backs were pummeled as painfully as if buckets of stones were being hurled from the sky. We were in a maelstrom of wind, rain, and ice stones.

Within minutes the slippery road became a river of white hail and water, making the bikes even more difficult to keep upright. Fields ran up to the road on both sides; there was no shelter.

The wind rose and howled as if it wanted to sweep us up and blow us away. We clung to our handlebars and fought to hold the five-hundred-pound bikes upright. We passed twenty white-and-tan cows in the middle of the road—and yet the sky was so black and the hail so thick we could scarcely see them. Our wheels slid about, and only our boots kept us upright. We were creeping along at four or five miles an hour when a cow, blinded by the storm, walked into me. My bike was knocked over and I was sprawled across the road.

Tabitha put her kickstand down and ran back to help, slipping and sliding on the mud and white balls underfoot. She helped me right my bike.

I should have listened to that policeman, and I should have stopped in that village. Here my impatience, my drive to move along, had put us in danger. Anything could happen out here—the road could wash out, a flash flood could overwhelm us, a blind truck could run over us.

She was terrified, in tears and in pain. "The hail—it hurts! I can't see anything!"

"What do you want to do?" I shouted. "Where do you want to stop?"

She didn't know. She shouted that she was worried about her bike—didn't hail destroy cars? I shouted that we had to keep moving to get out of this. There wasn't any sense standing here and letting the storm beat up on us.

I've never been one to stand still. If we left our bikes there in the middle of the road and walked somewhere, who knew what would happen to them or to us? We cranked the bikes up, put them into the lowest gear, and, still blinded by hail, hugged the edge of the road and pushed them along.

Even that was hard, because we had to peer through the gloom and the hail to make sure we were still on the road. It was hard to keep our footing with hailstones underfoot. We pushed the bikes for a long while.

Finally the storm lifted and the sky turned light again. Under the summer heat, the hail melted.

We had never had a chance to put on our rain suits. We were soaked, and so were our saddlebags and almost everything in them. In the middle of the road Tabitha stripped down to her underwear and put on her rain suit, the only dry clothes she could find. On every side the landscape was windswept and beaten down. Tons of water rushed down the sides of the hills and roads. Stones the size of footballs and grapefruit had been blown out onto the unpaved road. Branches, leaves, and trees were strewn across the road. In places the roadbed was washed away.

"Maybe *sturm* means 'tornado' in Russian," said Tabitha.

"Something might have been lost in translation," I said.

"The next time the police announce a *sturm,* we're stopping."

"Right" was all I could answer.

In a small town, parts of which were under a foot of water, we tried to get gas, but the electricity was out, which meant the pumps wouldn't work.

One of the locals sold us gas from his spare jerry can. Now the sky looked fine, so we again set out for Chita, this time with some of the local fellows in cars as companions, because we were always exciting to the Russians who stumbled across us.

They led us out of town. One dashed ahead and came back with the news that the storm had washed out the bridge. We figured this now was the end of the day.

"No, no," they said, "we'll show you something else."

We went back to the fork in the road with them and took the other way. After a couple of miles, we came upon a paved road. Unbelievable. Glorious asphalt. Not a road sign, not a car, not a manmade object, only flat paved road.

We roared out. Our new friends rode along, waving and shouting like teenage boys. Well, I was happy. It was late in the day, we were driving straight into the sun, I was wet from the "sturm," but we were making great time. I had on my electric vest and my heated handle grips, trying to dry myself out. My stereo was blasting, first Willie Nelson's "On the Road Again," and then Mozart's *"Eine kleine Nachtmusik."* We ran into another fabulous Siberian light show, lattice works of lightning flashes to the left and sunset colors the like of which I'd never seen to the right. I couldn't think of any place in the world I'd rather be, or anything else I'd rather be doing.

I was having a wonderful time, but I kept asking myself, What's this road doing out here? Why isn't it on any of the maps?

Finally the Russians wanted to go back. They explained that this was a secret military road, one used for the transportation of missiles. Of course it was flat and fast. Of course it wasn't on the maps! We said good-bye. With some trepidation, we moved on toward Chita.

The entire way there we encountered no one. We arrived in Chita near midnight, found a decent room, and collapsed into bed. At first Tabitha was too wound up, tired, and sore to sleep, but finally she dropped off. We had the best night's sleep we'd had in days.

The Hotel Siberia in Petrovsk Zabaykalskiy—yet another hotel in yet another town where nothing worked.

The light fixtures didn't work, nor did the elevators. We considered ourselves lucky to get a bathroom that worked, as out here lots didn't. As usual, the tub and the sink were fed from a single faucet that swung between them, an economic installation. There were long dark corridors, unpainted, run-down, and seedy.

If there hadn't been somebody at the desk, I'd have thought this dump was an abandoned slum, the hotel from the graveyard, yet it had been built only eleven years before we'd arrived. I couldn't figure out how the Russians did it, but we constantly ran into public buildings like this, almost new and transformed into an instant slum.

After four or five drunks accosted us in the streets, we realized people all over town were drunk.

The officer at the police station where we stored the bikes explained. "Two weeks ago the town ran out of vodka. Our boxcar came in today with our shipment, so everybody bought all he could and got drunk."

Back at the hotel, a ruddy-faced, jovial Russian in his seventies introduced himself as Nikolai. Normally he shut down the hotel's boilers at ten o'clock, he said, but tonight he would leave them on till eleven so we could bathe. He drew us aside.

"I was stationed with your army in the Great Patriotic War," Nikolai said in a conspiratorial whisper. In contrast to the usual fractured English we encountered, his was fluent. "In Belgium. You know Hershey bars? Fords?" Clutching my hand, he glanced around furtively. "I've never told any of them. Keep it quiet. They'll put me in a camp if I say good things about Americans."

"It doesn't matter anymore," I said. "All that's changed."

His face darkened and he put a finger to his lips. "It's changed before."

With tears in his eyes, Nikolai told us stories of his wartime adventures with American troops, for whom he was filled with admiration. For forty years he had treasured these memories, but fearful of the concentration camps that might follow his saying that Americans were good, he had shared none of them with his countrymen.

The next morning we asked if we could take his picture, but he refused, saying they might take it from us and use it against him in court.

Banned by the Communists for decades, town markets had sprung up in many of the villages through which we passed.

However, in Siberia there were still no roadside restaurants, no Howard Johnsons, Dairy Queens, or McDonald's to stop in for a snack. Travelers carried their own food or did without. We bought bread from the bakeries, and in these emerging markets stocked up on vegetables and fruit. Often we found potatoes, onions, tomatoes, scallions, cucumbers, yogurt, raspberries, and a delicious fermented blueberry preserve.

In contrast to the decrepit public buildings, we rode through villages that looked as if they'd stepped out of picture books. Every house was brightly painted and decorated with Victorian gingerbread, and each had its own well. Carved shutters and intricately designed latticework around the roofs showed how much their owners cared. Flowerbeds glowed in front, and huge vegetable gardens lay out back, many with greenhouses. Each house was unique and cheerful, and each strove to outshine its neighbors.

Nearly all the houses had blue-and-white or green-and-white shutters with picturesque designs, as did the gates to the yards and cemeteries. Reflecting layers of Russian history, some graves were marked with a double cross, its top bar aslant, the symbol of the older religion; some were marked by the cross that stood for the later Russian Orthodox faith; others had the red star, emblem of Communism and atheism.

Seeing these self-sufficient villages, I realized the Siberians were never going to starve. Russians might starve in Moscow, they might starve in Leningrad, but not here. These people had lived this way for hundreds of years without the Communists bringing them any food. After all, in none of these villages was there a single store. Except for the aid of an occasional telegraph office and train station, the villagers were completely self-sufficient.

We stopped in a couple of villages to find out who these people were and what this was all about, because their houses were in such contrast to the grim cities, where everybody lived in big apartment buildings that were allowed to fall apart.

The villagers always pressed vegetables on us. Occasionally they gave us meat, too, which always turned out to be as tough as a ten-year-old cow, which it probably was.

Inside, these houses were clean, whitewashed, and neat. Not much furniture, but they all had a TV. There wasn't much programming—I noticed Mexican soap operas and the news—but I wondered how they got a signal at all. Then I remembered that Russians were good with military satellite technology. Here was a country in which little except the Trans-Siberian Railroad and the telegraph system worked—and television! It suited their propaganda purposes, I supposed, to keep the people of one mind about whatever their bosses wanted them to be of one mind about.

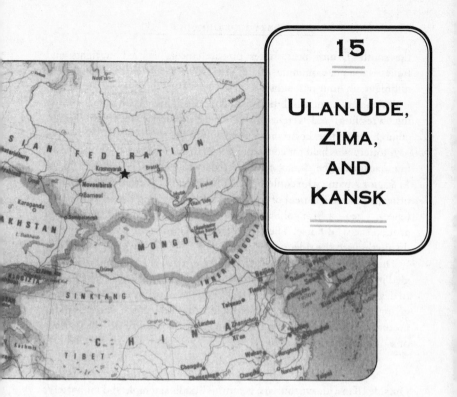

FOR SEVENTY YEARS the Communists had banned the Buriat Mongols' annual festival, the great gathering of the clans that had been a glorious rite for centuries.

These were the descendants of Genghis Khan, proud mountain people who reveled in this religious and nationalistic festival. This year they didn't ask Moscow if they could put it on, they just did it. More and more Tabitha and I kept noting examples of the Communists losing their grip over their subjects.

The opening ceremonies in Ulan-Ude, the capital of the Buriat Autonomous Republic, were held on a Saturday night. Four bonfires were lit at the corners of a huge field symbolizing the four corners of the earth and the four directions from which the clans had come. As a large crowd of Mongols watched, a trumpet was blown and another bonfire was lit at the field's center.

Drums banging, the clans from the traditional homelands marched in—clans from the east, west, north, and south, including the nation-state of Mongolia, each displaying its characteristic red, gold, green, and purple dress. Girls from the west skipped in and danced, then those from the south. Drums beat, flutes piped, dancers swirled in tights and tunics—none in Communist Party gray. Lit by bonfires, this went on till midnight, an hour past sunset.

On Sunday came exhibitions and contests in archery, hammer throwing, wrestling, and weight lifting, as well as horse and trotter races, enough events to take up the entire day.

A lottery was held for consumer goods such as refrigerators and washing machines. The climax of the festival was a thousand-ruble prize, or $160, for anyone who could ride an unbroken horse around a track. The officials cleared the field of spectators, grimly forcing the crowd behind fences. The first Mongol broncobuster stripped off his shirt and danced around the wild horse. The police drew their guns, for this beast might do anything to the rider or the crowd.

This killer horse had been tied to a stake all day. He had become tangled in his ropes, but nobody dared untangle him, afraid of being kicked to death. Yet, the Mongol horse was in no mood to cooperate. Instead of giving us fireworks, the exhausted animal walked the shirtless rider around the track. The crowd sank back in disappointment, cheated out of a display of Mongol daring.

Outside Ulan-Ude we toured a beautiful Buddhist temple and monastery, built in 1975 to replace one that had burned. In all the Soviet Union, this was the only surviving Buddhist temple.

With its exotic prayer wheels and drums, it made what was happening in the Soviet Union sink in yet deeper. The revival of Judaism in Birobidzhan, the blossoming of Islam in the Central Asian Republics, and the resurgence of Christianity everywhere along our path made it clear how far Communism as a faith had failed. Across the entire Soviet Union people were spiritually bereft and grasping for something to believe in, a faith to clasp. Desperate for a collective identity—something we all need—this was frequently either their religion or their ethnic group, and often the two fused together.

Had the Communist Party developed a successful economic theory, one that produced true wealth, these drives back to ethnic roots would not exist. Create a true boom and everybody wants to join you.

Back in the twenties, thirties, and forties, those who had immigrated to the States wanted to be Americans above all else. They insisted that their children learn English, the faster the better. It is no accident that by the nineties our immigrants are clinging to their roots and that the demand for bilingual education has exploded. Multiculturalism is a force in America as in the Soviet Union because our immigrants no longer feel it's as easy to rise to the top. The decline in our currency and the stagnation of real wages is making being an American less alluring.

A reverse example is Poznan, once the summer home of the Prussian kings but given to Poland after both World Wars. Under Communist rule no one in the city had claimed to be or admitted to being German. Now, however, to take advantage of the rise of German prosperity, 40 percent of these Poles can prove that they are Germans, we were told, and thus must be allowed into Germany.

I began to believe that the concept of the giant nation-state, the great melting pot, as economically sound was diminishing across the world. The British Empire had collapsed, the Chinese were ignoring their central command, and the Russian empire was falling down around me. I wondered if the American republic, overburdened by the heavy machinery of its federal government and spiraling debt problems, was destined to lose some of its parts, too. As a single example that could be multiplied by the thousands, since 1932 the number of Department of Agriculture bureaucrats per American farmer has multiplied by *sixteen times*.

There are two major forces at work as the world moves into the twenty-first century, globalism and tribal control. How these opposing forces resolve their contradictions will be one of the new century's great historical dramas.

The truth is, people need the psychic glue of deeply held beliefs to bind them to others. That we all drink Coca-Cola and eat McDonald's hamburgers is not good enough.

We have a powerful need for a strong local identity, one we can comprehend and control, something close to home that we think we can reach out and touch. We resent its being destroyed by globalization and gigantism.

We met our first political protestors, two hunger strikers, camping out in the main park in Irkutsk. They sat on a bench surrounded by posters that detailed their stories.

One had lost her job at a drama institute. The other person was a dedicated human-rights advocate trying to obtain the release of an electrician jailed for accusing his boss of embezzlement. He had been in the park for six days.

That both were being ignored by the authorities was a major step forward for the people. A year before they would have been arrested the first day they had shown up.

· · ·

We approached the town of Zima on a dirt road made slippery by a slick coating of thin, watery mud. The rain was wearing us both down.

Although we drove cautiously, I took a spill. I wasn't hurt, but one of my saddlebags was ruined and much of my gear was spread behind me along the muddy road.

I gathered up my mud-streaked maps, shirts, toothbrush, and socks. Muttering to myself, I spent a couple of hours scrubbing mud out of them in the bathroom of the sports complex where we were staying. Many cities in China and Siberia had one such center where all athletic contests were held. There were always locker rooms and guest rooms for visiting teams.

We learned that Zima means "cold." I couldn't imagine what this town in the middle of Siberia called "cold" must be like in the winter.

Here we met Ramis Yukus, a visiting Lithuanian about twenty-five years old, and his first cousin.

Ramis's uncle had been exiled to Siberia in 1948 by Stalin when he had refused to turn his farm into a cooperative. Three years after the uncle had arrived, while working as a woodcutter here in the Lithuanian community, a tree had fallen on him and killed him. He had been buried in a local cemetery for thirty-nine years.

For a long time Ramis's parents had talked about the tragedy of his uncle's being buried so far from home. Ramis, finally, had been told by his mother, "Go to Zima and get my brother."

So, a little bewildered by the strangeness of Siberia, Ramis and his cousin had traveled thousands of miles with a small copper-covered, lead-lined locker to find his uncle's grave and bring the bones back to Lithuania for his mother.

They had found the grave in a cemetery near a settlement of Lithuanians, marked by his name, the single word *Randis* on a large traditional cross. The ancient grave-keeper said he had known the uncle and verified that this indeed was his grave.

The youths' initial excitement had turned to frustration on encountering the Soviet bureaucracy. No local official wanted to give them permission to remove the remains. Each had thrown up objections, handing them more forms to fill out, citing further permissions needed before his department would issue a permit.

Ramis had visions of returning to Lithuania empty-handed, disappointing his mother. For more than a week the two had trudged from one government office to another in this small town, documenting who they were, who was buried in their uncle's grave, that the body was indeed that of a relative, and that their uncle had not died of a disease too frightful to unearth.

Finally, however, Ramis had everything he needed. The two young men were excited and apprehensive at the prospect of opening up a thirty-nine-year-old grave.

As they dug, it began to rain. At the bottom of the grave the shovel struck old wood. The remnants of a pine box and a suit of clothes were brought into the light of this sodden day. They tossed the bones out one by one and put them in the lead-lined box for their uncle's long ride home.

Before they left, they used a rusty nail to scratch onto the huge, sagging cross in Lithuanian, "Gone home."

In most towns there was a gas station that sold the only two qualities of gas available in the Soviet Union, 74 and 93 octane. Most drivers, looking to save a few kopecks, changed the compression on their cars to burn 74, although over time this ruined their engines. Gasoline cost us the equivalent of six cents a liter, or twenty-five cents a gallon at the official ruble-dollar rate. Of course, at the black-market rate it was half that— twelve cents a gallon.

In Siberia we always went to gas stations for gas. When they didn't have 93 octane, we went to the police station and asked for it. They either had it on hand or could get it from the military.

At one gas station, Olga, the lady attendant, said in broken English, "Look, I only can sell ninety-three to police or ambulance drivers."

"Yes, but we have to have ninety-three," I said, pointing at the seventy-four sign and crossing my two index fingers. In Russia, this all-purpose gesture means *nyet*—"I can't do it," "No way," or "Broken." I went on to lay my usual rap on her in sign language and simple English, using the map of the world to show our journey. Hoping she could follow me, I said we had legitimate visas and that we had to have the right gas for these bikes or stay here forever.

Olga was firm. "I tell you, it is law. I no give good gas to nobody but police and ambulance drivers."

"I know we're an inconvenience," I said, "but our bikes must have ninety-three octane. By the way, do you like Western cigarettes? We don't need this carton of Marlboros."

Now Olga was adamant. "Don't you listen?" she shouted, drawing herself up to her full formidable height. "Don't you hear? I tell you two times already. I no give good gas to nobody except police, ambulance drivers, and American travelers driving motorcycles!"

More bad stretches of road—little pavement, of course, mostly loose gravel, deep ruts, and potholes. We started off fresh each day, thrilling to the scenery and life in the remote villages through which we passed, but by the end of an eight- or ten-hour day our shoulders ached, our legs were cramped, and we longed for a hot shower. No, our butts weren't sore, a question I've been asked a thousand times. That may happen on horses, but rarely on a motorcycle, no matter how long the trip or rough the road's surface.

It was a constant struggle to stay focused, although mercifully here the weather was dry. We counted every mile on the speedometer and hoped the end of the bad road was near. When we got to good patches—dry packed dirt—it was a joy to speed up to thirty miles an hour. Each mile gave us a sense of accomplishment, although it also reminded us of how long it had been since the last one had ticked over, how slowly we were going.

Despite the hardships, there was no other place that summer I wanted to be. While we pushed ourselves on travel days to make all the time we could, in between we'd rest and absorb our new surroundings, spending days poking around, visiting, and exploring. This was travel the way it was done in the centuries before the car, the airplane, and the steamship. I loved the leisurely pace and the sense of personal mobility, as if we were ambling around the world on a horse, seeing, hearing, and smelling everything firsthand.

I reveled in the wind in my face and the unobstructed view of fields, mountains, and streams, the beauty of which was often staggering. The honeyed perfume of flowers would be followed by the excited buzz of bees. When we stopped we heard the warm wind sigh through the trees. It was fun to be out where no one from back home had ever been, meeting villagers who had never before met foreigners and were delighted to see us. I loved their rough faces, harsh like the Siberian weather, but also untainted by too much civilization.

We never knew who and what adventure lay right over the hill. It was a thrill to get a close view of what the world was like, to see for myself what was going on globally. To my mind, we were like Europeans meeting the natives of North America hundreds of years ago. As happened to the Americas, Siberia would become open, would be explored and tamed. We were the precursors of many more like ourselves who would one day arrive.

Wherever we stopped in the wilderness, in the much vaunted *tayga,* we were attacked by trillions of black flies. For some reason they didn't bother us as we drove, but once we stopped, they made that rest stop a torment. Where they came from I never could figure out. What did they do all day when we weren't there? All year?

In the towns, restaurants were often covered with flies. Once we saw a manager doing her accounts, oblivious to the dozens of flies on her dress and her books. No Siberian had ever seen a fly swatter. Some entrepreneur could make millions producing them.

One morning, we pulled over for a break. While I dodged flies, Tabitha explored the lush green field near the road. She called out excitedly, holding up a tangle of green. I went to her.

She was standing in a field of green peas that back in the South we called sweet peas. Well, Tabitha loved raw peas, so we pulled up a bunch and sat by the road. We swatted black flies and shelled and ate a mess of them.

I was worried about our eating so many raw, green vegetables, that we'd get sick the way you can after eating green apples, but the peas were delicious and went down well. In other parts of the world, China, for example, neither we nor the Chinese would dare eat anything straight from the field because they used human excrement as fertilizer. Nobody in China, not even the Chinese, would drink untreated water. But in Siberia there were so few people that there was little pollution of vegetables or the water.

Afterward, despite the flies, we were so contentedly full that we took a nap. The field of peas was out in the middle of nowhere, far between towns, a field gone wild. We filled a plastic bag and took several bunches.

Part of our excitement in finding the peas stemmed from our experience of the Russian diet, which appalled us. For breakfast they ate every artery-clogging, cholesterol-filled food they could find: a hard-boiled egg or two, a piece of bread covered by a layer of butter as thick as the slice itself, and a glass of *smitanya,* maybe twelve ounces of the stuff, sour cream with the consistency of yogurt. Their other meals were as bad—fatty meat, more bread and butter, fried potatoes, and few vegetables, followed by sweets and cakes.

This diet, the general lack of exercise, smoking, and rampant alcoholism combined to shorten lives. The life span of Russian men averaged only sixty-four years. In the United States the average was seventy-two years, and in Japan, an even more impressive seventy-five years.

We found more green peas along the road and continued to eat our fill, along with the vegetables and fruit we had bought in town markets.

Coming into Kansk at about ten-thirty we saw a light show of lightning on one side of the road and a glorious sunset on the other, pinks and yellows like I'd never seen. Then the first end-to-end double rainbow of my life appeared, and I kept staring at it in disbelief.

The road here was another disaster, dry but with lots of loose gravel. It took us ten hours to drive 130 miles. Both of us fell several times. We were going so slowly that these falls weren't dangerous, just frustrating. I tried to take the spills in stride—after all, I'd never expected anybody to pave our way around the world—but Tabitha was disheartened by the endless bad roads. We had been in Siberia several weeks and had covered three thousand miles, yet we had another three thousand or four thousand miles of doubtless the same bad roads to go. We were discovering the hard way how large indeed was the world's largest country.

We approached Krasnoyarsk, a large industrial city closed to foreigners.

Its population of nearly a million people made it one of Siberia's largest cities and the capital of the huge region that stretched from central Siberia to the Arctic coast. I understood that it was a center of the Soviet defense industry, and that it produced plutonium. It was here in 1989 that the Soviet government had admitted it had a missile-tracking radar station, in violation of the ABM (antiballistic missile) treaty and which it promised to dismantle. Rumor had it that the Russians were building the world's largest underground nuclear-waste dump near the city, with part of it to reach under the important Yenisey River. This seemed stupid to me, but I didn't put it past a government that had destroyed the Aral Sea.

All this military activity, according to a policeman we asked about the roads, meant we had to go around Krasnoyarsk. Our map showed that the road in and out of the city was good, whereas the northern route around the city was, as usual, unmarked, which meant impossible roads—and an extra two days and three hundred miles at that.

I wondered who would stop us if we disobeyed our permits. So far the soldiers with guns on every bridge only stared in disbelief as we passed. We had been stopped only once in three thousand miles.

"Well, we certainly can't stay in a hotel there," said Tabitha.

I agreed. At night, when we would park our bikes at the police station, we only sometimes had to show our visas, but we always had to show them to the suspicious hotel management.

"We'll just drive through," I said.

"Sure," she said, perking up at the idea of bypassing all the bad roads. "We'll stay at a room on the other side. For a good road, I'll even camp out."

I nodded. "No accidents. I don't want the KGB down on us because we're not where we're supposed to be."

"No accidents," she echoed with a knowing smile.

So we set off on a beautiful paved road toward the closed city of Krasnoyarsk. Shortly, we approached a bridge that was heavily guarded by Russian soldiers. They made me nervous, but I stared straight across my handlebars and pretended I belonged here. Both of us kept our speed steady. To our relief they only watched us go by.

A second bridge came up, again guarded by a patrol of gun-toting soldiers. Again we stared straight ahead and didn't slacken our speed. I felt their eyes raking us.

We drew abreast of them. No one shouted. We passed them. No shots were fired in the air. I didn't dare look back. We'd made it!

A few minutes later we were in downtown Krasnoyarsk: grim broad streets, seedy modern buildings, and scores of people fishing below the big main bridge.

Then it hit me. The KGB was in Moscow telling them what to do in Krasnoyarsk, but out here nobody was listening! This country was disintegrating around us.

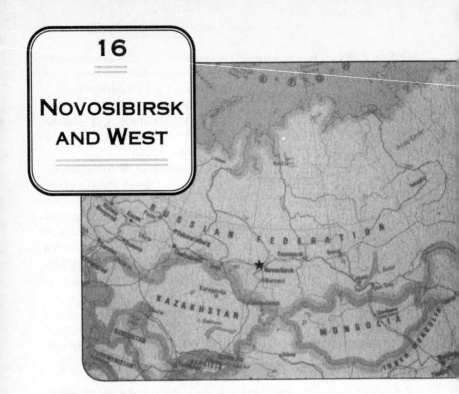

A T KEMEROVO, where the coal miners had gone on strike in 1989, we met the head of the union and some miners.

This was the union that had stunned the USSR with its first strike in decades. Militant, they told us they supported Yeltsin and that they wanted to change the government. They knew they would have to strike to do it. Then we went to see Oleg Glazunova, the head of a new independent newspaper, which was being threatened with closure. An employee translated our conversation.

While we were there, in walked an army major, quickly followed by Colonel Solovyov, both from Novosibirsk and intent on getting the paper to be less antimilitary. Colonel Solovyov's message to Oleg was that if the paper didn't stop saying rude things about the army, next week there was likely to be a severe paper shortage.

Over a picture of tanks coming back from Hungary, the newspaper had asked, "Why are the military sending tanks here, a town that doesn't have room for them? We think it's to suppress the coal miners. We think they're building up the army for the time they can crack down on us."

Oleg pointed out the caption to the colonel, who replied, "No, no, that's not the reason. We learned that lesson in Tbilisi. In the future the army will stay neutral. We're bringing in troops and tanks because we've been thrown out of Europe and this is the only place they can put us."

I was amazed that their discussion was this rational and that we were allowed to hear it. That it was being held at all was progress, because not too many months before, the KGB would have come over and said, "Close the damn paper," or they would have shot Oleg.

However, the miners supported its publication. If the army got too heavy-handed the miners would go on strike. The Soviet Union was one of the world's largest coal-producing countries. All their steel mills, generators, and trains ran on coal. The apartment buildings of the party members in Moscow, not to speak of everybody else, were heated with Siberian coal. Despite the nation's gigantic oil production, coal was what kept Soviet heavy industry going. All hell would pay if the army blundered into shutting down the Siberian coal mines.

I wondered if the Soviet workers had wised up about their masters. It seemed such a good deal for the workers that no price ever changed. What worker wanted prices to go up?

The Communists had a sweet racket.

To begin with, they had the world's largest country, 8,650,000 square miles, a sixth of the world's land area and almost as large as the entire North American continent. While difficult to exploit—Siberia hadn't yet been properly surveyed—Russia was also the world's richest country in energy resources and minerals. The Soviets probably had at least a quarter of the world's oil deposits, 40 percent of its iron ore, and a third of its phosphates. Even today no one knows the full extent of the nation's wealth. Pushing hard, the Soviets had come to produce more steel than Japan, more fertilizers than the United States, and more oil than Saudi Arabia. This fervid lunge for producing more and more, however, meant that quality, environmental concerns, and efficient production had been ignored.

If Russia produced a lot, the theory went, and kept the price of bread and rent and cigarettes and vodka low, then it would never have to raise wages. The theory was interesting: If the price of gas for the tractors never went up, surely, then, the price of wheat and thus bread never had to go up.

The reason, of course, that Communism had survived here as long as it had was that prices went up in the outside world. During the commodities boom of the seventies and eighties, when the Soviets had sold huge amounts of gold, palladium, coal, silver, lumber, natural gas, copper, platinum, and oil to the outside world, they had paid their subservient citizens nothing to drill and mine and plant and harvest. As the price of oil went to forty dollars during the 1970s, Moscow had reaped a bonanza. All the money had gone to the Communist hierarchy and for the space program, to intercontinental ballistic missiles and world-class Olympic teams. The Party managed things so poorly and the system was so rotten, there had been nothing left for the 275 million working toads except subsistence wages and a subsistence existence. If you counted all the Central European workers slaving under the umbrella of the empire, there had been yet more slaves.

Well, why couldn't it have gone on forever? If they hadn't bought anything from the outside, if they'd had a closed system, if they were so smart, why did it collapse?

Because the system hadn't been efficient; because nobody had had any incentive to produce more, sell more, or make a profit. A perfect analogy is the U.S. post office or our state-run educational system. Imagine an entire economy run for seventy years by the U.S. postal system!

That was the old Soviet Union.

The problem is the real world keeps intruding. In the real world, real prices are the only mechanism that brings in the right amount of supply. All a government has to do to deal with a shortage is let the price go up. We didn't need gas lines back in the Carter years. All we had to do was let the price of gasoline rise and oil would have been found under every service station. As the price goes up, people drive less. The price always matches supply and demand. That's what the price is, that matchup.

If you run out of copper in a closed system in which the price cannot go up, then nobody has an incentive to go out and find more, unless he's told to. "To hell with that," he'll say, "I'd rather go to the movies or drink vodka." But if the price of copper does go up, then lots of people say, "Hey, wait a minute, I can make a lot of money if I go out and find me some copper." Owners start to produce their marginal mines; those that weren't profitable at fifty cents a pound become extremely profitable at a dollar and a half. Scrap pipe comes out of walls and old car radiators and goes to the smelter.

If you had complete abundance of everything, without shortages and dislocations, in theory I guess a closed system would work. That was always part of the Soviet theory, that "We'll have an abundance of everything because we are Communists, we plan centrally, our people work hard, and it's a new mankind."

Well, the new mankind was certainly one part of that formula they didn't quite swing. People don't change. They haven't for the past five thousand years I know about, and I have no earthly reason to believe they will anytime soon.

One effect of low prices in the Soviet world was constant shortages. Every time the price of oil went up in the great outside world, there was an internal shortage. The Communists, however, never told their citizens that they couldn't have gasoline because they, the Communist leaders, were selling it for hard currency in Europe and Africa.

As we drove into Novosibirsk, the largest city in Siberia, we were excitedly flagged down by a couple in a fairly new Lada, the basic Soviet car.

Igor Kulikof, and his wife, Valentina, introduced themselves in broken English as the only private producers of motorcycle helmets from the Urals to the Pacific, or three quarters of the Soviet Union.

As was true back in the twenties, when the United States had been poorer, the Soviet Union had lots of motorcycles. The Kulikofs' customers didn't buy the helmets for safety, but because they looked Western. They made a fashion statement, announcing that this motorcyclist was up-to-the-minute and cool.

The helmets cost thirty-two dollars at the official rate, sixteen dollars at the black-market rate. There was enough of a demand to furnish the couple with an imported Jawa motorcycle, matching yuppie clothes, and gold chains. They were the Soviet Union's new entrepreneurs. They were so successful, they had even acquired a second one-bedroom apartment—nearly impossible to obtain in the Soviet Union—which they used as their factory.

They insisted we visit them. Their home was furnished with tiles bought on the black market, a washing machine, stove, stereo, and other consumer durables. They brought out black-market caviar, wine, and pâté to celebrate our visit.

A couple of years before, when it had become legal to produce goods privately and sell them, they had given up their factory jobs to concentrate on helmet production. They'd crafted their helmets from fiberglass, aping the models they'd seen in foreign pictures, and sold them on the black market. Working together at a kitchen table, they'd made ten times what they could have made in a factory, even though they'd had to give half their profit to the state.

"This country can't go back," Igor told us. "We have to move forward, become like the West. We won't let the old bosses go back to the old ways. The past is dead."

We also met their shell-shocked Afghan-war neighbor, fat and unemployed. I couldn't help but think that Valentina and Igor represented the future of this country; their sad, pathetic neighbor, its past.

For a few days Igor and Valentina traveled with us on their bike, wanting to spend time with us and loving the idea of crossing part of their country with Americans.

In the poor hotels in which we stayed, rooms rarely had double beds, yet they told us they always woke up in the same bed together because sometime during the early morning one of them crept into the bed of the other.

They had been married as teenagers, had a child, and after ten years they still did everything together, supported each other completely. Romance was clearly still in the relationship.

I saw in their marriage something I'd never seen before. I realized such long-term relationships were actually possible. I was very sorry when they turned back.

The Hotel Novosibirsk refused us service because the rooms weren't "good enough" for foreigners. Ha! They should have seen where we'd been. So we stayed at the Hotel Central, which took foreigners but almost refused us too, since the only rooms available weren't "good enough for Americans." Ha, again! They finally gave us a suite, which was what we usually got in our quest for a minimum standard of comfort. At least the refrigerator worked.

A bright banner arching across the street drew our attention. Special events were so rare here it made us stop and ask what was going on. A festival was being held. Everybody would bring his accordion for a combination folk festival and dance. Yes, indeed, we wanted to go.

That afternoon, accordion players and dancers gathered on an outdoor stage. We were introduced to Genadi Zavolokin, the folk accordion star, and his wife, Svetlana. He had a broad Slavic face, warm and generous. In the Slavic part of the Soviet Union, in Mother Russia, he was very famous, with his own television show and albums. We learned that he, his folk music, and his dances were part of the revival of the Slavic spirit. The accordion spun such soul-captivating Slavic notes that the adoring public gave these festivals a special name, Play Garmonica.

He introduced us to the crowd. Tabitha and I danced on the stage with the rest of the celebrants. This seemed to be a combination church festival, country-music hoedown, and square dance. Certainly it was a throwback to the days before the Communist Party. Genadi wanted to keep his music separate from politics, but I gathered that the Slav nationalists wanted to conscript his music into their cause.

I asked him to define for me the Russian soul. "Ahhh! Fire! Stars! Talent! Joy!" he declared, his eyes shining.

To him this festival wasn't political—and yet it was. He was one more manifestation of what we'd seen in so many places in this part of the world, people grasping for an identity that was theirs alone. The Slavs were reaching for their heritage through Genadi's music and dances, reaching for their traditions the way the Mongols and the Muslims were.

We went to our new friends' dacha with their kids, sixteen-year-old Anastachia and eleven-year-old Zahar.

What was strange to us was how the dacha was situated. Out here, still three thousand miles from Moscow and in the very heart of Siberia, there was nothing but vast tracts of unused land in every direction, yet the government would set aside only five acres for the entire town and say, "Okay, you can build all the dachas you want on these five acres." So, there would be forty or fifty summer cabins—with no running water and no electricity, with tiny yards and tiny gardens—all crowded together on a few acres in the middle of this immense wilderness.

We swam in the River Ob and then sweated in their *banya,* the Russian steam bath. Genadi stoked up the woodstove, then after he had heated up some rocks, he threw water on them, creating clouds of steam. We were given a particular type of birch branch, one as fragrant as eucalyptus, with which to lash ourselves. The women and girls undressed in the house, wrapped up in towels, and rushed into the banya. When they couldn't stand it anymore they came back and the men went in till we couldn't stand it anymore either.

We ate and danced and drank and banya-ed till one in the morning, having a fine old time.

In Novosibirsk we saw our first really big demonstration, scores of people gathered around the ubiquitous Lenin statue, demonstrating against the Communists.

One man protested that he was a war hero, had been decorated several times, and wasn't getting his military pension. There were others with similar gripes. Most of these people were protesting that they wanted more democracy, a better economy, and an end to the life-draining shortages.

We went out to a think tank at Academgorodok, the local university, a gigantic one built by Khrushchev, second-largest in the Soviet Union. I was hoping to get a better fix on these enormous changes. I met an English-speaking economist, Svetlana Muradova, who taught courses in capitalism here. We talked about what was happening.

The command economy, she said, planned from the top down, had been reasonably effective in the early stages, when the Soviet Union had been trying to leap into the industrial age, but was hopeless now. The country had to move to a market economy.

While it was hard to swallow, I remembered that Kiev mathematicians were said to have calculated that to plan in adequate detail just one year's industrial production in the Ukrainian republic alone, the entire world's population would need to be employed for 10 million years. Besides being inefficient, such a command system devolved into bureaucratic delays, shoddy goods, no consumer power, no competition, no innovations, and perpetual shortages.

"After seventy years of Communist teaching and sixty years of planning," Svetlana said, "our people expect the state to take care of them. They are used to taking orders, not taking initiative. We can't get it out of our heads that people who get rich, speculators, or people starting a co-op, are inherently evil." She sighed. "The truth is, the capitalist system works. The Communist system doesn't.

"We have two big shocks going on," she further explained. "Loss of hard-currency income, which led to Gorbachev's twin reforms of glasnost and perestroika. We sell commodities abroad like a Third World country, not quality goods like a superpower. With the collapse of oil prices, we have to sell three barrels of oil to buy the same German machine tool we used to buy with one barrel."

I knew their trade amounted to only 2 percent of the world's total, pitiful for a superpower.

They had never had inflation in the Soviet Union, she explained. It was an evil of capitalism that they bypassed because they never raised prices.

At a time when a ruble was officially worth sixteen cents, a hundred kopecks to a ruble, the bus cost two or three kopecks—less than a tenth of a penny—and newspapers two kopecks. In our money, it cost anywhere from ten to eighty cents to stay in a hotel room, for the best room in the house. Newspapers were so cheap, people bought them for wrapping paper. In the state store a bottle of vodka was ten rubles, a dollar and a half. A tomato was five kopecks, a tenth of a cent or so, if you could find it, whereas on the private market a pound of tomatoes cost fifty cents. The only thing the state store had lots of was birch juice.

The economist said they were only now starting to figure out how to measure inflation. She was baffled by what she saw around her, obviously sensing that events were occurring that were momentous but not knowing what to do or say about them.

"Isn't standing in line a form of inflation?" I asked. "Isn't all that time and energy a tax, one that increases the price of goods?"

She shrugged and gave me a weak smile.

As if to give myself a living example of the absurdity of their pricing, at a poster store in Novosibirsk I bought about a hundred posters—which weighed more than fifteen pounds—for twenty-four rubles, about $2.50. No wonder there was a paper shortage if posters were this cheap.

Then I found a 1991 calendar for forty cents with pictures of all the czars on it. The czars! I couldn't believe my eyes. Had glasnost come so far that the former "oppressors" could be celebrated? Figuring it would be valuable after the Soviet Union fell apart, I bought it, too.

This was like being down the rabbit hole in *Alice in Wonderland*. Nothing had a real price. At the post office it cost me twenty-eight rubles, less than three dollars, to mail these fifteen pounds of posters to New York.

The babushka there wrapped up my purchases lovingly, but I wondered how they could make it halfway around the world at such an absurd rate.

Tabitha was tightening the heads on my bike when she realized the wrench wasn't clicking; it just kept turning. She found that the threads of two of the long studs holding my cylinder to the crankcase had become stripped, ending the mystery of the source of the knocks in my engine.

She surmised that this had been caused by overheating compounded by the pummeling the bikes had taken on those bad roads. In addition to my driving this air-cooled engine at such low speeds that it hadn't properly cooled, my large fairing had further boxed in the heat. We couldn't go any farther till these studs were repaired.

We asked around, the way you shopped for everything in the Soviet Union. Certainly there were no motorcycle dealers. Somebody's kid's history teacher knew somebody at the auto plant. Armed with a sort of introduction, we drove out to the factory, hoping the automotive engineers there would help, as well as have tools.

Yes, they would help. Tabitha got into a collaborative process with the workers, and they all tackled the problem. I tried to imagine what would happen in the States if you pulled up to an automobile factory and asked for help with your motorcycle.

They said, "Okay, the first thing we'll do is make a part." Someone remembered a Czech truck engine that had metal studs of about the right length, also threaded on both ends. Czech meant quality, they bragged.

The stud was larger than we needed, so they had to lathe it down to the proper size. This international crew took a tap-and-die set, tapped out the holes, and rethreaded them. I hoped they knew what they were doing, since I certainly didn't. To make sure the stud didn't wiggle loose, Tabitha insisted on using a little of the Loctite we'd brought. When completed, the repair was supposed to make the bike as solid as new. However, the autoworkers presented us with a couple of extra truck studs in case we had further problems.

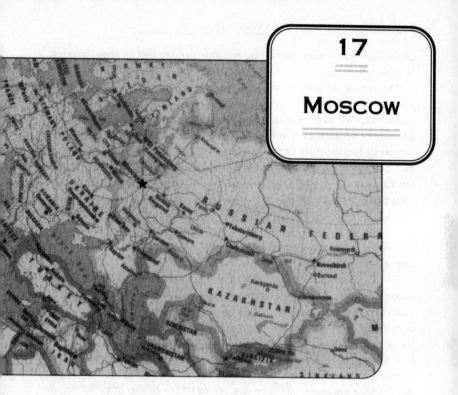

AT LONG LAST we were on the M-5, the main road into Moscow. Not only was there more traffic, but here it was faster and more reckless. Our excitement, too, was rising at nearing the capital.

Now the traffic-guard stations were all manned. Also, there were many more cars than trucks, whereas out in Siberia it was by far the other way around. Despite this traffic, the vast, empty spaces we'd been across made it hard to believe that the Soviet Union was the world's fifth-largest producer of cars, turning out 1.3 million a year. Under the thirteenth five-year plan, the one for the nineties, car production was supposed to double, but I had every doubt that this would happen.

Back in the States there was a diversity of vehicles on the road: campers, big trucks, little trucks, motorcycles, station wagons; European, Japanese, and American cars. But here there was only one kind of car and one kind of truck. Oddly enough, the cars looked like small Italian boxcars, with no refinements, no padding, and no real dashboards— just tiny stripped-down boxes. For twenty years the Russians had made the same car in the same factories, changing them very little. Our motorcycles had more horsepower, more cubic centimeters to their engines, than did these cars.

The reason, of course, was that when the Russians said, "We gotta have a car factory," they went around to see who was going to build them a factory and show them how to build cars. The Italians won the bid partly because at that time the Italian Communist party was the largest in Europe. Fiat came over and built the car factory for them. In fact, the Russians renamed the town Tol'yatti, after the leader of the Italian Communist Party. So to this day the Russians turn out only sixties-style Fiats, but with the brand name Lada.

The closer we came to Moscow, the more ordered and clean became our surroundings.

We stopped at a collective farm. Factory workers from Moscow were there harvesting what was supposed to be a bumper crop, their wages paid by their factory. There was an excellent chance, however, that despite the good harvest, half the grain and vegetables wouldn't reach the consumer because of tractors, combines, and trucks that sat idle for lack of spare parts and gas. The factory and office workers who were working the fields told us they thought their coming here was a stupid policy. One engineer said it was a waste of his talents for him to be pulling up carrots.

The farm's manager said this year they would again have to import wheat from the United States. He felt private farms and adequate machinery would solve Russia's food problems even though, yes, this would make some people rich. Poor Lenin! He had led the revolution and made himself into the father of the new world order for the peasants, and now they thought it was all a mistake. Every farm worker had productive private plots, while the state farms never met their potential.

As we pressed on, more and more gas stations were out of gas or limited us to ten liters each. Because I listened to the BBC shortwave news broadcast nightly, I knew that the Gulf crisis over Iraq's invasion of Kuwait had raised the world price of oil. I was certain the USSR was selling its petroleum products overseas at top dollar to get hard currency, but the Russians assumed it was only another mysterious shortage. Naturally, they didn't know that for years their oil production had been the world's largest.

Whenever there's a national problem and the government explains things to its citizens, don't believe the explanation. Figure out where the money trail goes, and you'll almost always know what's going on in the real world.

The hundred and fifty miles from Ryazan to Moscow were all four-lane.

Despite the crowded roads with their aggressive drivers, we felt wonderful. When we had landed in Siberia two-and-a-half months before, Moscow had been only a dot on the map, Siberia a vast expanse of paper. Every day I'd draw a new line on the map, showing what we'd done—and here we were, we'd made it!

Both of us were exhilarated. And now we were about to see Moscow itself, the capital of the largest contiguous empire the world had ever known, one larger than that of the Chinese, the Romans, and the Spanish. As someone who had studied history and politics, I could not conceive that anyone would ever again conquer so many square miles, and here we were charging into its capital on 1,000-cc steeds.

Had you ridden into Xi'an and Rome and Samarkand at their heights, you would have found rich people and unparalleled luxury. Moscow should have been the richest city in the world, but it was a place where you couldn't buy a carton of cigarettes without a riot. You couldn't get a bottle of vodka. You couldn't get soap. You couldn't get toilet seats. You couldn't get anything. Even though Moscow dominated this gigantic empire of hundreds of millions of people, what we were driving into was a large, poor city, a city of the Third World. It was huge, there were big buildings and wide roads the way you'd expect at the seat of a powerful empire, but there was no vibrancy, no texture, no depth. This was a bland, dismal city, a gray monument to a dying faith, a city without a soul.

Odder still was the fact that since the days of the czars, Moscow has never had much. Moscow was the richest city in the Soviet empire, yet Birmingham, Alabama, had more. Harlem had more of the everyday necessities of life, available to anyone who simply walked into a store. African cities often had more to offer in terms of luxury goods—even regular stuff like toothpaste, shoes, beer, a shirt, a pair of socks. Here, even if you had money, little was available at any price.

Tabitha was from the Upper West Side of Manhattan, and she lives about four blocks from where she grew up.

She loves cities. After two-and-a-half months of Siberian wilderness she was ready for a city, a big city. Back in New York she loved to walk and observe street life, the souvlakia man and the different shops and the West Africans selling fake designer watches on Broadway and the incredible variety of people, everything that makes New York's streets vital. When we came into a wonderful city she always made time to take long walks. She would plan strolling tours along the city's most famous streets, viewing them as urbanologist W. H. Whyte did, as rivers to be swum and played in. The first time she was in London she had walked eight or nine hours and had been exhilarated by her tramp.

So on two different days she went walking in Moscow, every minute expecting it to become interesting. If you started walking in Paris at the far end of the Champs-Élysées it might be boring, but the closer you got to the Arc de Triomphe, the more interesting street life would become. As she walked along Moscow's streets—ulitsa Gertsena, Pushkinskaya ulitsa, Kuybisheva ulitsa—she kept thinking, Any minute now it's gonna start happening.

She tramped about Moscow for four or five hours at a stretch and it never became interesting. The city's continual gray sameness was oppressive. On the street there was no life, no vitality. Nothing seemed to be going on. Along Broadway back in New York there were always deliveries being made. She told me that night that she couldn't remember seeing even one. There were few shops, maybe two every three or four blocks, one of which was likely to be a bakery. By the end of Tabitha's Moscow walks she was exhausted, not exhilarated; downtrodden, not stimulated.

We had heard of Suzdal, the legendary town outside the capital that a thousand years before had been larger than Moscow, but nothing prepared us for its score of ancient churches.

If Tamerlane's mosques in Samarkand and the Emperor Qin's terracotta armies will provide Uzbekistan and Xi'an with tourist dollars for decades to come, so Suzdal and environs will bring visitors by the tens of millions to Russia.

Over our entire journey of seven thousand miles across the Soviet Union we had not seen more than a dozen architecturally significant buildings. Out in the hinterlands the ancient churches were crumbling from disuse. Many had been destroyed or converted for other uses. Often the glorious onion domes had been dismantled and replaced by flat roofs. Here in the Suzdal area, a few miles from Moscow, were dozens of ancient monasteries, museums, convents, and churches, many lovingly preserved on a green country plain.

Set in what was originally a fertile wheat-growing area, Suzdal became a center for monasteries after it came under Moscow's rule in 1392. Later, in the seventeenth and eighteenth centuries, rich Moscow merchants had displayed their Russian Orthodox spirituality by putting up little churches in Suzdal—sometimes one for summer and one for winter—each merchant striving to outdo the last in pious splendor.

I was amazed that the Communists hadn't razed them all. Maybe because the town was small, nobody had ever thought of turning these religious gems into apartment houses for state workers. Maybe the churches had never been torn down to make way for industrial progress because the Moscow-Nizhni Novgorod railroad passed by twenty miles to the south. Anyway, luckily for the world, to this day the area has kept its glorious religious buildings and its rural charm, forgoing air pollution, big-city noise, and ugly modern buildings.

The most magnificent church was called, oddly enough, the Kremlin, or "fort." Building was started in the twelfth century and completed in the eighteenth. An enormous onion dome, cobalt-blue with gold stars and topped by a cross, was surrounded by four miniature replicas of itself, all five towering over scalloped gables and whitewashed stone.

The Nativity Chapel was filled with brightly lit gold panels of late-seventeenth-century icons. Many were painted in a combination of Byzantine and Russian Orthodox styles.

Suzdal didn't only have magnificence, however. The wooden church of St. Nicholas, brought here from the village of Glotovo, held no more than twenty worshipers but brought home the importance of religion to eighteenth-century Russian villagers.

The churches might have been built by rich merchants in a vain display of spiritual worthiness, but the quiet buildings, the long arched walkways, and the faultless skies had a calming effect on us. Nothing we'd seen so far in the Soviet Union had been as remarkable.

To our amazement, one of the churches had a plaque that said it belonged to the Russian Orthodox Synod in New York.

I was stunned. The New York Synod had been founded by White Russians, czarists fleeing the Bolshevik Revolution. In Red Square, I thought, Lenin must be whirling in his glass coffin over the fact that a local church had pledged allegiance to his worst enemy.

Inquiring how this could be, we met Father Valentin, the church's spiritual leader. Several months back, he said, he had been asked by the KGB and the bishop of Moscow to spy on foreign visitors. He had refused and was transferred to another church, one out in the boondocks. His parishioners made such a fuss over his departure, however, that he was brought back. Yet a proviso was added to his return—that the renegade church couldn't be part of the local synod—punishing its parishioners and Father Valentin alike.

He wrote New York and asked permission to join the synod outside of Russia, which was granted, which is how the synod on Ninety-third Street in Manhattan has a branch in Suzdal.

In Moscow we visited Maxim Kruglova, a young doctor who had been not only the first in his class, but number one in the country-wide medical competitions. While he was passionate about medicine, he was forced to work for a trading company because there was no money in medicine at that time in Russia.

At Moscow Medical School, the Soviet Union's chief medical school, he said there was a small specialty in preserving Lenin's body. Every five or six years the school turned out a graduate; it didn't need too many. The chosen few were selected to go down to Red Square and work on Lenin's remains.

Maxim said that because an ear once fell off Lenin's head, visitors weren't allowed to talk or make a sound while viewing the remains. Visitors also weren't allowed to put their hands in their pockets, as they might be saboteurs.

Today people will periodically stand up in the Russian parliament and ask, "Why don't we bury this guy? This is absurd, he's not even our hero anymore." But his tomb was a big tourist attraction back then, so they couldn't afford to bury him.

Actually, Maxim said, Lenin had wanted to be buried. He'd left specific instructions to be buried in his mother's church cemetery or some such place. Then Stalin had come along and said, "No, we have to build him up as the hero of the revolution, so put him out there in the Square." He had known that the people needed an icon, and he'd had nothing else. Stalin had wanted to be displayed there, too, as if to show that he was another hero of the glorious revolution. Originally he had been placed in Lenin's tomb, but one night Khrushchev had moved him out under cover of darkness.

Maxim wanted to come to the United States to practice medicine. While there was nothing wrong with Soviet medicine as it was taught, doctors were forced to work the way local mechanics worked on cars: They made do. You might be a superb doctor, bursting with the knowledge of your specialty, but without CAT scans, penicillin, scalpels, and vaccines, how could you do your job?

Moscow. The extremely inexpensive subways were nicer than New York's, each station with magnificent chandeliers and designed by a different architect. Stalin had built them, one of the few things he had done right, but we found little else over which to marvel.

We still couldn't find Moscow's heart, its hub, nor any glitz or glamour. Even Red Square, the putative center of Moscow, was not bustling with Muscovites. The city was as dull, lackluster, and lifeless as a day-old pot of oatmeal.

The huge government department store, called GUM, had few goods. Long queues were everywhere, the people in them as stolid, somber, and grim-faced as mourners at the funeral of a distant relative. We supposed they didn't have anything to smile about, or that they didn't want to be caught in public smiling, afraid somebody might ask, "Why are you happy? What's going on?" In private people laughed and giggled with us, but in public they were always grim.

In Tokyo, New York, and Buenos Aires you constantly run into a corner restaurant, a bistro, or an antique shop in which it's fun to poke around. There was none of that here. It didn't exist. In Moscow, you didn't stumble into some unique little shop, because it wasn't there. In the Soviet Union the idea of a pet store was incomprehensible. In all of Moscow's vastness there were maybe three cafés in which you could sit down and order a cup of coffee. The meanest café in many African or South American cities had a better menu than the best of these.

In a Moscow kindergarten we visited a former dissident, Tatiana, a trim, attractive woman who had been four years in a labor camp and another four in internal exile.

"Our people are finally waking up," she said. "For seventy years we've been like these children here, waiting to be told by our parent, the Party, what to do. We took no initiative, the way five-year-olds expect their parents to do for them. It's hard to break out of that old mind-set, but now we're all seeing we have to fend for ourselves. Hunger, scarcity, that's what's doing it. The Communist Party is dead."

At a huge outdoor flea market near Moscow, German military uniforms, equipment, and medals from World War II were on sale, items abandoned by the defeated Nazi battalions hastily retreating to the fatherland. The Russians' former enemies were coming back from Berlin and Munich as tourists and buying at outrageous prices the equipment their fathers and grandfathers had abandoned fifty years earlier.

We cranked up and left Moscow. We stopped at Borodino, the great battlefield. As it happened, we were there on the same day the battle had begun, August 26. Poor Napoleon. He had won the battle here in 1812 but lost so many soldiers that his ultimate chances at victory had been doomed.

As I read Napoleon's speech to his soldiers, in the wind I heard the strains of the "1812 Overture."

"This is going to be a great battle," Napoleon told his men. "Someday you'll tell everybody with great pride you were present at the Battle of Borodino. Let's win this battle and race to Moscow so we'll all have warm apartments for the winter."

Winter started here in September. Even this early we felt a sharp drop in the daytime temperatures from a few weeks before in July. I felt it on my neck; the air had a real chill to it, cool in the morning and cool in the afternoon.

Those soldiers must have felt that chill, too, and said to themselves, "Oh, Christ Almighty, we don't want to be in this place for winter, we'd rather be back in Paris."

But Napoleon said, "Don't worry, guys, we're all going to Moscow and get apartments."

What he didn't know was that Moscow was going to burn the whole place down. "Okay," the Russians said, "you want it, take it, but we just burned everything in sight. Take the whole city." So Napoleon lost the war. Would it really matter three hundred years later who had won?

I was certain that those scores of thousands of dead twenty-year-olds on both sides would have preferred living out their lives rather than dying here in the "great" battle few now remembered and even fewer cared about. Some might say this particular battle had changed history. Does anybody really believe that France would have still controlled Russia nearly two hundred years later even if Napoleon had won this war?

Tabitha and I were glad to be getting out because winter was roaring in, the one I had worried so much about earlier back in China and Siberia.

Finally we reached Brest, our last city in the USSR.

Properly speaking, Brest was Polish. But Stalin had wanted it and made it his after the Second World War, another example of a border drawn by a victorious army. People cry out these days for stable borders, but if this one is left unchanged, it will only endorse Stalin's madness in setting borders and his lust for more territory.

We'd been almost three months in the Soviet Union on this leg, June through August. I was ecstatic at having made it and depressed at leaving. Ecstatic at knowing that most of our road problems could be easily solved in Europe, where we would find good roads, tires, spare parts, medicines, and money. I would be able to communicate with the world we'd left behind. I might even be able to get a real newspaper, which I hadn't seen since Tokyo. But I was depressed that this once-in-a-lifetime trip was over. This had been special, the panorama of a giant country in transition. The Soviet Union was coming out of a decades-old winter into a spring whose nature would be cruel.

At the border we found a gigantic queue. The Poles had already freed up their prices and their currency. Their money was fully convertible, and they had legitimate pricing. Of course the Russian Communists hadn't yet. So while there wasn't much to buy in Russia, all the Poles and Hungarians were piling in to buy whatever they could at absurdly low prices. In Poland gas was two dollars a gallon; in Russia, twelve cents. With everything else—cars, sheets, pots, pans, refrigerators, TVs—there was the same discrepancy. The Poles would take these low-priced goods back to their country and make a killing, selling Russian products for twenty to a hundred times what they'd paid for them.

Naturally, having made the same mistakes for seventy years, the Russians didn't just fix their currency or their prices. Instead, they put on export controls. The border guards had long lists of what you couldn't take out of the country. One guy had a bunch of sheets taken from him. We had souvenirs and Russian medals we were anxious about, but the guards didn't seem to think we could take out many refrigerators and sheets on our bikes and so they gave us only a cursory exam.

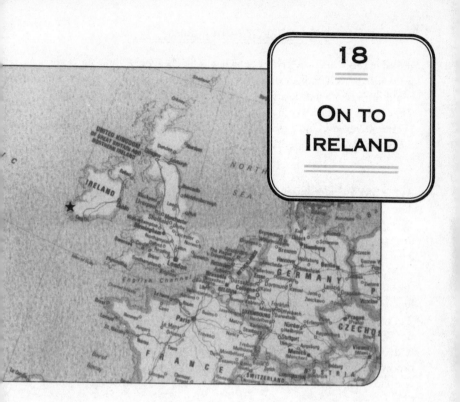

RIDING THROUGH the Polish countryside felt like pure freedom. We could go anywhere we wanted. The currency was convertible, so we didn't have to worry about black markets. We didn't have to worry about where to find food and gas.

A year previous the Poles had freed up everything. In Warsaw on every block, vendors were selling Marlboros and Pepsi-Colas from kiosks. Back in Russia there had occasionally been kiosks, but they sold mainly Russian cigarettes and only after you'd been in line for three hours. In Polish kiosks you could buy dresses, candy, whiskey, sodas, radios, batteries, flashlights, consumer goods of every stripe and variety, nearly all imported, which we hadn't seen since Tokyo. Few people in Warsaw had a real job, so they'd hit the streets selling to hustle up a zloty.

With completely convertible currency, the nimble ones could go to Berlin, buy goods, and bring them back to sell at home.

After struggling through Turkey, China, and the Soviet Union over the past several months, we weren't in the mood for old-world charm. We stayed in the Warsaw Marriott, which was like heaven. All the hot water we wanted! Well-cooked meals on white tablecloths! All the coffee we could drink! Soft sheets, and the beds made for us! Newspapers. Faxes. The phones worked. I could pick up the instrument and talk to anybody I wanted. I even found a gym nearby. I had forgotten it was possible for the world to work properly.

At the BMW dealership in Berlin the mechanics were agog at how much damage we'd done to the bikes. The bikes looked as if they'd been through a war, banged up, with jerryrigged parts, fork seals gone, mud in every part, loose wiring, wobbly brakes, beat-up tires. They had to put a new crankcase in mine, and the head bearings were blown, too.

We explained that these were the wrong bikes for the trip we'd just taken, that we'd needed cross-country bikes, their GS model, which had higher wheels and fenders and stronger shock absorbers.

As it happened, both of our bikes were under their original warranties. BMW had never assumed they were warranting such hard riding, but with a smile the BMW executives said they would honor them. So they proceeded to rebuild the bikes, giving us thousands of dollars of repair work in what seemed to be a salute to our trans-Siberian journey.

We went to the world's largest motorcycle show, in the Cologne-Essen area.

I was struck by how extraordinarily modern, neat, clean, rich, and vibrant these cities were. I wouldn't have had the same impression on riding into Pittsburgh or Cleveland. These cities were dynamic and bustling. Everything was new, well maintained, gleaming. And this was the Ruhr, Germany's Rust Belt, where the Allies had blown up all the factories they could, and through which their armies had marched.

I'm often asked how we could have won the war by blowing up the German industrial heartland and then find ourselves fifty years later on the short end of the stick.

The guys who lost had had a good workforce to begin with, real craftsmen with real discipline. After the war they hadn't been arrogant or sassy, but eager and grateful for a job.

In America everybody had been making a higher wage than those in Germany. Our currency had been worth something, whereas those guys had had nothing, no assets, no currency. Their workers had to work for a lot less and work a lot harder because they knew they had been beaten and they felt suppressed. They didn't have a choice. No pretensions there, absolutely none.

During the Depression our citizens had hoarded every penny, fearful of the future and putting off purchases. During World War II, even if they wanted to spend their savings, nothing was available on which to spend them.

After the war, fifteen years of pent-up demand exploded. No matter what you manufactured, you could sell it. To gear up for the demand, vice presidents of production were promoted to company president. Marketing people wouldn't be needed at the top until the sixties and seventies, when demand would become sluggish as other countries brought their factories on stream. The reality of the late forties for the United States was that the rest of the world had been destroyed and our business managers could sell everything they could produce.

Also, when you build a new factory, you use the most modern technology, whether in your manufacturing process or in the products you develop. Back in America we said, "Look, this is how we built phonographs in 1939. We've gotten a little better; here's the 1947 version. We haven't innovated for eight years because we couldn't, everything was going into the war effort, and why do we need to now?"

The Germans weren't hidebound by their success; they had leapt forward in processes and products.

People don't change their ways till they're forced to. Even if a visionary sits there and tells them what's going to happen, if it ain't broke, they'll do nothing. It takes real vision for a guy making a pile out of a ten-year-old phonograph design to revamp his product and cannibalize his own success with a cheaper product that has twice the features. It's not human nature, especially when currently you can sell all the machines you can make.

However, it leaves you vulnerable to the guy who *will* produce such a product. Over the past thirty-five years these have been the Germans, the Japanese, and only a few American manufacturers, such as Hewlett-Packard with its laser printers, who have made a vigorous policy of leapfrogging not only their competitors' products but also their own.

A people's mindset becomes wrapped up in the way things are. Even if people can believe something will happen a few years from now, they'll still say, "Well, that's in years, that ain't now."

After World War II, Memphis, Birmingham, and Atlanta were approximately the same size and had approximately the same commercial chances. The business leaders of Memphis and Birmingham decided to rebuild and modernize their railway stations. Atlanta's leaders, however, decided to put their money into a new and large international airport.

Atlanta became an international city—even able to attract the 1996 Olympic Games. Lacking reputations or infrastructures suitable for the big time, Birmingham and Memphis didn't make themselves into international laughingstocks by applying.

However, I wondered if there wasn't a dangerous worm in the apple of this economic paradise, one that would gnaw at the center of Europe until it consumed the best part of this lovely fruit.

The European Common Market was a trading group of 500 million people that had finally broken down the centuries-old economic walls that had divided them. Nearly everyone within its umbrella was benefiting from this large new open market. Now they could trade freely, just as citizens of Virginia could trade freely with those in California. This major economic development had huge ramifications for the world.

The economic effect of integration, however, had been far less positive than had often been argued. At the same time these countries had been opening up their borders to each other, they had been erecting protectionist walls against the outside world. In the past two decades these restrictive trade policies had protected sectors such as motor vehicles, consumer electronics, and office machinery. This would seem good for a while, but Europeans had been sowing the seeds of their own destruction. The Common Market's share of world markets since 1970 had been concentrated in less sophisticated products. It could make wine efficiently, but not computers or electronics, since there was less pressure to innovate. In five to fifteen years, I believed, they would pay a heavy price for this protectionism.

Protectionism exists because local producers always clamor for it. French wheat farmers want to be protected from American wheat farmers. German steelmakers want to be protected from steel manufacturers in Korea. American autoworkers want to be protected from their counterparts in Japan and Mexico. Japanese rice farmers want to be protected from those in America. In turn, American sugar growers want to be protected from Latin American producers. The list is endless—and highly organized and loud. In every country around the world such groups contribute to political campaigns, hire lobbyists, and call for protection.

After all, it sounds as patriotic as Mom and apple pie to protect American autoworkers' jobs, as well as those of Northeastern shoemakers and Southern textile workers. We all want that, don't we?

The answer is no, we don't. Protectionism not only picks our pockets, it robs us as a society. We consumers, however, have no political leader active on our behalf, we have no lobbyists, and we aren't all that vocal. If Congress erects a wall to keep out foreign steel, the price of a tin can will go up, but perhaps only by an eighth of a cent a year, scarcely enough to notice. The cost of a car might rise by 4 or 5 percent instead of 2 or 3 percent a year; again, not enough to make you hire a lobbyist and hit the streets in protest.

Over time, however, the effect is ruinous. Protected industries stagnate and don't innovate. Their products become shoddy and overpriced. American cars back in the sixties, without foreign competition, are a prime example. Once Chrysler, Ford, and General Motors had all the business, nature took its course and gave us poorly built cars at high prices.

The world over, politicians face constant pressure from well-organized special interests clamoring for favors. The rest of us aren't organized well enough to clamor for our eighth of a cent off tin cans and cheaper Fords.

Over the past couple of decades, the Common Market has tended to look backward and preserve itself from change rather than embrace it. It has used protection to avoid industrial restructuring, which has contributed to its falling behind the United States and Japan in producing high-tech goods. It has been doing okay relative to India and Africa, but not so well relative to Taiwan, southern China, and Korea.

But an iron law of modern economics says that countries cannot protect themselves as the world changes by avoiding restructuring, by dodging the need to redeploy assets constantly into the most productive, most efficient facilities.

And the world will change. Anybody who doubts that is brain-dead. Not only will it change, but it will change with even more speed as the new decades arrive. The only question is how nations will meet these changes, whether they will innovate and compete or put their heads in the sand. Was America to produce 1970s shoddy cars forever while the Japanese sold their well-designed, cheaper ones to the rest of the world? Were Americans never to buy Walkmans until an American company knocked off the design?

A government's job must be to set up an environment that forces its culture, society, businesses, and institutions to adapt or perish. This sounds harsh, but the changes come almost unnoticeably—but it's a lot

more gradual and less harsh than economic stagnation, high unemployment, and finally catastrophic collapse, which is the result of long-term
protectionism.

Cases in point? The Soviet Union, Africa, Mexico, and every country
in Latin America.

Back in civilization as we know it, Tabitha again had doubts about continuing. Our original plan was to cross Europe, dive through Africa to
the Cape, jump to Australia and New Zealand, fly to the tip of South
America, and drive up to Alaska. Crossing China and Siberia had been
feats enough for her.

We bumped into a German, Felix, who had ridden a BMW motorcycle
through Africa. He gave us information about the roads, visas, and problems. On the Theresienstrasse in Munich we window-shopped at Därr's,
a large store that outfitted overland journeys through Africa.

Felix and Därr's seemed to bring Tabitha around, sweep her up into
the potential adventure. After all, here was Därr's, a good-sized store set
up specifically to outfit travelers crossing the Sahara and plowing
through the jungle. We had certainly never seen a store that outfitted
anybody to cross Siberia, and we had made it, hadn't we? Därr's made it
appear as if traveling through Africa was something a lot of people did.
If there was an entire store devoted to it, how remote and difficult could
it be?

Africa! Had we really meant all that talk about going around the
world?

Africa by motorcycle, through the Sahara Desert and the mud swamps
of Zaire. We'd heard of people—the lucky ones who came back—partially paralyzed or blind, others crippled or missing limbs, others mere
skeletons with protruding eyes, discolored skin, and lips drawn away
from their teeth.

While Siberia was wild and unknown, at least there had been no war
or epidemic. Africa, however, meant elephantiasis, lice, leprosy, typhoid,
guinea worm, two kinds of hepatitis, yellow fever, yaws, tuberculosis,
and, of course, malaria. Africa meant plague, brucellosis, beriberi,
typhus, amoebas, cholera, smallpox, polio, three kinds of dysentery,
giardia, river blindness from running water and bilharzia from still
water, plus the tsetse fly and sleeping sickness. If we got sick, much less
very sick—at least one was inevitable—there would be few drugs and
fewer hospitals. Books on Africa described travelers succumbing to sun-

stroke, dehydration, delirium, vomiting, prostration, and two kinds of diarrhea that lasted days on end.

Other African travelers had to fight for their lives or were killed for no ever-discovered reason. We knew about the bribes and payoffs. Someone asked me my greatest traveling fear, and I said it was crossing the borders. Border guards have complete power over travelers, with no appeal granted. Even if our consular officials figured out which route we had taken, once we disappeared, few questions would ever be answered. Most African border crossings were too remote, too isolated, with little if any outside communication.

Then there were the wars—tribal, civil, guerrilla—many undeclared, unreported, and spontaneous. In Africa there is no such thing as a "civilized" war where the participants are delighted to help two naive travelers on some quixotic adventure. In these wars, everyone is desperately trying to survive and kill in a primitive struggle.

More important still, I wasn't much of a prize other than for my bike, the traveling gear, and some money—but Tabitha! Tabitha was young, tall, blond, and beautiful. Did I dare take her any farther?

Where would we stay? Could we ever be safe? Animals in Siberia were one thing, but we didn't even know all the animal dangers that awaited us in Africa, and beyond there, South America. We knew nothing about the predatory habits of crocodiles, hippos, rhinos, puff adders, hyenas, mambas, boa constrictors, panthers, rabid bats, wild dogs, lions, tigers, cheetahs, leopards, elephants, gorillas, poisonous spiders, baboons, and pythons. All these and more were in the jungle. The leopards were exceptionally bold and clever, we'd heard. They would wait patiently in your tent for your return.

Yet suppose all this was just the imagination of some soft American? Suppose all this was a bygone Africa? We still had to worry about gas, money, spare parts, roads, languages, food, water—who knew what? We did not even know what we did not know.

Tabitha and I had driven our motorcycles from Ireland through China to Tokyo, then from Tokyo back across Siberia to Ireland, and now we paused in London. If we were going around the world, Africa was next, Tunis to the Cape.

"I'm game to carry on," I said to Tabitha after a week of rest in London. "I've started around the world, gone halfway, and I've got to finish it right."

For another few days we discussed it, and once again I wasn't sure she would come.

Finally one night at dinner she said, "Okay, I'll go, but promise me we'll take it easy. No more pushing."

It wasn't a hard promise. The twenty thousand miles of roads across China and Siberia had been rough, often unpaved, full of mud wallows and potholes. In Africa they would be in even worse shape.

There was so much to do—get vaccinations for yellow fever, cholera, tetanus, typhoid, polio, and hepatitis. Round up the dozen visas necessary for African countries. Buy tents, mosquito netting, and a water filtration system. Buy spare parts for the motorcycles: gaskets, spark plugs, points, filters, fuses, and cables. Find chlorine tablets. A folding shovel. A compass. Antibiotics, salt tablets, and bandages. Chap Stick—Chap Stick was essential for lips constantly dried by the wind and sun for hour after hour, day after day. Maps, we needed maps. The list seemed endless, the time short if we were to avoid the winter.

After hours, Tabitha and I wandered around the streets of London, happy to be with each other. I couldn't imagine anyone else in the world with whom I would rather have made this journey.

To make it a true trip from the Atlantic to the Pacific and back again, we lit out for Ireland.

For her fiftieth-birthday present, we invited Tabitha's mother, Biffie, to come stay with us, hoping a visit would lessen her worries about her daughter. She flew over. She had Irish ancestry, but she'd never been here. A Wellesley graduate, she had been a beauty queen as a young lady, and now wanted a second career, in nursing, after a first as a wife and mother.

Biffie wept and pled with Tabitha not to go with me any farther, begging her daughter to come back to the States before she became a paraplegic. By now Tabitha had made up her mind and was determined, but she tried to reassure her mother.

In Dublin, we examined the *Book of Kells,* three hundred forty pages handmade in 806 A.D. and justly described as the most beautiful book in the world. Modern tourism had caught up with the *Book.* In its honor, the library that housed it had special guides, souvenir shops, and tours. Back when I was a student you simply went up to the library and looked at it; now we had to go through a whole rigamarole to view it.

I wanted to see the Nelson Pillar, a monument to the great British hero, which I remembered climbing as a student, but the IRA had blown it up. A hundred and fifty years of history, and *bam,* gone. People always do these things—destroy George III's statues in the States and Lenin's in the Soviet Union—as if they can change history by blowing up and pulling down.

At Dunquin we looked up Mrs. Campion, the postmistress, who howled with delight that we'd driven all the way to Tokyo, through China and Russia, and had come back to see her. More cups of tea, more postcards and displays of maps, lots of loud stories.

Down on the southern coast we found the motorcyclists, Kevin and Barry, who had helped us out the first time. We took Biffie with us on the back of my bike when they invited us to a motorcycle bar. This Connecticut matron in a leather motorcycle bar was perplexed by our entire trip but had to admit she liked the wild freedom of riding motorcycles. She was also perplexed by her reaction to bike culture, a little stunned she should find the rough bikers charming and delightful.

She rode with us for a week, back into England, unable to tear herself away, afraid it might be the last time she would see her daughter alive.

In London we visited the Algerian, Zimbabwean, and Nigerian embassies, seeking visas. Tabitha had made up her mind; she was ready to go. Next stop, North Africa, then right through the Sahara Desert, central Africa, and South Africa to Cape Town. After all, we'd now been about a third of the way around the world, why not go all the way?

SEEN AT THE EMBASS
REPUBLIC OF ZA

valid for ...... S/e......

within........ 1 .....

reof, provided passport

THORITY

GNED .....

TE.....

E PAID Z.12,25

EMBASSY OF THE REPUB

2 2. FEV. 1991

KINSHASA

ZAMBIA

REPUBLICA DE NICARAGUA

12 Ⅶ 11 2 D

OCT

PART III

DUNQUIN TO THE CAPE OF GOOD HOPE

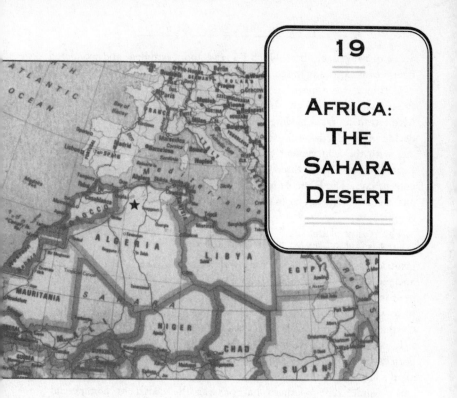

LIKE SOME UNSTABLE EXPLOSIVE, the machismo produced by the combination of Arab and Italian mentality in Tunis was the worst Tabitha had ever encountered. Men leered at her, followed her when she was out alone, and made obscene noises in her direction. In the street she was deliberately jostled. Even though the majority of Tunisian women wore Western dress, her black leather jacket and sunglasses probably screamed "loose Western blonde."

Moreover, we arrived in November 1990, a couple of months before the Allies began bombing Iraq, and the air crackled with political tension. Tunis was a haven for Islamic political activists from the Arab-Israeli conflict. It was a modern city, the Switzerland of the Arab world, and a meeting place for many Islamic supporters whom the West considered criminal.

Ten miles away to the northeast stood Carthage. Over the past three thousand years the name alone has evoked terror, dread, envy, respect, and wonder throughout the world. The idea of seeing such a fabled city was as awesome as seeing the Gobi, Siberia, the Sahara, the Andes, or the

Strait of Magellan, all of which I'd read about, studied, and wondered over, never expecting to see.

Carthage was a maritime republic founded by Queen Dido from the Phoenician city of Tyre. Its near thousand-year rule in the western Mediterranean was challenged by Rome in the three Punic wars. Rome decided that Carthage must be destroyed. The struggle ended in 146 B.C. with the achievement of Cato the Censor's dictum, *"Delenda est Carthago."* A siege of three years climaxed in a battle that raged for seventeen days. The Romans leveled the city, then plowed up the ground and laced it with salt to make sure their enemies were utterly without resources.

The reality of the small site that was the remains of Carthage contrasted sharply to whatever I'd expected after several thousand years of historical references. Despite the dominance Carthage had held over the ancient world, the Romans had done such a thorough job of demolishing it—for centuries even using the city's foundations as a quarry—that its ruins were disappointing. Most of what there was to see was Roman, not Carthaginian, and there wasn't much of that.

It was hard to believe that such a meager port, two small basins, had been used by a navy that had ruled its world. From here, however, Hannibal's legions set out for Europe, eventually to cross the Alps and challenge Rome. The southern harbor was the center of commercial shipping, at which the Carthaginians were superb. The northern one was the naval base, and the island in its center Carthage's naval headquarters. To my amazement, historians reported that as many as 220 warships could be anchored there.

The city's location over the bay was magnificent, but at its peak its population couldn't have been more than twenty thousand. In the same way that I was so forcibly struck by the early inhabitants of Samarkand, Moscow, and Xi'an, I wondered who they were and how they had done so much. All I could figure out was that expert sailors in small ships could achieve dominance if everyone else was struggling in small boats and canoes.

Two hundred years after the Roman sack, Carthage was again one of the Mediterranean's great cities. From 439 A.D. to 533 A.D. it was the capital of the Vandal kingdom, a status it kept even after the Byzantine reconquest and up to its next sack by the Arabs, in 697 A.D.

The history of Tunis was far less imposing. The Carthaginian stronghold of Thynes, destroyed with Carthage, rose again as Tunes, a small but

At last! Tabitha's bike, all dressed up and ready to go:
Off to Aer Lingus for the flight to Ireland.

Dunquin Post Office on the Atlantic Ocean—the westernmost point in Ireland.
Documenting the start of our attempt to be the first to ride
from the Atlantic to the Pacific.

Ashkhabad on the eastern side of the Caspian Sea. Then, a remote city in the USSR; now, a major center of Turkmenistan. The bikes always attracted the curious here.

Samarkand—Tamarlane's capital. These ancient madrasas will be discovered by tourists and pilgrims now that the Communists are gone.

At least in Bukhara, the centuries-old Islamic city in Uzbekistan, we found something besides drab Communist buildings.

Finding a "gas station" in western China was always an adventure. "Pumping gas" came to take on new meaning if and when we found it.

Jiayuguan, the western outpost of the Great Wall. Traditionally, anyone going west from here was leaving civilization and entering the land of the barbarians.

A tile factory in western China. After the clay cylinders dry, they are split into quarters to be used as roof tiles.

If you can find the bird market in Xi'an, you'll discover one of China's most startling experiences.

*The first road signs of any kind for thousands of miles—
none since Central Europe.*

In Siberian cemeteries, a red star on a grave signifies a Communist/atheist.

Siberia wasn't all drab Communist apartment houses. Some villages were filled with locally crafted gingerbread log houses.

We actually found a road sign as we neared the end of Siberia— still 2,470 kilometers to Moscow.

We rode our bikes right up to St. Basil's in Red Square for an obligatory photo opportunity.

The Old Square in Poznan. While it is currently part of Poland, Poznan has been alternatively part of Germany and Poland over the centuries.

A bad stretch in the Sahara. It's hard going when your muffler pipes are buried.

A better stretch in the Sahara—a much better stretch.

If Dr. Ekpo from Kano can deal with all these problems,
he could make a fortune on Park Avenue.
Tabitha wouldn't let me stop for a consultation.

We pitched our tent on the deck of a barge
floating down the Ubangi and Congo Rivers
in Central Africa.

The tugboat Fleuve Congo
was pushing thirteen barges
by the time our trip was over.

The captain and the first officer
of the Fleuve Congo ran a tight ship.
They also kept our beer cold.

The main highway
connecting Zaire's major cities.
Mobutu, the local dictator,
is a rich man; the country,
a shambles.

The Cape of Good Hope—
we actually made it.
Memories of geography
lessons and history texts
overwhelmed us.

We sailed Australia's Great Barrier Reef—
diving and snorkeling down under.

Every country has its own road signs warning of wildlife on the highways.
A kangaroo almost hit Tabitha later on this stretch.

Port Arthur in Tasmania was a prison colony for nearly one hundred years. After the British lost the American Revolution and their North American prison colonies, they were forced to find a replacement: Australia.

Perito Moreno in Argentina's Patagonia. The ice at the front of the glacier froze in the Andes hundreds of years ago and has been inching its way down to this lake ever since.

Tabitha crossing the Andes from Argentina to Chile. Bandits, wars, epidemics, and wild animals weren't our only problems on this trip.

Machu Picchu in Peru's Andes is and deserves to be South America's most visited tourist site. What an extraordinary civilization the Incas developed!

In Guatemala's former capital, Antigua, I stumbled upon a classic antique BMW still running after decades.

Would we really make it?
I was sad the trip was nearing an end,
but exhilarated that we were triumphant.
As we took this photo, a friendly Texas driver
deliberately ran over my bike.

prosperous Roman and then Byzantine town. In the ninth century A.D., the fourth Aghlabid ruler, Ibrahim Ahmed I, made it his home.

The modern French portion of the city was plain and functional, with few interesting features. Here Islam took a liberal form. In wandering around the new part of the city it was hard to tell that we were in a Muslim country, let alone in Africa. To me, the combination of nearby ruins and this functional, unhurried city was yet another vivid lesson in how nothing was permanent.

As this was the hometown of the PLO in exile, we kept a low profile. To keep even more out of sight, we had new license plates made. Our new plates gave our proper license numbers but neglected to include "Alabama" or in what country we were registered. Since this was the norm throughout the world, no one noticed.

The trek across the Sahara Desert loomed before us, another challenge of motorcycle touring.

The size of the lower forty-eight United States, the Sahara is the largest desert on the planet, two thousand miles north to south, as far east to west as Los Angeles is from Washington, D.C. At its northern and southern edges lie paved roads, while at its heart are nearly five hundred miles of lifeless dunes and rocks without any sort of road, paved or unpaved, across which we had to drive.

We planned to go along the edge of the Grand Erg Occidental, or Great Western Sea of Sand, which anywhere else in the world would have been a first-class desert in its own right. Here, it was only seven thousand square miles of rock and sand in the midst of a wasteland scores of times larger.

Six thousand years before, the Sahara had been a savanna much like today's East Africa. In fact, before the fifth century B.C., hunter-gatherers had roamed here. In Roman times the inhabitants had herded animals and took up a more settled existence. Before the Christian era, horses had been used for transportation; only afterward, as the region turned into desert, did the camel become dominant.

Here was another example of nature doing what man today is often accused of doing, "ruining the environment." If the Sierra Club had been around it would have obtained a court order from the Supreme Pliocene Court to keep the Grand Canyon from eroding a perfectly good tract of Western real estate.

Although it stretched across all the countries of North Africa, most of the Sahara was in Algeria, a country three times the size of Texas, yet five-sixths of which was taken up by the desert. Only 10 percent of the country's 26 million people lived in this vast wasteland.

To get to and then across it posed one of the great challenges of modern travel. It was not for those who needed their comforts, for in the Sahara proper there were not only no roads, but also no hotels, no gas stations, and no restaurants. Every means of transport across it was rough, for no railroad or bus crossed it. Its climate ranged from fiercely hot to fiercely cold. Except for occasional oases, there was no water and no food. Its trails ranged from awful to nonexistent.

We bought hats with large brims, water cans, gas cans, and dates, a desert travelers' standby, which didn't spoil. I wanted to buy or hook up with a truck and a driver with whom we could travel south, since for this leg of the trip it made sense to have backup transportation as well as an extra supply of gas, food, and water.

Just as we hadn't wanted to cross Siberia in the winter, we didn't want to cross the Sahara in the summer, when the temperatures would overheat the bikes and us.

I was looking forward to the trip as one of the great thrills of my motorcycling life. Tabitha had a sense of dread, as if she were sure something was going to go spectacularly wrong.

I couldn't decide if her female intuition was operating on target or working overtime.

We cranked up and drove to Algeria.

We passed European military cemeteries from wars, insurrections, and rebellions of long ago, acres of uniform white crosses, each well maintained. It was a surprise to come upon them, and it made us sad to think of young English and French men buried in the desert, thousands of miles from the green fields of home. And for what? I know their descendants did not have a clue as to what they had died for. In many cases they didn't even know that Great-great-great-grandfather Pierre had died in some supposedly noble but forgotten cause.

Who remembers today that Napoleon, out to topple the divinely crowned heads of Europe, bringing terror from revolutionary France, had been hated far and wide? Can any of us say why countless thousands died in the eighteenth century's Polish-Swedish War? Back then the Polish and Swedish kings had ruled important empires, but today not only have those dynasties vanished, the borders that so many twenty-year-olds died to preserve have changed and changed again. That we view such a war as a joke today in itself displays the sweep of history.

On this trip we stumbled across the artifacts of scores of ancient wars. Few, if any, of those wars seemed worth dying for. If history is a natural panorama of changing borders and shifting centers of power, why should twenty-year-olds die to speed up or slow this inexorable process?

My antiwar fervor began back at Oxford. I often passed a stone passageway at Balliol on which were carved the names of hundreds of English youths, captains and lieutenants, killed in World War I. At the end of the passageway was another section filled with names, those of German students at Balliol killed in the same war. In 1905 England and Germany were the fastest of allies, as evidenced by the number of German youths sent to Balliol to study, yet by 1914 they were at each others' throats. It seemed absurd.

On another night I was singing and drinking with a group of Spanish friends, twenty-two-year-olds like me, when the thought struck me that if my government decided it was the thing to do, I could be shooting these drinking companions in a matter of weeks. I was horrified. That night something in me shifted. I've never been able to see the utility of war in the same way as before.

The city of Algiers was bigger and older than Tunis. To Tabitha's eye it didn't look as interesting as Cairo, although it did have a Casbah.

Many of us know the Casbah from 1940s films, a marketplace surrounded by old buildings, overhead passageways, and screened-in balconies. During the Algerian revolution, the rebels darted into it as if the French were cats and it was a mouse hole.

As visas are perishable, it was impossible on a trip like this to obtain them all beforehand. Here in Algiers we began to collect the rest we'd need for our route to Cape Town, those for the Central African Republic and Cameroon. We hunted up the Zairian embassy, which took two days of searching to find. At last we found the house of the ambassador himself, and his embassy turned out to be across the street.

Economically Algeria was a real mess, another statist government that had misfired. It wasn't a small economy as African nations went, $53 billion in gross domestic product with a per-capita GDP of $2,170. In comparison, the countries of sub-Saharan Africa, excluding South Africa, had a per-capita GDP of $400, compared with the major industrial countries' GDP of nearly $12,000. However, the socialists had mismanaged their potential riches from their huge oil and gas reserves.

In reference to statism, I certainly don't want to be misunderstood. I'm no anarchist. There are many legitimate functions governments must handle, mostly involving public safety, such as those of national defense, police and fire protection, air traffic, the inspection of buildings and food, and flood control. It's just that after a century of experiments we can now see clearly that governments are terrible at engendering prosperity and wealth.

Algeria is a prime example. During the sixties and seventies it was touted by many as a model for Third World liberation movements. The socialist government attended to social welfare needs while the economy grew rapidly, but now we can see this was not the result of good management, but of rising oil prices. What appeared then to be sound economic policy was actually one more case of a country riding the commodities boom of the seventies.

Today petroleum and natural gas account for 95 percent of Algeria's foreign-exchange earnings. When the price of oil fell, the country was socked hard. At one time it was self-sufficient in food production, but now it is highly dependent on imports. Algeria's unemployment is at 25 percent, inflation more than 20 percent, and its people need housing. A couple of years before we were there, spiraling prices and shortages had led to riots in which the army shot hundreds of people. The widespread sense that government officials are corrupt continues to this day.

The black market is rampant. Virtually nothing from the outside comes in, not even Western newspapers and magazines.

The country had one of the more absurd currencies we'd encountered. On the black market we could get thirty dinars for our dollars, while the official rate was ten to one. This large discrepancy told me that the government had run its nutty economic policies about as far and as long as it could. At a 200 percent premium, it was worth everybody's while to change money on the black market, whereas at, say, a 20 percent premium, otherwise law-abiding people would be reluctant to break the law.

Because nobody was allowed to bring in outside goods legitimately, it was difficult to find any. The country had an external debt of $20 billion, which was serviced by most of its hard-currency earnings. If the central bank had had extra hard currency, legitimate merchants could have bought Sony TVs, cars, Italian shoes, and New Zealand lamb and sold them to legitimate customers. But since its hard currency was being used to service the debt, the central bank had none, merchants imported virtually nothing, and everybody was suffering.

Compounding their economic problems were low gasoline prices because of price controls, which encouraged wasteful consumption just as low bread prices had encouraged boys in the Soviet Union to use state-baked loaves for footballs. To dampen demand here, the government should have sold gasoline at world-market prices and shipped all it could overseas for much-needed hard currency.

These economic problems were the principal reason for the rise of Islamic fundamentalism here. The Algerian people were looking for somebody to blame for this mess. As always, they had to have a scapegoat, such as the government or Westerners.

Since Westerners had been gone since the early sixties and the secular socialists had run things for the three decades since, the people said, "It's the fault of those godless ones."

Not having allowed an entrepreneurial sector to develop, the statist government was now faced with the choice of either continuing its policies, import and currency restrictions, or devaluing the currency, which would make not only import prices but also domestic prices rise sharply. Continued restrictions, on the other hand, would naturally lead to a larger and larger currency premium on the black market. Eventually no hard currency would be left in the country, which would mean nothing could be brought in from the outside world, as nobody wanted dinars. Since the economy didn't produce much—certainly nothing to match Japanese cars, Italian shoes, and New Zealand lamb—life would become yet tougher on the people. Finally the government would be forced to devalue the dinar, but that of course in a single shock would make foreign and domestic goods that much more expensive.

So the government had arrived at a point where it thought it could do nothing that was not political suicide. I knew its only hope now was to have a freely convertible currency, and to try to weather the political storm that sudden massive price increases brought. At least at that point goods would again become available.

At the end of their rope, forced by the marketplace to face a similar situation, Polish politicians had done this. Their people, like the Algerians, produced little and could import nothing. They made the currency convertible, and it had worked. The conversion rate of the Polish zloty skyrocketed, but it didn't matter, because this new high level was what the real rate was. Goods poured in, the government survived, and everything had been fine.

Unfortunately, the Poles hadn't had staying power. They and their ivory-tower Western advisors had been so sure democracy would cure their ills—all you had to do was look at the U.S. and Germany to see that democracy meant enormous prosperity—that they hadn't seen the need to take other measures. Yes, Marlboro cigarettes and Toyotas were available, but they hadn't realized that they needed to sell something to the outside world to pay for these new cigarettes and cars.

Decades of shoddy workmanship, mismanagement, and little capital investment meant the Poles weren't efficient producers of much that the outside world wanted. Still, the government felt it couldn't fire the unproductive workers on its payroll. It feared that would have been another form of political suicide. So it printed money to pay these workers, expecting with childlike faith that any day democracy would explode into prosperity.

These wheelbarrows full of money made the whole mess start all over again. Inflation came back. Since the government now couldn't go back to exchange controls and nobody wanted the yet more worthless zloty, its value eroded again. Once you start printing money without anything behind it, nobody ever wants it. The public ain't that dumb. Even if you call it money, nobody's going to buy something without real value.

Around me I sensed Algeria was seething and ready to explode. Yes, it was tightly restricted now, but how long would this last? Here was another country where socialism and the revolution had failed badly. As in the Soviet Union, the people were going to demand a big change.

As we drove toward the Sahara we passed more Roman ruins. The village markets were lush with produce, big mounds of pomegranates, dates, pears, and apples, but little else. Gradually the surrounding countryside became more desertlike. The closer we drew to the Sahara, the more expensive the markets became. Only gas, controlled by the government, was cheap, a fraction of European prices and a third of that at black-market rates.

The Sahara proper began four hundred miles south of Algiers. Tabitha was still uneasy, but I was growing excited. I'd always enjoyed traveling through deserts. There was a romance to them, a poetry of starkness. A desert like this was like a tough market. It did not forgive mistakes and it forced you to be attentive, to be fully awake—and God, was it beautiful!

Moving steadily south, we carried all the water we could, and extra food and gas. The terrain became dryer and rougher. Vegetation became sparse. Gas stations were farther apart. The landscape became more and more inhospitable to animals and plants alike.

Two days of southerly driving brought us to the M'Zab, a scrubby valley occupied by the Mozabites, a puritanical Islamic sect. The people of this valley lived in a pentapolis, five villages that had developed independently of the country.

We stopped in the main town, Ghardaia. Like the other four, it was built on a hill and crowned by a distinctive, unadorned minaret. We weren't allowed to enter Beni Isguen, or "the pious," the religious town of the M'Zab.

We had passed from the urban civilization of Algiers, where few women wore veils, into such fundamentalist backcountry that the women exposed no more of themselves than one eye, which could be seen through a fold in the cotton cloth that covered them from head to foot.

We stayed on a hill overlooking the town in the three-star Hotel Rostimedes. We'd been on reasonably good two-lane blacktop, but the ocean of sand we were about to plunge into kept looming before us. Still looking for someone to carry extra provisions, we drove out to the local campsite. We moved from truck to Land Rover, asking who was going south, who would carry gear and supplies for a few dollars.

We met a French graduate student called Pierre who was going our way and needed extra cash. We'd form a partnership. In return for our paying his expenses, he was delighted to carry our tents, spare tires, water cans, and fuel cans in a battered pickup truck whose grill and lights were shielded by steel bull bars. His pockmarked face had a ready smile, and he seemed charming and civilized. He would make a fine traveling companion.

Over the next three days our small caravan covered a thousand miles along a desert road that was mostly paved, the easy part of the trip.

And what a desert! What finely sculpted dunes and daring sand formations! Hour after hour, mile after mile, the dunes' elegance, grace, and voluptuousness bore down on us. The monotonous beauty wore down my ordinary way of looking at the world. Molded by the wind's harsh caresses into daring waves no sculptor or engineer could dream of duplicating, the dunes began to remind me of the sensuous curves and swooping arcs of Tabitha's body.

Early in December we reached Tamanrasset, the fabled jumping-off city on the northern edge of the roughest part of the desert. Named after a famous beautiful woman, it was the geographical center of the Sahara.

Tamanrasset is one of my favorite towns, a jumble of Land Rovers, mud houses, and hardened desert travelers. We stayed here several days to rest. Even though it was newly built, clean, and active, goats wandered the streets. Along with donkeys, camels were parked outside modern houses. The supermarket offered mainly canned food, peaches, and meat.

Most of the locals were extraordinary in appearance, with stately turbans and white robes. From time to time the Tuareg, the nomadic blue-robed Berbers of the Sahara, sailed through on camels. These tribespeople went back and forth across the border between Niger and Algeria, not recognizing any national boundaries and proving the absurdity of having borders in the middle of the desert.

Originally Tamanrasset had been an outpost of the French Foreign Legion. In 1950, it had thirty people, but now it had thirty thousand—a real boomtown.

It was a major crossroads for long-distance African travelers. Everybody traveling on the continent was either here, had just been here, or was due to arrive. Camaraderie sprang up between travelers as we shared maps and travel stories.

"Watch out for the owner of the Antelope in Nigeria."

"Stay at the Moon Inn in Zimbabwe."

"This road here is washed out; take the route through the mountains."

The hotel bar was a good place to hang out, one of the few in Tam where you could get a cold beer—or as close to cold as you could find in an Islamic desert. Pierre joined us with a Malian woman he had picked up at the campground.

We swapped tips with Makoto Yamamoto, a Japanese who had spent eleven months traveling around Africa. Another Japanese we met had been a student in Africa for two years and was now visiting as many African countries as he could pack in. We met single hitchhikers and bicyclists as well as couples from Parisian society in designer clothes and designer Land Rovers who had brought along designer meals from Därr's back in Munich.

The main street of Tam was lined with two rows of rough-and-ready restaurants, each with a few battered tables outside and inside and surrounded by vendors selling chicken on rotisseries. Travelers gathered at these cafés and table-hopped, asking questions and gathering information in a swaggering yet egalitarian spirit.

Parked out front like horses in the Old West were trail bikes, Japanese bikes, Toyotas, and Land Rovers festooned with sand ladders and bull-catchers. Shovels were bolted on, and strapped on top were sleeping bags, camping equipment, and steel boxes of clothes. Every vehicle carried a plentiful number of green or gray jerry cans loaded with gas and water, as well as extra tires.

The talk in the street cafés came to center on three topics: border officials, bribes, and the risks presented by crossing the Sahara. Due to breakdowns and the lack of fuel, dozens of Europeans and Africans died every year in the desert.

A year before, a French family's Land Rover, off the main route, had broken down halfway to Arlit. For days the mother had kept a diary of her, her husband's, and her two small children's battle against heat, hunger, thirst, and despair as they waited in vain for help to come. Her diary ended with the faint scrawl of a plea for help reflecting her and her family's fatal debilitation.

A few months before, a caravan of five cars and ten people had set out along the same route. As happens easily in the Sahara, where there are no roads but only the crudest of trails across hundreds of miles of rocks and dunes, they, too, had become lost. One car had broken down, and its occupants had piled into the other four. One by one, three of the other cars broke down or ran out of gas until the ten travelers all rode in the last car. Then it broke down under the strain, and the ten perished under the desert sun as they waited for help.

Story after story like this made us sober about the dangers we faced. Obviously we should stay on the main route at all costs, a feat we were told repeatedly wasn't easy because of the lack of a true road.

In other conversations, the travelers identified for us and each other those border guards who would help and those we had to bribe, and told horror stories about travelers caught with contraband. Desperate for hard currency, Algeria, like many African countries, had strict exchange controls, insisting that travelers exchange all their hard currency for the country's worthless dinars.

No traveler could afford to change all his money ten to fifteen times as he passed through successive African countries. Not only would he lose money as the local currencies depreciated and as he paid the money changers' fees, but he wouldn't be able to exchange some currencies at all. Outside of Algeria nobody wanted its dinars, and there were no banks at the southern end of the country.

Thus all travelers crossing the continent were forced to become smugglers. Finding this undeclared currency was an important source of revenue for the country—or for the border guards, who made big efforts to discover travelers' secret stashes. Frequently, in addition to confiscating the stash, they fined the "smuggler" two or three times as much as they found. All this led to much talk among Tam's café society about the best place to hide contraband, where on your person and where on your vehicle.

The only thing Tabitha and I ever worried about hiding was money, because we didn't carry drugs or other contraband. I wore a money belt, which to my delight was never discovered by any border guard on our entire trip. One of our motorcycles had a mud-splattered manual underneath the seat in a filthy, dusty pocket. We hid money between its pages because it was too grubby to examine. In the frame under my gas tank there was a hollow pipe into which we slipped money.

The adventurousness of the travelers in Tam astonished us. We met two Amsterdam schoolteachers who had taken a year or two off to travel Africa. A New Zealander was making his way by ground back to New Zealand from London. There were 3 million people in New Zealand, he said, and seventy thousand of them—or 2 to 3 percent of the population—were in the United Kingdom at any time. But traveling through Africa I never saw any other Americans except for one missionary family.

Tamanrasset was the last town on the paved road, so we had to check out with the customs and immigration office. Here we had our passports, carnets, and currency declarations stamped for exit. Our minicaravan of two cycles and a truck pushed off into the Sahara proper.

We asked our way out of town, as there were no signposts. Up to Tam the roads had been good, two-lane blacktop in fair repair. As we knew from the other travelers, however, from here on south the roads stopped and turned into a nightmare of sand. Thirty-one miles out of town the pavement indeed petered out and we hit sand, hundreds of miles of it in every direction, just like in the movies. We dipped into a ravine and started a descent from forty-five hundred feet.

Because the desert is flat and open a traveler can make his route anywhere. The route we followed was a band of truck tracks, perhaps two miles wide. If a sand storm had hit, the tracks would have been blown away and we would have had to use compasses to navigate an empty sea of sand.

For a quarter of an hour I suffocated on Tabitha's billowing cloud of dust and then called a huddle. Because of the dust, we would stretch out, Tabitha in front, me a half mile or so behind and a quarter mile to her right, and Pierre several miles farther back.

The terrain became more desertlike the farther we moved into the Sahara. Dunes of sand and scrubby rock rose on both sides. The way was overblown with sand, threatening to throw us over and preventing any speed.

Sometimes road markers, fifty-five-gallon drums or tall poles stuck in the sand, showed us the way.

Where the sand hadn't covered them, Tabitha followed tire tracks. She hoped whomever she was following knew where he was going, that we weren't following bandits, smugglers, or someone who himself was lost. As perhaps fifty tracks wove back and forth in front of her, she stuck to those more heavily traveled. Every three or four hours a truck, perhaps a mile or so distant, passed heading north, or one overtook us, heading our way but never getting close, making us again wonder if we were on the main route, if in fact there was such a thing. The trucks always made us feel better, that we were more or less in the right place, but shortly after they disappeared, doubt would creep back.

The clusters of burned-out wrecks of cars we came upon made us feel better, too, indicating we were probably on the main route. As spare parts were in great demand, these were completely stripped.

As the lead vehicle, Tabitha drove slowly, working to pick the firmest surface across the ocean of sand. Despite her best efforts, however, she would become stuck in sand so deep it covered her tailpipe. Here was where teamwork was most important. I would get off my bike, put a board underneath its kickstand to keep it from falling over, and with her on the bike, push or dig the sand away from her wheels so she could inch forward. We carried a fold-up military shovel, but it wasn't particularly useful. Using my hands to scoop away the sand worked better.

Once I'd removed it, however, Tabitha couldn't simply accelerate. She had to release the clutch slowly to prevent the wheel from spinning and digging her deeper into the loose sand, yet she had to release it far enough so as not to burn up the clutch. Every time we smelled asbestos burning it alarmed us; an extra couple of clutch plates weren't spare parts we had thought to pack. In one patch of sand it took three hours to cover fifteen miles; we were constantly getting stuck, constantly digging out, constantly pushing.

Once Tabitha's bike was freed, I would walk forward several yards to find the best way to continue. Often we couldn't drive straight, as the loose sand ahead was even worse, and we would have to plot another path to the side.

Sometimes we passed over a stony area sporting a patch or two of scrubby bush. Other times the sand became firm and we hummed over it at thirty-five miles an hour. We had to be on the lookout for deep pockets of loose sand, traps that had wrecked the numerous stripped, burned cars along the way.

The first day we covered only seventy-five miles, even though we were on the road for ten hours.

That night, exhausted yet feeling triumphant that our teamwork was mastering this ocean of sand, the three of us camped in the desert. We brewed tea and cooked on small butane stoves. There was no need to put up a tent, as here the terrain was as bare as the surface of Mars. It was not going to rain, the air was dry and cool, and there would be no dew. We didn't have to worry about animals or insects attacking us, as there was no wildlife for hundreds of miles, not a leaf, not a lizard, not an ant, not even a midge.

The desert's silence was so clean it was like nothing I'd ever experienced. Without life, the Sahara lacked the background chatter we normally experience. No bird chirped, no remote insect buzzed, no faraway airplane droned, no leaf rustled. I realized I'd never been in pure silence.

It seemed a sacrilege, but I broke the silence by tuning in the BBC. The tension between the Allies and Iraq had increased again. We were glad to be putting miles between us and Arab Islamic culture.

In the middle of the night, Tabitha and I both woke up, sure someone had turned the lights on. We jumped out of our sleeping bag and walked around.

The canopy of stars was even clearer than in Alaska or Siberia. The full moon had come out, made exceptionally huge and bright by the desert atmosphere's lack of moisture, dust, and pollution. Nimble and vivid, our moon shadows followed us everywhere. We got out a book, and we were actually able to read by the extraordinary moonlight.

The brazen moon . . . the deep quiet . . . the sensuous dunes—this exotic yet comforting nightscape brought Tabitha and I close and was so wonderfully romantic that I think of it as one of the world's most perfect honeymoon spots, tough to get to as it is.

The next day we rose early and pushed on.

At the top of rises the sand, blown away by the wind, wasn't so deep but snowy drifts had been deposited in the dips, causing us to flounder. A couple of times when one of the bikes fell over, gas spilled from the tanks and carburetors. The desert was wrestling with us, trying to take charge.

We encountered more stripped and abandoned cars, always near thick sand, often in clusters and on their sides or backs, victims of sand traps.

Probably they had been traveling at high speed, hit a pocket of deep sand, and flipped over. I was reminded of old cartoons about the desert showing bones around a water hole, but here it was cars that hadn't made it.

Navigating continued to be difficult. Any of the tracks might be the main trail, if such a thing existed; any might lead into trackless wastes and death. At times, without a visible marker, the trails shot off in so many conflicting directions that the only way to navigate was by climbing on top of a wrecked car and peering southward to spot the next marker or, failing that, the next cluster of abandoned cars. We hoped these vehicular skeletons marked the main trail.

We passed a Land Rover stuck in soft sand. Its passengers had put two ten-foot sand ladders under its front wheels and were inching forward. They would repeat this till they were through the soft patch.

Even though it was December, it was blazing hot, the sun roasting us an hour after sunrise. The white sand absorbed the sun's rays and reflected them back, throwing heat at us from above and below. In the middle of the day we sweated profusely, especially when bogged down in sand. Afraid of spills, however, we continued to wear our leather jackets and chaps. A few times I sweated right through both my jeans and my chaps, something which, except for rugged days in Siberia, hadn't happened before in all my twenty-five years of riding.

Several days into the Sahara, I thought I saw my first mirage, a tandem bicycle ahead of us carrying two people dressed completely in white.

Amused, I watched and waited for this shimmering white image to disappear. As we clattered abreast of the mirage, the white-outfitted pair turned their heads, focusing on us black swimmer's goggles, aliens out of a feverish dream.

I was so startled I flagged them down and asked, "God, what are you doing here? Where are you from?"

They were a French couple on their honeymoon who had set out to bicycle across the Sahara. They were remarkably chipper and in good spirits. It had taken them ten days to pedal across what so far had taken us five days.

A few miles later we came upon an Italian headed north whose motorcycle had broken down. We offered to take him back south to Arlit, but he refused, fearful of losing his bike to bandits or the desert.

Our tanks were low, so we swapped him water for the gas he no longer needed. He hoped a truck would come along and give him and his motorcycle transportation north, but I had major doubts. Suppose this was one of the less frequented desert trails?

Remembering the stories we'd heard in Tam about people never returning from the desert, I've often wondered if that Italian motorcyclist is still there waiting for a truck, his stripped bike and skeleton a grim reminder of the Sahara's unforgiving harshness.

Finally we hit the flat part of the desert near its southern rim. Small thorn trees told us there had to be water nearby.

Tabitha was grinning madly as we moved along at thirty-five miles an hour, the dust in long, high coils behind us. She was delirious we'd made it across, shouting and waving.

I felt good, too, relieved we hadn't been one of those who had died in this Martian landscape of beauty and death. This had been a tough part of the trip, days of sweaty effort, but we'd come through without undue mishap. As we barreled along, over and over again I sang:

> Oh, see, C. Rider
> See what you have done.
> You've made me love you

When we stopped for water, still grinning Tabitha said, "When I was in the first grade, I went ice skating one Sunday for the first time. I remember how I felt when I was able to skate across the whole pond by myself—I kept saying to myself, 'Proud! Proud! Proud!' That's how I feel today—Proud! Proud! Proud!"

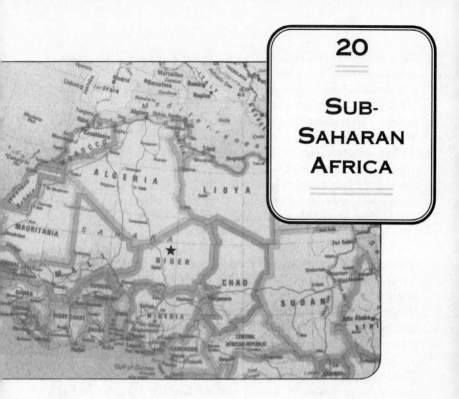

EVERYTHING CHANGED as soon as we crossed from Algeria into Niger.

We were coming out of North Africa, an Arabic-Islamic culture, into Arlit, which, while still Islamic, was the first big city of black Africa. As we crept south, the monotonous dunes turned into broken rocks, weeds, and scrub, the first growth we had seen in days.

With only a few miles left to Arlit, we saw smoke. We passed a French-run uranium mine and an airstrip.

The closer to Arlit, the better the road. The sand here was packed hard and we made great time. We hit a four-lane dirt road, doubtless here to provide access to the uranium mine.

Arlit, another travelers' town, was a mixture of old and new, mud huts and modern houses. From time to time topless buxom women with goods on their heads and babies on their backs sauntered past the open butcher shops and vendors cooking meat and doughnuts on fires.

We sat in a café and drank big brown bottles of African beer, impossible to order on the street back in a strict Islamic culture. A wave of relaxation spread over us as the paraffin lamps flickered in the dark and black faces smiled in our direction. After our jitters about being Americans in Arabic North Africa, it felt incredibly good to be here.

Pierre had found a local girl whom he bragged was his for the price of a half-bottle of whiskey and a pack of Marlboros.

Like Tamanrasset, Arlit was a place to swap stories, get your vehicle repaired, and buy spare parts. We spent a day there, reconnoitering and pulling ourselves together. The next hundred and fifty miles south were over a well-paved road, we learned—an amenity that was created because the local uranium mine needed to ship out its ore, and that, as a by-product, developed the general prosperity of this region.

The town stayed open all night, its lamps gleaming a welcome, as its principal occupation was serving foreign travelers.

Tabitha didn't feel well. She had a fever, and over our first day here it got worse, making her woozier and woozier. She tossed and turned much of the next night. She took some aspirin and finally got a couple of hours' sleep.

We decided to stop here another day to give her some rest. The evening was passed in several cheerful cafés where we drank Cokes, sodas, and beer and ate shish kebab and goat cheese.

The next morning we drove to Zinder, three hundred miles south. Tabitha felt worse, by now gulping aspirin and forcing down fluids. To give her more rest, we stopped a couple of days here, too. She still had a fever, which I was afraid was a result of heatstroke, perhaps from the Sahara, perhaps from walking around in the sun in Arlit.

Entering Nigeria we hit one of the worst border guards we'd ever encountered, a large fellow in a green uniform whose badge identified him as Lieutenant Ibrahim.

"Well, you're American," he said in a snotty tone, "so I'm going to treat you the way I'd be treated at Kennedy Airport. I'm going to search you completely, because that's what you do to us at Kennedy."

He was right, I thought.

When the lieutenant saw we had BBC radios, he said, "Are you listening to it in Hausa?" the local language and in which the BBC did indeed broadcast. As Nigeria had been an English colony, he spoke fine English.

Staunching my impatience, I said, "No, we don't understand Hausa."

He became indignant because, after all, he understood our language. He wanted to know which tribe we were.

"We're not in any tribe."

This made Lieutenant Ibrahim yet more overbearing.

By oversight I showed him the carnet that didn't have Nigeria stamped on it.

He became furious that it didn't list his country.

"We're the largest and strongest country in Africa," he ranted. "We're not a Third World country, we're a world power, a rich world power. You'd better understand that."

He checked every single document we'd thought to bring: the international certificates for the motorcycles, international driving permits, certificates of vaccination, entry visas, proof of ownership of photographic equipment, travel insurance forms, carnets, and passports.

Seemingly disappointed at our preparedness, he and his men searched us completely, examining every item on our bikes. Fortunately, we didn't have to bribe them, although we left a carton of cigarettes on the counter, which promptly disappeared. He gave in. With a disgusted wave, he let us through.

By now we had begun to realize that guards like this Hausa would force us to budget an entire day for crossing each border, an extra two weeks to cross Africa alone.

Tabitha was still feverish, still taking aspirin. As we moved on through Nigeria, we encountered one military checkpoint after another. Each one ate up long stretches of time. As the guards checked our papers and our bikes, I frequently questioned them: What was the point of these stupid inspections? Didn't they know they were driving away travelers bringing much-needed hard currency into their economies?

As Pierre hadn't had the foresight to obtain visas in North Africa, he wound up needing more money for bribes than he anticipated. I wound up forking over more for his expenses than I had expected, but it seemed worth it to have the safety margin of extra supplies.

Tabitha was still sick. I was sure it was just a little sun. I suggested she eat as much salt as she could and drink a lot of liquids—sodas, bottled water, whatever. Although she needed rest, we were afraid to stop in Nigeria because we were having so many problems with military checkpoints and visas. Despite her fever, we both wanted to get to Cameroon as fast as we could, and put these checkpoint problems behind us.

We hit a terrible section of dirt road for the last five miles of Nigeria, and it took quite a while to drive across it. Water had run over the road, which had then dried like a riverbed. The surface was hard, rutted mud with potholes a foot or two deep. We had to pick our way across it.

Even though we'd just been through the Sahara, Maroua seemed even hotter, even more suffocating. Here we found the first decent hotel we'd seen since Algiers. It even took credit cards, which was a help because we'd been burning up cash since Algeria. Its clean, new rooms, air-conditioning, swimming pool (with water in it!), and modern bar made me a little giddy with disbelief; nor could we believe it had hot water until we took showers. To an American it would have been the equivalent of a nice Holiday Inn in a small American city, but to us it was the Ritz. Despite the toll on Tabitha's health, we decided we had made the right decision in pushing through Nigeria.

Tabitha had developed a cough, and the first night here it got worse. She took more aspirin, but the pain was so overwhelming that it didn't help. Whatever was in her chest had now gone into her ear, giving her a piercing earache. By now this had continued, on and off, for nine days, and she wasn't winning the battle.

"I've got to get some help," she said. "This thing is getting worse."

As it turned out, we were lucky. We had pushed on to the right spot. Next door was a private clinic run by a Chinese couple named Chang.

I took Tabitha there. Dr. Chang wanted to run some blood tests, thinking she might have malaria.

Having heard stories of used needles in African clinics transmitting AIDS, Tabitha was apprehensive. However, Dr. Chang had a drawer full of disposable needles, all nicely wrapped in sterile cellophane, so she accepted his care.

This Chinese doctor not only had modern equipment but a private room. It wasn't much more than a cement-block cube with a bed, but it had an air conditioner and a bathroom.

I brought fruit and sodas, held her hand, and soothed her. She stayed in bed for forty-eight hours, right through Christmas Day.

After hitting me up for a few extra bucks, Pierre found himself a cheaper hotel, where he entertained a different local girl every night. I mentioned the possibility of AIDS, but he laughed and brushed aside my warning.

Dr. Chang diagnosed Tabitha's illness as a bronchial infection. He gave her a course of antibiotics. He was delighted to have our hard currency. I was amazed that the bill wasn't more—just a couple of hundred dollars for the antibiotics, the room, his care, everything.

Maroua turned out to be an interesting place, and I was glad we spent nine days there resting.

We became friendly with a shaggy-blond expatriate German called Dietrich Reinhardt, owner of an inn and a restaurant, with whom we spent several evenings.

Back in the seventies Dietrich had stumbled on a mode of making big money in Africa. He drove cars down from Europe and sold them at a profit. Over several years he had made twenty-odd trips, sometimes transporting two cars at once. For a while he earned a large premium, then other sellers piled in, which always happens in a market with a big profit. Once the premium was driven out of the business, it made no sense to continue.

In their mid-thirties, he and his wife now ran a restaurant, souvenir shop, bar, and inn. He also owned an auto-repair business that catered to travelers. They had an easy life, with two children and lots of servants.

However, it was clear from discussions with them that their business was drying up. Travelers weren't coming through as they once had, nor were the automobile smugglers. During the late eighties, African travel had became more and more difficult. Currencies had deteriorated; restrictions grew more burdensome; and as African economies got into trouble, wars had spread and deterred tourists.

These countries learned from the West only too well how to stick it to visitors. In the old days you drove up to an African border and sailed right in, possibly leaving a tip of a carton of cigarettes or a bottle of whiskey. In those days many travelers didn't have visas or the right papers. They might have been running from trouble in their own countries, or they might have been misfits starting their lives over.

The Reinhardts loved their life, but things were getting tougher. Their kids were growing up. They didn't want to raise them here because Africa didn't look as promising as it had when they were in their twenties, back when the continent was an adventure.

That was the problem with the life of an expatriate. Usually, an expat was dodging something. The Western expatriate in Africa was often a big fish in a small pond who did well because he didn't encounter much competition. Since the days of Lord Jim, expats had found they didn't have to run too fast.

Now Reinhardt was looking for a way out. He was going to be in a terrible bind when he had to go back to Germany.

Once Tabitha was back on her feet, we went out to a posh French restaurant near town for a bang-up meal.

It was called Le Saret. We had a wonderful meal yet a sad experience. For forty-five years the French owner, Luc Phillipe, now in his eighties, had maintained the equivalent of a first-class Parisian restaurant, complete with white-liveried waiters with impeccable manners, French wine, and everything cooked to a fine French turn.

Monsieur Phillipe and his wife had brought everything from France—the culture, the manners, the dishes, the cutlery—and now the business was finished. The game hunters had stopped coming, and after the independence movement came, the tourists had slowed, too. He had tried to entice his son into the business, but his son had gone to Hollywood to make movies.

After his wife had died he closed the restaurant for a while. Now it was back open and he was trying to sell it, but in a year or two it would be gone. Nobody was going to buy this white elephant of Parisian lavishness on the rim of the Sahara.

Like many others, Monsieur Philippe was going to lose his life's work. Throughout this trip, we heard this story over and over. No matter what a person built, no matter how wonderful the house, the museum, the culture, the country, it was going to disappear. There was nothing permanent. We visited dozens of once-powerful cities like Carthage that had been overrun and knocked apart, scores of once-stately homes that were now in ruins. No matter how magnificent the castle, in two hundred, five hundred, one thousand years, its ruins will be overgrown with vines. No matter how vast and powerful the empire, the country, the company, or the dynasty—it won't last.

Monsieur Phillipe would run his restaurant until he couldn't any longer, probably until he died, when it would be taken over by the state. The state would run it into the ground because no Cameroon bureaucrat could manage it Monsieur Phillipe's way. He had had some good years, and that was all there was and all there could be.

The papers here were full of the bloody revolt in nearby Chad.

Marauding soldiers had broken into the national parks and zoos and machine-gunned the animals and eaten them. In Angola the faction backed by the United States was having pitched battles with the dreaded Communists. Zaire would break down into a bloody shooting match any year now. So many conflicts remind me of barroom brawls on Saturday night, important to the drunken combatants but rarely to anyone else.

Despite these nearby troubles, I was optimistic about the future of Cameroon. The democracy movement here was beginning. The country had an educated, civilized population. In the 1990 World Cup, Cameroon got to the quarterfinals, the first African country to do so.

At some point this country, with its abundance of natural resources and an educated and outward-looking population, would be quite an investment. It would help a lot that the country was officially bilingual, speaking French and English, and that it was absorbing progressive information from not one but two outside cultures. The population was not only aware of the outside world but was encouraged to know about it. This was rarely true in dictatorships.

At the right time, an investor here could put his money into agriculture, metals, lumber, and food production. He should buy into any company that is well financed and sells to its neighbors down south, such as South Africa and Botswana, or north into Europe.

Cameroon was also small, which meant there weren't so many tribal factions. Borders here would probably not have to be redrawn, or at least not as extensively as those in the rest of Africa.

Many borders in Africa were artificial, drawn by colonialists going off into the woods on a horse and deciding where a country should begin and end. For example, Zambia had only 7.8 million people but twenty-five different tribes. A glance at a map made you wonder how the country had been formed. There was no geographical or ethnic sense to its boundaries. They were just where Cecil Rhodes happened to go.

In the same way that the USSR would split up and the borders in Eastern Europe would be redrawn until they made ethnic sense, here in Africa there would be upset until its borders were drawn in accord with natural geographic and ethnic divisions.

Rested and well, we took off south. The roads weren't too bad, and we could make fair time. A thousand miles later, stiff and sore, we pulled into Bangui, the capital of the Central African Republic, a former French colony, after an exhausting twelve-hour day of driving. We had camped out the night before, so we were keen to get to civilization.

We arrived after dark on New Year's Eve and checked into the Novotel. Dazed and weary, wanting a hot dinner, we went next door to Le Tropicana, which turned out to be a nightclub boisterous and stylish enough to have been located on Paris's Left Bank. A Western-style New

Year's celebration was in full riot, including champagne, special French dishes, whistles, streamers, blowers, and oddball party hats. Our weariness miraculously fled after a couple of glasses of champagne. We stayed up till the small hours, dancing, trading party hats, and blowing whistles with the best of them.

Like many Third World countries, the Central African Republic had prospered in the big commodities boom but now had collapsed. Its buildings sagged and poverty was everywhere. Like rats sensing a sinking ship, the savvy Indian and Arabian merchants who turned up in Africa wherever there was prosperity had sold their businesses and fled.

The police hadn't been paid for three months. Walking to a restaurant at night, we often had to pay a bribe to those who stopped us to examine our passports. They called it a *cadeau,* a "gift." One to five dollars satisfied them. Had they insisted on more, they knew we might report them and get them into trouble.

The C.A.R.'s biggest problem was its currency, yet the problem was the opposite of the one troubling so many other African currencies—it was too hard. Decades ago the currency known as the CFA had been pegged to the French franc, which itself was now pegged to the deutsche mark. If the C.A.R. could assign a value to its currency now, its government might peg the CFA at a fraction of this rate, but the CFA had been set when commodity prices were high. Changing the value of the currency now would be hard to accomplish (as all of Francophone Africa discovered when the CFA was devalued by fifty percent in early 1994; I suspect the problem is not yet solved completely).

Since world commodity prices were denominated in dollars, the country had received a double whammy. As the dollar had declined 60 percent in value against the deutsche mark, the C.A.R. was receiving that much less in value than twenty years before. On top of this, commodity prices had come down drastically, often by 50 percent. The hard truth was that the C.A.R. now often received 20 percent of its former effective income for its products. To make matters worse, the C.A.R. maintained large police and military forces, which produced nothing of economic value for the country.

What an odd place! In a city with dirt streets and without phones were a number of fine French restaurants that served meals as exquisite as those in Paris and New York. Because of the absurd currency, the prices were the same as in Paris and New York, too.

Here in January we even drank fresh *Beaujolais nouveau*. At Freddy's, the restaurant that became our favorite, I fell in love with *capitan lasagna*, a dish made from a giant river fish that looked like a grouper. Afterward we ate sherbet laced with vodka, which Freddy called *colonels*. We were in the depths of the Third World, light years away from Marseilles, the last place we'd had such meals, yet Cuban cigars and espresso topped off several sybaritic evenings.

Bangui, named after the nearby rapids of the Ubangi River, was being flooded with immigrants from the countryside come to town for jobs. Its modern blocks and broad avenues were shaded by mango trees and scarlet-flowered flamboyants, while its central market bustled with commerce.

The black part of town, called Kilometre Cinq, was fabulous, its nightlife justly famous for its wildness. Bars, restaurants, and discos were full of every kind of exuberant activity. We went out on New Year's Day. The town was booming, nightlife throbbing at noon.

Pierre had a field day, squiring a succession of comely African girls to the honky-tonks. He hit me up for an increase in his rates, which I wouldn't give him, but then he wheedled an advance out of me.

In visiting government offices to obtain permits and visas, I came to the conclusion that the Central African Republic was still a French colony, albeit a secret one.

For every black administrator there was a Frenchman in the next office or at the next desk to whom many matters were referred. French officers were "advisors," the same word used in the Kennedy years for our military in Vietnam.

I immediately noticed the contrast with former British colonies. French influence was everywhere, much more evident than the British in their former colonies, which had made a cleaner break. Even the C.A.R.'s president's chief of staff was a Frenchman, as was the commander of the presidential guard. The French gave French schoolteachers bonuses and tax breaks to come out here to teach. Several times Giscard D'Estaing, president of France, had come to hunt with Jean-Bedel Bokassa, the former "emperor," who had made him gifts of diamonds.

That had caused a scandal back in Paris, where they didn't seem to value the true nature of post-colonial African politics.

We rode by a set of buildings that looked like a public-housing slum. The windows were broken, bricks were falling out, and the lawns were unattended.

My new African friend Jean said, "That's the university."

"How long has it been there?" I asked.

"About twenty years," he answered.

I was amazed. The French government had built it as part of their foreign aid. Whether it was Peace Corps aid or the heritage of the European colonialists, everywhere we turned in Africa the waste of the West's legacy was appalling.

We then passed a stadium, ten years old and crumbling from lack of maintenance. Some European agency had come in and said, "What you need here is a soccer stadium." It gave them one, and ten years later it was falling apart.

Here we had to make a decision, one we had been wrestling with for days.

Two routes presented themselves, neither attractive. Should we now drive through Zaire—a rain forest a quarter of the size of the United States, across what we had come to hear were the world's worst roads— or should we push through Angola, in the midst of a fierce civil war?

Bangui was like Tam and Arlit, a traveler's crossroads. Tabitha and I pored over maps and consulted every traveler for news.

"It would have been tough," said Walter, a traveler coming west, "but you might have made it over Zaire's roads if you'd been here a few weeks ago, in the 'drier' season. It's too close to the rainy season now. Even the best jungle roads turn into mud gullies."

I thought of Isak Dinesen, who had lived in Kenya only a few miles from the capital. Kenya didn't have near the rain Zaire had, yet in *Out of Africa* she wrote that during the rainy season she wasn't able to travel even into town.

The maps said the roads were better in Angola, but we couldn't be sure. Because of the war no travelers came through there. The fighting had died down, but any day it might flare up. On the other hand, Zaire wasn't at war, but due to the rainy season its roads would shortly become officially closed and there would likely be no gas along them.

The rains would become so steady we might be stuck for weeks or months in a village hundreds of miles from any city, ruining our chances of crossing Tierra del Fuego or the Andes before the South American winter locked up travelers.

Weighing the considerations, we decided to go through Angola. Better a danger that was abating—the BBC's shortwave broadcasts confirmed the war had cooled—than a known hazard. To motorcyclists who had wrestled with the dunes of the Sahara, Africa's "passable" roads, and Siberia's dirt highways, a war zone seemed preferable to hundreds of miles of mud wallows that the locals called roads.

Back in New York, Eunice, who ran my office, had decided to retire. She had hired a young man named Judd as her replacement. He was a wiz on a computer, she said. Enterprising and efficient, he obtained permission from the consulate in New York for us to go through Angola and sent it to us via express courier. I was relieved that we had such a firm anchor back home.

Having made this decision, we now faced the problem of getting to Angola.

There was no road from Bangui to Brazzaville and Kinshasa, our twin-city jumping-off point. The only way to get to Brazzaville with our three vehicles, said the French consul, was to take a barge down the Congo and cross to Kinshasa, the westernmost city of Zaire. From there we could drive south into Angola.

"Remember," he said, "there're no people and no food on the barge. Buy everything you need in advance."

"Come on," I said to Tabitha and Pierre. "Let's go see this barge."

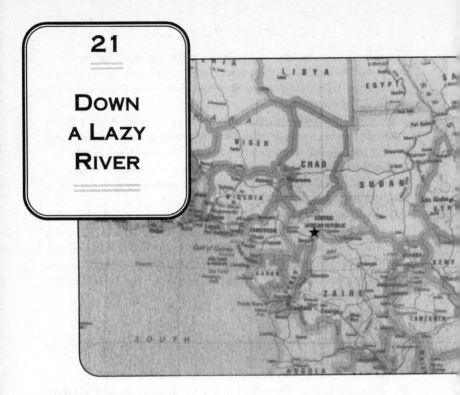

21

DOWN A LAZY RIVER

THE BARGE WAS as long as a football field, rusty and beaten up, with stacks of logs and freight containers in its center and crowds of travelers around its deck. It teemed with people, naturally all black Africans. It would chug down the Ubangi River, which fed into the Congo, "the river that swallows all rivers," as the Zairians put it. The trip would take eight days because the rains hadn't yet come.

I was excited—a trip down the Congo through the jungle! We'd have to rough it on the deck in sleeping bags and tents. Not only would it be an adventure, but it was the only way south.

Late in January we loaded our motorcycles and the pickup truck onto the barge and pitched our tents on the back deck.

On schedule, a tug came along and collected us. We were on one of four similar barges lashed together, a floating village containing hundreds of people, pushed downstream by the tug.

Business was being done on every side at makeshift tables displaying bread, medicines, nets, salt, and soap. The aisles were jammed with people shouting and haggling even over items as cheap as a box of matches.

I was offered catfish, eel, and a strange bottom fish with large lips and tentaclelike feelers.

Farmers, fishermen, and their families were taking their fish and produce downriver to the great market in Brazzaville. They not only smoked the meats and ground the grain into flour as we sailed downstream, they sold their products in villages along the way. A live seven-foot crocodile, tied to a pole, was stuck under one table, his furious eye glaring as if he would show us a thing or two if he could only escape the ropes binding him.

Hunters and fishermen pulled up next to the barge in pirogues and offered pigs, antelope, bananas, and fish to merchants standing at the rail next to us. Whenever we stopped, villagers crowded on board to sell turtles, lizards, pigs, snakes, and even baskets of caterpillars.

Slaughtered and alive, ground, cured, and smoked, the harvest of the jungle and the river was gliding down the great waterway to Brazzaville.

For breakfast our fellow passengers had bread and tea. Often in the late afternoon they ate a bowl of manioc and beans on manioc greens. We never developed a taste for ground manioc, a root vegetable that grew wild, which reminded us of chewy dough. Smoked crocodile, however, was light and tender and surprisingly like chicken. Sometimes we were invited to share our neighbors' meals of palm grubs, plantains, caterpillars, and roast monkey. We decided that the barge's "no food and no people" referred to by the French consul meant no *Western* food or people.

For the first time on the trip, Tabitha could set up housekeeping and a rudimentary kitchen. In addition to meals made from ingredients all around us, we had the European food bought before we'd left. We ate sumptuously.

To our right lay the Congo, the former French Congo, and to our left, Zaire, the former Belgian Congo. We were chugging through one of the most fertile regions on the planet, which some scientists call "the lungs of the earth." A hundred inches of rain fell here every year. Heated by the roaring tropical sun and dumped into the Congo basins' nearly two million square miles, this rain erupted into thousands of forms of life. The shore beyond our rail teemed with hundreds of species of trees, more than a thousand varieties of flowers, scores of different mammals, and hundreds of types of birds, reptiles, and amphibians.

.   .   .

The barge itself teemed with life.

As usual Pierre made himself available to the local *demoiselles,* hopping from barge to barge, always quick with debonair compliments, Western cigarettes, and trinkets for youthful ears, necks, and wrists.

On every side of us unfolded the drama of birth, death, mating, deals, squabbles, and reconciliations. Living so close to our shipmates, we came to know all their habits, as they did ours.

At night we zipped ourselves into our mosquito-proof tent and carefully killed every mosquito. In the morning we were usually awakened by the whine of a few more, they having somehow infiltrated the tent's defenses.

Whenever we stopped, the fellow with the goats went ashore to gather leaves and branches for his herd. A barnyard odor hovered over parts of this floating village.

The official latrine was in the back of the tug, from which naturally our wastes dropped into the river. Near the latrine stood two river-water showers, available for everyone. Queues formed in the morning and the evening. Tabitha and I showered in the middle of the day, when there wasn't much of a line.

The showers' water couldn't be turned off and on, as the tug's motors continuously pumped up water from the river. Since there was no separate changing room, we had to undress inside the stall without getting our clothes wet, not easy. The river water was cooling, but still warm. After the shower, with the water still raining next to us, we had to dry off and dress without getting wet again.

Our barge was not only a floating village, it was also a floating shopping center.

From time to time we pulled abreast of villages. Housewives crowded up our gangplank to buy salt, soap, and other household necessities. Traders left the barges and went into the villages to buy fish and game.

These villages were sometimes a collection of thatched huts standing on poles over the river, at other times mud huts with thatched roofs. Most had yards that were swept daily, on which no grass or twigs grew, which reminded me of the yards of many black people back in Alabama. I wondered if sweeping yards clean of vegetation was a bit of cultural heritage that had survived the migration west and slave times.

Clotheslines held the wash, and pirogues were pulled up amid the roots of the jungle's towering trees. Children dashed about while the men, often in blue jeans and tank tops, pushed their pirogues through the lagoonlike waters.

Whenever we hit one of these quiet villages Tabitha and I went for a walk.

Frequently we came across a lone Arab in traditional garb in the village's only merchant's stall. He would seem out of place in the jungle, a single turbaned merchant in a village of six hundred Congolese. I figured these Arabs to be expatriates like Reinhardt, able to thrive where there was less competition.

In one village, a white guy drove by in a beat-up Land Rover. About four minutes later he roared back and asked in French, "Who the hell are you?"

Jean Dieppe, along with his wife, Angelique, had left Paris three years before to develop a logging business. The Congo was trying to bring in entrepreneurs again. He'd been sent by a French logging company to ship out mahogany and other exotic woods. Intelligent, quick, urbane, and sophisticated, he seemed the wrong sort to be living in the heart of darkness.

By now we'd been on the barge for days without a good wash. Our new friend invited us to his house for hot showers, which sounded like hog heaven to us.

We drove by a building that I thought was a school.

"No," said Jean, "it's a match factory. It's fully staffed, but it hasn't produced a match in years."

I asked, "The workers don't do anything?"

"They go in to work and sit," he said; "six employees and a boss—seven of them."

Twenty years before, the North Koreans, for whatever political reason, had decided to make a gift of a match factory to the Congo. The country had nothing if not wood, so I supposed it made a kind of sense.

Unfortunately, as with almost all statist endeavors into commerce, the factory turned out to be inefficient and noncompetitive. The state couldn't sell the matches partly because the Congo, too, was tied to the overpriced CFA (Central African franc), and partly because nobody here knew how to make matches. This was a national enterprise, however, so the government wouldn't fire these workers. I remembered that the Congo national airline had only two planes and more than four hundred workers, a similar statist boondoggle.

Every day these seven people came to work in the match factory, did nothing, took vacations for two weeks of the year, and returned to do more nothing. They hadn't made a match in twenty years.

We left Bangui as four barges pushed by a tug. By the time we joined the Congo River, we had become seven barges.

The Congo River! At 10 billion gallons moving past each second, it was the world's second most powerful river after the Amazon, and a transportation system of more than eighty-five hundred miles of navigable waterways. Joseph Conrad called it "an immense snake uncoiled, with its head in the sea and its tail lost in the depths of the land."

A larger tug took over. Captain Joseph served as captain, mayor, and judge over what was now a floating town. At one point, when a local cop tried to shake us down for the usual *cadeau*, Captain Joseph stepped in and sent the fellow packing. He was happy to store our beer in his refrigerator, and several times we had a drink with him.

This wasn't just a boat, he informed us with a grave smile, but a social service. This part of the world, with no roads and few boats, depended on his barge service.

"I am this region's only market," he explained, his ebony face shiny with pride, "its only pharmacy, clinic, and bar for a couple of hundred miles. I bring the town to the people."

The view from the captain's bridge showed how right he was. We were now eleven barges crammed with more than a thousand people. Smoke rose in a haze across the decks from cook stoves and braziers. Masses of passengers filled every passageway and aisle. Some women nursed babies and yelled at children, while others washed clothes and sang. Men played cards and shot dice. Here and there the odd barber cut hair. Over the back rail of one of the barges a bearded man was butchering a monkey.

As we moved downstream, commerce became more diverse. Now traders' tables displayed unwrapped bars of brown soap, cellophane bags of crackers, loaves of bread, bags of rice, and perhaps underneath, a smoked antelope. A witch's table contained vials, potions, amulets, feathers, and charms of all sorts, along with a dried gorilla's hand that was supposed to give its owner particularly powerful magic. Yet other tables sold mosquito coils, tetracycline, malaria pills, vials of penicillin powder, hypodermic needles, and piles of brightly colored capsules.

One table held big porcelain and tin bowls of roasted caterpillars and palm grubs, which seemed to have the appeal of potato chips and french fries for the passengers.

Finally we were thirteen barges, all still pushed by the single tug lashed in the middle of the four rearmost barges.

More barges gave Pierre a wider field through which to roam, allowing him to pick off a different Congo lass on every deck, sometimes several in a day.

One day as we were chugging along, the deck shuddered underneath. There was a loud thud, and Tabitha and I were thrown to the side.

Around us everyone lost his balance. Soap and salt containers shot off the makeshift tables. We rushed to the rail. This was the tail end of the drier part of the year, on the cusp of the rainy season. The water was low. We'd gone aground on a hidden sandbar.

At the front of the barges Captain Joseph shoved the tugboat in reverse to push us off. The tug pushed and pulled for a quarter of an hour without any success. We were stuck.

With some unease, we watched the captain's roustabouts unlash the tugboat from its surrounding network of barges. The tug maneuvered away into the river. I was worried. Was he leaving for help? Suppose the barges floated away? Maybe he knew what he was doing, maybe he didn't. How much training did a Congo river pilot get?

From his position in the middle of the river Captain Joseph fired up the diesel motors of his tug. He rushed toward us as if to ram us—which he did—no gentle nudge, either, but a hard blow. It worked, however, knocking the left-most barge loose from the sandbar.

Now our thirteen barges, all strapped together, were gliding down the mighty Congo without guidance.

With another belch of smoke from the tug, the captain revved up his engine and raced toward the rear of the barges. If he weren't skillful enough to navigate the current, manipulate into position, and hook the tug back up, our thirteen barges would float downstream and crash into the bank, one into the other, a real mess and a real danger.

But the captain knew what he was doing. He skillfully maneuvered into position and hooked up again, and we proceeded downriver.

Finally, we reached the end of the line, Brazzaville.

Thirteen days of life on a floating African village. The merchants on board piled off and in jig time set up a marketplace on the dock. Like

Americans meeting trans-Atlantic supply ships in colonial times, thousands of urban dwellers streamed down and bought fresh supplies. In a day everything would be purchased.

Brazzaville, the Congo's southernmost city and capital, was more developed than Bangui. It had been Charles de Gaulle's headquarters back when the Free French were headquartered here in the Second World War.

On the side of a warehouse was a huge picture of Lenin—hand lifted over his head as he led the workers forward—which momentarily made me think I was back in Russia and struck me with culture shock. I remembered that the Congo had gone completely Communist at one point, one of the two or three countries in Africa that had totally bought Lenin's philosophy back in the seventies, when it was all the rage in the Third World.

Outside Brazzaville we visited the world's first orphanage for gorillas.

Its twenty orphans had been brought in by rangers who by law were now able to confiscate any gorilla offered for sale. The orphanage was funded by a British conservationist, John Aspinall, who owned two wild-animal parks in England. So far he'd spent $1.5 million to build and maintain the orphanage, and he planned to spend another million building yet more facilities. This park would also become a center for the study of primates, whose numbers were steadily declining.

Many of these orphans had seen their mothers slaughtered by hunters, and their teacher, Henry, told us they were often as wounded by the experience as a three-year-old child would be. These baby gorillas needed twenty-four-hour monitoring. Henry, an English zoologist in his early thirties, explained that gorilla mothers didn't wean their young for a year and often kept them by their side until they were three or four.

Like a roomful of six-year-old humans, each orphan had his own personality and antics with which to gain attention. Henry told us that research on chimps had shown them to be 99 percent genetically related to humans. Watching these gorilla orphans, I could believe that they were closely related to us.

One slapped me on the bottom and ran off, only to do it again when I wasn't looking. Several were shy. Some were playful and others show-offs. They interacted so strongly with us it was almost as if they were talking to us, letting us know their personalities, unlike, say, a roomful of cats, which wouldn't let us know what they were thinking.

The goal of the twenty-acre camp was to prepare these orphans for life back in the jungle. Henry assured us that despite their camp existence, they retained their instinctive ability to learn jungle ways. I remembered that dried gorilla hand back on the barge. I shuddered as I wondered if one of these orphans' hands would wind up for sale on a witch's table.

One two-year-old climbed all over me, making something of a pest of himself. Henry scolded him and he pulled away, patting me on the back to make sure I wasn't offended.

HOME OF THE ALWAYS VICTORIOUS WARRIOR

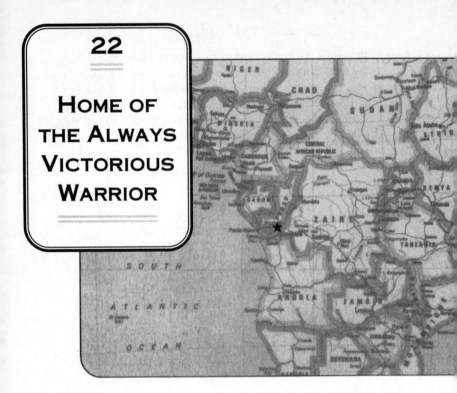

K INSHASA, Zaire's capital city, was the first major city we'd been in since Algiers, but nothing seemed to work. Upper-class Zairians walked around with walkie-talkies and mobile phones because their hard-wired phones were useless. At the hotel many prices were in United States dollars. Those in the local currency, the zaire, were raised daily, even the prices of newspapers. Restaurants didn't list prices on the menu; they inserted a new price list with every meal.

Two days before we were to set out, a BBC shortwave broadcast informed us that intense fighting had broken out along the route we planned to take through Angola.

We struggled again with our decision: drive through Angola or Zaire. What a choice! An active war or a trek along roads that by every account were far worse than Siberia's. Even the main road that went south to Lubumbashi, capital of the southern region and through which we had to pass, was described as a river of mud.

At the American embassy we explored our options with an officer, Phil Cowan. We asked what was going on in Angola, just down the road. Knowing that UNITA, the combatants the U.S. favored, were being supervised from this embassy, we knew he wasn't allowed to say much.

"Just tell us what to avoid," I said, having come to understand how much embassy officials hated to see citizens from their countries. "Don't tell us any secrets." Embassy personnel had wonderful jobs at good pay in fabulous locales. They were honored in the exotic countries in which they were posted. But then in came their bedraggled citizens with problems, requests, complaints, and grievances, spoiling a perfect succession of perfect days.

Even though Angola was only a few miles away, he airily waved his hand and said, "I have no idea." He promised to call a friend at the political section to see what he could find out.

When we came back the next day, however, Phil was cooler, downright icy.

"Nobody here knows anything about Angola," he said with a straight face. "But don't go there."

I gathered this meant he wouldn't go out on a limb with information that might get us hurt, or that he and the political section thought we might be spies. We were on our own.

Over the next twenty-four hours the BBC reported that the heat-up of the Angolan war was increasing, but I still resisted driving through fifteen hundred miles of jungle mud to Lubumbashi.

Everybody who had ever been through Zaire had horror stories to tell, and I wasn't eager to supply more.

On the other hand, even if the Angolan roads were better, I didn't want to be shot or taken hostage. Every traveler warned us of Angolan land mines. More one-legged people were said to live there than any other place in the world.

Each time Zaire seemed more attractive, I shuddered. It was the model of the post-colonial disintegration of African nations.

The second-largest country in sub-Saharan Africa, Zaire was the size of California, Texas, and Alaska combined. Potentially, it was rich, with large deposits of cobalt, copper, diamonds, tin, manganese, zinc, silver, cadmium, gold, and tungsten. Coffee, rubber, palm trees, cocoa, and tea grew easily there. Its vast system of inland waterways provided access to the interior and was the foundation for a major part of the hydroelectric potential of Africa. Despite all this, its per-capita income was one of the lowest in Africa. For years its economy had hovered on the brink of disaster because of corruption, depressed prices for major exports, massive foreign indebtedness, capital flight, and inflation.

In short, it was a potential economic giant reduced to one of the world's ten poorest countries.

The currency rate was three thousand zaires to the dollar and depreciating daily. Zairians went to the bank every day to check the rates. As I write this, the rate is several million zaires to the dollar, up from seven hundred thousand a few months ago. This is hyperinflation, usually a last step before political, economic, and social collapse.

Besides the fall-off in commodities' prices, Zaire and many African regimes were disintegrating because the Americans and the Russians were no longer propping up the thugs running them. Back in the Cold War, the two superpowers had spent tens of billions of dollars currying favor on this continent. Like many African dictators, Mobutu, Zaire's dictator, had played both sides against the middle until he realized his diamond, copper, and cobalt mines were more valuable to us than to the Russians.

He now had become so afraid of his own people that he spent most of his time on a barge in the Congo River, protected from them. President Mobutu Sese Seko Kuku Ngbendu wa za Banga, which meant "the always victorious warrior who is to be feared," was one of the richest men in the world, his personal fortune estimated at $6 billion to $8 billion. He had ruled for twenty-six years. We heard nothing about him but stories of his corruption, thievery, and abuse of his native land.

When he moved around the country, he was surrounded by secret police and accompanied by suitcases full of money. Everywhere he doled out zaires to his subjects to curry goodwill. All enterprises of any economic importance had been nationalized; in other words, Mobutu had stolen every decent business. As the government, he had spent no money on the country's infrastructure except to pave a road through the village in which his family lived and to prop up the national airline. Even the greediest colonialist would not have treated his plantation in such a sorry fashion.

He had forced the country to spend more on him than it did on its schools, hospitals, roads, and social services combined. During his years of rule, he had built eleven lavish palaces. He owned a sixteenth-century castle in Spain, a posh town house in Paris, a thirty-two-room mansion in Switzerland, and twenty-three other estates around Europe. According to *The New York Times,* he spent five thousand dollars every couple of weeks to have his hair cut by a barber flown in from New York.

He wasn't the only corrupt official in Africa, but he was the continent's worst. In Togo, General Gnassingbe Eyadema, its military dictator, had billions stashed in foreign bank accounts. The list of guys who got rich as African dictators in the past thirty-five years is endless. The Western press disclosed that Nigeria, its national treasury systematically looted over the years by thousands of government officials, was poorer by more than $30 billion, which had been socked away in Switzerland. Six Nigerians were reported to be billionaires, six thousand were multi-millionaires, and fifty-five thousand were millionaires, while 22 million Nigerians earned less than ten naira, or $1.50, a day.

The United Nations reported that 40 percent of all children under age five in Africa suffered malnutrition so severe it caused mental or physical damage. Estimates of what greedy African rulers had taken out of the continent ranged well over $100 billion—nearly all of it from foreign aid—enough to have established an infrastructure that would have staved off immense suffering by tens of millions of people.

So much for these assorted socialists, Communists, and fathers of their countries.

The tiny elite who ran Zaire cruised the decrepit roads in new Mercedes-Benzes. To them the rest of the country hardly existed. They shopped and educated their children in Europe.

For the rest of Zaire's 35 million people, life was very hard. The rail-roads, built back during colonial times, ran infrequently because of a lack of fuel. Most of the roads had fallen into ruin. Schools had no books and paper and few capable teachers. There was very little equipment, labs, or drugs in the hospitals. Commerce had come to a virtual stand-still. Zairians along the Congo River were lucky that they could still trade. We passed falling-down barns, houses, and water towers, and large inland rubber and cotton plantations turning back into jungle. What little rubber and cotton that was raised often went unharvested because trucks could no longer reach the villages. No one dared to dream of a better life.

Zairians knew they had a rich country and that the elite had stolen everything from them. They suffered and saw all their neighbors suffer-ing. They knew damn well they were a good people trapped in a terrible system.

We saw this reflected in the street. There were dealers for Mercedes-Benz and BMW cars, but none for motorcycles and bicycles, the poor man's efficient means of transportation, nor for inexpensive cars like Toyotas and Fiats.

· · ·

The fighting intensified in Angola. It was drive through Zaire or fly to South Africa, but that would violate the spirit of my dream.

We would drive. We set out south for Lubumbashi, our first stop Kikwit.

To our relief, the road wasn't bad, mostly hard, packed earth. The first day we made three hundred miles. Not too happy to leave behind the pleasures of civilization, Pierre followed along. As the slow, clumsy truck held Tabitha and me back, we sometimes pushed on ahead.

Having taken a wrong turn and left the main highway, we came across a village of Pygmies, which we discovered were the underclass of Africa, regarded as uncivilized. About four-and-a-half to five-feet high, they were perfectly proportioned. Shorter than average myself, I felt an affinity for these small folks. For once, I was a giant towering over other adults. As a souvenir I bought a Pygmy crossbow.

Although in towns a few blacks had Pygmy servants, for the most part these people lived in the jungle without clothes, not migrating to the cities like other tribes. Why go to a city and be subjugated?

I was surprised to find gas was only $2.50 a gallon. I couldn't figure out if the government sold it cheap to keep people happy or if the currency had collapsed too fast for the price to be raised to keep up with it.

"Come on, Jim," Pierre begged in the village of Mukoko, "you have money. Give me a little for tonight."

"No, I've given you all I said I would," I answered. "No more."

From the way he ground his boot heel in the dust I thought he was going to say more, but he spun away. I was sick and tired of his wheedling more and more money out of me. I figured I was playing some role from his Parisian childhood, a remnant of unfinished business with his father. Well, this was the real world, not the Paris of his pampered youth.

Sullenly he agreed to meet us at the Catholic mission in Mapangu. All day Tabitha and I sweated along Zaire's main highway, little more than a pair of deep mud ruts.

At sunset we stopped, worn out, at the compound of the Mapangu mission. No hotel; we considered ourselves lucky to find hospitable missionaries. Monsignor Francis allowed us to use the guest house to the right of the main building. With a number of empty rooms, this was a low, square building nearly surrounded by a wide, covered porch whose roof was supported by arches and columns. Unlike in many other missions, only Africans were present.

We'd had a hard day on the road, but Pierre had had an even harder time. He arrived two hours after us, having been stuck in mud for several hours. He was exhausted, sweaty, and covered with dirt. Soon after he arrived, he confronted me, again demanding money. I refused. Hell, I didn't owe him a nickel.

I'm told that one of the many fatal flaws in my character is that when anyone pushes me, I push back. Back home in Alabama, we were brought up properly and played by the rules. I never had any reason to push anybody. But once I moved to New York I met people who broke the rules, and I've become far more assertive.

I suppose there's more to it than that. There's an anger in me I've seen in my parents, siblings, and grandparents, too—all these smart, spunky people who kept missing opportunities and ending up with little. My grandmother Gladys was a wire-service reporter in Hugo, Oklahoma, during the 1940s and 1950s. She'd been a maverick in that macho, frontier society, a tiny little lady—no more than five feet one—who was always marching down to the sheriff's office to interview murderers. But she'd married a man called Dutch, who'd reached his peak when he was student-government president and captain of his college football team. By the time I knew them, their years of early promise had become no more than faded memories, and both knew it.

Grandmam, as I called Gladys, had missed all her best chances. She understood life had had much more to offer than she'd ever gotten or would get. There was a frustration in her—a fury—that I'd seen even as a boy. Much as I loved her, I didn't want to end up like that. That's another reason I don't like it much when people try to take away what's mine.

So I refused to give Pierre any more money than I'd promised, knowing it would never stop once I gave in.

We stood on the driveway, with people from the mission all around us. He kept demanding money, drawing closer, and I kept refusing. He got mad enough to throw a punch, making me stagger backward. He was a lot bigger and stronger than me. Several of the natives pushed us apart. They talked me into walking away. Rattled and angry, I left Pierre to camp out on the front porch, while I went around to the opposite side of the building, where Tabitha and I had been given a room.

Hyped up by what to do about Pierre, I didn't sleep much that night. Instead, I experienced my first all-out tropical rainstorm, with thunder loud enough to knock you out of bed. The rain caused so much flooding that the ground eroded from under Tabitha's bike, toppling it. I had to go out in the middle of the night and wrestle the two five-hundred-pound bikes up onto the porch outside our bedroom door. The storm continued until almost dawn.

I'd hoped to drive away before Pierre woke up, leave him here to fend for himself. No such luck. He hadn't slept, either. First thing in the morning, Tabitha and I went around to the front of the building where we'd left most of our gear. Ten or fifteen other people, all Africans, were gathered there, gabbing in French with Pierre.

He came up and asked, "When are we leaving?" He looked even more exhausted than the night before.

"I don't know what you're doing," I replied. "We're going on, but you're not coming with us."

As I packed, he mulled that over. Then he reached into his backpack and took out his bowie knife. I'd seen it many times before, but now it frightened me.

Knife in hand, he slunk toward the rear of the mission. I instantly knew he was going for the bikes, our only way out of here.

Instead of following, I raced around the building in the opposite direction. By the time I turned the last corner, Pierre was already leaning over my BMW. He seemed to be looking for something to slash—maybe the tires, maybe the fuel line. You can't stab an engine, but there's a hell of a lot of other damage you can do. It looked like he was going to demolish my motorcycle.

As loud as I could, I shrieked, "Get the hell away from that bike!"

Pierre looked up, startled. Then he came after me, knife raised.

"Jeemee, I kill you!" he shouted.

As I ran away from Pierre and his knife, splashing wildly through mud and puddles, I couldn't help thinking he was calling me Jimmy just to piss me off, because he knew I didn't particularly like it. It was sure working.

When your life is at risk, you think fast. I didn't want to fight him, not with that knife of his. I did want to lure him away from the bikes, and I figured the jogger in me ought to outrun him even though he was twenty-five years younger. He smoked cigarettes, and I'd never seen him do a lick of exercise. So I ran full-tilt toward the front of the building, hoping to beat him there. I prayed that somehow those other people would save me.

While I ran, I kept looking over my shoulder to make sure he was following and not going back to the bikes. I kept screaming, too, in English,

"Help me, he's got a knife!" Pretty dumb, since everybody in Zaire spoke French.

They may not have understood my words, but the men hanging out in front of the mission realized something was wrong. By the time I was halfway around the building, four or five of them were running toward me. I ran right past them, and kept running until I saw them stop Pierre.

I'm not sure how they did it. The men had him outnumbered, and more people soon joined them. Somehow they calmed him down and got his knife. They took him inside the building and sent for the police.

To my satisfaction, the police were soon there. I told the ranking cop, a captain, the full story. He asked Pierre for his side of things, which came out as my refusing to pay him his wages. I'd brought him this far into the jungle as his employer, he said, and now I ought to put up the money for his passage back to Paris.

That wasn't the deal. He had tried to kill me, I explained, and I wanted him held. We wanted to go south, and we didn't want him following us. As far as we were concerned, he could be released in a couple of days.

The captain's smooth, dignified face was troubled, as if a dispute between unruly foreigners wasn't something he knew how to handle. About six feet tall and with a bushy mustache, he weighed a couple hundred pounds. Yet even with the crowd of spectators milling around and yelling, he was calm and unflappable, as if he often adjudicated disputes in the midst of commotion.

"Do you want me to arrest him?" the captain asked me in French. As I have only a nodding acquaintance with the language, Tabitha translated.

"You're damn right!" I said. "He tried to kill me. Ask any of these people."

"All right." He gave orders to his men, who moved near Pierre. He said to me, "You'll have to pay two hundred thousand zaires."

I was flabbergasted. "Pay! What for?"

He shrugged. "There're many costs involved. May I see your passports?"

"Of course," I said. "Everything's in order. We have visas, too, everything."

He scanned them and stuck them in his pocket.

"I think we'd all better go back to town together until this is sorted out," he said.

This meant going seventy miles on to Ilebo, a good-sized regional town with a military garrison, which at least was in our direction. Hating any delay, I argued we had to be on our way, that we had a schedule to meet, but even in my fervor I realized that the bubble-of-the-Antarctic-winter-looming-at-the-southern-tip-of-South-America argument was not going to be a persuasive one here at the African equator.

Ilebo had one main drag, dirt, of course, or rather, mud. In the center of town stood a police stand, one of those overturned garbage cans policemen stand on and direct traffic, but no one had used it in years.

We got the best room in the town's main hotel, the Hotel du Palme, which the colonialists had built for a visit from the King of Belgium in the early 1920s. The richly paneled rooms were gigantic and surrounded by large open terraces. The huge bathrooms sported fixtures from the twenties. Downstairs was a dining room, but it served virtually nothing.

"Sir," asked the houseman in stiff English, "how many buckets of water do you want?"

A bit startled, I asked Tabitha how many. We settled on two.

We soon found out why we had been asked. While our bathroom had in fact been the king's, it no longer had running water. To wash, take a bath, or flush the toilet, we had to use river water from the dozens of buckets we finally had lined up across the tile.

The Palme had its advantages, though. It cost only a dollar a night. As in the Soviet Union, the rates had been set a long time before and hadn't been adjusted during the collapse of the currency.

The first order of business was getting out of there. We hot-footed it over to the captain's command post.

The captain's position was that we had to pay for all the trouble we'd caused, for all the expenses we'd run up, and that two hundred thousand zaires would cover it.

"What expenses?" I asked.

Tabitha translated. We had to pay for Pierre to be in jail, pay to feed him, and pay to guard him. I could pay in zaires, although he would rather have dollars. He was no dummy. His country's currency was collapsing at the rate of 1 percent or 2 percent a day.

I asked for our passports back.

He said they would be safer with him. Whenever I asked him his name, he changed the subject or ignored me.

I asked to call the American embassy in Kinshasa. The captain's face lit up—what a wonderful idea! He himself would take us to the town's telephone.

I would get the ambassador on the blower and insist he get someone down here to straighten out this mess.

With the captain at my side, I marched triumphantly through the sun to the town's single phone, located in the community center, a compound with a swimming pool, basketball court, and bar, none of which was open.

The captain picked up the instrument and fiddled with it. "It's not working," he said with an apologetic shrug and a smug smile.

Back at the Palme, I gave the problem more thought.

I rummaged in my saddlebags for a pen and stationery. I ambled over to the post office, little more than a twenty-by-twenty-foot shed. I stuck my head into the clerk's cubby hole and handed him a letter to the United States embassy in Kinshasa, a few hundred miles back north.

"You can't mail this," he said.

"Why not?"

"You don't have the right postage."

"What's the right postage?" I asked.

He shook his head. "You can't mail this. We don't send letters to that embassy."

By now everybody in Ilebo knew of our situation. Nobody wanted to cross the captain, whom Tabitha and I had dubbed El Capitan for lack of any better name.

Outside I looked around to see if there was a postal box into which I could drop a letter, but there wasn't one, nor would it matter if there were, because this lone bird was in charge of the town's entire postal system. Like Mrs. Campion back in Dunquin, no letter or postcard went in or out that he didn't know about.

Number two in the Ilebo police system was a thin, mean guy with a pencil mustache who was introduced as the town's immigration officer. The purpose of an immigration officer this far inland was never explained. Several times he told us with a vicious smirk that he was going to put us in jail. Here in the middle of the jungle we were getting the good cop–bad cop routine.

Like El Capitan, he wouldn't give us his name. Between ourselves, Tabitha and I called him Rayon because he always wore slick rayon shirts and pants in gaudy African colors.

These two were cops on the make, cops after *cadeaux* big-time, not like the street hustlers who'd demanded a few dollars in Bangui. If they never gave us their names, they would more easily dodge trouble from their higher-ups in case we pressed the matter. I fully intended to.

The next night El Capitan ate with us as our guest at the Palme.

As always, he was in uniform and carried himself with dignity. We learned he was from another part of Zaire, and was not a member of the local tribe.

Unfortunately, it was hard to put on the dog for him when there wasn't much to eat. The hotel offered wild boar, manioc, pig, and chicken. After dinner he took us to a disco next to the police station.

The disco was an open space surrounded by a wall. A band played on one side, and under a covered area in the center stood the bar. Hundreds of people danced here until three or four in the morning to a combination of Western and African music.

The captain didn't come here much, as this was a younger crowd. We all sat at a table and had big brown bottles of beer. Naturally we paid for everything, straining to be his friend, trying to jolly him into giving us back our passports and speeding us on our way.

Pierre's passport was held, too, and he was put up in a low-rent hotel. None of us was going anywhere. My conversations with the captain made me understand that in addition to his wanting money, he claimed to be genuinely perplexed about what to do with us.

He could read the intentions of his own people and make moral adjudications, but we were so different from his usual disputants that he wasn't sure who was right and who was wrong. He came up with what he thought was a brilliant idea. He would take us to the local Catholic missionaries, who would help him interpret the situation.

Father Jean-Pierre and two other Belgian priests, in their seventies, had lived in Ilebo since World War II. Their compound contained a big house and several guest houses, all erected fifty and sixty years before. They generated their own electricity.

These three priests educated and healed only on the side. Their main calling was managing the local beer monopoly. Perhaps on Sunday they performed a mass, but the other six days they distributed beer, as if malt were doing more to further their purposes than sacramental wine.

We told them our story, that Pierre had been hired to carry extra supplies, that he'd run out of money and attacked me, and that he now insisted on money to use to return to France.

Father Jean-Pierre said, "Let's get everybody together—you, the captain, this young Frenchman—and sort this out."

We were elated. This sounded like local justice, jungle style, and perhaps with their favorable endorsement we'd shortly be on our way.

A day or two later we all gathered at the priests' compound. Tabitha had been tense and anxious throughout our stay, but had kept a stiff upper lip. As her French was far better than mine, she was needed here to translate even though she would rather have stayed back in the hotel.

While we were standing around, we were drawn aside by an elderly Belgian, Monsieur Gilbert Tilburg, who told us he lived a hundred miles away. He was waiting for the diesel-fuel shipment to come in, which he needed for his mining operation. He was staying with the priests, who were old friends and the only white people for hundreds of miles.

"Let me alert you to two or three things about disputes and problems here," said Monsieur Tilburg in a low growl that didn't carry to the others. "If you get into them, it's best to work them out quickly. If you fall into the local courts, it'll go on forever, maybe years. You'll never get out." He paused, reflecting. I had a sudden vision of a mountain of *cadeaux* needed to prize ourselves out of the clutches of local lawyers and judges. "We who are here—there aren't many of us left—never want anything to happen to the few foreigners that come through. It makes things more complicated for us."

I saw what he was saying. If we lost in court, the idea that the foreigners could be preyed on would take further root. If we won, the Zairians would lose face and want to take it out on somebody, probably him and the priests.

"These things are best resolved as speedily and simply as possible," he said.

I heard him loud and clear: Pay up and get out. Forget about being a man of principle.

I offered to give Pierre enough money to get back to Kinshasa. He could go to the French embassy there, and it would help him get back to Paris.

Father Jean-Pierre asked him if it had been in our agreement that we'd pay his way back to Paris. To his credit, Pierre didn't lie. No, he said, it wasn't.

The priest asked me, "Have you paid him all you owe him?"

"Yes," I said, "and more."

Father Jean-Pierre asked him where the money was, and he shrugged. The priest asked me what he'd done with it. I told them he'd spent it throughout Africa on booze and women. With sullen braggadocio, Pierre acknowledged as much in what seemed a fear of lying to three priests.

They retired to deliberate. After a bit, we got a verdict.

Father Jean-Pierre said we didn't owe Pierre anything, that his being stuck here was his problem. If we would help him get back to Kinshasa, it would be generous of us.

Of course, this was an informal ruling, as the father had no legal authority. I'm convinced there was no such thing as a true legal authority in Zaire. The entire country was Mobutu's rundown plantation, and anything he or his thugs said went.

Father Jean-Pierre told the captain we were honorable, legitimate, and responsible people and ought to be let go. Back in town the captain smiled and said he agreed with the priests' decision. As soon as we had paid for the operation of justice in Ilebo, we were certainly free to leave.

In short, no matter what the priests decided, he still wanted his bribe of hundreds of thousands of zaires, a sum that escalated with other charges as each day passed.

Like vultures settling near a dying calf, more of the captain's staff gathered each day during our visit to the station. They, too, wanted in on the captain's good fortune.

Tabitha and I had a complicated discussion about skipping town. We'd heard that we couldn't go any farther south on our bikes, that from here to Lubumbashi, six hundred miles distant, the roads had been officially closed until the end of the rainy season and that there was no gas.

I wanted to hot-rod it back to the American embassy in Kinshasa.

Tabitha said that was stupid. El Capitan would surely race after us in a four-wheel-drive patrol vehicle, or he would use the radio, drums, or some mysterious other means of African communication to have us snared along the way.

I had to admit she was right, and I gave in.

On the sixth day, the captain took us home to dinner, where we met his family. All the while that we were his semi-official prisoners, under hotel arrest, I suppose, with our passports in his desk drawer, he was unfailingly dignified and polite. Scuttlebutt said not only was his salary fixed, a big problem in a hyperinflating economy, but that he hadn't been paid in months. In a major financial bind, otherwise honest, upright people will do unprincipled things. Possibly, preying on us was his sole means of economic survival.

After all, he told everyone we bumped into—we were a source of enormous curiosity for everybody: grandmothers, shopkeepers, schoolchildren—that we were civilized, cultured people, that Rogers here was a professor, not an evil person. The bad guy in this situation was Pierre, a crook. Yet the captain still wanted the money and wouldn't let us go. Once he suggested he'd use some of the money to put Pierre on a barge heading back to Kinshasa—the opposite direction from us—thus guaranteeing our safety by putting more distance between Pierre and us.

So I put my pride in my pocket and made a deal with him for a couple of thousand dollars in zaires that would allow us to leave Ilebo.

I didn't have enough zaires to pay the "expenses," but he would solve that problem. The banks might be closed, but a local money changer would open up for him.

At the money changer's, stacks of hundred-dollar bills and zaires were brought out. After some dickering I exchanged dollars for what was needed.

Once the captain had the zaires in hand, he said all we had to do now was be vetted by the town's immigration officer.

Vetted? Immigration officer?

He meant . . . Rayon!

We'd been tricked! Over the past few days, Rayon had been giving us greedy looks, and now I knew why. He wanted in on the hot action. Doubtless he had worked out an arrangement for this pair of plump geese to be shuttled to him as soon as his crony, the captain, had done his plucking.

My temper hadn't been in good shape throughout this ordeal, and now my outrage exploded, breathing fire and sprouting horns and hooves.

"Don't worry," said the captain, his tone soothing. "It's over. Let him check your passports and off you go."

My new friend put a gentle hand on my shoulder. At the touch a tremor went through me. I couldn't tell if he was being friendly or guiding a truculent lamb to the slaughter.

"I'll take you over there," he said with his usual broad smile.

Rayon worked out of his house in the sparsely furnished office favored by all country Zairian officials: a desk, a couple of chairs, nothing on the walls, and of course no glass in the windows, only wooden shutters when there was anything at all.

Rayon was a man who looked seedy, whose every movement shouted "shifty character." He would look seedy in New York, he would look seedy in London, and he looked particularly seedy here in the outback of Zaire.

A room off to the side of his office was the jail. As we passed, the door opened and I glimpsed a prisoner. He was in his underwear, his briefs, without other clothes. Soldiers went in and started beating him. This was the jail they hadn't put Pierre into, too terrible for a European.

I asked a guard what this fellow had done. He had stolen four pigs. He had to stay there until he paid for them, one hundred thousand zaires.

From behind his desk, delight exuded from every shiny fold of Rayon's face and slick clothes at having us in his clutches. Right off he asked for our papers.

I almost laughed. If papers were his game, he was in trouble. Ours were in perfect order.

He went through the documents one by one, then again.

"This can't be right!" he exclaimed.

He went back over them a third time, page by page, card by card, slip by slip. Yes, we had visas. Yes, we had permission to travel in this section near the diamond mines. And, yes, we had all the special permits and carnets for our vehicles.

I felt a bit smug. I was glad now I had listened back in Kinshasa when a consular official had asked, "Oh, by the way, do you have your economic-sector permit?" It had taken us another day to get that particular document, but better to have spent the day there than here, where it would cost a hundred times as much.

Rayon now insisted that everything of ours be searched. He had our bikes brought over, and under his supervision his minions took our luggage apart. We scrutinized the searchers to make sure no contraband was slipped in. They missed the money we had squirreled away in various places on the bikes. He could find nothing about which to raise even an eyebrow.

Unable to find so much as a comma out of order, Rayon reevaluated the situation and charged us with having two persons of the same sex in a room. Several days before, two male travelers, an Australian and a New Zealander, had shared a room at the Palme. Now they were gone.

"Those guys weren't in our party," I told him. "We don't even know them."

"But you were there," said Rayon in a triumphant tone. "You knew about it."

"But this doesn't make sense," I said. "If you knew about them, why didn't you arrest them?"

"They didn't have any money," said Rayon.

For once in my life I was too flabbergasted to speak. I remembered seeing people of the same sex in the same room in other parts of Zaire and said so.

"On top of that, you've changed money illegally," said Rayon, ignoring my response and rearing back with an even greater flourish.

"The zaires—we used for the captain's payoff?" I stammered.

Smugly, he nodded. I was even more flabbergasted. According to every guidebook and bit of scuttlebutt, this was perfectly legal. He was inventing charges, hunting for something, anything, with which to stick us.

"That can't be illegal," I told him. "The captain himself took us there."

"I'm in charge of immigration," he said, "not the captain."

We showed him several guidebooks that said changing money was legal.

"I don't care," he responded. "I am the law in those matters."

I held out. He insisted on a fine. I refused. He shouted. I shouted back.

Finally he threw me in jail, which meant he stuck me in one of the bare rooms in his house. True, I could've crawled out the window, but a soldier was standing in the yard and I wouldn't have gotten far.

I paced about and seethed.

Finally, I gave in again.

I agreed to pay Rayon a few hundred dollars only if he ensured that we could leave Ilebo. We could leave, he said, but only by train, as the roads south were closed. Not only had I arrived at a state of not believing anything he said, but his shifty expression told me he had some ulterior motive, one I couldn't read. Part of the deal, however, was that we had to eat dinner that night at his house.

We loathed the man, but this wasn't an invitation we could refuse. I saw his game plan, and it wasn't going to work. He wanted us to feel good toward him so we wouldn't rat on his conduct once we reached Lubumbashi. Fat chance.

That night his wife, his kids, everybody was there. Like all African men, he used his wife as a servant and then ignored her. Tabitha, being a Western woman, could sit and eat with Rayon and me, but his wife had to wait on us.

Afterward he said, "Now we all have to go out and have a beer together. We have to be friends and make up, so that everybody has good feelings about all this."

Again it wasn't politic to decline, so we went to the disco. The captain joined us. At the table they started hitting on us for more money.

I blew up. "Now, wait a minute! You told me I don't have to pay any more. I'm not going to pay any more, and that's that."

They giggled and pointed at me, smiled, and said, "Okay, no more money."

While we were drinking, I said, "Since we're all happy together and friends, let me take some pictures, give them to you so you'll have something to remember this." They might not give me their names, but with pictures I could identify them.

I took a dozen Polaroids and with great fanfare handed them around, managing to palm two with shots of Rayon and the captain. I pictured myself at the interior ministry in Lubumbashi saying, "Okay, here are the bastards who did it. Let's put them in jail, have an international incident and all the rest of it."

So, nine days after our detention, we were escorted down to the train yard by the captain, Rayon, and a raggedy troop of local constabulary.

As for why they insisted we leave by rail, I gathered that now that we had been plucked clean, they wanted to make sure the indignant geese were shot off by the iron horse as far as they could be sent. It's the only time I've ever been run out of town on a rail.

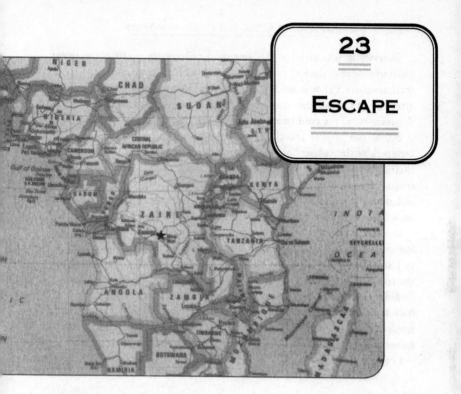

WE BUMPED AND RATTLED our way south on a flatcar through a long stretch of lush jungle.

The good news was that Pierre, El Capitan, and Rayon were behind us; the bad news was that this creaking, swaying train was obviously going to take a lot longer than the two days promised by the stationmaster. Both of us were full of relief to be away from Ilebo, but we were also acutely aware that if for any reason the train masters tossed us off this flatcar, we'd wind up smack in the middle of one of the densest, most dangerous jungles on the planet.

We learned that every railroad car in the world has its own brakes. We also learned that for safety reasons, only one car with broken brakes could be attached on each train. Naturally, our flatcar didn't have brakes, nor did another which carried a half-dozen self-important Zairian soldiers and a Mercedes-Benz. I figured they had stolen a car for a general and were taking it to him, or perhaps transporting it for repairs.

With its roads washed away by the continual rains, the lifeblood of Zaire were these trains and its river barges, which transported copper and diamonds. Without them everything in the country would die.

Everything was chaotic in Zaire, and rail service was no exception. Not only were there lots of stops and hours of waiting, but in the major stations every car was uncoupled and a new train was made up. Some stretches of the railroad used diesel locomotives, and some used electric. To compound the confusion, there was rarely any fuel.

So, as our flatcar traveled from station to station, we kept getting bumped by the soldiers and that damn Mercedes-Benz. At every station their flatcar would be the one car attached to the next train, ours the one forced to wait. I repeatedly asked the rail officials to give us another car, one with brakes, but out here in the jungle there was no depot platform on which to unload and reload our heavy motorcycles.

In every town the police found us and asked for our papers. Luckily for us, Africa had chiefly been colonized by the French and the English, so language was no problem. Back in Russia and China, English was still the second language of choice, although Japanese is rapidly supplanting English in China. Indeed, nearly half the people in the world speak some measure of English, and up to here we got by virtually everywhere with English, Tabitha's French, a smattering of local words, and sign language. I was worried that these local cops would pull the same stunt as the captain and Rayon had, but they didn't.

It was astonishing to realize that the Siberians were more efficient than the Zairians. In Siberia we had also traveled about six hundred miles by flatcar. But there it had taken us two-and-a-half days; in Zaire, nine.

The long waits gave us time to explore the villages, towns, and cities along the tracks. We stopped for hours in Kananga, a major city. Near the tracks were hundreds of old rails, ripped up and thrown to the side along with thousands of crossties.

The waste was staggering. Here in a country short of good steel, rails lay rusting. I supposed a clever foreigner could simply come through here, sprinkle around a little largesse, pick up this stuff, and make a fortune.

Why hadn't the locals melted it down into something useful? Because this was Zaire, because nobody here was organized enough.

We walked through Kananga, which had once been a bustling, thriving city. Now the old Belgian colonial buildings were dilapidated, sagging with decades of neglect, and shuttered.

"Look," I said, "that used to be the post office."

"There, that used to be a hotel," Tabitha said.

"That used to be a fancy restaurant."

"That was a tailor shop."

"A school."

"The city hall."

"A warehouse."

The train station had been built fifty to a hundred years before and hadn't been painted in decades, probably not since the Belgians had left. Most of its rooms—the old waiting room, the men's room, the ladies' room, the restaurant—were closed off and locked. A couple of offices were open, one of which was the train master's. As usual, it was spare, a small bare room with a desk, a lamp, and a decades-old telephone that only sometimes worked.

An almost new four-wheel-drive Land Rover passed us.

"My God," I said, "where did that come from?"

On its door was painted the answer: DONATED BY THE BAPTIST CHURCH OF JACKSON. A fat, well-dressed African was behind the wheel, obviously the king of the local economy, the baron of these parts, driving a vehicle that the Jackson Baptists back in the States had given him. He certainly didn't give the impression that he was on churchly business; he seemed to be using the vehicle to consolidate more earthly arrangements.

On our way out of Kananga we passed the defunct Dodge-Plymouth dealership, which looked to have once been large. There was the garage, on the wall were fading posters of sixties cars, and over there the showroom, but now the glass was broken and the front boarded up. In my hometown of Demopolis, Alabama, the Dodge-Plymouth dealership had closed thirty years before. From the similar style of these ancient posters and the out-of-date logo, I guessed this dealership had been abandoned at about the same time.

We explored many towns like Kananga, all of which saddened us. Water towers rusted and falling down. Two- and three-story buildings on either side of once prosperous main streets, in ruins now, boarded up, crumbling. An entire people had spent money, energy, and the capital of their souls erecting and maintaining these now-collapsing structures. Not only was city after city in ruins, but also the farms, plantations, and ranch houses we passed; vast amounts of capital and energy and lives tossed away by the careless Zairians.

The train stopped again. To pass the time, we went to the marketplace, where we found grasshoppers and locusts on sale. Tabitha turned up her nose, but I bought and ate some locusts, finding them tasty, crunchy and sweet.

One entrepreneur in a corner of a vast, nearly empty store displayed an extraordinary collection of secondhand T-shirts, three hundred or so. They were printed with Western designs, everything from the stuffy Yale Divinity School logo to funky pictures of the Grateful Dead.

Although his shirts were used, he had a well-stocked display, a selection that would have done proud any college shop in America.

This I understood: Here was a guy who realized his specialty was T-shirts, and he was in the marketplace working hard at his trade.

Where had he gotten these shirts? In another corner of this store were boxes of used clothes for sale, each carton marked with the names of various American churches that had donated them.

"Do you think the people who donated those meant for them to be sold?" Tabitha asked. She was still a card-carrying liberal from Manhattan's Upper West Side, but the card was becoming tattered.

"I somehow doubt it," I said.

No country in the world is wetter than Zaire. If you need water, all you have to do is put a bucket outside for a day. Yet we came across one Peace Corps volunteer whose job was to dig wells. True, the wells fell in within a year or two from neglect, as the Zairians didn't need or maintain them, but his job was to sink them, and sink them he did.

"I wonder if I can ever vote for foreign aid again," Tabitha said. "We haven't seen one good use it's been put to on this whole trip."

In fact, foreign aid's chief by-product is to prop up bad regimes. What foreign aid teaches dictators and the political hangers-on around them is how to obtain foreign aid, not how to make their countries productive. What foreign aid teaches a country's best and brightest businessmen is how to suck up to the politicians who administer it, not how to build businesses that earn hard currencies. In a country suffused with foreign aid, the military doesn't learn how to defend the state from external enemies, but how to protect its dictatorial masters from internal dissent. Foreign aid drives Western state-department types, International Monetary Fund bankers, academics, and UN bureaucrats to concoct endless studies on how aid should be spent, studies which few of the official brigands who receive the aid bother to read.

What we need to teach developing countries is how to open their markets, how to make their businesses competitive with those in other countries. How can a country become prosperous without prosperous businesses? Have there ever been prosperous businesses without entrepreneurs having the guts to risk their capital, time, and energy to increase their wealth? Isn't this so elementary it's self-evident?

To take its rightful place in the global marketplace, each country needs to develop its own competitive advantage, its own products that it produces cheaper and better than any other. Foreign aid postpones, even cripples, this development of its businesspeople, leading at best to economic stagnation, at worst to a loss of pride and spirit, which are vital to every successful society.

Deciding to chance the roads, we left the train one hundred and fifty miles before Lubumbashi. After nine days and five hundred miles of stop-and-go riding, the torpid pace was driving us crazy. We were told there were no gas stations till the city, but I figured we had enough in our tanks to reach it. Besides, surely the trusty black market wouldn't let us down.

They were right about there being no gas stations, and I was wrong about the black market. Even when we got to Lubumbashi, even though this was a major city—a gigantic city—at the first gas station there wasn't any gas. No, the attendant didn't expect more any time soon.

"Where can we get gas?" I asked.

He gave us directions to another station.

We drove the thirty blocks and said that we didn't have gas.

The attendant shrugged and said, "Well, who does?" His station was out, too.

We pressed him, and he directed us to yet another station.

Finally, we arrived at the city's main gas station. They had a little and agreed to sell us twenty liters. Between them, our bikes held sixty. A carton of cigarettes helped us buy thirty liters, fifteen for each bike. Naturally, I tried to get him to sell us more, but he was afraid to, figuring he could go only so far in doing us a favor.

This was the only gas in Lubumbashi, the south's major city.

Gas here wasn't expensive, simply unavailable, the way it had been cheap and hard to get in Siberia and Russia. But this made sense: Fix a price too low, and no one wants to supply it—not individuals, not corporations, and not governments.

We went back the next morning and got another ten liters. We drove to the other gas stations, trying to get more gas, but we had no luck.

We came back to the main station later, precisely at the time the attendant had told me to.

No gas, he said with his usual shrug.

Out of frustration I shouted, "What kind of country is this? Why isn't there any gas?"

Which meant absolutely nothing to this guy—what kind of country was this? How can you not have any gas? It made as much sense as screaming, "Why don't you have any kryptonite? What kind of planet is this?"

A white woman pulled into the station, her small son in the front seat. With a stunned expression she asked, *"Qu'est-ce qu'il ya?"* ("What's going on?")

The station attendant murmured, "The boss's wife."

She had the look of somebody who wanted to ask, "Have the Martians landed? Have the colonialists returned?"

Over and over we'd been told that nobody could save Zaire except for the departed colonialists, but they no longer wanted to come back.

Tabitha and I, a little astonished ourselves, explained our situation. We gave her the whole song and dance, how we were trying to go around the world on motorcycles, and here this station didn't have any gas. We threw ourselves on her mercy. What did we do now?

Her name was Eloise, and it turned out that her husband was the regional head of Petro Zaire, a part of the large Belgian oil company that had continued its presence here. He managed the southern triangle for the company, a third of the country.

At her suggestion, we followed her, and she led us to her home. She and her husband lived behind big walls in a spacious villa.

There we were given something cool to drink. We met her mother, Madame Toussant, more than seventy years old, who had been born in Zaire. This elderly lady had been trying for five days to get to Kinshasa by air. Nothing special—just passage on a scheduled flight between two of the country's three major cities, like flying from Chicago to New York in the States.

Every day Madame Toussant went to the airport, ready to fly, and every day she had to return home because there was no fuel. I was amazed. We were in the house of the fuel czar of the southern triangle, and his wife's mother not only couldn't fly to Kinshasa, but because of the lack of telephones and the general muck-up of the economy, she had to trek out to the airport every day to find out whether there was fuel.

It took hard foreign currency, not zaires, to buy that aviation fuel abroad. Doubtless, the airline had to pay for it in advance. No sensible businessman was going to advance credit to Zaire, particularly not to its state-owned airline.

Eloise sent a servant around back. He reappeared with a twenty-liter jerry can and topped up our tanks.

We tried to pay her, but she wouldn't think of taking money, and invited us for lunch. Her husband wasn't in town. He was in Kinshasa trying to deal with the lack of fuel, which was a major crisis. There was always a major crisis in Zaire.

Her family had been here since 1921, she said. We listened to stories of her school years in Belgium, how she'd often come and gone in those halcyon days. Her father had been an engineer who'd come to put in the railroad. She wistfully recalled how good the roads were all those years ago.

"Back under Belgian rule," she said, "each town was responsible for the road that came through its part, and they took care of them. The roads were always paved. Now nobody is responsible for anything, so all the roads have collapsed."

Eloise described the rich plantations that used to be here, the lush farms outside of town, how much food the farmers had produced, the plentiful produce in the markets.

I said that someone should bring in the Chinese to farm, that they would go wild in such fertile conditions.

"No, they tried that," she said. "Even the Chinese gave up because the government was so hopeless. No cooperation, no spare parts, no gasoline—nothing."

I was shocked. The Chinese didn't need a lot, and if they, the most frugal and efficient producers in the world, had given up, it really was hopeless. It meant nobody could work with Mobutu.

Madame Toussant said that back in the old days there had been three thousand working plantations around Lubumbashi. Today you could count them on your fingers.

In Lubumbashi we met a middle-aged black businessman, Moise Quela, a former economics professor fluent in English, who had grown up in colonial times.

"I've known both," he said, "colonial days and these awful times now. Things will only become worse here. We need somebody to come in and organize us, bring in capital and sell our products abroad. We need that, we need the money, we need the discipline, and we need the know-how. Trouble is, even if companies from America, France, and Belgium wanted to come back, their own left wing would raise a hue and cry. The current fashion in political thinking won't allow its capitalists to set this country right. What we need is to be colonized again, but nobody can or will be bothered anymore."

The record bears out Moise's thesis. Even though both were oil-rich countries, thirty years ago Nigeria on a per capita basis was wealthier than Indonesia. At the same time Ghana was wealthier than Thailand on a per capita basis; both then were agriculture-based economies.

Over the past thirty years, Nigeria and Ghana renounced colonialism, foreign capitalists, and foreign expertise, saying they would use African expertise and African capital. They sought foreign aid, flirted with Marxism, had an affair with socialism, and married statism.

Like the United States in the nineteenth century, Thailand and Indonesia embraced foreign capital and foreign expertise. They took little foreign aid. Today Nigeria and Ghana are among the world's poorest countries, while Thailand and Indonesia are booming, prime examples of the economic miracle on the Pacific Rim. Their peoples have become wealthier.

These aren't arguments in musty economic journals; they are experiments over decades involving the lives of tens of millions of people, tests that pit vital economic ideas against each other. I can't imagine a better test, one that much of the world, outside the United States, is seeing and taking to heart.

One day Zaire will break up, probably into four parts around its largest cities—Kinshasa, Kananga, Lubumbashi, and Kisangani—but possibly into many smaller divisions. The roads are such mud wallows no one travels between these cities by surface transportation other than by rail and slow-moving barge.

True, the geography and climate make maintaining an infrastructure difficult. Even in the dry season it is always raining, and no sooner do you put in a highway or a railroad than a section washes away. However, when the Belgian colonialists ran the country, they built an infrastructure and kept it together. The irony is that if there were a good economic base and a decent political system, Zaire would be enormously rich.

If an investment company married American agricultural technology with Chinese farmers, it could make a fortune here. Even now, the crops grew without supervision. You didn't even have to speak to them, much less water them. The soil is incredibly rich and lush, and because it is so near the equator there are three growing seasons a year.

At one time the country exported food to Europe; now it imports food. Even though there is no more fertile place on the planet, Zaire can't feed itself. Instead, in the Zairian markets we found only manioc, along with locusts and grasshoppers, certainly not domesticated forms of livestock. Once in a while we came across a half-dozen misshapen, withered tomatoes, which always made us wonder where the hell they had come from.

Zaire will fall apart completely. The only forces that have held it together this long are Mobutu and American money and arms, along with whatever Russian support the dictator could sneak in. Both superpowers claimed they kept Mobutu in power to create stability in Central Africa.

Now that the Cold War is over, there is no reason to support him. His people hate him, and he is going down.

Other countries in this part of the world, Mozambique and Angola, have already experienced their vicious civil wars. Their currencies have already collapsed. These, not Zaire, are the places on which a smart investor should keep his eye. Zaire hasn't had its final civil war yet. That horror will come as local chiefs and barons snatch at the country's wealth after something dislodges Mobutu.

As an investor, I wait until the wars are fought, the borders are redrawn, and the newly elected democratic governments are eager to make something of the country's resources. Here, I thought, there ought to be a period of stability once the borders were redrawn and Mobutu was gone. That would be the time to pile in.

Once war starts here, the end will be near, because nobody is left who wants to finance a conflict in Zaire. There is nothing in it for anybody, because there is nothing left to Zaire.

What must happen in the real world is that Zaire must emulate Thailand and Indonesia and welcome unfettered outside expertise, management, and capital—as the United States did in the nineteenth century—or disintegrate before it can return to true economic health. I know there are a lot of decent people with good intentions in the West who think we should ship in aid to help countries at this point of dissolution. However, the Red Cross, the United Nations, and other charities should let them go, let them disintegrate instead of propping them up. Unfortunately, shipping in aid will only prolong the agony and the time the Zairians must spend fumbling at the bottom of their economic cycle. Instead of one or two years at the bottom, they would then have to spend three or four.

Only being on their own will give the Zairians a chance to regroup and make a solid new start. However this appears, it's not cruel, but the fastest and most reliable way to revitalize a shattered society and economy. How so? Because at the bottom people will say, Well, this is my tribe, my group, my whatever. They will work together and become self-sufficient.

Law and order will then return. Whether it's the Soviet Union breaking up, a Mafia chieftain running lawless and breaking kneecaps, or Zairian warlords pillaging, people demand the rule of order. During the breakup, yes, there will be a period of anarchy and chaos, but that will become too exhausting, too chaotic, for everyone involved. Finally, they'll say, "We want stability." People can't take living in chaos and warfare for long. Better to let things collapse quickly than drag out the misery, as dragging it out will still lead to chaos and warfare, only far worse, like a wound that's neglected and left to fester.

Only after collapse can true peace come. After all, tens of billions of dollars in foreign aid have been poured into Africa by both the West and the Communists, much of it guided by the International Monetary Fund, the World Bank, the Scandinavians, and the United Nations. No one, however, can name one developing country in Africa that has become developed due to foreign aid.

Once there's peace, somebody will say, "Gosh, we're really good at growing tomatoes. Why don't we sell them to the guy down the street?" So they'll start a little business, one with a firm underfooting, not one imposed by a Peace Corps volunteer or an IMF banker.

There's been so much meddling in the twentieth century that, except for places like Taiwan and South Korea, which received military aid, it is hard to find a once undeveloped country that makes a good model of economic self-sufficiency. However, in the nineteenth century in America and Europe, there were booms and busts that weren't manipulated by foreign aid, and those economies still grew rapidly.

For thousands of years, African kingdoms functioned without the burden of nation-states as we know them. Many had complex social structures supported by solid economies, court systems, and wealth. If African tribesmen put together a civilization once, they can put one together again.

Out of these tribes would come true local government. These new states would make voluntary alignments with others that would take root, rather than have order imposed upon them by Mobutu or the United Nations. When you consider the dozens of ethnic groups forced together under one system of government here, it's easy to see that Zaire should never have been a country in the first place. It's been one for only a little more than a hundred years, a patchwork quilt stitched together by the Belgians.

The rest of us, particularly those who like to meddle in others' lives, should stay away and let Zaire disintegrate into its natural shape. Every time we prop it up we'll get it wrong. We should let nature take its course, allow these people to sort out their own problems.

In the West we have the hubris, born of statist notions, to think we can change history, force the world into a political, social, and economic configuration that we find pleasing or familiar.

We cannot. There aren't enough soldiers or money in the world to stop the coming collapse in Zaire.

24

ZAMBIA AND THE GREAT ZIMBABWE

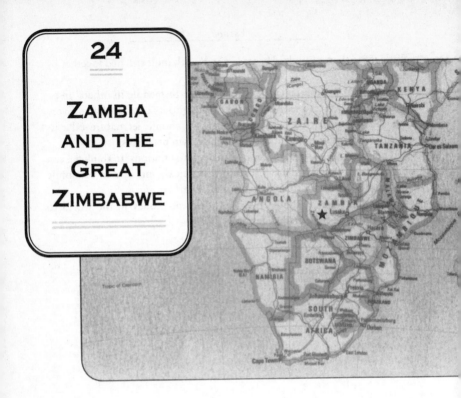

WE WERE DELIGHTED that Zambia was close to Lubumbashi.

By now we had been in Zaire almost five weeks. Both of us were heartily sick of it. We pushed on south and arrived at the border.

As usual, we dreaded the crossing with its crowds of people, cars, and trucks, its chaos, paperwork, and the bribes we would have to pay.

However, entering Zambia turned out to be simple. The border guards spoke Oxford English. We went into the customs shed and said, "We're tourists going through," and it was a snap.

All of a sudden, we were in civilization again.

Civilization by African standards, that is. If the average American were dropped into Zambia he would recoil at the primitive conditions. But here the roads were paved. The people were sane. The currency was declining but not collapsing. They had gas. There was food. You could buy vegetables. There was soda pop.

Even though everybody was nice as pie at the border, we jumped on our bikes and took off, obeying the first rule of crossing borders: When you make it across, get away before someone changes his mind.

. . .

We immediately ran into a military checkpoint, but we were waved through, as if they saw we weren't emerald or gold smugglers. Few, if any, white travelers come through here, and no long-distance travelers of any race, much less outlanders in chaps and riding what to them were exotic machines. What a relief after having gone through so many police and military checkpoints in Zaire!

Around the world, military checkpoints are often an attempt to deter smugglers. Governments want to prevent the export of the local product that brings them the most hard currency.

As emeralds were important to the Zambian economy, the government had instructed its citizens that it and only it was allowed to buy emeralds. The government set the price, naturally a good bit lower than the world price. If you wanted to sell emeralds in Zambia, you had to sell them cheaply to the government or run afoul of the law. It took emerald producers no more than a second to figure out they could make more money by smuggling their product outside the country.

Such government-established monopolies were a worldwide racket. To give a few examples, there was cocoa in Ghana, coffee in Colombia and other Latin American countries, gold in Russia, bananas in Nicaragua, tin in Bolivia, tobacco in Zimbabwe, oil and gas in Libya and Algeria.

Some of Zambia's roads near the economic centers were very good. Its markets had lots of produce, and gasoline and electricity were available. I couldn't figure what would happen here after its socialist leader and benevolent strongman Dr. Kenneth Kaunda departed. He was the glue holding the country's twenty-five ethnic groups together.

In the pantheon of Third World leaders, he was regarded as a hallowed saint. Saint or not, he was in the process of being thrown out because his statist policies weren't working.

Zambia's 7.8 million people had been jammed together without geographic, ethnic, or linguistic rationale, a collection of land and peoples that the British had cobbled together as Northern Rhodesia. I doubted Zambia would exist for long in one piece.

We heard the roar and spotted the steam cloud from Victoria Falls from six to seven miles away; the natives called it "the cloud that thunders."

The Falls were awesome, all the more so because we could walk right up to and into them.

Around the footbridge across the pool, the mist was so thick it actually made a rain shower. Baboons were everywhere.

The falls were one and a half times as wide as Niagara and almost twice as high. The water roared down in a canyon which has formed a pocket, not at all like Niagara and far more majestic. Over the centuries it had cut a deep river channel that wound back and forth in a zigzag through the jungle.

As we'd crossed from Zambia into Zimbabwe we noticed an immense difference in their approach to the falls. Both countries had full access to this tourist attraction to use to draw business. However, on the Zambia side, there had been only one decent hotel; socialism and government control precluded choice and competition. On the Zimbabwe side, tourist facilities were highly developed, with hotels, stores, villages, airplane rides, tour groups, every amenity a traveler might want. The five-star Victoria Falls Hotel, with its manicured lawns and 1907 fixtures, was as elegant as Raffles in Singapore or the Savoy.

This side of the border was capitalistic. Entrepreneurs could develop whatever business they thought would turn a profit, and so they met the needs of the market.

Back on the Zambian side, there was only that one drab hotel because Dr. Kaunda, elected in 1964 and still in power, controlled everything. After the transformation of the British protectorate Northern Rhodesia into Zambia, its citizens had been granted elections, one man, one vote—but only once. The country had been stuck with the socialist dictatorship ever since.

Naturally when tourists visited Victoria Falls they went to the Zimbabwe side.

Here was an object lesson in the difference between the free market and statism with its incredible restrictions. Capitalism was battling statism right across the river, and it was hardly a contest.

Zimbabwe had a checkered political history. In 1923 it had become the self-governing British colony of Southern Rhodesia. In 1965 it unilaterally declared its independence, and a white-dominated republican regime was established. In 1978 it became a biracial one, with a black-puppet administration controlled by whites. For a year or so the British returned to run the country. In 1980 it reached its independence again as the

Republic of Zimbabwe. As happened in many African countries, in 1987 it became a one-party state.

It had lots of natural resources and a relatively advanced economy oriented toward foreign trade and supported by a sophisticated infrastructure. In addition to large tobacco exports, asbestos, chromium, copper, and other minerals were shipped to a wide variety of foreign markets. For a while agricultural self-sufficiency permitted the export of corn and other crops to its neighbors.

Like other African countries, however, mismanagement, drought, and falling commodity prices had since contributed to fiscal difficulties, including budget deficits and persistent inflation. As in China today, the government still spouted Marxist-Leninist rhetoric, but it was being forced to explore relaxing its control of the economy in favor of private business, industry, and agriculture.

We stayed outside Hwange National Park in the Ivory Lodge, one of the world's most unusual resorts.

Each of its dozen suites was a treehouse in the middle of the jungle. Although the bathrooms were at the base of the trees, each treehouse had a full bedroom, one as big as you'd find anywhere, and was surrounded by a porch. There were never more than twenty-four guests at the lodge, all living in the treehouses with the birds. A nearby small water hole drew lions, giraffes, zebras, and other jungle animals, which guests could view from their porches.

The guests ate gourmet meals in the main lodge at a single large table. The owners, holdovers from the colonial period, had spared no expense. The fixtures were new, the plumbing modern, and the rooms well appointed. They figured to break even at 40 percent occupancy and to make a fortune at 100 percent.

Most of the guests rose before dawn to watch jungle animals gather at the larger water holes inside the park. After viewing the animals and taking pictures, they returned to eat a big English breakfast together.

One night Tabitha and I heard elephants making loud grunts and trumpet calls below us. These were young male elephants, about twelve years old, who traveled in packs because they were young bucks, a bit like our teenagers. When they were older than twelve they found a female and paired off, or whatever elephants did. We figured this would be a terrific chance to see them up close.

We climbed down, got a driver, piled into a jeep, and drove to the water hole to see them.

We were watching a dozen by the light of the full moon when something spooked them. They immediately charged, stampeding toward us. We were stuck, couldn't move—we were paralyzed. When they were fifty or sixty yards away it was clear that Tabitha, the driver, and I were going to be trampled underfoot. Somehow, at the last minute they veered away.

Later the lodge's owner told us elephants didn't like to step on anything squishy that would make them slip and fall. They avoid mud, slick leaves, and, I suppose, motorcyclists filled with slippery blood.

In Zimbabwe many farms were in ruins. These had been taken from the white settlers—expropriated—and turned over to locals to reward them for whatever. Today lots of them stand empty even though fifteen years ago they were prosperous and exported food.

The government of Zimbabwe had decided to have a cheap food policy so everybody could get inexpensive grain. What could be more benign? They set a low price for corn and forced producers to sell to them. Back in the mid-eighties, before this policy, the country had produced 1.8 million tons of corn a year—that's tons, not bushels. Now it was producing thirty thousand, a drop of 98 percent.

This was yet another example of a government stupidly setting an artificially low price and thereby getting a low supply, the same stupidity applied by Russia to virtually every product.

And how did the government explain this failure?

"It's the drought."

Was this the truth? My answer, as usual, was to check the flow of money to find out.

In its wisdom the government had never regulated the production and sale of flowers. Back in the mid-eighties the country's farmers had produced $5 million worth of flowers, which they exported to obtain hard currencies. This year they were producing $200 million worth. The ability of farmers to raise flowers had apparently gone up some forty times during this catastrophic drought.

How was it possible to raise flowers and not corn?

Because the government hadn't set the price of flowers. Farmers could obtain rand, dollars, and deutsche marks for them, so they raised all they could.

Had the government left the price of corn alone, people with capital would have been attracted, irrigation systems would have been laid down, and even inefficient growers would have made money. There would have been corn.

The government should never have set the price, and instead allowed it to rise naturally. The Russians got themselves into a pass where, to get the price of fuel to a market level, they had to raise it one hundred and fifty times. If they had let it creep upward over the years, nobody would have noticed. Here in the United States we all say, "Gosh, I remember when gas was twenty cents a gallon." But there aren't riots in the streets because it costs a dollar now. However, if it went from twenty cents to a dollar in one week there might be riots. It is only when a government artificially holds a price back and then all of a sudden releases it that the price explodes and a political crisis arrives.

Human beings don't grasp this intuitively. History has shown over and over that a government doesn't have to worry about high prices because they bring in supply and eventually drive prices down. The proper concept is certainly taught in economics courses, but it's so expedient to cap a price that politicians often try to do so. It's never successful, always diminishing supply and making the situation worse.

One of the reasons I was bullish on parts of the world was that over and over I saw countries realizing they could not control prices, that it wouldn't work. Statism was on the run. More and more governments had tried and had such obvious failures with this policy that they'd given up on it. For every Zimbabwe where price controls were still in effect there was a Poland allowing the marketplace to set the price—and the resultant natural increase in supply.

Once we got to Harare, the capital of Zimbabwe, we tried again to lodge a complaint against the captain and Rayon with the Zairian ambassador, as we had tried to do in Lusaka, the capital of Zambia. Once more we got nowhere. Since the next country we would pass through that had a Zairian embassy was the United States, there was little we could do after this. It would be a long time before we could even hope to pursue this matter again.

I went to see a government official and told him I thought his country's prospects were great. Sometime in the future I wanted to invest here.

"If I invest," I asked, "can I take my money out when I want?"

"No, once it's here, you can't," the minister said. "We want to build up our country's foreign-exchange reserves. It's in the best interests of everyone, including you as a foreign investor."

"But don't you understand what you're doing?" I asked, exasperated. "You're preventing capital from coming in, which you desperately need. Nobody's going to put his money into a country from which he can't withdraw it."

"No, we must have exchange controls," he said. "Otherwise, we won't have any capital. It'll all flee to Switzerland."

"Now, wait a minute," I said. "I'm here. I want to give you foreign capital. I want to bring money in, but you won't let me take it back out when I want to."

"We must protect our foreign reserves."

"Don't you understand that if you let the money go back and forth freely," I said, "a lot of money might leave, but eventually a lot more will come in?"

Mexico was finding that out now, having finally allowed a freely convertible currency. In Latin America over the past fifty years there had been an enormous amount of flight capital precisely because of regulations and exchange controls.

What these officials never realized was that when the system collapsed and they imposed exchange controls, of course people rushed to get their money out. In their efforts to stop it they actually created currency smuggling. Prosperous citizens would sell their farms and buy stamps, antiques, gold, and diamonds and sneak their wealth out—the ways were unlimited. But no one was ever going to sneak his money *into* such a country.

The twenty-first century will not look like the twentieth century.

One huge difference will be the incredible mobility of people, goods, information, and capital. A major theme of twentieth-century economics has been the limitations on capital through exchange controls.

In exchange controls' simplest incarnation, it means if an American went to London, he could take, say, only three thousand dollars out of the country without permission. He could not take more unless he paid a special tax—if at all.

Now, why would a government care how many zlotys, francs, or dollars a citizen took out?

If I take my dollars and exchange them for five thousand francs, there are five thousand fewer francs in America's foreign reserves, in the total of its citizens' and the government's franc holdings. When an American importer needs to pay for the wine he's brought in from France, there will be five thousand fewer francs here for him to purchase.

To Americans it seems as if there's an ocean of francs available, with no problem in obtaining them. However, the only way our banking system got those francs in the first place was from our selling something to the French.

For many years we sold more to the rest of the world than we bought. Therefore, we built up or saved a lot of foreign currency: yen, deutsche marks, francs, and pounds. Whenever an American wanted to buy French wine, in essence he went down to the bank and got some of those saved-up French francs and sent them back to France and said, "Sell me some wine."

As I have tried to explain, trying to solve the problem of a lack of foreign reserves with exchange controls doesn't work. These controls are a Band-Aid. Once again, one person, one entity—the central bank—will decide what's important for an entire society, even if the product is tractors. Only when the market is free—unleashed, if you will—and the local currency finds its own level, will people then start doing what comes naturally: dig up emeralds, sell them to France, get francs, and sell those francs to somebody who wants to bring in either a case of wine or a tractor. If the holder of francs is reluctant to sell them, then the wine and tractor importers will bid up the price until he can't resist.

It's this kind of vigorous activity that builds up a country's economy and its foreign reserves.

Even though a canny investor like John Templeton will invest in a country before the currency becomes freely convertible, I will only go in and get the lay of the land. I won't put my money into a country until it actually makes its currency convertible.

In this vein, I urge all my American friends to open a foreign bank account, if only as an insurance policy. Second best is to buy foreign currencies in a brokerage or bank account here. People have life-insurance and automobile-insurance policies and never expect to need them. If you have to use them, however, you're glad you have them. On that basis, every American should put some money out of the country. I don't know what's going to happen to the U.S. dollar over the next twenty-five years, but I know what's happened in the past twenty-five—it's lost a lot of value, over a third compared with other major currencies.

The fiscal situation in the United States is so bad that ultimately—during this decade—I'm sure we're going to have exchange controls. The dollar will have become so worthless that U.S. citizens will be as desperate for foreign currencies as the Italians are today. Our government will limit how much money we can take out of our country. You won't be able to go to England for a vacation unless you can do it on, say, twenty-five hundred dollars.

As of now, it's patriotic to send your money abroad. The government wants the dollar to go down, to be worth less. It is American government policy for the dollar to sink, because the government thinks then American goods will be more competitive on the world market. American steelworkers will have more jobs. American farmers will sell their wheat and corn more readily. Our government is encouraging its citizens to sell dollars, and I'm right in there with them. But unfortunately the dollar will continue to go down until its fall becomes so out of control that the government will snarl and blame our problems on "evil financiers." Once controls are put on, the currency will fall farther because everybody will try to smuggle it out.

A year or two after this, my mother in Alabama will call me and say, "I gotta get some money out of the country."

I'll know then we're near the bottom. Many of us will be on planes, two suitcases full of money, flying to London or roaring across the Great Lakes. Once again exchange controls won't have worked. Particularly today, with telecommunications and mobility, they can't work. But of course, being a government, ours won't acknowledge it's a root cause of the problem.

One of the reasons I'm so bullish on Latin America is that its governments have tried exchange controls for decades and have now eliminated them. Latin Americans have gone through the complete cycle. They know. That's why they're ahead of the Africans. The Latin Americans have learned after seventy years that exchange controls don't work. The Africans are just now getting to the stage of, "Okay, we know exchange controls don't work, so now let's try something else."

Unfortunately, the Africans also have a problem with their colonialist-imposed borders, whereas in Latin America the borders are reasonably stable and a bit more rational.

We visited the ruins of the Great Zimbabwe with our friend Stan Mudenge, a historian and nationalist who has written the only history of precolonial southern African empires, none of which, unfortunately, had left any written record. Thus by necessity he had to be somewhat more vague about his historical sources than he would have been if writing a Princeton doctoral thesis.

The ruins of this old stone city were the largest ancient structures south of the Sahara. According to Stan, in terms of importance they were on a par historically with the ruins of the Mayans, the Romans, and the Aztecs. To me, the Great Zimbabwe looked to have been a large fortress with outbuildings, perhaps like that of an extensive medieval castle with a good-sized town at the base of its commanding hill.

From the Zimbabweans' point of view, these ruins dated from when they had ruled the world. Obviously, these ruins were of some kind of kingdom that had been considerably developed. This said a lot to Africans, that long ago their ancestors had raised elaborate structures and presumably an intricate civilization.

This mazelike collection of stone ruins was set on a large, steep hill with various approaches. Every day workers would have had to bring up water, food, wood, and the other necessities of life, which would have required quite an organization of labor. So here was antlike behavior in Africa, maybe as well organized for its time as that of the Japanese or the Germans today. Here was hierarchy and discipline.

African nationalists use the Great Zimbabwe to make the point that the Africans are as historic as anyone, particularly when they're castigated for not having more in the way of ancient civilizations.

They had other such ancient civilizations, they claim. Unlike the stone buildings of Rome and Central America, their forefathers' structures had been built of wood. As wood rots—and in the jungle it rots fast—nothing of those magnificent civilizations was extant—no buildings, no ruins, no implements, and no historical records.

I wondered what had happened. Why had the Zimbabweans fallen back into tribe and jungle life? After all, we know Arab traders had come this far south. Zimbabwean gold artifacts had been found in Arabia, and if the Arab traders had taken science and outside exposure to Europe, surely they had been carried south to Zimbabwe.

In Zimbabwe we needed to get visas for South Africa. The two countries didn't have a political relationship, but fortunately there was a South African trade office here, which functioned as the local embassy.

In front of the building, black people were lined up around the block.

"What's this all about?" I asked the cab driver.

"Those are people waiting to get visas to go to South Africa," he said.

South Africa? I was shocked. We went in and asked for visas, but we were told there would be a four-week delay.

"Why?" I asked.

"Because all these other people want to go to South Africa, too," I was told.

Mercifully, we were able to persuade the trade representative that while we didn't want to jump the queue and give anyone a hard time, we needed to keep moving because of the oncoming South American winter.

At my side Tabitha, still lugging along her tattered card identifying her as a bleeding-heart liberal, spoke up in a puzzled voice. "Wait a minute. I'm missing something here. Why are all these people trying to leave a black-run workers' paradise to go live in the racist state of South Africa?"

The Zimbabweans were voting with their feet, the strongest ballot of all. For them, South Africa was the land of opportunity, and they were in a headlong rush to leave one Africa to get into another Africa that the Western press condemned so roundly.

We were eager to find out why.

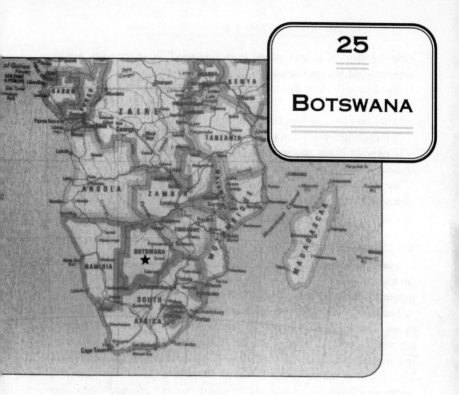

WE HAD HEARD that customs officials in Botswana were lackadaisical about travelers' bringing in money, but as we approached the border I was wary.

We were asked to fill out a form indicating how much money we were bringing in, as we had in all those wretched countries with exchange controls.

I asked the border guard, "Do we have to change all our money?"

"No, bring in and take out anything you want."

"When we change money, do we have to get this form stamped?"

Many countries with exchange controls not only insist on knowing about every penny you bring in, but each time you change money, they want the transaction stamped on your currency-exchange form. When you leave the country you must show the form.

"Okay," they'll say, "let's see the nineteen hundred dollars you have left." If you don't show them you still have nineteen hundred dollars they figure you exchanged it on the black market, and the central bank didn't get its whack at it. This was the same governmental racket as

Zambia's buying all its citizens' emeralds and Bolivia their tin, a state monopoly on foreign currencies.

"Do I have to show this form when I change money?" I asked again.

"No."

"Do I ever have to turn this form in again?"

"I think when you leave you have to turn it in, but I'm not sure."

If nobody knew much about it, this was clearly a form that was archaic, a holdover from the past.

We drove away on highways even better than those in Zimbabwe, which had been pretty good.

So I liked Botswana right off the bat.

One, it was easy to get into. Two, there was no black market in the currency. Guys on little chairs by the side of the road offered to change money for a small commission, a convenience to save a trip to the bank.

The mere fact that the currency was freely convertible made me think about investing here. You may be a brilliant investor, but if you have to get your money out through the black market, it's going to be an incredible hassle, particularly if a lot of money is involved. If someone local, like an arm of the government, knows about you, doesn't like you, and wants your money—no matter how smart you are, you've lost it if you can't get your money out.

Sometimes I won't invest in a country because I know it'll change the rules on me. Kuwait was one of those countries. The Kuwaiti stock market in the late seventies was a gigantic bubble, like the tulip bubble in seventeenth-century Holland. I wanted desperately to sell it short because when it burst, the profits were going to be unbelievable.

At that time in Kuwait, if you wanted to buy a million dollars' worth of stock all you had to do was write a check for a million dollars, postdate it for six months, and give it to your broker. Whether or not you had the million in the bank didn't matter. Naturally, the broker didn't—couldn't—cash it till six months later. If the stock went up, you made the profit. Under this system of financing, as you can imagine, stocks went only one way, up, buoyed by an ocean of worthless checks.

This was so much fun that many buyers decided to buy $10 million's worth. No problem, said the brokers, just give us a postdated check.

Government clerks wrote checks for $20 million and $30 million, all postdated. Six months later the investors were supposed to sell the stock and pay the money back.

But, of course, they didn't. They wrote another check, this one for $50 million or $100 million.

It was obvious that this had to explode. The Kuwaiti currency was freely convertible, which meant I should be able to whisk my profits out after the crash. Still, much as I was aching to, I didn't sell the market short because I knew just as sure as I was sitting there that the government would change the rules on me and I'd never get my money out. I'd probably lose money. It would say I was the evil speculator who had burst the bubble. It would change the rules and nail me. I believe even if I had been Kuwaiti it would have changed the rules on me as a short seller. It would have decided everybody had to suffer.

This is one of the big problems with international investing. It's hard enough playing the game in many countries, but if you go into a place where your money is not freely exchangeable, you're just asking for problems.

Kuwait? The inevitable happened. The market crashed. The clerks lost every penny of their tens of millions of postdated profits—and then some.

When we got to Francistown, I said, "Good God, look at this place!"

In addition to real shopping centers, the people had nice cars and trucks, new ones. Lots of Toyotas. In Zimbabwe, the cars and buses had been old and there hadn't been many of them. Here in Francistown, the buses were all new. A lot of construction was going up, with new buildings jutting up right and left.

Bells started going off: "Hey, something's happening here, something I ought to know about." What I had begun to sense, without knowing why or what the process was, was that the farther south we went, the harder the currencies became. It was a little like going through Central Europe: As one went from Bulgaria to Romania to Hungary, the currencies got sounder and harder. When one got to Austria, of course, the schilling was as hard as a rock.

Not coincidentally, as we moved south we also encountered more and more prosperity.

Zambia had been more prosperous than Zaire, Zimbabwe had been yet more prosperous. Botswana was even better off than Zimbabwe. At the tip of the continent, South Africa was the economic powerhouse of Africa, its Germany and California all rolled into one.

I learned there were lots of mines in Botswana: copper, diamond, copper-nickel, and coal. The country had only a little over a million people, yet it was about the size of Texas. Recent economic growth had been about 10 percent a year, four times as much as that of the United States. It was one of the world's top three producers of diamonds, which provided 75 percent of the foreign exchange and 60 percent of government revenue. The government's free-enterprise orientation and conservative monetary policies had attracted some foreign capital, although its investors still tended to be wary of the country's dependence on South Africa.

All in all, Botswana was intriguing.

The Second World War did much to unleash black Africans' expectations. War is always a major watershed in history. The war changed many of the social, economic, and political balances of the continent. Many Africans went off to Europe, where they experienced a different mode of life. Back home, they had certainly observed the English colonialists. After the war, many foreigners moved into Africa. They brought prosperity even though the Africans thought they were all colonialists out to exploit them.

When the British were chased from Ghana in 1957, Kwame Nkrumah, the first black prime minister, pledged, "If we get self-government, we'll transform the Gold Coast into a paradise in ten years."

Outside of Ghana many other blacks realized they weren't cashing in on the worldwide, post-war prosperity. They naturally thought if they got rid of the outsiders, their oppressors, things would get better.

They got rid of them and things got worse. Typical of the new democrats, Nkrumah turned dictator and jailed his enemies. He made court buffoons of the press and forced farmers to sell their output to his crooked cronies on the Ghana Cocoa Marketing Board, which destroyed the small farmers' farms with its low prices. By the time he escaped to Romania in 1966, he had created the pattern for African leadership for the next twenty-odd years.

All across Africa post-colonial blacks got one man, one vote—but only once. In came the dictators. Their first act was to snatch everything they could from the "exploiters," never mind building up their countries' economies. To them it looked as if they could make things all right forever if they could rip off the colonialists. They expropriated the lands and made themselves into what they called good Communists and socialists. Many of them were simply perfectly ordinary dictators and tyrants who covered over what they were doing with the theory of the day, socialism, which they said was the sound social policy.

This theory didn't work, however, any more than any statist theory of government can work. As their economies had fallen apart, the dictators had become more and more frantic to preserve what they had. To shore up their collapsing economies, they'd put on tariffs, import controls, regulations, licenses, and currency restrictions, everything they could think of.

Once again, here were governments employing Band-Aids instead of dealing with their root problems. These measures provided short-term help, but their economies had continued to spiral downward. They had a reprieve with the commodities boom in the 1970s.

Ironically, that boom itself was swelled by worldwide commodity shortages engendered by the colonialists leaving Africa a decade before. They had taken with them their knowledge of production techniques, administrative savvy, marketing contacts, and every scrap of capital they could repatriate to their homelands. Production of everything in Africa naturally declined. Before other mines and agricultural lands could expand to fill the economic void, prices rose dramatically. Without this boom in prices, these dictators, like the Communists in the Soviet Union, would have been tossed out long before.

By the late eighties, African leaders had no more room in which to maneuver. There were no more Band-Aids that would work. With new sources of minerals and agricultural products coming on stream, the commodities boom had fallen apart. Africans across the continent reacted by calling for change. Change meant democracy movements, since Africans were reacting to failed one-party dictatorships, as had happened in Boston in the late eighteenth century and in China in 1989.

Today only a handful of the fifty-odd African countries, such as Zambia, São Tomé, Mauritius, and Botswana, have open governments. My take is that unrest and clashing factions will produce many problems here. However, I don't think these problems will be as endless as those in Central Europe.

Why not? For the past forty-five or fifty years Central Europe has been thinking, Well, if we had democracy, we'd have prosperity. We in the West know democracy doesn't necessarily mean prosperity.

Central Europe will probably go the same route as Africa: elect statist governments that will become more restrictive as things go wrong and put on controls "to solve things." Thus, as in Africa, these Central European democracies will probably be stillborn. Ignoring the history of

Africa and South America, they will head down the same path, the one of massive regulations, high inflation, ethnic warfare, bad currencies, and ultimately dictatorships. In addition to the root problems of badly managed economies and irrational borders, Central Europe is filled with armaments, which will further complicate its political affairs.

Ordinary Africans, like ordinary South Americans, have traveled the hard road long enough to know they must be vigilant about what form of government they allow. Unlike the Central Europeans, they now have the collective wisdom to know democracy isn't enough, to know certain political and economic policies won't work.

They now realize they must no longer put up with oppression, that they must cut out regulations and controls, and that they must embrace a true open society. Those who are now running these countries are freeing up and privatizing the economies. No longer do they think the way to solve their problems is to centralize everything. They know state businesses don't work and that the only way to gain any prosperity is to unleash the entrepreneur.

Of one thing I am sure: Africa has to find its own solutions. Nineteenth-century colonialism, socialism, and Communism have been tried and have not worked. True democracy might work here, yet it might not. What would work would be a system that would unleash the spirit of the people to do better, one that would allow the market to help them find their own true way.

Even though neither they nor anyone else knows exactly where they are going, Africans are now on the right road for the first time in decades.

We drove down to Gaborone, which was so well developed we could have been driving into Montgomery—big buildings, paved streets, and good road signs. We exchanged currency and indeed didn't have to have our currency forms stamped. We spoke to bankers, brokers, and others in the financial markets. They all confirmed that the currency was freely convertible.

Not only convertible, but hard. I wondered why it wasn't at least deteriorating like the lira or some of the other weak European currencies.

One of the world's largest diamond mines was here, discovered only a few years before. The area also did a big business in ranching, even exporting cattle. In Central Africa we had seen only goats and pigs, but down here it was cattle. Raised on the open steppes, cattle had traditionally been a good livelihood here, the measure of a tribesman's wealth.

Botswana had another comparative advantage over other African countries.

A little more homework told me Botswana had a balance-of-payments surplus. In other words, every year it exported more than it imported.

It even had a government-budget surplus.

This startled me. A government-budget surplus would be rare anywhere, but was especially surprising in Africa. Botswana also had three years' worth of foreign-currency reserves. This meant if it stopped exporting tomorrow, stopped earning foreign currency—deutsche marks, rand, and dollars—it had enough foreign currency in the central bank to import at its present rate for three years. The same number of Sony TVs could come in, the same number of Caterpillar tractors.

Contrast this to Italy, where the foreign reserves were measured not in years, but weeks. Indeed, many countries had only a few weeks or months of reserves, their governments' living so hand-to-mouth that imports and currencies had to be rigidly controlled.

I did more homework and found out Botswana really did have democratic elections. I was warned by the opposition politicians, those out of power, that the police were getting a little corrupt. The other thing that worried me about Botswana was that diamonds as a commodity were a short sale. I didn't think the diamond market would collapse any time soon, but I certainly didn't want to be buying them.

I felt I had to be careful because the government might be foolish with all that surplus money. It had built a big soda-ash mine, which I wasn't convinced was a great business for this country. The government might invest in a joint venture with a large international company involving a show project only because it thought this was the proper way to do things, not as a sound way to make money. If that soda-ash mine didn't work, it could be evidence that the government would fritter away the country's assets.

Later I found out the soda-ash mine wasn't working, which certainly gave me pause about investing further here. The government had opened up the mine, it had turned out soda ash, but it wasn't profitable. The press had quoted the government as saying the lack of profits was due to technical problems and the price of soda ash. Well, that explanation wasn't news to me, because I was sure this government, like every other, was never going to say it didn't work because it was its own fault. What I had to do was figure out whether the price of soda ash had really collapsed or whether the government had been incompetent.

On the plus side, the government had decided the country should be full of capitalists and that it needed a stock market. If it were going to develop industry, with a sound economy and jobs and all the rest, it recognized that it would need a stock market to raise capital.

So it had passed laws, given tax incentives, and done everything it took to attract capital. It hadn't gotten too far with it. Since it was such a tiny market, there was only one stock broker in the entire country. This broker was in a joint venture with Barclay's Bank. That made me feel good, because I knew Barclay's wasn't going to disappear soon. The entire stock market was in one guy's office, and he had only a half-dozen employees.

In fact, the entire market happened at one guy's desk. He matched up buy and sell orders. There were seven stocks.

I kept investigating. I went to see the government minister in charge of the stock market. He confirmed the government's intentions to aid the raising of capital.

"Yes," he said, "we're going to build it up. We're going to continue to pass favorable laws to make it work well. We're going to give tax incentives for companies to go public and for people to buy and own shares."

At least the government had recognized you could not just start a market and sell stock if there hadn't been one before. People would then say, "What is stock? I don't want any part of it."

But if you said, "Stocks pay dividends, and we won't tax them," it doesn't take people long to figure out, "Well, if I put my money in the bank, I pay taxes on it. But if I put it in this newfangled stock market, I don't pay taxes." So, they'll put it in the stock market.

This government had learned all these tricks. So I asked, "Who's against this? Who's against a stock market?" You have to worry about this in any country. If there's an election and the other side comes in and says, "We're socialists, and we don't like this stuff. We're going to change the rules," you get out then—if you can.

"No one," he said. "The opposition is in favor, too."

I checked to see if these stocks were expensive. I looked at traditional measures, like price-to-book value. Were the balance sheets sound? Did they pay a dividend? Were the price-to-earnings ratios high? Were they viable industries? Did they have a good future in Botswana?

Things looked fine. I figured I was not going to lose any money. These stocks appeared cheap enough that the worst that would happen was they would sit there and give me no return. All I would lose, I hoped, was the opportunity cost. However, they all paid dividends, so it wouldn't be that unproductive. I would be getting dividends in a currency that was hard or at least semi-hard.

I had ascertained that Botswana had a sound economy and a sound social structure. I had ascertained that there was a new stock market and that the government wanted it, and that the opposition also wanted to develop and encourage it. I had further ascertained that the stocks were cheap relative to dividends and other traditional stock-market valuations. The final reason I invested here was because it was next to South Africa.

I knew South Africa was at a crossroads, and that it could either become Argentina—the old Argentina, where they printed money, had rampant inflation, and bought votes—or it would become open and sound. My analysis was that even though South Africa was Botswana's largest trading partner and even if South Africa didn't make it, Botswana was still not going to be a disaster. I was not going to lose money in Botswana, because its stocks were cheap and there were many other things going for it.

If South Africa became dynamic with explosive growth, I was going to make a lot of money in Botswana, its northernmost neighbor, just as Canada, our neighbor, had become rich because of our markets. I came to think that Botswana was the best means of investing in South Africa because it didn't have the political, economic, and social dangers South Africa presented. I had all the potential of South Africa without its risk.

I went back to the fellow who ran the stock exchange and bought all seven stocks because I couldn't see what difference it made to pick and choose among them. Obviously, if you're starting a stock market you don't start with Joe's Corner Liquor Store. You start with your largest, soundest enterprises—banks and mines. And that's what they were—not a whole lot of risk. In the beginning, I never go into these markets with a lot of money. I like to get my feet wet and see what kind of problems happen before I really pile in.

Several more companies have come public since then, the same sort of companies—big ones—which I've also bought. When Joe's Corner Liquor Store in Francistown goes public, that will be the time to get out. I hope that will be a long, long time from now.

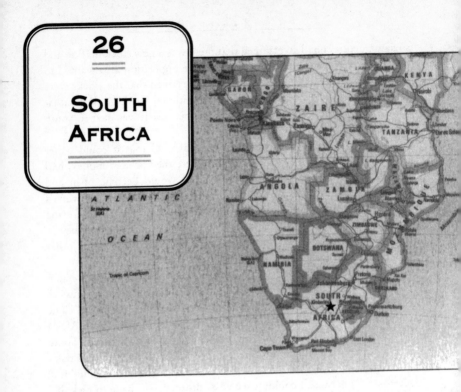

26

SOUTH AFRICA

WE STOPPED AT KIMBERLEY, which I had long wanted to see. It is the site of the world's largest manmade hole, called just that, The Big Hole.

Back in 1871 diamonds had been found here on what used to be a large hill. From that date until the site had been exhausted in 1914, not only had the hill been carted away, but an enormous crater eight hundred yards deep and covering thirty-seven acres had been dug into the ground. From all over the world tens of thousands of people had poured in to make their fortunes. A number of them did get rich. More than 28 million tons of earth had been removed by hand and sifted, and about six thousand pounds of diamonds had been found, 14.5 million carets, which at today's prices would fetch almost $200 billion.

The De Beers mine across town looked as if it would match in size and be even more valuable than The Big Hole had been.

In many cultures throughout history, emeralds, sapphires, and rubies have been more precious than diamonds. That diamonds were now more valuable than all other gemstones was a recent phenomenon. A hundred years before, emeralds had been far more valuable.

The De Beers Mining Company not only set up the South African diamond monopoly, it then set out to control the world price by keeping diamonds off the market. To build demand the company came up with the extraordinarily successful advertising campaign, "A Diamond Is Forever," that fixed in the public's mind that emotionally important events, such as engagements, marriages, and special anniversaries, needed a diamond to commemorate them.

At least since ancient China and the time of Christ, business owners have tried to establish monopolies. The early Chinese emperors forbade anyone to export silkworms, under the pain of death. The aromatic gum resin frankincense, which the Wise Men brought to Christ's birth, was the product of a monopoly. The two Arabian cities that produced the resin also forbade the export of the frankincense tree under punishment of death. Their monopoly kept the price at the equivalent of our price of gold, four hundred dollars an ounce, which is why frankincense was considered an extraordinary offering for a child in a manger.

Nearby Angola was going through a terrible civil war. Even so, about fifty thousand people were there digging up diamonds. Since Angola had no government, De Beers had not been able to get those miners under its control. Nevertheless, as soon as there was a government in Angola, the first thing it would do—both warring political parties had said so— would be to gain control of the diamond market "for the good of the country." They would pass a law that would say to the prospectors, "You can only sell your diamonds to us, the central buying unit, or go to jail."

To the buyers they would say, "For your own good we won't let you buy from the producers, otherwise the greedy capitalists will sell you counterfeits."

Actually, the measures would serve to control the price and enable the government to get its mitts on all the hard currency.

For the past sixty or seventy years, De Beers has succeeded in hiking the price of diamonds to an incredibly artificial level. There was never an economic justification for such a high price. Now that monopoly is starting to crack. Historically, De Beers has controlled 100 percent of production and sales. Today that number is about 80 percent. In thirty years, diamonds will have less value than they have now. Certainly they are not a gemstone in which to invest.

Why not? The law of supply and demand is once more hard at work. Since De Beers has set the price high, people are motivated to find diamonds. To maintain its high prices, De Beers has to buy from every producer who puts diamonds to them. If it refuses to buy, the producers will sell elsewhere. The price will crack and plummet. De Beers' inventory will become worthless.

On the other hand, if De Beers continues to buy all the diamonds offered by independent entrepreneurs, it will eventually run out of money and have to stop buying. Either way, the price of diamonds will drop. Nothing lasts forever, certainly not artificial controls, whether concocted by bureaucrats or capitalists.

De Beers' success depends upon its using the diamonds it has purchased as the collateral behind its bank loans. The banks, however, are waking up to this stupendous scam. Cautiously, they are wondering if they can tiptoe out the door before their peers also wake up and the exit becomes crowded.

Perhaps the end is closer than we expect. At this writing De Beers refuses to send annual reports to potential U.S. investors, in an apparent attempt to keep its situation under wraps.

My advice? Sell diamonds and buy emeralds, rubies, and sapphires.

A factor complicating South Africa's relationship with the world is the international media's fascination with its problems. Journalists seem more excited by violence than anything else. The media are hungrily waiting for South Africa to blow up, to give them a terrific story. What is unfortunate is that the media does not undertake any sort of detailed analysis of the issues. The blow-ups with the dictatorships in Zaire or Uganda were reported as flash fires and the media moved on. However, the media have their way with South Africa, refusing to acknowledge that they are a part of the problem.

This notion became clear to me when we visited Leon Louw, a white South African who ran his own political and economic think tank. He had analyzed the factors that had led South Africa into its present situation in a series of brilliant articles and best-selling books.

His books point out that apartheid should be dismantled because it is a horrible distortion of the marketplace, hurting whites as much as blacks. He had set aside moral arguments in favor of economic ones. He looked at the reality and practicality of the situation and said, "Of course apartheid's immoral, but even if it's not a moral question for you, if you just want to be richer or face reality, this is ruining our country. It will lead to war, rebellion, and a host of other problems."

Louw was selling white South Africans on the fact that they would be better off if they didn't have apartheid. In the West we think of South Africa as a land of black and white conflicts, of which it has plenty, but it also has a multiplicity of political parties and interests producing far more than bipolar racial conflicts.

Normally, Tabitha and I didn't look up people like Leon Louw, because we wanted our trip to be serendipitous, to encounter only the people we bumped into. However, South Africa was so interesting and we knew so little about it that this time we made an exception.

His think tank was in a big old home he had converted into an institute. Naturally, the house, like every large house in Johannesburg, was behind gates and walls. Because of civil war, robbers, whatever, there were walls everywhere, with electronics and all sorts of modern security. Jo'burg was a walled city with walled homes.

In the conference room we described our trip.

He said, "God, why aren't I doing this? As much as I like what I'm doing, why aren't I traveling with you?"

Louw struck me as a committed, smart, and perceptive guy, the kind who noticed the true nature of the emperor's new clothes. He saw clearly what had caused his country's problems. I felt enormous rapport with him.

As an illustration of what South African blacks could do, he described the local public-transportation system. Twenty years before, the government had had a monopoly on public transportation, fielding battered buses that didn't serve the population well. A system of gypsy cabs, minivans, and buses had sprung up. Since these gypsy drivers hadn't been allowed to use the government's bus stops, they'd employed a system of hand signals. Riders in the street would signal where they wanted to go, and drivers would respond with their hand signal, "No, I'm not going that way," or "This is the South Square bus."

This spontaneous system had worked so well that over time the government had been forced out of the public-transportation business. Now the private Johannesburg system is superb. Here is a classic case of customers and entrepreneurs meeting each others' needs—over the objections of their common enemy, government regulations established "for their own good."

Louw and I both agreed philosophically that if we could get the government out of most activities, as in his transportation story, everybody would be better off. He had also demonstrated in his writings that the blacks in South Africa were historically far better farmers than the whites. This had been one reason why the land had been taken away from them. Apartheid originated at least partially from economic interests.

It's hard to believe, but codified apartheid—another example of economic difficulties leading to ethnic strife—has existed only about forty-six years. When South Africa was having economic problems after World War II, the politicians had decided to save the economy and themselves with a lot of new regulations, licenses, and requirements—a way to protect some businesses. The blacks had suffered the most in the end. The morass became more complicated as ever more racially divisive laws had been enacted to prop up the entire rickety, jury-rigged concoction. It was another example of statism, one that had taken on a life of its own as a racist policy.

An international investor is forced to consider South Africa. It is such a marvelous country, chock-a-block full of commodities, with gigantic resources, huge assets, a wonderful climate, a big population, a large market, and a great infrastructure. In every way, South Africa is the California of Africa, in terms of geography, weather, size, variety, and potential. It not only has mountains and ocean frontage, it has amazing flowers, birds, and animals.

I asked Leon what was the future of his homeland.

His view was that apartheid was now crumbling under its own weight. Its restrictions on the economy had become so strangling that South Africans would have to start over. This meant, of course, that they would have to get rid of apartheid, because most of the country's regulations flowed out of solving the problem of how the whites could control competition, preserve their positions, and become prosperous at the expense of the blacks.

A big problem here was the African Nationalist Congress, Nelson Mandela's party. Mandela's heir apparent in the ANC was about forty years old and a Communist. In the days when it was Communism versus capitalism, the ANC naturally had chosen the Communist side. After all, the colonialists had all been capitalists, and nobody wanted to agree with them on anything. The ANC still embraced the passé, old-time left-wing mentality, which, though it hadn't kept up with the world, still ran the party. When Mandela died or lost power, the younger people would take over.

Many people in South Africa, especially the blacks, were of the radicalized, we-are-owed mentality, just as they were in other African countries that had become liberated: "You've stolen from us for three hundred years. Therefore, we're owed. We're going to take everything away from you."

Though not without justification, this attitude had destroyed economic development and spoiled these countries for everyone. Should the ANC come to power, its left-wing "reforms" would possibly set South Africa back a decade.

My view is that the country might have to go through a period of wild money printing, taxes, and deficits before a sensible investor should invest there. There might be more racial strife and civil unrest. The height of that unrest, however, when every other investor is fleeing the country, might be the time to buy South Africa's currency, the rand. Assuming the ANC wouldn't have gone to complete statism, this could be the currency's low point for decades.

Leon's view was more optimistic, and his could be right. He felt that one day Mandela's ANC would win the South African election, that eventually many whites and most of the blacks would vote for him. Leon figured the ANC would be in power for a single term of four or five years, depending on how the constitution was set up.

The ANC would be the rough political equivalent of the U.S. Democrats or Britain's Labour Party. After this single term, because of the ANC's international noncompetitiveness, the South African equivalent of the Republicans would win the next election. Politics would settle down and economic progress would reaccelerate.

Not that the "Republicans" worldwide have all the answers. They don't. The two-party system leads to a rotation between the left and right wings of society, which tends to establish the stability that is the best environment in which to invest.

When I reminded him of post-war Africa's "one man, one vote, once" tradition, he responded that the world press would never let South Africa go the way of the myriad northern examples, such as Zaire, Kenya, and Zambia. I wasn't so sure the rest of the world had that much say in the matter. Even if it did, there was still the unresolved threat of tribal civil war.

While I was fascinated by South Africa and its possibilities—who wouldn't want to invest in the Germany or California of Africa on the ground floor?—the best thing I could do was to wait until I was convinced of the nature of the coming change.

An investor is better off doing nothing until he sees money in the corner just waiting to be picked up. One of the biggest mistakes most investors make is believing they've always got to be doing something, investing their idle cash. In fact, the worst thing that happens to many investors is to make big money on an investment. They are so flushed, excited, and triumphant that they say to themselves, "Okay, now let me find another one!"

They should simply put their money in the bank and wait patiently for the next sure thing, but they jump right back in. Hubris! The trick in investing is not to lose money. That's the most important thing. If you compound your money at 9 percent a year, you're better off than investors whose results jump up and down, who have some great years and horrible losses in others. The losses will kill you. They ruin your compounding rate, and compounding is the magic of investing.

In Johannesburg we stayed with an old college friend and his wife, Humphry and Serenity Mullard. This was again an exception to our rule of not looking up old acquaintances, but I hadn't seen enough of him over the previous twenty-five years and I couldn't pass up the opportunity.

A white South African, Humphry had become involved, on his return to his homeland, with Serenity, a black woman twenty years his junior. The two had lived together at a time when he could go to jail for the rest of his life for the crime of "cohabitation." At Oxford, and even when he was president of the student body at his own South African university, he had been anti-apartheid. For years he and Serenity had lived together in a white neighborhood in Johannesburg, fifty yards from a police station. In South Africa, he said, there was much more interracial dating than the rest of the world imagined. Now they were married, with a son.

Serenity was a teacher in Alexandra, the hottest township in terms of violence, struggle, and bloodshed. Tabitha and I went to see what her school was like. Outside, the children played marbles on the well-swept earth, reminding me of my days shooting marbles back in the third and fourth grades. Older boys played soccer the way we'd played baseball and football. The teenagers, however, didn't appear as lively but seemed more withdrawn than we had been.

Her classroom had about forty desks, each jammed against the other. Her classes held seventy to seventy-five students, which meant only forty had desks. The rest stood, milled around, or didn't come to school. All the windows were broken out. Fortunately, the weather was good here, so that didn't present a great problem.

She taught the fourth grade. Her class brought back memories of my grammar school days in Alabama. Back then, we constantly made posters and put pictures on the walls. In Alabama in the fifties, there were atlases, charts, and other teaching aids pertinent to the work.

Not here. If Serenity wanted chalk, she had to buy her own, as there was no budget for supplies. Here there was no bulletin board, no pictures, and no charts. The paint was peeling, and she had no books.

She took us to the school library, and we were shocked it was called one. While it was the size of three classrooms, its metal shelves were almost empty, displaying only a handful of books. Its only magazines were *Africa Today,* a periodical from the Zulus, and another from the ANC local. We saw no other African periodicals and certainly no foreign periodicals. One atlas and one encyclopedia, both old and tattered, lay on the shelves. Once there had been more, but they had been ruined either by usage and age or stolen.

We were introduced as visitors from New York. The personnel and teachers struck me as dispirited, even numb, which was not surprising. It was a hopeless situation. The school had three thousand or four thousand students, a few hundred books, seventy-five people in classrooms with forty desks, and no materials. Earlier in the week three or four students had been killed in riots, which certainly contributed to making the school unsettled and uneasy.

As we moved through this depressing school, I thought a lot about teachers, how many good ones there were. They don't earn much money and often not much respect; they still go in and teach every day. Many of the teachers who had helped me had taught their hearts out. Despite the backwardness of parts of Alabama in those days, they had believed in teaching and loved it. They had wanted everyone to learn. And I had learned an enormous amount from them, even though when I got to Yale I hadn't thought I'd learned much, and probably I hadn't compared with someone from Hotchkiss. My teachers had insisted we master such basics as the multiplication tables and the rules of English grammar.

Serenity's colleagues also wanted the kids to learn. They went in every day determined to teach the children something, knowing many students didn't want to learn, that the conditions were overwhelming, that it was a hopeless situation. Even if these students did learn something, their future wasn't bright. We were awed by Serenity's courage, that with no resources, no materials, and very little support from her school district, she, too, came to class every day determined to make that day work.

. . .

At last we drove into Cape Town.

We had now made it from the top to the bottom of the African continent—five thousand miles as the crow flies—and covered almost eleven thousand miles. The trip had been a sensory feast, everything from the Sahara's windswept moonscapes to the lush richness of Zaire's rain forests.

Cape Town was such a beautiful modern city that we understood what a frontier Botswana still was. Even though South Africa was the most prosperous and well-developed country in Africa, I still had the strong sense that if Mandela's African National Congress gained power the country would go the way of old Argentina after Perónism ruined it. It was a shame, but so many blacks obviously felt it was their turn to get something back that they wouldn't be looking toward long-term economic development. As an investor, what worried me about Africa was that if South Africa didn't turn out well, the entire continent could become Zaire.

This was a country with a wonderful climate, lots of technical knowledge, good workers, and great opportunities. Nigeria, because of its natural resources, principally oil, once could have been the continent's economic engine. As a result of economic mismanagement, which had led to a resurgence of ethnic and religious pride, it was likely to split into two or three countries before its political problems were over. No country other than South Africa had the infrastructure, the heritage, the collective memory, and the capital base to be the engine of the African continent's growth.

As roads went, we could have been in Kansas, we could have been in Europe. The phones worked. There was gas everywhere, and restaurants, hotels, hardware stores, and all the other amenities of modern life. Thus, South Africa had a leg up on China, which needed more infrastructure. We hadn't seen many vehicles in China, and in its western half, roads hardly existed; but South Africa had roads, highways, telephone lines, electricity, and an adequate water system.

All this infrastructure existed because Cecil Rhodes and a few other fellows had stumbled upon diamonds and gold. If these fellows had stumbled on diamonds and gold in such profusion in Zaire, Zaire would have become an economic powerhouse. It wasn't just that Cecil Rhodes had exploited the blacks. He and his crew did, of course—they used cheap labor whenever they could. The real point was that the discovery of diamonds and gold forced capitalism to put in an infrastructure in order to get its profits out. This brought South Africa prosperity and gave it a base on which to build.

People forget that back in our nineteenth century it was hard-bitten capitalists like Commodore Vanderbilt and Jay Gould who not only became fabulously wealthy by laying railroad track but also built the infrastructure enabling America to make gigantic economic leaps. Cecil Rhodes did the same thing in South Africa. As another example of capitalism aiding infrastructure, remember that wonderful paved road back in Niger as we came out of the Sahara? The reason it existed was because it was needed by a local uranium mine.

In Third World countries—in fact, everywhere—there is no better way to develop an infrastructure. If there are profits, somebody will put down roads and telephone lines.

No politically correct way exists to lay down an infrastructure. Many of us would like to think bureaucrats from the World Bank can sweep into a country and figure out precisely what needs to be built in order to have that country develop successfully. Unfortunately, their projects tend not to be located in the right place economically. Often these bureaucrats will build a bridge over a river, but unless there's some potential economic activity to exploit that bridge, it will not raise the region's prosperity. Running water may be brought to a village because it's good for the people, but that doesn't necessarily lead to prosperity. The place to put roads, telegraph lines, and water systems is near beehives of economic activity—mines, factories, and cities built by entrepreneurs willing to risk their capital to take out profits.

Is it likely a bureaucrat earning a secure seventy-five thousand dollars a year will make a better judgment of what will work economically than an entrepreneur about to risk his own money, reputation, and opportunity? I promise you the entrepreneur will give the question far more thought and will examine a hundred times more variables and problems than the bureaucrat will. The entrepreneur will make sure he can communicate with his investments, house his workers, and get his products out over a decent road.

When you look back at the United States, you see the ideal pattern. Until 1914, America was the largest debtor nation in the world. Entrepreneurs had borrowed a huge amount of money in the nineteenth century to develop our infrastructure. We built railroads, canals, cities, and factories.

Today, there is an immense hoopla—and correctly so—over our deficit. There's nothing wrong with being a debtor nation if you are putting the money into productive assets for the future, which is what we did in the nineteenth century. The Europeans sent their money to our country because they could make a lot of money off us. We got the payoff in the twentieth century, when we became the richest country in the world.

This could happen to Zaire, too. If Zaire attracted entrepreneurs who would truly develop the country, in time its economy would become immensely powerful. Unfortunately, back in the sixties and seventies Zaire had thrown out all the capitalists solely because they *were* capitalists and colonialists, or exploitative.

Economically, nineteenth-century America was like Africa or Siberia today. Then, of course, there were no currency controls, regulations, immigration policies, and visas. There were no United Nations' studies and task forces saying money should be sent here and there. If the opportunity looked good, capital, which was fluid and without inhibitions, took advantage of it. Like water running downhill, capital flowed to wherever the return was the highest.

Capital never cares whether you're black, white, Communist, socialist, Christian, or Muslim. All it cares about is its safety and its profit. It goes where the opportunities are. Capital is not concerned whether it impregnates Israel or Egypt, electronics or diamond mines.

With this in mind, the Russians could solve their problems quickly. Legalize private property, tax everyone modestly, and make their currency convertible, and their mess would straighten itself out in rapid order. Foreign capital would find that attractive.

In the sixties and seventies, the Communist countries—China, Albania, and that whole crowd—said, "No, we're going to do it on our own. We don't want any outside capital because then we'll be exploited like the Africans."

The Africans said the same thing, but they were all looking at the wrong model. In the nineteenth century, America borrowed huge sums of money and invested it wisely. We didn't buy furs for the dictator, we didn't buy cars for Mobutu. The money went into productive assets, and we got rich.

Thus, South Africa now has a leg up on every other place in Africa because of an infrastructure laid on by its "exploiters," its true developers—an infrastructure any future government and all future generations will be glad to have. In the West we hear that everything in South Africa would rapidly resolve itself if only the Europeans would leave so the real Africans could run South Africa. After traveling close to the ground through the black-run countries of Zaire, Nigeria, Cameroon, Niger, the Central African Republic, the Congo, Zambia, and Zimbabwe, I was certainly not convinced that this was any inevitable path to African prosperity and social justice.

I wondered who, in fact, were the real South Africans. In Johannesburg, the population was indeed black and white, but in Cape Town it was multicultural and multicolored. Two centuries before the English had arrived in the nineteenth century to mine gold and diamonds, European settlers called Afrikaners had settled the Cape of Good Hope, establishing Cape Town. Through a former student of mine we met Hannes Myburgh, the ninth generation of a Northern European family that had arrived on the Cape more than three hundred years before. His family, which owned the oldest vineyard in South Africa, had been in the Cape area longer than most every black's.

He invited us to have lunch at the vineyard, where we and his other guests sampled not only his wines but also a number of competitors'. It turned into an exuberant day that lasted long past lunch and ended in our dancing on the table. In fact, if it hadn't been for a yet more complicated dance that evening, which resulted in a fall and an injury to my back, that ten-hour lunch might still be going on.

A day in bed gave me time to reflect on who were the real South Africans. Those blacks we'd seen crowding borders north of here to enter South Africa were typical of the immigration that had taken place over the past century, black Africans from northern regions migrating south for mining and then industrial jobs.

The earliest inhabitants of South Africa were the Khoisan peoples, called Bushmen and Hottentots by the white colonizers. Not large in number, they lived across much of what we today call South Africa but were concentrated in the Cape peninsula.

In 1652, the Dutch East India Company established a rest stop at Cape Town for its trade to China, Indonesia, and India. Some Europeans spread out from the town to grow food for the settlers, called Boers, and to supply food for the company's ships, which provided the Boers with European consumer goods.

As long as two hundred and fifty years ago, South Africa, particularly the area around Cape Town, wasn't a black country; it was more of a melting pot than New York City is. Europeans pulled in here, particularly the Dutch, English, and Portuguese, as they rounded the Cape of Good Hope and headed to China and India. Naturally some stayed and settled. Chinese, Indonesian, and Indian traders heading west followed the same pattern. Many of these peoples intermarried.

"Go back?" one Indian shopkeeper said to me. "Where? I don't speak Hindi. My family's been here since the late seventeen hundreds. I speak only Afrikaans and English. I wouldn't have any idea where to go if things become impossible for me here."

Force this shopkeeper and Hannes to "go home" and they would no more know where to head than would 95 percent of Americans. The ancestors of these two had been on their continent far longer than most Americans have been on theirs.

Hannes was no longer European; he and my new Indian friend were both African.

The farther south we had gone in Africa, the more beautiful and prosperous Africa had become. At that time, of the sub-Saharan countries, I considered investing in only Cameroon, Zimbabwe, and Botswana.

Despite everything you have heard about boycotts, black Africa's trade with South Africa was booming. Even though Mobutu, the dictator of Zaire, was a leader of the boycott, we had bought South Africa's delectable wines throughout Zaire. South African products were available in every black country through which we had passed. These countries had wanted the boycott to continue so they could get there first and capture the South African market. For example, Zimbabwe's trade with South Africa had been doubling every year for at least five years.

Here's my bullish case for Africa: In the sixties, seventies, and eighties, the Soviets and the Americans had financed dozens of African regimes through the CIA and KGB. Today there are no more struggles with Communists or socialists, nor any money to finance them. The movement has died. Neither the Americans nor the Soviets are propping up guerrilla movements now.

As a result of their leaders dying or simply stepping aside, African governments are collapsing, their people rising. The continent's status quo and its borders are ripe for change, which will bring some strife. Any wars that might follow will be short, however, since there are few armaments to speak of on the continent and little will to fight. In the political reformation to come, the Africans will adopt either the Western model or the Chinese model, that is, one mouthing social and political platitudes but allowing every kind of vigorous free-market activity.

The borders in Africa are even now becoming rational. After years of war, Ethiopia and Eritrea have peacefully agreed on how to split into two countries. The border problems in the Sudan are working themselves out. Until we intervened, a similar process was happening in Somalia.

As African problems get cleaned up, the entrepreneurs who already exist throughout Africa will be freed to develop real economies. Africa has huge natural resources. The commodities markets are depressed now, but someday the world will be desperate for Africa's resources, especially as production in the former USSR falls apart. Zaire, for instance, is wonderfully fertile. Let a seed fall from your hand and it grows. Zaire used to export food, and it could again. Even Angola will bounce back. As for the future of South Africa, it all depends on how the political struggle plays out.

What I know for certain is that big fortunes will be made on the African continent in the next twenty-five years.

Without doubt I'll be back in a few years to make more extensive investments.

REPUBLICA DE GUATEMALA

112-600-0700-11-21-11-102 VISA

No. 1434/c-11 CLASE 450

PASAPORTE No. 110173171

FORMA 63-A No. -- — Q. --

PERMANENCIA EN EL PAIS 30 dias

EXPEDIDA POR Embaguate

EN San José

FECHA 10-10-91

BUENA PARA ENTRAR Y SALIR DE GUATEMALA, EN
VIAJES SUCESIVOS HASTA 9-10-94
SEGUN CONVENIO DE VISAS CON LOS E. U. A.
DEL 20.5.56 MODIFICADO EL 9.8.82

Juan Espinoza Farfán

PRIMER SECRETARIO
Y CONSUL

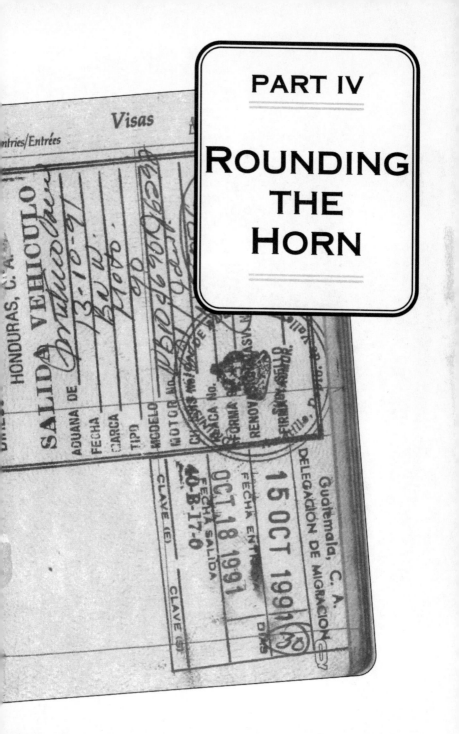

PART IV

ROUNDING THE HORN

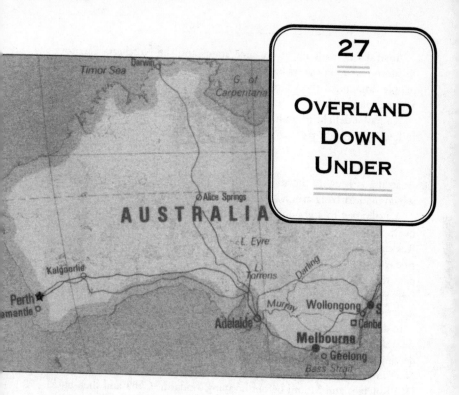

TABITHA'S GRANDFATHER had been a submariner in Western Australia during the Second World War. He befriended a young Australian family, and over the years he had stayed in touch. Now the husband, Francis Burt, was the governor-general of the state of Western Australia.

Not knowing what to expect, Tabitha called him when we arrived in Perth and explained that her grandmother had said she must look them up.

We were invited to dinner at the governor-general's mansion. She explained that we were on motorcycles and didn't have much in the way of fancy clothes, but this was waved away. We put on our best bibs and tuckers. Tabitha had brought along a pair of high heels and a single black silk dress for such occasions. I wore my leather jacket and boots, shined for the first time in months, put on a bow tie, and off we went.

The governor-general, we learned, was Queen Elizabeth's ceremonial representative here. He occupied a spot in the Western Australian government roughly equivalent to that of the queen in hers, a figurehead who cut ribbons and hosted state dinners.

Australia is made up of six such states and the Northern Territory. Western Australia covers half the country but contains only 1.6 million people. Imagine if the United States west of the Great Plains held only 1.6 million people.

We had a delightful dinner with Francis and his wife, Margaret. The following weekend we even witnessed the baptism of their grandchild.

Australia is roughly the size and shape of our lower forty-eight states, which made driving around three of its four borders a very long ride.

We planned to start out from Perth and ride along the western and northern coasts to Darwin. From there we would ride south to Ayers Rock and Alice Springs. After retracing our route back north, we would ride east to the Great Barrier Reef. We would then hit the east coast and pass through Brisbane, Sydney, and Melbourne, from which we would ferry over to Tasmania, then ride back to Sydney in order to fly to South America.

In distance, this was the equivalent of riding from Los Angeles to Seattle, taking a right turn and riding to the Minnesota-Canadian border, driving down to Tulsa and back up to Chicago. On to New York and the New England states, from which we would ride through Washington, DC, Raleigh, and Miami before hopping a boat to Cuba and then back to Atlanta.

Nine thousand miles of motorcycling.

Australian roads turned out to be different from those anywhere in the world, except perhaps Texas. For the most part the country is flat. The roads barreled forward for hundreds of miles without a curve. We put our rubber on the asphalt—the roads here were paved—and made terrific time.

The first time we went to pass a large truck we were taken aback. We were going around it—and going around it and going around it—until we realized it was a vehicle called a road train. Essentially, it was a tractor with three long trailers attached, each fifty to sixty feet long. Road trains shot down the highway because there was no reason not to, another example of mankind adapting to its circumstances. We had to goose up our motorcycles to get around them.

In Australia everybody lives along the coasts, inside of which is very little except desert. As we drove the long distances between towns there was nothing man-made—no gas stations, no houses, no mailboxes.

The vast distances of Australia were broken only by the occasional roadhouse offering gas, food, and beds, and the even less frequent towns. Every so often dead kangaroos and sheep appeared by the side of the road, victims of high-speed trucks and cars. The absolutely straight roads appeared surrealistic, pressing forward into the endless, empty, flat desert. It made me realize how much as travelers we expect a variety of scenery to sweep over us rather than to encounter the same scene without end.

We crossed Australia in a month and a half. Luckily we were there in the dry season, so we didn't have to worry too much about rain.

In the west, flash floods were a danger. We had seen photographs of stalled vehicles flooded out in the desert. Along the roads depth rods, four yards high, stood every mile or so to warn motorists how deep the water was during these floods. Later we saw these same rods as we crossed the Andes, warning of the depth of snow.

In the Sahara we sometimes covered as few as fifty or sixty miles a day. Here we had several days during which we covered seven hundred miles, our longest driving days on the entire trip, since there was little else to do but drive.

We were taking a trip the Australians themselves did not take. In the west we constantly met people who said, "I've never driven in the east. I'd love to go there." In the east people said, "I've never driven in the west." When you realized it is as big as the United States but mostly empty, you understood why.

Unlike the land mass of other continents, Australia has been stable, with few geological shifts to create mountains. The starkly beautiful landscape was interrupted only by salt lakes and infrequent protrusions, like Ayers Rock, the Olgas, and a few austere hills. In our Old West, a cow needed forty acres to survive; here, too, each kangaroo or sheep needed an enormous tract of grazing land.

The hours passed in a surreal experience of humming motor, paved road, red clay, and rocky scrub. One night Tabitha said she spent much of this driving time, which didn't require the concentration demanded by Africa, Siberia, and China, thinking back through much of her life, replaying her childhood, school, and college days in an effort to understand them better.

Tabitha and I began to talk about life after this trip, which seemed remote. We'd been away forever, and it seemed almost as if we would be away forever. Life when we got back? Well, yes, we wanted to refashion our lives, but neither of us was quite sure how it would work.

· · ·

We enjoyed stopping at the Australian roadhouses, perched on the never-ending, straight desert roads.

For hundreds of miles these were the only places a traveler could rest and resupply. A roadhouse sold gas, had a small restaurant and a convenience store, and let rooms, usually no more than eight to ten. Too remote to be whipped into any sort of conformity by competition, they had developed into crusty frontier hangouts, each individual and unique. An air about them encouraged the Australian passion for drink at any hour of the day. This was the first time I had ever been offered a beer for breakfast.

At night the travelers swapped stories and drank beer. Occasionally a few employees joined us, but the owner and his wife, understaffed like entrepreneurs everywhere, were usually too busy to sit down and talk.

The employees tended to be drifters. In one roadhouse, the staff was in revolt because the owner, going bankrupt, couldn't pay them. They were working there only long enough to get the money to move on to the next roadhouse.

I felt sorry for many roadhouse owners because their business was suffering. The road-train drivers, usually out in pairs, didn't stop at night. We guessed they swapped drivers and slept in the rear of their cabs.

This seemed to be a good time to buy roadhouses and develop a chain. I determined that their business was suffering because the price of oil had shot up as a result of the Gulf War and people weren't traveling. Buying Australian roadhouses in this slump would be an example of buying straw hats in winter. Whether for business or pleasure, travel is going to be a major trend in the world of the future. Those prepared to take advantage of it are going to reap fantastic profits.

Our tires made a satisfying sizzle against the asphalt as we reached sixty-five miles an hour. We'd just tanked up, the sun bore down, the road shot off straight before us, and we were ready for a three-hour run to the next roadhouse.

Pop! My bike wobbled between my legs. The engine had blown something, I guessed, and from its hard knocks and the way I couldn't steer properly, something major.

I pulled to the edge of the road. The bike lurched as I came to a stop. Ahead, Tabitha had slowed and looked back, wondering if I was adjusting my helmet or if something was wrong.

My back tire was flat. Examining it, I found I'd had my first blowout in twenty-five years of driving, a three-inch-long gash. The tire had become worn in its center, which I had also never seen on a motorcycle. Normally the wear is even, as motorcycles constantly bank on all surfaces of a tire, but there were few curves on these long, straight, flat, hot roads. As I assisted Tabitha in changing the tire we realized we had to examine our tires more frequently.

I'd always expected a blowout to be dangerous, but this happened at what for us was top speed and yet I'd had no difficulty in controlling the bike. I wondered what would have happened if the front tire had blown at high speed. I decided I'd be happy to wait another twenty-five years to find out.

We finally hit Darwin, a semi-Asian frontier town.

As Australia's northernmost city, the one nearest the Indonesian islands, it was striking how multicolored, multiracial, multiethnic, multieverything it was. People from all over Asia had crowded in here—Chinese, Koreans, Indonesians, Indians, and Pakistanis. In the street we heard a polyglot of languages, along with English spoken in peculiar ways.

A boomtown now, it would be one for a long time. As Australia opened up more, people would move into the frontier areas such as Darwin and Perth. It would become one of those world cities where a go-getter could strike figurative gold. People are always on the alert for where the gold is and rush to it. If a student asked me today where it would be over the next couple of decades and he insisted on speaking English, I'd send him to Darwin. I'd tell him to go into tourism or into any field having to do with trade between Asia and this crossroads.

Darwin's population had tripled in the past fifteen years. The entire Northern Territory was booming. Almost the size of Alaska, the Territory had great weather along with abundant natural beauty and touring sights. Though it was not heavily populated, immigrants were pouring in.

At this point Darwin wasn't connected to the country's railroad system, but this would certainly change in the future. The train came up from the south to Alice Springs and went down from Darwin a bit, but there was still a big gap. Once that was closed, Darwin would boom like crazy. From an economic point of view, it would be as important as the completion of the Trans-Continental Railroad had been for California.

To add to all this, just north was Papua New Guinea and Indonesia, both of which were exploding and dynamic. After all, Indonesia was the fourth largest country in the world in population. Indonesians were excellent businessmen, thriving in an old and crowded country. Here was a vast, empty country a few hundred miles south.

Australia is rich in natural resources. The world's largest industrial diamond mine was opened here only fifteen years ago. The country possesses an abundance of nickel, copper, undeveloped land, and water, as well as huge farms, huge ranches, huge everything. Throughout the history of Australia, whenever they've put in a dam or irrigation system, the entire area around it has blossomed with prosperity.

Here is another Siberia with abundant resources and another nearby China with abundant labor.

Decades from now, if and when the Indonesians become aggressive and militant about expanding their commercial operations, the natural place to look will not be north to crowded India and other countries with large populations, but south to Australia, where there is little population and a small army, nothing to impede them.

We set out south from Darwin toward Ayers Rock, which sits in the center of Australia.

The earth we traveled across was red dirt, a deeper, duller red than even the red clay of my native Alabama. Given the distance, Tabitha suggested we skip Ayers Rock because it was "just a rock in the middle of the desert."

She still talks about what a great mistake that would have been. It was another of those sights so awesome that photographs ought not be allowed. As we approached it on our motorcycles, it was startling. First there was a vast, flat plain, and then without warning a huge red monster that seemed to come alive was looming over us.

If not alive, Ayers Rock seemed to have a soul or be the home of spirits. Rising more than 1,100 feet from the flatness of the surrounding plain, the rock is the world's largest monolith. Even though it is two miles long, scientists say two thirds of it is buried beneath the sand. The exterior looks like the hide of a gigantic prehistoric animal. Up close, large holes like pockmarks dig into its surface. We drove around it on our bikes, and it kept shifting and changing reds in a way as fascinating as its size.

As the sun went down, the rock's surface became a darker and deeper red and finally became a ghostly gray.

At dawn the reverse happened. The rock's gray changed to a deep red and then to a lighter rust color. It didn't rain while we were there, but the pictures I've seen of it in the rain show it as a dark, almost black gray.

I certainly understood why the aborigines regarded it as a holy place, one haunted by powerful spirits.

Despite Australia's excellent roads, we never traveled at night. Travel by motorcycle isn't just the means to an end, but an end in itself. If we traveled at night, we wouldn't get what we'd come for, the thrill of enjoying new places by motorcycle.

Since safety is never a small issue on motorcycles, driving at night is far more hazardous than during the day. Seventy percent of motorcycle accidents are caused by cars. Over and over, car drivers say after they hit a motorcycle, "I never saw him." If they don't see you during the day, they certainly won't see you at night. At night, of course, people drink more. Other nighttime dangers were kangaroos, cows, potholes, gravel—everything.

Most important, if we were going to ride around the world once, we wanted to see it. Why go around the world on a motorcycle at night?

We loved Sydney, putting it on our list of cities in which we would like to live. My top three are New York, Buenos Aires, and Tokyo, followed by Sydney, Bangkok, and Rome.

Sydney was a dynamic capital, bursting with life and vitality, while Melbourne sported old money and old gentility, the difference between brassy New York and Boston's reserved tony demeanor.

When a traveler arrived in Perth, the joke went that people asked him, "Where are you from?" In Sydney they wanted to know how much money you made; in Brisbane, if you wanted a beer; and in Melbourne, what public (private) school you had attended.

About 30 percent of the people who live in Australia weren't born there. Huge waves of immigration have flowed over its shores, making it boom over the past twenty years. Yet it still had only 17 million people—a country the size of the United States with a population slightly larger than New York State's!

The Japanese had discovered Australia, too. We found Japanese clerks in every major store, hotel, and resort area. The marriage of Australia's natural resources with Japan is a natural, as is Australia's geographic location for tourists. You'll see Australia and Japan becoming yet closer in future years, as their long-term interests with each other are greater than those either has with the U.S.

Even with all this empty land, most people live in the cities. Twenty percent of Australians live in Sydney, and another 15 percent live in Melbourne. In nearby New Zealand, a third of the population live in Auckland. (If this percentage held true in the United States, New York City would have 85 million people.) The twentieth century's revolution in agriculture made this possible. In the nineteenth century, the technology did not exist to support such large urban populations.

We began to think now about our next hop, from Australia to South America.

It made no sense to worry about these hops much before we were ready to jump. First of all, we might not make it through the particular continent we were on, and certainly not on any schedule that could be relied on. Why flail around in Zimbabwe and say, "Hey, how are we going to get from Australia to South America?" when there was no one in Zimbabwe who could answer the question?

We would catch a flight on Aerolineas Argentinas. We would land in Río Gallegos and go from there to Tierra del Fuego, the tip of South America nearest the Antarctic, from which we would drive north.

The flight went once a week. The travel agent said that if we wanted to, he could arrange for us to stop for a week in New Zealand, then pick up the same flight the following week.

We jumped at the chance.

New Zealand is basically two islands, North Island and South Island.

If a traveler wants to drive in Australia and New Zealand but has time for only one, New Zealand is the country to choose because it is so compact and beautiful. For the sports-car driver, motorcyclist, or ordinary traveler with a yen for breathtaking scenery, snug New Zealand has sprawling Australia beat hands down. For a motorcyclist, New Zealand's roads are better because they wind and twist through exciting vistas and constant change. In Australia we often drove a thousand miles without change, days and days of breathtaking sameness.

New Zealand's pleasant climate and geographical features are similar to and as varied as California's. It's not a big country, but for sheer variety it's hard to beat. In addition to lush meadows and ominously smoking volcanoes, it has farmland, deserts, cities, bubbling-hot mud holes, geysers, icy glaciers, the ocean, sandy beaches, rugged coastline, and lots of mountains. The ancient South Pacific culture of the Maoris, who never developed writing, is expressed in elaborate carvings on war canoes and totem poles, which are on exhibit throughout the islands. Within a few hundred miles, visitors can fish, ski, and bungee-jump, as well as hike, scuba-dive, watch whales, and go white-water rafting. Planes and helicopters are plentiful, and visitors are offered "flightseeing" tours. Kiwis, as New Zealanders call themselves, love mazes, and construct gigantic ones out of hedges. They've even begun to export them, particularly to Japan, where the better New Zealand designers hire themselves out as consultants.

Being here was a bit like being on a honeymoon. New Zealanders are friendly, easygoing, and helpful. Tabitha and I both fell in love with this fresh, upbeat country and wanted to stay longer than our allotted week, but winter blew at our backs. We would be traveling across the Andes and Tierra del Fuego, a few hundred miles from the Antarctic, in June and July, the seasonal equivalent of driving across the Canadian Rockies in January. Every week we lost might throw us into the January and February of the South American/Canadian-type winter and might cost us six weeks of delay.

New Zealand is a country of 4 million people and 60 million sheep. After the lambs are born in the spring, the four-footed population often rises to 100 million. The country's economic history is written in the story of its sheep and wool. In the seventies, the Russians bought wool with hard currency as part of their effort to keep up their standard of living. The price of wool went through the roof. With the prosperity of the Middle East resulting from the oil boom, the Arabs indulged themselves in their taste for lamb. The price of mutton went through the roof, too. This continued into the eighties. As always happens when there's great demand, everybody piled into sheep. Shortly, there was too much mutton and too much wool.

Demand slackened off as the Russians ran out of steam and the Arabs could no longer sell their oil at high prices. The New Zealand government, wanting to keep the boom going and its voters happy, came up with a bright idea. Obviously this was only a "temporary dip" in the ravenous world appetite for lamb and wool. Any year now things would turn around. In the meantime, why should its citizens suffer?

The government set up a special board that said, "We'll buy all the wool you farmers produce to keep the price up."

As De Beers had done with diamonds, this board subsidized and stabilized a high price. The farmers, no fools, raised more sheep, produced more wool, and put it to the government. Over the years the board bought and bought with borrowed money till it finally couldn't take any more. Then the Russians ran out of money, and the Middle Eastern war killed its markets. Under a United Nations embargo, Iraq certainly wasn't ordering any lamb. Occupied by the Iraqis, Kuwait was out of the market, too.

It was unfortunate that the government had kept the price up for so long, because when this bear market came, prices had that much further to fall. Markets always go down much more than they should when someone has put a Band-Aid on the problem. That's what's happening in the United States now. The government has been putting Band-Aids on our financial situation for so many years that when the day of reckoning comes, it's going to be horrible.

In essence, the New Zealand government was borrowing money to buy sheep in order to finance its farmers' lifestyle. In America we've borrowed money to build armaments and hand out transfer payments and entitlements. If we borrowed to invest in highways, railways, factories, and telephone systems, that would be one thing. But to borrow to keep up the price of wool so farmers can buy TVs, that is quite another.

Of course, from the politicians' point of view, what was being bought were votes. The merchants who sold the farmers their TVs didn't have to suffer, either, nor did the fellows who sold them automobiles, repaired their TVs, or outfitted them in designer clothes. While it lasted, it was wonderful. Plato, Jefferson, and De Tocqueville, among other political writers, warned of this supreme danger of democracy, that politicians will sell the nation's birthright for a mess of votes.

Now some people might say, "Wait a minute, don't we have warehouses full of wool? Isn't the wool ultimately valuable?" But I say if you put the money into a road, when everything is said and done, you have the road, which can increase productivity. There's a vast difference between creating a cartel to support the price of an expendable item and building up a country's infrastructure. The economic history of the world is full of cartels that attempted to support a price and failed.

Anyone who buys mammoth amounts of a product with the idea that he can keep up the price is doomed to fail. It's one of the oldest and soundest rules in economics: You can control the price, you can control the supply, but you can never control both for long.

As an example, think of OPEC. OPEC tried to control the price of oil, but after a time the entire mechanism collapsed under the weight of greater supply brought on by high prices. In another example, the Malaysians almost went bankrupt supporting the price of tin.

Part of New Zealand's problem was that in the seventies and eighties the socialists were running the country. They borrowed to keep the workers and farmers happy—doing what good socialists ought to do. Better to keep employment up than build for the future.

New Zealand's finances got so bad that the voters threw the socialists out and hired the conservatives again. What I mean by "bad" is very high inflation, very high interest rates, and very high unemployment, since nobody was buying anything because prices were so high. The currency had become so weak, nobody could afford to import the foreign goods a small, isolated country like New Zealand desperately needed, since no transistors or automobiles were made there. Voters came to realize loans were expensive, inflation was way up, and they couldn't buy Sony TV sets or Japanese cars. Nobody could get a job, either. They became furious with the socialist government.

Then came one of the more extraordinary stories of the relationship between a people and its central bank. At the beginning of the decade the new conservative government went to the bank and made a contract with it, a written contract which specified that it, the government, could not abrogate the contract. The government officials saw that if they simply passed a law or replaced the governor of the bank, such measures could be changed. They insisted on something more permanent.

This contract said the central bank had to get the rate of inflation down to less than 2 percent and keep it there. "You central bank fellows do whatever you have to do. We government fellows will do our part, but in case we don't, you still have to do your part because we're politicians and can't be trusted."

The Tories said this because they had the sense to know they were politicians. They were afraid the political will of the country would shift and they would be stuck back where they had started.

Lo and behold, the central bank did its job and got the inflation rate down; and it has kept it under 2 percent ever since.

As we rode through New Zealand, I couldn't help noticing all the sheep. I got out commodity charts and checked the price of wool to scrutinize what had happened. Sure enough, here the big collapse was laid out in graphic form.

At the same time, all around me I saw a hardworking labor force. They, like everybody else, were grateful for a handout, but they were far away from the centers of the world and knew nobody was going to take care of them. Even though they had been cradled in a welfare state for more than a decade, the basic New Zealand personality was rural and self-reliant.

I took a look at the New Zealand stock market. I was aware it had been one of the worst, if not the worst, performing major stock market in the world during the past decade. Of course, I recalled the worldwide commodities boom of the seventies and eighties. New Zealand had absolutely nothing but natural resources: wool, sheep, and other agricultural products, so it had been one of the biggest beneficiaries of the boom. When it ended, however, it had gone in the tank first. Simple economics would tell you this had to be the worst-hit developed economy in the world because it had nothing else besides agriculture, and it was marginal in the first place. The smart money knew that the boom had come to an end and put its money somewhere else. So there were sound and understandable reasons why New Zealand had been the world's worst performing stock market during the past ten to fifteen years.

That whetted my appetite. First I saw a depressed area of investment, the stock market. Then I saw a depressed country, because of the nature of its economy and bad public policies vis-à-vis wool, sheep, and other agriculture products. Then I saw a government that was doing all the right things to strengthen its currency and make its economy strong. The New Zealanders had come to know that they had to do the right things because they didn't have any choice. Otherwise, their currency was going to disappear the way currency had in many African countries, and they were going to suffer as horribly.

It was obvious that I had to invest in their stock market. I opened an account and put in some money.

As usual, I worked through the country's largest broker. I wasn't too worried about the risk of bankruptcy with a company of this stature. If the broker looked as if he were about to go under, the government was likely to take the company over or force it into a merger.

I opened a small account first to make sure there were no hitches. I worry about having the wrong account number on the paperwork or my money getting lost in the transoceanic netherworld through which international cables are laid. First of all, I want to see the system work properly.

Outside of my normal reading of the world press, I had not done any special study of New Zealand, but being here told me a lot. In the broker's office I looked through various books about the market, including its stock-market annual. I looked back to see what had happened in the country during the past ten or fifteen years, the basic facts, including the balance of payments and an overview of the country's economic situation.

I wanted to make a direct investment in wool in New Zealand, but if I bought wool futures, I'd have to worry they would expire sometime or that I might get a margin call. So I tried to buy a seat on the wool exchange. Whenever there's a savage bear market, the seats on the exchange—whether for stocks, sugar, gold, or bonds—become seriously depressed. The best way to invest in a depressed market is to buy a seat on the exchange and forget it. Frequently there's not even maintenance to pay.

Unfortunately, the futures exchange down here was all-in-one. If you bought a seat on the wool exchange you were buying a seat on the entire futures trading market. That wasn't what I wanted. I wanted a pure play in wool and lamb, but I couldn't get it with a seat.

Another reason I liked having an account in New Zealand was that it gave me a presence on the Pacific Rim. These were the first markets to open in the day because of their time zone. Sometimes I wanted to put on a trade in the middle of the night and I might mind waiting until Europe or Tokyo opened. New Zealand came first to the extent that anything opened "first" these days.

How might I use this? Say on Saturday afternoon I came to believe the dollar was going to cave in on Monday morning, that it was all over for the dollar. Well, I could short the dollar in New Zealand long before the markets opened in Asia, Europe, and New York. I could buy gold. If I thought the stock markets of the world were going to collapse Monday morning, here was where I could sell first, because it was going to be the first one open. If I thought there was going to be a big boom for some reason, again here was where the first market opened. In fact, Monday morning in New Zealand is still Sunday afternoon in New York.

The New Zealand stock market had a few hundred choices. I picked out twenty, each in agriculture and raw materials and each with a strong balance sheet. While I was at it, I put a smaller bit into Australian agriculture, too. I looked for companies that would survive in case I was wrong about when to jump into this market, and the country's hard times weren't over.

28

THE UTTERMOST END OF THE WORLD

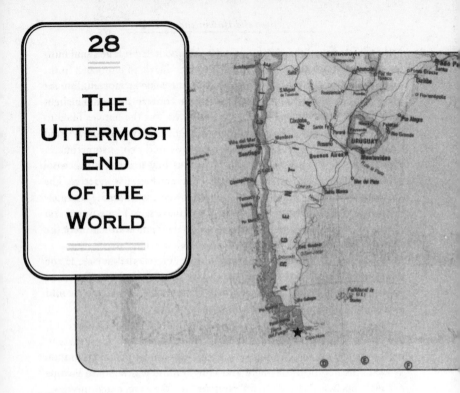

I N MANY WAYS I was still a starstruck kid from a tiny town in Alabama, agog at the sights and the strangeness of the great world through which we passed. To ride across the Strait of Magellan! To roar across Tierra del Fuego! For most of my life these had been only exotic names on maps, and now I was within hailing distance of Magellan's historic route.

Much less frigid in winter than we'd expected, Tierra del Fuego is mainly flat, windswept, and lovely. It is occupied by sheep, geese, a few people, and guanaco, a llamalike animal.

To attract people to visit and settle, the island was duty-free. Indeed, the Argentine government encouraged people to move into all the regions below Buenos Aires. Although it is a huge country, eighth largest in the world, a third of its people live in the capital city.

Tierra del Fuego's largest city, Ushuaia, is the southernmost city in the world. The city certainly needed to provide all the incentive that could be dreamed up to attract settlers. A bank manager told me the area needed hotel and fishing development. Empty stores and half-built lots said business wasn't doing as well as it might.

At this time of the year, June, sunup was at ten in the morning, sunset at four in the afternoon, providing us with short driving times. The light down here at the "Uttermost End of the World," as the natives liked to call it, was an ever-changing source of wonder, otherworldly, pale, and bleak.

Tourism will boom here. The scenery is breathtaking. Fabulous cross-country skiing could easily develop. The king crabs were wonderful. The town provided one of the few ways to get to Antarctica, which I was convinced was about to become a great tourist site. Just as Tamanrasset, on the edge of the Sahara, had boomed because travelers wanted to see the desert, Ushuaia would boom, too, as they visited Antarctica.

Ushuaia might have a small population, but I felt the rumble of the coming boom. I was tempted to buy land.

After all, the town had just come by its first real estate agents—could big growth be far behind?

We took a boat out. On both sides of the choppy water steep craggy mountains rose, giving the Beagle Channel a haunted feel. Rocky islands were scattered about, one covered with cormorants, another with seals.

Young seal bucks put on a diving show around us, bobbing, weaving, and torpedoing. On the rocks the seal social hierarchy was on full display, a king on top challenged by another big seal, while below younger males challenged each other. Farther away, other, older seals had opted out and weren't bothering to contest the pecking order.

Was there a lesson here?

We were on the home stretch of our trip now. We'd been away from New York for fifteen months. My odometer, recorded in my notebook each morning before we left the hotel or campsite, had logged forty-three thousand miles. I figured we had another twenty thousand to go.

I was very much looking forward to seeing South America. I knew Chile was booming, an economic miracle, and I wanted to see the effect it was having on other South American countries. My take on the continent was that it was coming out of a seventy-year bear market and was poised for a continent-wide economic boom.

Even though we were near Chile there was no decent road north to Santiago, its capital. The only paved road north was up Argentina's coast to Buenos Aires. Since no one here had any clear idea of how to drive to Central America beyond following the Pan-American Highway, we decided to wait till we reached Buenos Aires to gather more intelligence.

We headed north to Buenos Aires over the pampas, plains differently colored and textured than those anywhere else in the world. Prairie hares bounded around us, and eagles soared overhead. Wild ostriches, smaller than the African variety and gray with white-trimmed skirts that fluttered, hopped across the plains.

At Lake Argentina the sight of dozens of pink flamingos stopped us. The drive around the lake was a wonderful motorcycle ride, mountains to one side, the vast lake on the other. The forest and boulder-strewn terrain appeared primeval and spectral, the tangled moss and grotesquely shaped trees and rocks seemingly drawn into monsters by the magnetic attraction of the nearby South Pole.

A huge, bluish mass appeared at the water's edge on the horizon. Over the next five to ten miles its color deepened and the object grew larger as we drew closer.

It was the Moreno glacier, one hundred and fifty miles long, one of the few in the world still moving. The air filled with groans and loud cracks that grew into rifle shots and booming explosions. The glacier became compressed as it pushed between two mountains, then spread again and broke up. When it finally met Lake Argentina, the glacier's front was a 160-foot-high wall of ice that had taken hundreds of years to inch its way down out of the Andes. Its path cut the lake in two, like a moving dam. Occasionally large pieces cracked off and plunged into the blue water, creating blue-tinged icebergs and sending waves to thunder against the shore.

Once this moving ice dam had cut the lake in two, every three or four years it burst under the immense water pressure behind it and collapsed in a spectacular scene lasting several hours. This created a remarkable sight few had ever witnessed because it was so unpredictable and sometimes happened at night. With collapse, the seven-hundred-year-old ice melted back into the blue lake, evaporated into the air, fell again as snow, and became glacier all over again.

Considering how remarkable all this was, I was surprised at the meagerness of the tourist promotion. The southern tip of South America is remote, but so are lots of popular places. Part of this doubtless was due to Argentina's insularity, which was changing as the country opened itself again to the larger world.

The glacier presented someone with a great opportunity to become rich. All that was needed was an airport so people could fly down from Buenos Aires. Foreigners could fly into Argentina, go to Iguaçu Falls in the north, visit the glacier next, and later sail to Antarctica, all stellar attractions. A similar tourist boom had happened to the Galápagos. An airport was built, now thousands flocked there, and vast fortunes had been made. The town nearby, Calafate, is just sitting there waiting for the same thing to happen.

We made friends with a sheep farmer and rode along behind his battered pickup. Most farmers here were in dire straits. His Ford truck was eleven years old, but he couldn't afford to buy a new one anytime soon.

We went out to the sheep farm of the Rudds, our new friends. The family had come from the Falklands more than a hundred years before and obtained land grants. As in our Old West, the Argentine government gave away land to entice settlers into taming the frontier.

The size of acreage here was like that of Texas. The Rudds leased out to others a couple of fifty-thousand-acre spreads. Their land was a bit marginal, as each sheep needed ten acres to graze, but the Rudds were nevertheless working the farm in these hard times after many others had closed up.

The Argentine government still owned much of the nation's land, especially down here. To become a landowner, a citizen proposed a project to the government and executed it—built a house, say. After four years and lots of red tape he owned the land at a low price.

The Rudds' grandfather had owned 750,000 acres here, but the grandchildren had broken up the station, as ranches are called here and in Australia. Back in the grandfather's time, around 1900, Argentina had been richer than the United States. Today we say someone is as rich as a Texan, an Arab, or a Japanese; in Europe before World War I the expression had been "as rich as an Argentine." The Rudds' grandfather had been one of the wealthy ones.

How it happened is a lesson in technology and being in the right place at the right time. In the sixteenth and seventeenth centuries the Spanish mainly settled in Mexico, Peru, Bolivia, Ecuador, and Colombia. Argentina had been no more than a vast, lightly developed territory of plains, without gold and without interest. Many of the cows and horses the Spanish had brought over escaped and went wild. Without natural predators—there were no wolves or lions in Argentina—they multiplied and became good-sized herds.

Over the years, these cattle were chased down by Argentine riffraff called gauchos, who had to become great horsemen if they wanted a beefsteak. As there were few people in Argentina, the market for the meat they killed was small, so the herds kept expanding. In Europe, where there were no large plains, beef was a much desired delicacy, yet no matter how good a horseman a gaucho was, he couldn't drive a herd to Paris.

In the late nineteenth century, refrigerated transoceanic ships were developed. All of a sudden Argentine cows became unbelievably valuable.

Whoever was in the pampas, whoever was horseman enough to ride down wild beefsteak, became rich. As in Texas, huge ranches were developed. The successful gauchos transformed themselves from riffraff into wealthy ranchers.

At that time the United States did not have many cattle. We jumped into the European market, but the Argentines had the stock, left over from the Spanish strays. Vast numbers of immigrants flooded into both countries. It was a toss-up in Europe whether the North or the South American plains would make you more prosperous.

These things sometimes take a while to clarify. It wasn't until later in the twentieth century that it was clear that Argentina was the wrong choice. When entrepreneurs around the globe realized how lucrative the cattle business was, many jumped in—Americans, Australians, and Africans. Losing its easy money, the Argentinian government sought to compensate with protective tariffs, regulations, and exchange controls, all of which compounded its ever-worsening economy. As in New Zealand during the eighties, during the twenties, thirties, and forties the Argentinian economy spiraled downward. The government borrowed to maintain living standards in the short run, and debt accumulated. Perón, Argentina's man on a white horse, promised easy prosperity and completed the destruction of the economy.

Meanwhile America was building factories. Argentina had had it too easy, had hit the gold mine too quickly. They didn't need to invest for the future because they were so rich. They chose Band-Aids to cover their wounds rather than the surgery needed to correct deep-seated cancers. Decades of suffering followed.

. . .

We'd had so much fun viewing the seals off Tierra del Fuego, we hired a boat to take us off Península Valdés.

July was the best time to visit whales here. Not only was the rest of the year too windy, but this was the mating season. There were few travelers since it was winter. At one point our boat was surrounded by a dozen right whales, most of which were so busy copulating they paid no attention to us. We might have been flies to humans similarly engaged. The boat maneuvered so close, we could reach out and touch their slick hides.

These were called right whales by old-time whalers because they had the right oil, the right bones, the right blubber, the right everything. They came here every year to mate, and as usual each female had captured the attention of three or four males.

Our guide pointed out two females on their backs, floating within a few yards of our boat. This was a female's signal to the boys she'd had it for the moment, to leave her alone.

We hiked down to a beachful of male sea elephants, resting and fattening up for the return of their females in August. When the females arrived and mating season began, the males had to stay on land to guard their harems from marauding woman-stealers. This meant for several weeks they couldn't go fishing or eat, thus the rationale for fattening themselves up. We walked among them, huge, great sausages laid out in the sun.

This peninsula teemed with animals. Another beach was full of sea lions sleeping, fighting, swimming, and squawking. We came across an injured penguin in from the ocean; a mara, a large rodentlike rabbit; sea elephants; burrowing owls; sheep; dogs; cows; pink-breasted thrushes; upland geese; and Antarctic pigeons.

The days lengthened rapidly. We drove up the Argentine coast toward Buenos Aires through a countryside with few people. The roads were long and straight through the broad, empty pampas. For an entire day we didn't see a single tree. These vast plains certainly contained abundant room for development.

It was true, Argentineans ate more red meat per person than any other people in the world. Every little town had a big barbecue place, or, I suppose, grill, and in the cities there were scores of them. With the mixed grill they served blood sausages, cases crammed with baked blood and spices, which I found surprisingly tasty.

Argentina will become a tourist's paradise. Along with dozens of exotic animals, it has mountains, beaches, deserts, the Antarctic, skiing, hunting, the vast, wild pampas, and horseback riding—everything a traveler could want. Up north is extraordinary colonial Spanish architecture as well as the wonder of Iguaçu Falls. Now that the government is stable and has gotten rid of the military, or at least calmed them down and stopped the atrocities of the seventies and eighties, real development can take place.

While our bikes were being repaired in Buenos Aires, Tabitha and I flew up to Iguaçu Falls in the north, one of the world's ten largest waterfalls.

Located on the Iguaçu River where Paraguay, Brazil, and Argentina come together, the falls were breathtaking: a 300-foot drop that pounds the water below so hard it constantly produces a giant rainbow in its cloud of spray. Like Victoria Falls, Iguaçu Falls make Niagara look minor. Hundreds of years before being stumbled upon by Don Alvar Nuñes in 1541, the falls were a sacred burial place for South American tribes.

From the precipice over the Devil's Throat, the falls roared below, drenching us with mist. Rainbows arched over the water, while parrots and hawks cruised over the deep green jungle. Swifts dropped like stones into the mist to spear insects.

All this made us feel a bit embarrassed by Niagara Falls, our continent's answer to these falls. I first figured that somebody had done a great PR job up there, but then I realized Niagara's reputation was the result of another of those historical tides that come and go.

The northern part of the U.S. was a great boom area in the later part of the nineteenth century—a time when the railroads, not the airlines, gave definition to the word *mobility*. The newly prosperous wanted to see new things, and the railroads had seats to fill. Voilà!

Niagara Falls were certainly stupendous, if that was all you knew, so a self-reinforcing process started. The railroads hyped the falls to fill seats, inexperienced travelers were impressed easily, and the cycle had begun. Stunts and more press followed until Niagara Falls had become—*Niagara Falls!*

But like most things, the market became saturated, the falls even déclassé. Transportation technology advanced, allowing travelers to fly ever farther afield.

Niagara does have one superior feature that the world's great waterfalls cannot match, but it doesn't do much for the tourist trade. During January and February, Niagara freezes and produces the most extraordinary ice formations that one can visit. You won't find ice sculptures at

Iguaçu Falls ever, but how many people want to go to Buffalo in February?

Twenty miles away on the Rio Paraná is the world's largest hydroelectric plant, Itaipu, and a frontier city, Ciudad del Este, or "City of the East." It is a real boomtown, booming because of the tens of billions of dollars spent to build the dam. Nearby Foz do Iguaçu grew from 35,000 inhabitants to 150,000 as the dam was built. Here is a perfect example of an infrastructure laid down by entrepreneurs to construct the dam, and now available to service travelers and any industry that can take advantage of it.

Itaipu means "singing rock" in a native dialect. Built as a joint project by Brazil and Paraguay, it is powered by the Paraná River, which divides the two countries. Financed by World Bank debt, the $25 billion dam is five miles wide and eighty yards high. Recently completed, it had taken seventeen years to build. The last generator had just come on stream, and now the dam produced 12,600 megawatts. Egypt's Aswân Dam is puny compared with it, and our own Hoover Dam isn't even in the running.

Tabitha thought visiting the dam would be a waste of time, but since I'd read about it in the press for a couple of decades, I was eager to see it. It is as stunning as any man-made thing I've ever seen, and I include in this assessment the Taj Mahal, India's Ellora caves, Easter Island, Machu Picchu, and Tikal. It is an engineering marvel, a most extraordinary product of mankind's capacity to build. In addition to its size, it contains entire cities for workers and supervisors, including self-service elevators and an intricate latticework of interior catwalks and crossways. As at Ellora, everything had been planned and then carefully put together over a period of a couple of decades. It is a wonder of the modern world.

Tabitha was impressed, but still not as impressed as I was. Although the guidebooks barely mentioned the site, I cannot recommend it enough for those with the turn of mind to appreciate the beauty and imagination of such a monumental human accomplishment.

The political situation engendered by the dam was interesting, too. Paraguay, with only 4.5 million people, owned the dam fifty-fifty with Brazil, which had a population of 155 million. Naturally, the Paraguayans couldn't use all of their half of the electricity, so they had sold 90 percent of theirs to the Brazilians for hard currency. With this infusion of hard cash, the Paraguayans were retiring their foreign debts.

Someday they will be sitting very, very pretty. With a great balance sheet, they will be able fully to develop their country.

I did see a political problem that could arise in twenty years. When their economy was grown, the Paraguayans might well want their electricity back. Rather than surrender its vital supply, Brazil would likely come up with a ruse to invade its smaller neighbor, or "renegotiate" the treaty. A treaty infraction would develop or a national slight would occur to justify such an invasion or renegotiation, and there wouldn't be much tiny Paraguay could do.

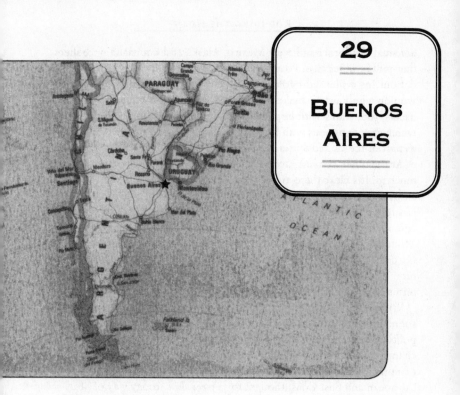

W ITH THE WINTER largely south of us, we decided to stop for a
few weeks in Buenos Aires, which became one of our favorite
cities, full of energy and bustle, nightlife and street activity. Here restaurants didn't start filling up till nine at night, and even people accompanied by their children came in at eleven. The days were back to regular
length, and the climate was mild. Buenos Aires was about the same distance from the equator as Charleston, South Carolina.

We decided to take Spanish lessons. I had always thought Spanish
would be one of the languages of the twenty-first century. Ever since I'd
quit working so hard, I'd had it in the back of my mind to come to Latin
America for six months to learn the language.

Why will Spanish be so important? There are two major languages in
the western hemisphere, English and Spanish. Chinese will also be
important to the world, but China is a long way from the Americas.

In the next century, as the South American countries become more vigorous and richer, and as our own geographic area becomes less dynamic
and poorer, a Spanish separatist movement will develop. There will be
political and historic justification for its arguments, because after all we

did steal California and New Mexico. Alaska and Louisiana we bought, but not the other two. People have long, long memories for such depredations, as evidenced by Poland, the Ukraine, Russia, and Hungary. It wouldn't be hard to make a case that we stole Florida, Arizona, and Texas, too, states with large Hispanic populations, and the last two of which are contiguous with Mexico. In the end, half of Mexico wound up as part of the United States.

At the other extreme are the Yukon and Alaska—the northern end of our trip. It's clear these areas, too, are ripe for future change. I am not surprised to discover that some U.S. and Canadian visionaries want to create a separate nation out of their part of the world, a country to be composed of Alaska, British Columbia, Alberta, Washington State, Montana, Oregon, and Idaho. They propose to call their new nation Cascadia. Geographically it would be larger than the European Community. This region now ranks as the world's tenth largest economy in terms of its annual gross domestic product, with $250 billion in sales.

Will these two provinces and five states secede? Probably not, or not soon. This is more a growing regional identity rather than an ambitious politician's grand design. This is a grassroots revolution, the product of a changing world, a new way for the region to see itself. Cascadia is a state of mind, one in which its inhabitants are throwing off the shackles of European and East Coast thought for a freer, less stodgy way of life.

In the twenty-first century, with every people yearning for more control over their lives, the world will be full of new regions like Cascadia.

Splits and recombinations of nations will be a historical theme of the next fifty years. In addition to Canada splitting into three parts, I expect India to split into three, too, probably Hindu, Muslim, and Punjab; Italy to divide into North Italy and South Italy; and Brazil into North and South Brazil.

After seventy years of mismanagement, the countries of Latin America are finally getting rid of the old practices that destroyed their economies, except for legalizing what are now illicit drugs. If and when they do that, the continent will become even more dynamic.

Latinos in the United States will say to us, "Historically, this land is ours. You took it by force of arms, and we want it back. You're discriminating against our people. Our people no longer want to be with you because you're a bankrupt country. They want to be back with us; we're prosperous." The familiar provocations that produce war will reoccur and intensify.

People have different goals. If our goal is to keep this country together as one, it's a huge mistake to educate immigrant kids solely in their parents' language instead of English. It only breeds separatism, which worldwide is a leading cause of strife. If our goal is to bring along kids in the language in which their parents are the most comfortable, then by all means teach them in Spanish, Chinese, and Urdu. If the overall goal is to make whatever political entity we're talking about survive and be dynamic and successful, then we need everybody to speak the same language. In a country like the United States, a melting pot of many immigrant groups, a common language is the only thread connecting all of us. Multiculturalism—the philosophical, political, and pedagogical movement—will lead to the destruction of the United States as its borders are drawn today. All you have to do is look at what the French-speaking people are doing to Canada's unity.

In the past twenty years a malaise has crept over America. Everybody here knows there's something wrong. Most Americans don't know quite what it is, but they know their standard of living has not become better. Average real American wages haven't gone up for twenty years, largely because so much money has gone into nonproductive uses, into consumption, which has led to gigantic debt, which has led to the twenty-year decline of our currency.

All this will become worse, much worse, and will feed the separatists. Nobody's plotted, infiltrated our society, and corrupted it. We have handed over our birthright.

Nobody has said, "Okay, what we're going to do now is make all our kids fluent in Spanish by teaching them only that in school, forcing them to identify with our Latin culture. We'll have Spanish neighborhoods, Spanish athletic teams, and Spanish newspapers, radio stations, and TVs. We'll wait thirty or forty years till hard times come. Then we'll develop a separatist movement, pull away, and destroy the United States."

That's the way it's going to work, although the scheme won't be consciously plotted. Through multiculturalism, we will have given it to them. Our politicians, ever seeking votes in the short term, will have sold our destiny.

We're pandering to everybody. In California you can get a ballot in any language you want. In its last election there were a handful of ballots cast in Eskimo. There are always a hundred amendments on the California ballot, so somebody had to sit down and translate all that complicated prose into Russian, Eskimo, Vietnamese, Urdu, whatever anyone asked for.

Americans have been spoiled by the past hundred years, and spoiled by our special, one-time dominance over countries like Japan and Germany during the first few decades after World War II. We think we are exempt from universal laws, but we are not. People who think they are exempt from universal laws have a moral disease called hubris, frequently fatal.

I am not trying to be clever or outrageous; this is simply history, the way the world has been ever since we've been recording it. Separatism is a fact of history at all times of economic distress. Most people will maneuver to maximize their economic lives, always have and always will, and in the process new societies and structures will be established. Sooner or later political structures around them must shift to deal with the change.

Americans find it hard to believe that such laws apply to their country, that even their borders can change. They shouldn't. Borders and governments move to follow economic interests, which shift constantly, as Adam Smith, Marx, and Keynes all noted; then come religious, ethnic, and linguistic reasons. There is no border in the world that has lasted centuries, much less forever. With our short-term myopia, we think it's different this time.

For example, an investor will say, "This stock has a lock on the market—a monopoly—it will grow at twenty-five percent a year forever."

I ask, "What about high returns on equity bringing in competition or substitution?"

"Yes, that was true for IBM and Penn Central and oil, but this time it's different because of [its patents, its management, its market position . . .]"—you fill in the blank.

Well, in the laws of economics, in the laws of history, in the laws of politics, and in the laws of society, it's *never* different this time. The law of gravity isn't ever suspended for someone's convenience, and these laws are just as rigorous, though more subtle and complex. If they weren't universals, we wouldn't call them laws.

"Oh, come on!" I hear all the time. "This is *America*. It's different here."

I wish it were, but unfortunately, it's never different anywhere, never different anytime. Every piper has to be paid. Fall off a cliff, and no matter whether you're Spanish, Argentine, Chinese, or American, gravity still operates, no different from any other time.

. . .

We enrolled in Spanish classes. Tabitha had a far better facility for languages than I. I am lazy, dyslexic, brain-dead, or grew up tone-deaf—who knows? Equally important, I was diverted by a lot of other things. It was that motorcycle-mechanic's school back in New York all over again. I didn't have time to go to classes as much because I was worrying about the stock market as well as the endless details of the trip.

Now that I could make telephone calls easily—Siberia and Africa had been hopeless—I was constantly talking to New York, buying new bonds because the old ones had matured, or moving money to Europe. We needed spare parts and chart books, so I called Judd in the New York office and had them flown in.

I decided to invest more in the New Zealand stock market. I sent Judd a check to record and send on to the brokerage. Despite my following up daily, the check never arrived in New Zealand. I debated whether to wait a few more days or cancel it and rewrite it. My hands were too full for intensive Spanish classes.

Tabitha, on the other hand, studied six or seven hours a day and lapped it up. Her French was good, so she made amazing progress.

I was investigating the Argentine stock market, visiting the president of the exchange, brokers, finance ministers, and lawyers, trying to dope out whether it was a market worth investing in. I sensed that here was a country that was beginning to realize, after decades of failure at trying, that the state had limited powers to make prosperity happen. The newspapers said the new president and the new finance minister were determined to change the face of Perónism, which had nationalized everything, as the Labour Party in England had. Perón, of course, had promised "the shirtless ones" that the government was going to buy the important industries and businesses and save the people, guarantee them jobs, provide for them. He printed money, put on regulations, guaranteed jobs, and protected the economy. A free lunch, if you will, not to speak of breakfast, dinner, and afternoon tea.

You don't have to be too knowledgeable about finance and politics to know such statist policies ruined the economy. It led Argentina into a long-term downward spiral. I wish politicians could order economies to create and protect jobs and make money grow on trees, but unfortunately the world doesn't work that way. It didn't work for King Canute to order the ocean to roll back, and it doesn't work for a politician to protect jobs and an economy from the world's ceaseless change. Perhaps it will work for a short time—until the next elections, say—but never long-term.

In the late eighties the Argentines had bouts of 20,000 percent inflation. The currency collapsed. If Americans think a mountain of debt is hard to live with, wait till they go through a collapsing currency. Just read about Argentina, Zaire, Russia, and Germany during hyperinflation. If something's not done, and done quickly, the same thing is likely to happen in the United States.

Argentina suffered during the Great Depression. Unlike many countries, however, World War II didn't bail it out. Juan Perón offered to save his people, who were not as rich and glorious as they used to be. Which is probably what will happen in the U.S., too. Somebody will come along and "save" us, another Roosevelt, another false savior who will gather all the votes. Our mythology says Roosevelt saved America, but most don't realize that in 1940 unemployment here was still 16 percent, a situation that wasn't corrected until World War II broke out.

Not only was the former Argentine political establishment discredited, but so were the generals. If the military launched a coup in Argentina today it wouldn't be successful because the people wouldn't allow it.

I liked what I saw. The country seemed to have learned its lesson. The public had learned what we in the States have yet to learn, that even if the government hands it to you there is no free lunch, that everything has to be paid for, now or eventually.

Now interested in investing here, I asked these officials if they thought the government or the country would go back to the old ways.

"I can understand why you're so suspicious," said one. "Nobody knows for sure if the government means it this time—we've heard a lot of this before. But every time in the past when they put on currency controls, you could always go down to the corner and change your money." He meant, of course, on the thriving black market.

"We might be talking about a lot of money."

"You aren't the first person who's needed to get a lot of money out of Argentina. We've been doing it for decades. I won't help you, but dozens will." In other words, he was letting me know my capital wouldn't be trapped even if things went wrong again.

I was convinced. The government had announced it was targeting three industries for growth—telecommunications, tourism, and mining—all three of which made sense for Argentina's development. Argentina would ease taxes on these three, which, without any investment or micromanagement on the part of the government, would cause them to boom. Mining had been woefully underdeveloped because in Argentina a landowner didn't own the mineral rights to his own land. All those people on cattle stations of 750,000 acres could not drill for oil or dig for gold or diamonds because they didn't own the rights to them. That was Perón. Of course, nothing became developed.

Argentina fit my two basic investment criteria. One, change was coming—I'd been in the country several weeks and could see it—and two, investments were still dirt cheap. Money would now be thrown at these three industries and others, and shares would skyrocket. I wanted to buy the biggest companies because when the market started to move up, various money-center institutions would be interested and create special country funds, establish local offices, buy seats on the exchange, and spread the word about Argentina throughout the world. This crowd would buy the biggest, strongest companies, bulling them up yet further.

I looked over the market and bought nineteen of the stocks whose industries made sense to me, companies with strong balance sheets to give me downside protection.

"Oh, there it is again!" cried Tabitha, grabbing my arm.

She pointed to a gold necklace in the jeweler's window. She was right; it was the same necklace she'd admired in a fancy jeweler's back in Iguaçu Falls. Gold with medium-sized links, the chain sported nearly two dozen green, red, blue, and yellow semiprecious stones in a clean modern design. We went in and she tried it on again.

Her birthday was coming up in December and I wanted very much to make her happy. Hoping to surprise her, I snuck back around to the jeweler's that afternoon and bought the necklace.

Back on the street in the sun, I asked myself how the hell I was going to get it back home. I didn't want to carry it across the remaining fifteen borders, where repeated searches were likely to expose it to her view. Since I didn't trust the Argentine post office, I arranged for a courier.

We were now five thousand miles away from the United States, and we began to plot our way homeward. We knew we'd covered the easiest part of South America, that north of us in many countries, including Peru, Ecuador, Colombia, and Brazil, were a cholera epidemic, civil wars, bandits, bad roads, drug dealers, and greedy policemen and guards.

Unlike crossing the United States, where you can huddle with a guide from AAA and receive accurate information about routes and hazards, we had to piece the situation together from a variety of sources. Not the least problem was finding maps.

Two routes presented themselves: up the east coast or up the west coast. Most of the east coast was taken up by Brazil. The route west would allow us to see Chile, Bolivia, Peru, Ecuador, and Colombia, a real cross section of South American cultures. In addition, I wanted to see the economies of these countries, for I wanted to invest in several, even though this route also led us through guerrillas, drug wars, bandits, and epidemics.

Everybody knew about the Pan-American Highway, but the local touring clubs knew little about any other route. The Brazilian Automobile Association in Iguaçu Falls had one map of the country, which I induced them to sell to us, but they knew nothing of how to drive through Brazil to such exotic far-north locales as Colombia and Mexico. This ignorance of travel conditions is precisely what you can expect in most parts of the world.

With little more intelligence than this, we decided to head west to Santiago and make the rest of the trip up the west coast. I also hoped to visit Easter Island, Machu Picchu, and the Galápagos Islands, sights I'd long read about and was eager to see.

It would have been difficult to get to these sights from Brazil. On the other hand, we were very worried about the Shining Path, Marxist guerrillas who seemed to be increasing their attacks against anything and anyone connected to Peru's establishment. We decided to stop at every Peruvian consulate along the way to check on the insurrection's progress. We could always turn into Brazil if the war got too hot in Peru.

Finally, after seven weeks, it was time to leave Argentina for Uruguay, something we hated doing since we loved the ambiance, people, and vibrancy of Buenos Aires.

Montevideo certainly lived up to its reputation as the Switzerland of South America. A huge number of foreign banks were here, including Swiss, Dutch, and German. One reason tiny Uruguay, with only 3 million people, still existed was because the establishments of Brazil and Argentina wanted it here. They needed it. Everybody in South America needed a haven for money, just as European countries all needed Switzerland. Once Uruguay had lost all its money after the cattle boom collapsed, it had adapted by becoming the place its giant neighbors could stash their money. Its neighbors voted with suitcases full of cash to keep Uruguay in business as Latin American countries kept imposing currency controls.

Today enforcing the controls is becoming harder and harder to accomplish because of low-priced air fares, increased travel, wire transfers, and various other ways of circumventing them. And are governments today going to destroy international trade? Put on exchange controls and I might just buy Swiss watches with dollars and sell the watches in Germany for marks, which I might leave in Munich. With global trade booming, and with governments acknowledging their countries' need for it, it is going to be much more difficult than in the past to control currencies.

Uruguay filled a basic human need, a place where people could protect their hard-won assets. If the country didn't exist, South Americans would have invented another to hide their cash from their confiscatory governments. Perhaps with the easing of restrictions in South America, it won't be needed as much, but Uruguay will still benefit from the boom times of its neighbors.

There was virtually no stock market here. I tried to find a broker to buy me some issues, but several balked, as the market was inactive and no one bothered with shares. All this whetted my appetite, made me want them all the more. Eventually I found a willing broker and started buying.

We drove through central Uruguay and were delighted by the country. We would cross the continent by reentering Argentina and driving to Santiago. We passed through a rolling landscape and isolated but friendly towns. Plenty of sheep. No one here had ever seen the likes of us, a couple of Americans on German motorcycles. A continuing parade of old vehicles rolled by, many from the twenties, bought new in palmier days and maintained till now since no one could afford a new car.

As usual, a few days before the border crossing, we looked at the maps and doped out where to cross. Americans, used to traveling to Mexico and Canada, think one border entry is much like another in that a country's central bureaucracy issues orders and the guards obey them. Nothing could be farther from the truth. Border crossings differ enormously, and we spent lots of time asking other travelers about their experiences and consulting guidebooks for the best places to cross. We always wanted frequently traveled crossings, where holdups would engender complaints from many travelers and where the guards had plenty of experience with foreign vehicles and carnets.

To leave Uruguay and reenter Argentina we picked the crossing at Colón, which the guidebook said was easy. Normally we budgeted a day for crossings, but as we had been weeks in Argentina, we arrived just after noon, figuring to spend the night across the border in Colón.

"Wait a minute," said the guard, "both these carnets are in the same name. A single person can't be driving two motorcycles."

"No," I said, "these are my carnets, and these are both my motorcycles. This is my wife, and we're traveling around the world. From the stamps, you can see we've been through all these other countries."

He gave me the look of a country bumpkin who knew when a city slicker was having one on him. "Señor Rogers, you can't be driving two vehicles, can you? She has to have permission to drive your vehicle."

"Well, she has permission. I'm standing right here, and I give it to her."

"No, no, we must have it in writing."

"Okay, I'll write it down."

"No, you must have special permission, notarized by the embassy. It has to be written up in four copies, with the ambassador's signature."

"What are you talking about?" I said, my patience evaporating. "We've already been in Argentina. We've already brought those vehicles into the country once. We've driven through Argentina's entire length, been here seven weeks, and there was no problem."

As I pointed out the stamps of his own agency back in Buenos Aires, I remembered that the country had a long history of its people being desperate for bribes. Indeed, when we flew the bikes in we went through a mind-numbing amount of paperwork, making me reflect on how regulations were stifling trade here.

"Isn't there some sort of special fee we can pay to settle this?" In my experience this was the best phrasing to use to see if bribery was the object. While I detest bribes, I wasn't going to let a few bucks delay us for days.

He wouldn't bend. I asked to see the head man. With pompous, weary shakes of his head, Corporal Mendez agreed with his minion. We had to have such permission throughout the world.

"The world!" I said. "I've been around the world. I've been in forty countries, including yours, and never needed it."

"Well, everywhere in Latin America, certainly."

"I've been in Uruguay and I've been in your own country, and I didn't need it."

Despite an hour of argument, Corporal Mendez wouldn't give in. There was an Argentine consulate back in Paysandú, he said, back in Uruguay, where I might obtain the documentation that would satisfy them.

As we cranked up our bikes, Tabitha said, "Jim, it's Sunday. Are consulates open on Sundays?"

"God knows. Let's go see."

Through a miracle it was open. That day was election day in Argentina, and since its citizens by law had to vote, the consulate was open so expatriates could cast their ballots.

We found a young consul-general, Raolf Santos, who had been in fancy capitals around the world, obviously a youthful comer in the diplomatic trade. Along with his eight-year-old daughter, Juanita, he was in the consulate for the afternoon to help out with the election. He was in this hick post for a couple of years so his and his wife's parents, just over the border, could see their grandchildren while they were still children.

In small talk, we learned he was quite a dynamic guy, bringing art shows to the consulate and doing everything he could to promote international relations. As this was a small consulate, he had all sorts of duties. For instance, when Argentines were killed in traffic accidents, mainly from rushing to and from Brazil, he had to return to Argentina to buy coffins because those in Uruguay—wood only, instead of wood and lead—didn't pass the Argentine health code. Even the coffin makers in Argentina had a strong guild.

"We've had constant complaints about that crossing," he told us in better English than mine. "Let's go there. I have no direct command over them, but theoretically they report to our service."

With Juanita perched on the front seat, our new friend drove his car to the border. We followed on our motorcycles. He argued strenuously with the guards, but it didn't help.

"I don't want to lose my job," said Corporal Mendez.

Outside, Raolf said, "My wife and I even came out here and cooked a big Christmas dinner for these fellows, trying to make friends with them."

"What do we do?" I asked.

"You need a notarized permission," he said, "which means finding a magistrate on Sunday to certify the papers."

We asked for his help. First we had to find a lawyer, he said, because it wasn't enough for a mere mortal like me to write out permission by hand and in English. It had to be in Spanish, it had to be phrased right, it had to be typed, and it had to be properly sealed and stamped by an officer of the law.

Raolf made some calls. He found a magistrate-lawyer, a half-hour's drive away, who was willing to give up part of his Sunday afternoon for a fee.

In the magistrate's home office, we gave him all the necessary information—passport numbers, vehicle numbers, carnet numbers, every number we could come up with. Covering all bases, I even had Tabitha give me permission to drive both vehicles. I wanted extra copies in case we ran into this north of here. Every copy had to be stamped and sealed. It wound up costing a few hundred dollars.

A couple of hours later we returned with Raolf and proudly handed Corporal Mendez our shiny new documents.

He scrutinized them as well as our registrations, licenses, passports, and carnets. Thank God I hadn't brought that gold necklace. I'd never have gotten it through this inspection without Tabitha seeing it.

"We can't stamp these carnet things," Corporal Mendez said at last.

In the ensuing argument it became clear he didn't know what a carnet was. This border crossing was so out of the way, and Corporal Mendez and his detail so ill trained, that they had never seen one. So much for guidebooks.

We explained several times, as did their own consul-general, that it was no skin off his country's back if he stamped the carnets saying our vehicles had entered his country. In fact, his country would make hundreds of thousands of pesos if we left without having our carnets restamped. Argentina would automatically apply to the Royal Automobile Club in Great Britain and receive the full amount of the vehicle's import duties from our failure.

Nobody can go around the world in any sort of vehicle without a *carnet de passage en douanes*. Imagine having to post $20,000 in dinars on entering Algeria to guarantee that you don't sell your motorcycle while you're there. At the other side of Algeria you would receive your 200,000 dinars back, maybe, or it might take weeks, months, or years for the bureaucracy to get around to sending you a check—in dinars, of course. Travelers' stories were full of bonds posted that had never been returned. Meanwhile, how would you deal with Niger? With Nigeria, Zaire, and Botswana?

"I don't care if Argentina gets millions of pesos," said Corporal Mendez. "I care about my job."

After Raolf worked him over again, he said, "Señor, here is a form I have to fill out saying a vehicle came in the country. Now, if I stamp this carnet document, too, I will now have certified the vehicle has come into the country twice."

Incredulous, I pointed out it didn't mean that at all. "And so what?" I added. "It's simply two different forms for one event."

Corporal Mendez gave me the look an adult reserves for a child who has asked a particularly dumb question. "Señor, it is only one vehicle."

Fuming, I considered simply having him stamp his form and our entering Argentina with it alone, but I was worried about getting stopped inside the country or upon leaving it. He didn't know about carnets, but the next dozen policemen might. And, too, perhaps Corporal Mendez was playing a far deeper game—let us in on his form, call a cop friend down the road, have us stopped without a carnet, and between the two of them share a really big bribe.

Finally Raolf called up the guards' boss, head of customs and immigration, at his home, this on a Sunday night. Pull counted for something. Señor Sanchez would see us.

Leaving Tabitha to look after the bikes and gear, I piled into Raolf's car and we drove into Colón.

First we had to apologize for bothering Señor Sanchez on a Sunday night, then we had to sit and talk. Bone-tired, I had to show him our map of the world and tell a few spirited stories about our adventures. I met his wife and children. As the Latin American small talk wound on, I was beside myself, impatient and barely containing it, aching to be in a hotel room in this wretched city.

Raolf explained he had been posted in many world capitals and had never had a problem like this. Mr. Rogers here, a learned professor, had been around the world and had never had such a problem, either. In a delicate fashion he suggested that Argentina might appear a touch backward and a laughingstock if this weren't handled right.

Finally I pulled out the carnets. It was immediately clear to Raolf and me that Señor Sanchez, too, didn't know what a carnet was. I supposed when Uruguayans went into Argentina they filled out the local form at the crossing and that was enough.

Finally Raolf came up with an idea to handle the "two documents, one vehicle" problem. Why didn't the guards simply staple the two papers together?

I almost groaned at the stupidity of the suggestion, but Señor Sanchez thought this was an exceptional idea. He wrote a letter instructing his people to do just this, in essence to make two pieces of paper into a single form.

After much handshaking and mutual good wishes, we drove back to the crossing. By now it was nearly ten o'clock.

I didn't think anything was going to work. Staple two pieces of paper into one? Didn't there have to be a wax stamp sealing the two together? A notarized cover letter in high-flown Spanish from an officer of the court describing the procedure? How many more hours, how many more hundreds of dollars would that take?

What worked were instructions from the boss. The documents were stapled together by Corporal Mendez in jig time and the ten-hour international snafu was over.

Outside the guard station Tabitha and I swore undying devotion to Raolf, exchanged addresses, and invited him to stay with us when he was next in New York. As commemorative gifts, we had brought along a few Susan B. Anthony dollars. We gave him one each for his two daughters, his wife, and himself.

We arrived at the hotel in Colón at midnight, and a bed has rarely felt as good.

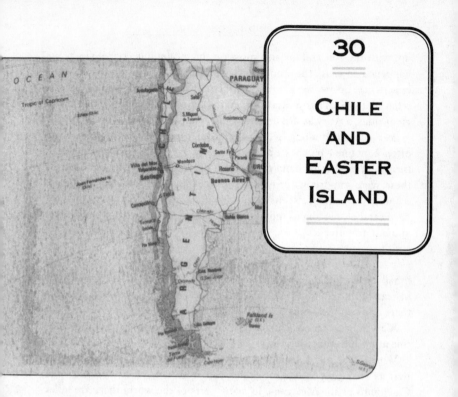

COMING OUT OF ARGENTINA toward Chile, the Andes rose in the distance, sixty or seventy miles away. Around us across the pampas stretched huge vineyards.

As we drove into the mountains the temperature dropped. Every two or three hundred yards stood depth rods, four yards high, marked to show how deep the snow was.

Around six thousand feet it began to snow, but we kept going, afraid we would become snowed in. We arrived at Puente del Inca at four or five in the afternoon. I was torn, wanting to go on, feeling we should continue so as to get through what might be a blizzard, yet wanting to spend a night in the Andes. By now we were nearly ten thousand feet high and there were ski lodges along the road.

We found a delightful place to spend the night, so if we were snowed in, it wouldn't be the worst thing in the world. At the hotel they told us we didn't have to worry, the roads would be cleared. We'd be able to travel even if a blizzard hit.

The next day was a beautiful sunny day, and we drove along the top of the world. At least that was what it felt like, more than ten thousand feet up, with the sun and air and snow on the mountains crystal clear. We happened to cross the Andes not as a struggle, but as an exhilarating experience. So we were on top of the world in two ways, high up and relieved it wasn't like Siberia or the Sahara. It turned out to be one of our great rides, as easy as driving across the mountains in the summer.

As we zoomed along, we learned to be careful of shadows, as these often contained patches of ice. I wore my electric vest, and Tabitha turned on her heated handlebars. With the frigid air blowing around us, these were important, providing lifesaving warmth and psychological comfort. Something else that kept up our energy and concentration were hard candies, feeding us minute hits of sugar to keep up our metabolism and our attentiveness.

Finally we left Argentina, which took two minutes in the guard post instead of the ten hours it had taken to enter. And you guessed it: No one there or ever after asked to see our "permission papers."

We were now in no-man's land, the several miles between the Argentine and Chilean border posts.

When I was a kid, I thought border posts were always back to back, that as soon as you left the States you were obliged to deal with the Canadians or the Mexicans. In many parts of the world there are miles between posts, with only an isolated sign saying you've crossed the border. Governments don't want to maintain posts in extremely remote areas; guards don't want to work there; and in the desert or the mountains, there might not be water. People leaving Argentina could go only one way, along this road, which led right into the Chilean border post a few miles away.

We took advantage of this extended no-man's-land to change our license plates. We had new plates and new numbers to replace our out-of-date registrations from the States, and we'd had to get new carnets. Just as we had done in North Africa, we had a local shop make up new plates with the correct numbers, and naturally they were in the Argentine colors. As we had several more war zones to go through, we didn't want to be easily recognized as Americans. Since we had to make our carnets conform coming in and going out with the same registrations and plates, it made sense to change them between borders. This is an example of the sort of thinking we had to do, planning ahead, thinking through the details of each step.

· · ·

I'd heard a lot about the new Chile, the Chilean miracle, and I was eager to see some of it. My first tip-off that the Chileans were running a tight ship was the border crossing. They seemed only to want to make sure that we weren't bringing in any diseases on fruits or vegetables. I didn't like the holdup, but at least preventing plant disease was a legitimate interest of Chile's, since agriculture is its major industry.

The border crossing reminded me of the necklace. Had it made it to New York? I kept reminding myself to ask Judd to see if the package had arrived, but I kept forgetting to do so.

Several miles inside the border we were whizzing along, mountain peaks and snow on both sides, when we hit a flat stretch, one well paved and bare of snow.

Without warning we came across a long patch of snow, several inches deep. Several bulldozers were plowing the road, bearing down on us. We inched forward, careful not to allow our wheels to slip. As usual Tabitha was in front.

To my horror, two bulldozers drew up on either side of her, closing together toward her bike. I yelled. Either they didn't see her or were playing a bizarre game of tag. I shouted a warning.

She turned to one and then the other and cursed the drivers, raising her fist, her helmet snapping back and forth from bulldozers to the patches of ice on the slippery road. If she lost her nerve and skidded, she'd be under the clanking iron treads of these behemoths.

She shot free, sliding and skidding, and pulled away. A hundred yards farther, she pulled over and turned and gave them hell in English, both fists raised and shaking with fury, berating them for almost killing her.

I was overwhelmed with relief, pride, triumph, and adoration. I immediately understood the delight she'd felt that night we'd finally made it to Istanbul. An extraordinary heroine! My partner!

In Santiago we saw at once that this was indeed the most prosperous country in South America. Everybody in Chile noticed the difference between this economy and that of his neighbors—in fact, between Chile now and the Chile of twenty years before, when it had been a basket case. Here was a currency that was even appreciating against the dollar.

I grabbed one of the last seats on the weekly flight to Easter Island. Wanting to rest and shop, Tabitha stayed behind. While I was gone she would do what she could to find a clutch cable and some chart books I needed. That check for stock purchases still hadn't arrived in New Zealand. She would cancel it and send a replacement to New York.

Easter Island is a triangular island of about sixty-five square miles, formed by three volcanoes that stand extinct in each corner. Lakes lie in the centers of the volcanoes, surrounded by rolling grass and volcanic soil broken by frozen lava flows. I wondered how its original inhabitants had gotten here—twenty-three hundred miles from Chile, eight thousand miles from any Asian landmass, and thirteen hundred miles east of Pitcairn Island, its nearest neighbor.

Of course, the astounding thing about Easter Island is its giant heads, the *moai*. A thousand or so in number, carved in nearly identical styles from volcanic rock, many weigh twenty tons and stand ten to twenty feet high. The largest weighs ninety tons and rises thirty-two feet. The chief difference is between those carved with short ears and those with long.

Majestic and disturbing, scrutinizing with brooding and disdainful expressions, these stone heads, standing on giant *ahu*, or altars, have been a mystery since the island was first encountered by Europeans in 1722. The few thousand surviving islanders lived in thatched huts and scratched out a living from the sparse plant life. They were demoralized by years of internal strife. War and cannibalism were common, perhaps an outgrowth of earlier population pressures and a shortage of protein. They didn't even remember the stories behind the *moai*.

Who built these heads, and why did they build so many? How were they transported miles to their perches overlooking the sea? How were such heavy monoliths stood upright? And how were the red topknots, separate stone carvings of red scoria weighing as much as twelve tons, raised onto the *moai*? How had an island twenty-three hundred miles from the South American mainland become peopled?

The ancient stonework in Bolivia and other South American countries so resembles the *moai* and *ahu* that I am convinced that the islanders must have come from there, not Asia or the Polynesian Islands. Periodically earthquakes in South America produce tidal waves reaching all the way to the island.

My guess is that a tribe of South Americans, on a sailing expedition, maybe trying to escape the aftershocks of an earthquake, were caught by one of those giant waves and driven the necessary two thousand three hundred miles to their new home.

The largest platform of all had supported fifteen massive *moai*. As late as 1960 it was still in pretty good shape, but a tidal wave has since scattered it beyond recognition.

Near one volcano were the ruins of a sizable town, but all that was left were scattered rocks giving no clue as to why the carving had stopped. Scientists estimate, as they did with the Sahara, that hundreds of years before, the island had been covered with trees and denser plant life.

This is on a par with the mystery of how the pyramids were built. Scientists calculate that to carve, transport, and raise Paro, the ninety-ton *moai* that is the largest example of these stone-carvers' art, took approximately twenty-three thousand man-days, nearly seventy-five man-years. And Paro is only one of a thousand such monuments. If the completion of an average *moai* took a third of this time and a thousand were carved, then this tiny island devoted twenty-five thousand man-years to sculpture. And how long had it taken to carve the *ahu* and the red topknots?

Three hundred *moai* had been in the midst of being carved in place in the side of Ramo Raraka, the mountain from which the heads were produced, when the carvers had suddenly stopped, their work now frozen in both its early and late stages. When finished, these *moai* would have been severed at the back and moved down the mountain, sometimes fifteen miles away, where they would have been erected on stone *ahu* built for the purpose. A few finished statues had even been on their way down the slope.

As these *moai* in the quarry and on the way down hadn't yet had their eyes carved, they were called the Blind Giants. Archaeologists wondered if the eyes would have been carved only after the *moai* had been placed facing the sea, at last enabling them to see.

I figured the people who carved the heads must have entered a period of great prosperity, because at one point they were making a lot of them—to my eye it looked like a bull market that had gotten out of control. After all, a poor society cannot develop such extensive art. Somehow this tiny island piled up enough of what here counted as capital to afford what, for the size of its population, must have been one of the largest art projects ever constructed. The question remains, how many people can prosper on a sixty-five-square-mile island?

As the boom expanded, the heads became ever bigger. In the quarry where they were produced, some were twice the size of the finished ones, a full twenty-one yards long. I guessed the market had become saturated when carving had stopped for an unknown reason. Was it famine, earthquake, tidal wave, epidemic, civil war?

The ancient stories had it that this once-glorious civilization had been reduced to a primitive state by a war to the death between the island's two factions, one tribe called the Long Ears, the other the Short Ears. Armageddon in a compass of six and a half by ten miles with no exit— and today no one even remembers why. Madness. One more absurd war.

Yet another Saturday-night brawl at the bar between power-drunk plug-uglies prepared to ruin not only their own lives but also those of their families and friends.

In a few hundred years nothing of all this will be left, just as other wonders of the world have disappeared.

In Santiago, I saw that Chile was not only a perfect lab for the war between statist and capitalist ideas, but that the experiment was almost complete. After a good deal of socialist mismanagement, Chile was completing one of the world's most profound economic transformations, its economy roaring, its exports soaring. It had been the first South American nation to undertake deep structural reforms. After fifteen years of efforts, it was reaping huge benefits.

Salvador Allende's Marxist government ruled Chile from 1970 to 1973. His statist regime was marked by four-digit inflation and daily demonstrations against shortages of basic necessities. In this economic debacle, Chile lost many years of work. If ever a country was behind the economic eight ball, seemingly doomed forever to Zairian-type poverty, Chile was it.

In 1973, Allende was overthrown in a bloody military coup. General Augusto Pinochet returned six hundred expropriated companies to their former owners, privatizing part of the public sector. His seventeen-year rule was marked by massive human-rights violations, including two thousand to three thousand deaths and disappearances.

In 1976, his government implemented free-market reforms, established a sound-money policy, and raised interest rates. Whenever a fiscally unsound household, company, or economy faces reality and bites the bullet, the initial stages are always terribly painful, as these steps were. This was part of Chile's process of recovering from decades of statist mismanagement. Overseas goods became cheaper and Chile's more expensive. Now domestic producers had to learn to compete or fail. By as late as 1982, Chile's GDP had fallen 14 percent. Many inefficient companies went bankrupt, a necessary part of making a country more competitive.

In spite of making some mistakes, the finance minister instigated a number of sound policies that worked for the economy's good. State enterprises were sold off. The government lowered import tariffs and deregulated the economy. Companies were forced to compete globally or die. The government replaced the state social-security system with obligatory individual retirement accounts, a savings plan used in parts of Asia for decades with excellent results to create investment capital. State subsidies to private businesses were eliminated. Interest rates were allowed to be set by the market, not the government, and wages were set by the supply of labor.

The results of these fifteen years of tough economic decisions have been significant. Exports have zoomed from $4 billion in 1985 to $10 billion today. The GDP has grown at 6.5 percent annually since 1984, and since the nineties it has grown by 10 percent. The government has run a surplus since 1990 while increasing expenditures on health, education, and housing. Inflation has been controlled, and the GDP doubled to $36 billion, in two decades. Unemployment has fallen from 20 percent in 1982 to 4.8 percent today. Per-capita income has neared $3,000, on a par with that of Korea and Portugal. Chile has even run a trade surplus with Japan, its leading trade partner. The country had become the engine, the model, of South American growth.

Very important, the political parties, the unions, the military, the church, the universities, and the entrepreneurial sector all had a stake in the new democratic system. It has become respectable to be a businessman, to own property, to build a company, to create jobs, even to acquire wealth.

We saw prosperity everywhere. American companies such as Procter & Gamble, Pepsico, Pizza Hut, and Kentucky Fried Chicken were making large investments. Au Bon Pain and Baskin-Robbins, two specialty-food retailers, were planning to open outlets. Chilean businessmen were making investments in nearby countries. But it wasn't only the rich and managerial class who were benefiting. Telephones were now easily available—something that never happens under Communism—and malls with inexpensive items for workers were opening.

Chile might become South America's first developed country—without the benefit of socialist, Communist, International Monetary Fund, or United Nations planners. This has happened because the government stopped being a drag on the economy, got out of the way, and allowed its citizens' natural desire to do better economically to be put to work.

As important as what the Chileans did was the time it took to accomplish the change. Having lost many years of development from their roll in the hay with Communism, the country had a lot to rebuild. Chile's was a transformation that took fifteen years, and might have taken many more. People everywhere want results now, but unfortunately economies aren't transformed in two or three years.

In any event, Chile did it. Other statist governments in Latin America are going to have a lot of explaining to do to their citizens if their economies aren't doing as well.

Naturally, this hadn't gone unobserved by Chileans, who so bid up their stock market that news of it was on every front page.

While I wish I'd been here five years before, when I would have put money in, I don't invest when the stock market is on the front pages. I normally sell markets short at that point. Chile's growth and structural position, however, was too strong to short. The market might pull back temporarily, but I would bet that, having tasted blood, it would roar ahead for a long time.

Chile is now democratic and prosperous for the first time in decades.

I was further amazed that Chile had sharply reduced poverty. According to government and United Nations figures, during the past three years the government had reduced the ranks of the poor from 5.2 million to 4.2 million through widespread prosperity. To raise the standard of living of the poor, the Chilean government did more. It injected capital into micro-companies, lending sums as small as $350 to tiny companies, such as sewing-machine factories, in the poorest districts. These loans enabled families to buy machines and take in piecework from overburdened factories. These micro-companies, many working out of a spare bedroom, were surprisingly efficient. They employed 40 percent of the workforce and 80 percent of the country's very poor.

In the United States, as you might expect in a country becoming more statist every day, it's illegal to farm out piecework so women can care for their children and simultaneously earn money. Better for them to be on welfare or find a job taking them away from their children. The cant is that these women have to be protected for their own good from making a voluntary arrangement with evil factory owners, who will mysteriously take advantage of them. The truth is that the unions have rammed through a law protecting their factory jobs and that they have effective lobbyists to make sure the law stays on the books—otherwise the unions won't vote for the lawmakers. Women with children have no union, lobbyists, or block vote.

In addition, the Chilean government grants scholarships to thousands of students to keep them in school, paying for books, meals, transportation, and prizes, such as bicycles, for those who excel. As well, it has work-study programs, subsidizing employers to employ students and give them on-the-job training at a small salary. When it started, many thought the kids wouldn't be interested, but this program quickly became oversubscribed.

Although prosperous Santiago is lively, it isn't Buenos Aires. Smog is heavy even though strict laws keep some cars off the streets every day.

Normally I would call my New York office in the afternoon. One day I called at an odd hour to check on a late shipment. Judd wasn't there. In his stead was a temporary bookkeeper, Sally. This puzzled me. Judd hadn't said he had hired anyone to do his work.

"How should I handle this eight-thousand-dollar transfer to Judd?" Sally asked.

"What eight-thousand-dollar transfer?" I asked.

"And what do I do about the fifty-thousand-dollar loan he's moving out of your brokerage account?"

"What the hell are you talking about?"

"You don't have to shout, Mr. Rogers. I can hear you perfectly fine."

Calmly I explained, "I've never agreed to loan Judd any money."

Thoroughly alarmed, I called Barbara Robinson at Debevoise Plimpton, my lawyers in New York.

"Great connection," she said. "But slow down."

I briefed her.

"I could go right over," she said.

"Please."

"Does he know we'd be coming?"

"No, I've never even met him. Maybe you'd better bring a guard or something, too."

"Right away," she promised. "Give me your number. I'll have them call you down there once they reach your office."

I paced around the small hotel room. Fifty-thousand-dollar loan! What else was missing? All those excuses about shipping services, about their losing packages in Miami, about their mixing things up, the little things in his reports that hadn't dovetailed—what was going on? Had he "loaned" himself more? He couldn't take money out of my brokerage accounts—could he? How clever was he? He didn't have signatory power over them—but suppose he'd forged my signature? I might win in a court battle with brokerage firms, but not without a long fight with their insurance companies. I would not only be deprived of my money, but whatever foolish investments he made might be locked in place— even now they could be declining. Here I'd been meandering around the world, supposing myself well heeled enough to afford a couple years away, and this kid—my God, an employee of mine whom I'd never met—might have bankrupted me. What had I done? How could I have been so stupid? This was the kind of elementary mistake I sneered at others for making. Not only was the trip ruined, *I* might be ruined. I would have to cut everything short and fly us and the bikes back to New York to straighten out this mess.

The phone rang.

"Jim," said Barbara, "I'm in your office. What would you like me to do?"

"What's going on? How much has he taken? Where is he?"

"Slow down. One thing at a time. I'm just not sure what to do now."

"Is he there?"

"No, the bookkeeper says he's taking flying lessons today."

Flying lessons? He was supposed to be working for me full-time. Was he going to fly to Mexico or the South Pacific on my money—*with* my money?

"Jim, are you there?"

What would I like her to do? It wasn't the stereo or air conditioner I was worried about. How could Barbara figure out if something was missing?

"The books," I said. "Go over them and see if there are suspicious transactions. This fifty-thousand-dollar-loan is a good example. See if Judd loaned himself any more money. See if there are any loans to him at all, as there shouldn't be."

Quizzed about unusual transactions, Sally said she hadn't understood how I had bought stereo equipment on Long Island with a credit card when I was in South America.

"This place is a mess," Barbara reported an hour or so later. "Stuff heaped on the desk, papers, bills, and files in disorderly piles, very little filed. We have no idea what's been paid and what hasn't."

"Has Judd come back?"

"No. There are a couple of checks here made out to a New Zealand broker. What should we do with them?"

He had had the missing check all along? He hadn't mailed off the second check? What was he planning—some scam to make off with my funds?

"I want him fired," I said, "and I want that office sealed so he can't get in. Have someone call that credit-card company and make sure I'm not responsible for whatever he's run up. Get an accountant in to go over the books to see what's missing."

I was as agitated by this as about anything on the trip. I knew where the bulk of my assets were, and he surely couldn't make withdrawals without my authority—could he? The brokers had clear instructions about this. Surely the worst was that the phone would get turned off, one of our credit cards would get shut down—wasn't it? Was I broke? Would I have to go back to work?

I set out with a grim face to enjoy the local sights. There didn't seem to be any more I could do for a day or two, so I would enjoy my stay here—if it killed me.

Barbara discovered that Judd had been trying to shift fifty thousand dollars from one of my brokerage accounts to a particular bank account over which I'd given him power of attorney.

Judd finally showed up. They fired him and sent him a certified letter. Bills and papers were in piles everywhere, records were in chaos, and God knew what was paid or not. It was a horrible mess, she said, and it was essential that I fly home right away.

Yes, she had changed the office lock. Yes, she had canceled his power over any bank and brokerage accounts. Yes, she had found the package with the necklace, and would put it in a safety-deposit box. No, she couldn't find any more attempts at embezzlement. When was I going to be back?

Sally, the temp bookkeeper, was unable to focus on much, which doubtless perfectly suited Judd's purposes. Ask her what the weather was like and fourteen minutes later you still were trying to find out. You had to grab her mind and shake it and shout, "Stop right here. Now, how is the weather today?" We needed her, though, because we needed a home base to take care of our credit-card charges and cash advances. Those bills had to arrive somewhere and be paid. She knew where the checkbook was and how to find everything, so I decided to hire her full-time, do an audit, and chase Judd legally.

"I'm not sure hiring her would be wise," said Barbara. "She feels guilty about turning Judd in, for biting the hand that hired her."

"Who's been paying her salary? It was my money! What about loyalty to me?"

"No need to get excited, Jim. She's just incompetent in some matters."

"What do you suggest?"

"Well, we could put an associate in here."

"What would you charge?"

The per diem she proposed charging would be enough to send a platoon around the world. Already her bill was likely to be more than the embezzlement. All I wanted for the next three months was someone to answer the phone and pay the bills. Without a method for paying them, we couldn't move.

Saying for the tenth time I ought to fly right up, she promised to hire Sally. I would keep trying to grab her mind during telephone conversations.

Quelling my unease, I decided to push on with the trip. This was the dream of a lifetime, and interrupting it by flying back to New York would violate its spirit.

We drove along the Pan-Am Highway and then down to the small town of Algarrobo, where we hired a private boat to take us out to a penguin colony on a small island. The boat turned out to be a skiff that I was sure was going to capsize in the chop.

We were delighted to find a pelican colony and even sea lions. A private yacht club had built a sea barrier out to this island to protect its cove. This allowed predators to steal out and eat the penguins' eggs, causing their population to decline.

This ride through the Andes is stunning, some of the best motorcycling in the world. At times the Pan-Am runs along the sea, sometimes midway between the mountains and the sea, and other times it cuts back into the mountains and meanders along the top of a plateau. It then dips through long valleys with mountains towering on either side. The climbs into and down from the mountains are thrilling. Even the colors are out of this world: deep emerald-green grass; small bushes of a dark kelly green, except for the new growth on top, which is a bright light green. The cacti are an all-together different green, paler, yet no less intense.

The Chilean Pan-American Highway is another feat of extraordinary engineering, with good pavement, banking, and drainage despite the heights and depths. At times as we shot through the mountains it was terrifying to peer down into bottomless gorges.

As we neared Vallenar, plant growth thinned out. According to our map, we would soon be in another desert. Along the highway were small monuments, crosses, and shrines to mark the places people had died in accidents, many more than we had seen in Argentina or the USSR. Many of these were on flat, straight surfaces. Why? Had the drivers fallen asleep? Had they been drunk? Too young or inexperienced to understand the dangers of driving?

These certainly caught our eye. Perhaps we ought to erect black spots or something equivalent in the United States.

Finally we reached the desert, much of which looked as barren as the landscape on the moon. The section in Chile, six hundred miles up the Pacific, is known as the Atacama Desert. The desert continues up through Peru almost to Ecuador; sometimes it is only a few hundred yards wide, sometimes several miles. Normally the area between the sea and the mountains, such as in California, is green and fertile, but not here. Called the driest desert in the world, there are some spots of it where rainfall hasn't been recorded for more than four hundred years.

So we rode through the desert past snowcapped mountains just to our right and the Pacific Ocean just to our left. The desert, mainly red but sometimes white, constantly changed from dirt to stones to sand to boulders and always smelled of the sea.

My relationship with Tabitha had changed over the trip, as I suppose it would have with over fifteen months alone together. I remembered vividly back when we were coming out of Bulgaria and the plug had fallen out of her carburetor. We'd scrounged around and found an old rubber tube, and using the miracle 3M tape, put plugs into the carburetor, which had worked. At the hotel that night she had been excited, happy, pleased, with a beautiful expression on her face. We had triumphed. We'd had a breakdown and we'd been resourceful enough to fix it without anybody else's help. I'd been too tired or insensitive to relish the moment.

A few months later, in Russia, I had been amazed by the tender relationship between Igor and Valentina, the husband-and-wife helmet manufacturers.

They had opened my eyes to the possibility of still feeling this way after a long marriage and children. Maybe there was something to the idea of true and lasting love. As we drove up the west coast of South America, I realized how much my entire feeling about Tabitha had changed and was still changing. I found myself wildly happy to have her with me. Both of us woke up glad to be with each other, excited at how happy and delicious it was to be together.

We felt triumphant that our love was deepening. I now knew I could make a lifetime commitment; I wondered if our partnership would last after the trip, or if I could find someone else with whom I could have a lifetime commitment.

We decided that even though we were going through these romantic feelings here in South America, we would do nothing for six months after we got back—not break up and not get married. We'd been out of our world back home for a long time, over fifteen months, and we would need a period of adjustment.

Life on my return to the States? My adult life seemed to have been divided into two parts, before 1980, when I was on Wall Street, and after 1980, when I was doing a variety of things culminating in this trip. The trip marked the end of the second part of my life, and I was ready for part three. I didn't know what that would be, but I wanted a new life, and I was ready to work at it.

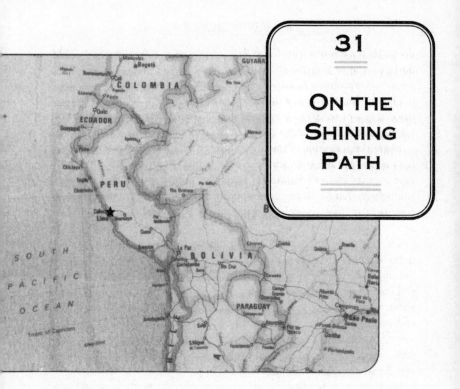

W E NEARED PERU, home of the Shining Path.

The Shining Path was a decade-old guerrilla movement, the only Maoist guerrilla movement left in the world at the time. Chairman Gonzalo, a Peruvian academic-intellectual trained in philosophy, had decided he was the world's "fourth sword," the merciless successor to the three prior blades of Marx, Lenin, and Mao Tse-tung. His organization, the Shining Path—officially the Peruvian Communist Party—was going to take over Peru and then South America and lead the world into a worker's paradise.

To him, every socialist regime of recent times, including Albania, North Korea, and China, had gone in the wrong direction, selling out. The true struggle was not between the Path and the army, with whom his cadres had regular shootouts, but against Peru's capitalist structures, which he was determined to destroy. His cadres threatened anyone—priests, Peace Corps volunteers, and foreign-relief workers—who wasn't working through bloody revolution to improve the lot of Peru.

When we were in Australia, the press was full of stories about three Australian nuns, in Peru to minister to poor Peruvians, who were gunned down by the Shining Path. The Path's logic went something like, "You nuns are supporting the state by working to make things better for the poor, so we're going to do away with you."

Here in South America the newspapers were full of stories warning of the Path's vow to kill all foreigners. It gunned down innocent travelers to kill tourism and hurt the currency in order to damage the state.

In another example of the Path's ruthlessness and bizarre reasoning, a few weeks before we came through it had captured three Japanese agronomists at an experimental farm fifty miles north of Lima. Its reasoning was that any foreigners working in Peru must be working for the state because they weren't working for the Path. The Path executed the agronomists.

The Japanese government pulled out its fifty-two agricultural engineers from Peru. The Path's five thousand rebels were paralyzing a nation of 22 million people and an army of 120,000 soldiers.

These stories naturally gave us pause. Not only were we North Americans, which I supposed to Maoist guerrillas made us worse than Australians and Japanese, and not only were we travelers, whom they had vowed to gun down, but I was what the Path's theoreticians might call an arch-capitalist, the anti-Christ, a capitalist prince of darkness—at the very least, a capitalist running dog.

In addition to reading the press, we stopped in many Peruvian consulates along the way to ask, "All right, how is it these days? Where are they now?"

Of course, the embassy officials always said the Path was under control. Consulates and embassies were being paid to say, "Come to beautiful Peru."

The country sounded worse than a war zone. In a war, neutrals might have been protected by international conventions. Yet in addition to these fanatical guerrillas, Peru was in the midst of the worst cholera epidemic of the twentieth century.

At the border we went into the Peruvian consulate on the Chilean side. This was our last chance for information. If the news was bad, we would skip Peru, cross the Andes on an unpaved road, push into Brazil, and somehow drive north through hundreds of miles of Brazil's outback to Central America, none of which would be as good as driving the Pan-American Highway.

We started with the easy questions, asking the consul about the highway north.

"For the first sixty miles or so it's not too good," he said, "but after that it's fine all the way to Lima."

This was a relief. Bad roads are a motorcyclist's nightmare. I asked, "Can we change money on the other side?"

"Yes, of course," he said as if I had asked something as stupid as if Peruvians wore clothes. "There's a bank right across the border."

Now for the big question. "And the Shining Path?"

He paused. "Are you sticking to the Pan-American Highway?"

"Yes."

He smiled. "Then you won't have any problem. The Pan-Am is my country's major transportation artery. It's very much in the interest of my government to make sure the rebels don't take it over."

This all made sense, so with a feeling of relief we set out north.

On the other side of the border, however, there was no bank. We asked the police for the bank, and they sent us to the next town, ten to fifteen miles down the road, where we found the vestiges of the black market.

The consul was also wrong about control of the Pan-American Highway. The Path attacked towns along large stretches of it.

We wound up staying in one town with no electricity. The day before the rebels—its saviors?—had blown up its only generator.

The hotel here was a rathole compared with many of the other South American places in which we'd stayed. Imagining a Path sympathizer driving by at night, seeing our foreign bikes, and spreading the word to Path higher-ups, we found a neighbor who for a dollar allowed us to store our bikes in her living room.

As we drove north along the ripped-up highway and went through devastated village after village, it was clear in leaving Chile we'd left prosperity and plunged back into the Third World. How the Path expected to persuade the majority of Peruvians to follow them by blowing up generators, killing innocent nuns and tourists, destroying the economy, and holding up banks was beyond me. The Path was led by a former professor. One would think he would have enough intellectual honesty to send a lieutenant—or even go himself—to see the economic miracle in his southern neighbor. Any honest person might wonder if maybe he'd made a mistake. Wouldn't a fearless rebel leader have enough intellectual honesty to examine the past and the present socialist economies of Peru, North Korea, Russia, and Cuba and compare them with their democratic and free-market counterparts in Chile, South Korea, Taiwan, and Botswana to see what he could learn about helping his people? God save us from true believers, whether devoted to religious, political, or intellectual theories.

In keeping with the Peruvian consul's batting average, the Pan-American Highway was in bad shape all the way to Lima. Despite the few police checkpoints, the guerrillas came and went as they damn well pleased. That consul's job was to sucker travelers into the country. More probably he was a typical bureaucrat, with no idea what he was talking about. He had succeeded in bamboozling us.

We must have been his only customers for months. The Shining Path had done its work well. From the bottom of Peru all the way to Lima we didn't see a single foreign license tag, whether from other continents or Chile, Bolivia, or Argentina. Actually, we saw very little traffic.

Every factory we passed had walls around its compound, big walls with guards at the corners with guns. If there weren't signs saying copper refinery or whatever, we would have thought these were prisons. At one point the newspapers said the Path had blown up forty banks. Every bank we saw had about fifteen armed guards standing around looking nervous. The huge amount of money the Peruvians were forced to spend on security was a drag on its economy. If it ever got this war behind it, Peru would become much more competitive worldwide.

I wasn't sure I wanted the trip ever to end. I decided I would do it again.

"Sure," said Tabitha, "but next time I'll stay home, worry, and write the checks."

"I'll do it in twenty-five years," I said. "I'll follow the same route in the log, stay in the same hotels, and see how the world has changed."

Twenty-five years. I'd be seventy-two, not so old, really. I'd write another book about how all the countries, people, places, and I had changed.

At the end of every day we always stopped and got gas before we checked into a hotel. One day after we filled up I gave the attendant a credit card. Despite signs saying that the station would take them, he didn't know how to process it. Nobody had ever given him one before, so I had to go inside to see the owner. Frantic examining of manuals, a huge hassle over how to deal with this bizarre transaction. Finally the owner discovered he couldn't charge more than six dollars at a time, so I gave him three cards, which totally flummoxed him. This provoked another hullabaloo, with the owner calling three separate banks to make sure this wasn't a North American scam at his expense.

Impatient and hopping from foot to foot, I was in there quite a while. Tabitha was outside watching the bikes. A truck pulled up and five guys piled out, all with AK-47s, the revolutionary weapon of choice. Since they weren't in military uniforms, she knew at once it was the Path. As they filled up the truck, a guy cradling an AK-47 drifted over and started flirting with her.

Tabitha leaned over to wipe off her Argentinian tag and immediately formulated another essential rule for traveling around the world: If a guy with an AK-47 flirts with you, flirt back. Don't say, "Mind your manners," or "Don't be fresh"; giggle and laugh. She flashed her wedding band and said her husband—her big husband—was inside. All the while she laughed at his jokes. His chums filled up with gas and paid the attendant with cash, as the Path didn't issue company credit cards.

Finally the AK-47 asked, "Which way are you going?"

She giggled again and asked, "Which way are *you* going?"

"South."

She looked disappointed. "We're going north. It's too bad."

When I came out, the tail of the truck was rounding the corner. She was white with terror.

"What's the matter?" I asked.

"Thank God you took so long," she said and told me the story.

"I had to show the owner—" I stopped short. Had my life been saved by the slow processing of a credit card? "Let's get out of here."

She shivered. "Nothing I want more."

Lima had once been the capital of the vast vice-royalty of Peru, which included Ecuador, Colombia, Bolivia, Chile, and Argentina as well as Peru itself. During the sixteenth, seventeenth, and early eighteenth centuries it had been a city of wealth and luxury that no others in the Americas could rival. For several centuries, when Europeans thought of America they thought of Mexico City or Lima.

I have mixed feelings about the development of the Spanish Empire in America. Somebody eventually was going to discover these two continents, which would lead to their integration with the rest of the world. This was good. Unfortunately the conquistadors were not the noble explorers about whom we read in school; they were thugs. Like the Huns sacking Rome, they destroyed the thousand-year-old civilization they encountered, giving no thought to the cultural treasures they pillaged. They melted down tens of thousands of priceless gold artifacts and shipped the ingots back to the motherland to swell that country's war chests.

Sanctioned by their clergy, the conquistadors didn't view their behavior toward the *indígenas* (the native South Americans) as subject to the rules of God or decency; they were a subhuman species on whom committing any atrocity was justified. The first Spaniards, only a few hundred strong, were able to prevail against tens of thousands of Incas because they were in a fierce civil war. Pizarro used treachery to capture the Inca emperor. The Incas paid a huge ransom in gold for his return, but Pizarro slaughtered him anyway.

Pizarro and his men kept some of the gold but sent much of it back to King Charles. The news of this treasure attracted thousands more Spanish thugs to descend on the New World for their share of the booty.

Later, the Spanish viceroy, who had been granted virtually unlimited authority over his domain, handed out land, and labor in the form of the native Indians, to colonialists. The pope's gift of America to the Spanish crown was justified by the king's mission to convert the heathen *indígenas* to Christianity. The system became disguised slavery, as adult male members of the tribes were forced to work for the Spanish for certain periods a year for a tiny wage.

Founded in 1535, Lima was almost completely destroyed by an earthquake in 1746. It is now South America's fourth largest city, its population about five million. Though it is surrounded by endless shantytowns filled with mountain people who've come for work, the center itself is quite compact.

While parts of its center retain a colonial flavor and the Plaza de Armas is impressive, much of the surrounding area is dirty, decayed, and strewn with litter. Only in the richer suburbs of Miraflores and San Isidro and along the Paseo de la Republica in the center is any effort made to plant trees and tend gardens.

In years past, Peru was more hamstrung by regulations than Argentina, which is saying a lot. If a businessman followed the rules and didn't set up his business on the underground economy, it took nine years to obtain a license. It even took several years just to buy a house. The government had finally started eliminating all this red tape. We saw budding entrepreneurs everywhere, in stores and countless street stalls. For sheer bustle and activity, Peru was rivaling China, the Middle East, and Africa.

This shouldn't be a surprise. It happens everywhere in the world once a government stands aside. Governments often think the method to get an economy moving is to give large businesses incentives or to cap prices. But the real way is to give the ordinary citizen a chance to jump in, to stop meddling with voluntary transactions—as they say in medicine, to do no harm.

Peru excited me. Once the richest country in all the Americas, it had been in a bear market for two hundred years. To the seventeenth-century Spanish, everything north of Mexico had been on a par with how we think of northern Canada today, a vast undeveloped scrubland. Not only had there been gold in the vice royalty of Peru, but the Spanish had discovered Potosí, a mountain of pure silver that at today's prices might fetch $200 billion.

Peru had enjoyed a silver boom on a par with that of the Saudi royal family and the Sultan of Brunei with their oil and gas wealth. For a while—everything is for a while—Lima was the richest city in the world. "The people here live on another level from the rest of the world," wrote a Spanish chronicler, "and the getting and spending of money is a fever that burns and possesses the whole population. They always go in cloth of gold and silver, or in scarlet silk. . . . In general, they eat and cook off silver plate."

To this day you can see the ancient wealth in Peru's leftover, deteriorating architecture. After viewing so many Peruvian cathedrals, altars of gold, fancy coaches, and lavish homes, I was staggered at the unproductive ways the wealth had been spent. No wonder the Spanish Empire hadn't sustained itself.

Some day Lima will be an exciting city again. When we were there prices were terribly depressed by the Shining Path, decades of government mismanagement, and the cholera epidemic, but I saw that the new government was removing the decades-old bonds that had been strangling the country. If I were right, that the turning point was near and prosperity would return, then a higher percentage would be made here off shares than almost anywhere else.

I figured the Path was far better at PR than fighting; it had little chance to bring down the government. This was nowhere near the successful revolution Fidel Castro's had been.

So, the anti-Christ invested a small amount in shoring up Peru's capitalist structure against the depredations of the Marxist-Leninist toads.

"They called from Queens about changing your skydiving lessons," said Sally, the temp bookkeeper on one of my calls to New York.

"Sally, I'm not taking skydiving lessons. I'm in Lima—Peru—South America."

"I wondered about that," she said. "You're sure you haven't been to Queens in the past few weeks?"

I sighed. "No. Why?"

"I know this is complicated, Mr. Rogers. It makes me nervous."

"Sally, what skydiving lessons?"

"Thank you. The woman said it had been charged to your Master-Card. She wanted to know since you hadn't made it if you'd like to come another time."

"Judd! He's done it again! What's the credit-card number?"

We checked, and it wasn't a number on any of my cards. He must have sent in one of those preapproved applications with his address. I dragged Barbara Robinson, my lawyer, back in. On the card were ten thousand dollars in charges, and every now and then a thousand or so had been paid to keep it in good standing.

Not knowing what else he might have taken, Barbara recommended canceling all the old cards and starting fresh. That seemed like a wonderful idea—till I had to resuscitate them in Lima.

From Lima there was no direct dial. The hotel operator became snippy because I was making so many calls to New York. Despite my paying the hotel an extra dollar just to pick up the phone, it made work for her. To get new cards, to sign the right papers, we had to drive to hell and back in the Peruvian suburbs. We spent a lot of time in banks, where squads of soldiers, dressed in flak jackets and carrying machine pistols, nervously eyed our motorcycles, jeans, and black leather jackets.

Ten cards, ten banks. Every bank officer, too, was suspicious of this guy in jeans and a black leather jacket who wanted to resuscitate a credit card that a lawyer in New York had canceled. They figured I was probably the thief who had stolen the credit card in the first place. Maybe my moll and I had killed Mr. Rogers and stolen his motorcycle, wallet, and gear and were now engaged in a bold, clever operation to obtain yet more booty at the bank's expense. The cables north smoked with telexes, phone calls, and faxes.

We flew to La Paz to look around.

Near twelve thousand feet, it was the world's highest capital city. It sat at the bottom of a natural canyon several hundred yards below the level of Bolivia's altiplano, with snowcapped Mt. Illimani towering over it. As we flew in, the skyscrapers in the center of the city resembled scale models surrounded by the reddish and pastel houses of the *indígenas*, which climbed the steep slopes of the canyon.

La Paz was founded in 1548 following the discovery of gold by the Spanish. Despite skyscrapers, the old part of the city retained a colonial Spanish flavor.

Even though Bolivia was the poorest republic in South America, La Paz appeared more prosperous than Lima. Maybe the gold and drug money showed up here and not elsewhere in the country.

Even more *indígenas* here. The women wore wonderful little bowlers, which they managed to keep on their heads in some mysterious fashion. Their style of dress had been prescribed by the Spanish several hundred years before and they still maintained it.

Witches had set up stalls where they sold potions that brought you luck in love, business, marriage, having children, whatever you were having problems with. Taking no chances, I bought the giant-sized, high-ticket talismanic vial that was all-in-one, good for every domain of your life, which I keep on my dresser. So far, so good.

India has its soothsayers, and the Indians consider it bad luck to build a house or marry without consulting one of these wise men. In China we'd come across *feng shui,* much the same system, and Africa had its witch doctors. Our pharmacologists now acknowledge that so-called primitive healers know much more about biologicals and medications than we used to give them credit for; today ethical drug companies even hire these backwoods healers as pharmacological consultants. People all over the world use the local witch to help them make decisions, as they have for centuries—even in advanced civilizations. Is there a lot more to this than our literal-minded science understood? After all, aren't coincidences really only scientific truths that haven't been discovered yet?

The traffic was as bad here as anywhere in the world. The roads weren't made for it. Hundreds and hundreds of stalls, as well as money changers and typists, were set up on the street. Some stalls even had phones and charged for calls.

The stock market here was only one-and-a-half years old and still had no stocks. Without a public market, I was forced to leave an order to buy stocks "in the street" or privately. I wanted a beer company, the convertible bond of a bank, and another coming new issue. The travel company here, Crillon, will be a terrific buy if it ever comes public.

As they have for hundreds of years—long before the Spanish came—every day Bolivia's miners consume up to a pound of coca leaves, the raw material of cocaine, for energy and endurance. Ever curious, I tried some of them the way the Bolivians do, by chewing them. My first wad was bitter, but the second and third were better. I learned to hold on until the momentary bitterness passed, then keep the wad in place the way Alabama country people chew tobacco or a cow mashes its cud. I also tried *mate de coca,* tea made from coca leaves, which tasted a bit like Japanese green tea. It's even served in the U.S. embassy in Bolivia. The locals used it to ward off hunger and altitude sickness.

I got less of a buzz off all this than from a cup of strong coffee. In its natural state the leaf was harmless. But maybe that was the point. Our people had taken tobacco, a herb sporadically used in a ceremonial fashion by the Native Americans, and smoked it ceaselessly. "Civilized" rich countries had taken a mild stimulant like coca leaves, used here the way the more sensible of us use tea and coffee, and cranked it up into a strength dozens of times its normal potency and used it several times a day, abusing it.

The Bolivians have chewed and made tea from coca leaves for more than four thousand years. The Incas restricted its use to royalty, priests, doctors, and the empire's messenger runners, who could travel more than a hundred miles a day by chewing the leaves.

Modern scientists agree that the traditional way the Bolivians use coca is harmless, nor is it even slightly addictive. The U.S. had often barged into Bolivia with programs to defoliate the plants, however, provoking violent demonstrations from *campesinos,* or peasants. They could see no reason to give up their best cash crop, one from a hearty, resilient plant they could harvest four times a year. I wondered how we'd react to Chinese or Koreans barging into our country and telling us to defoliate our tobacco plants, that we were selling their citizens poison.

Despite the stupidity of the drug habit, many of the financial and social problems of both South and North America won't be solved till we legalize drugs. I know all the arguments against doing it, that we'll have twenty-one-year-olds buying cocaine and designer drugs in the local pharmacy, but the vast crime and security apparatus we employ now to deal with this problem is crippling producer and user societies alike. Tens of billions of dollars a year are stolen in the United States to finance a drug trade bloated by illegal profits. It makes no more sense to make drugs illegal than it did to make alcohol illegal. The same basic problems have arisen—large criminal enterprises and corrupt officials. We're handling cigarettes and alcohol by jawboning successfully against them, by turning them into a déclassé activity, and the only solution is to legalize drugs and educate people against them, too.

The world is spending hundreds of billions of dollars fighting a hopeless battle. We are corrupting our entire criminal justice system. The police don't want the drug trade stopped; for them it's good business. They can now confiscate anything they want so long as it's in the name of "the war against drugs."

We saw the corrosive effects of this drug trade everywhere in Latin America: corruption, deaths, smuggling, entire societies undermined. Why not just legalize the stuff? The hundreds of billions we would save on law enforcement if drugs were legal and the taxes we'd collect on legal drugs could be better spent on prevention and cure of whatever cases of abuse arise. There would be enough left over to deal with alcohol and tobacco use and still cut taxes.

Little will happen until there's a huge scandal in the United States. Perhaps the president or a member of the Supreme Court will be found to be corrupted because of drugs. Today more than fifty of the several hundred federal judges refuse to try drug cases because they find the laws useless in solving the problem and harmful to our society. If all federal judges took the same action, that would be scandal enough.

After legalization, the freed-up jail cells could be used for corrupt politicians.

When Peruvians talked of Titicaca, the world's highest-altitude navigable lake, they never failed to mention it had waves. That was their way of emphasizing the size of this bright blue body of water separating Peru and Bolivia. And large it was, covering more than three thousand square miles. But while its skies were sunny and the land around it was gentle terrain, it wasn't that hospitable. Its water was frigid year-round, the result of being more than 12,000 feet above sea level.

According to local folklore, from Lake Titicaca sprang one of the most important cultures the world has ever known, the Incas. For them, the lake had been sacred and its islands holy. Legend had it that when the Spanish reached Cuzco, the indigenous inhabitants had taken the two-ton gold chain of Incan Prince Huáscar from its resting place at Qoricancha, the Temple of the Sun, and hurled it into the lake to hide it from the invaders. Some years ago oceanographer Jacques Cousteau spent eight weeks with a mini-submarine exploring the bottom. He found no gold, but he did discover a twenty-inch-long tricolored frog that never surfaces.

On Titicaca's surface were islands, the best known being the floating reed islands of the Uros tribe. Here was a remarkable method of self-defense, further proof of man's great adaptability in the face of necessity. Around the world we'd seen caves, castles, moats, and underground cities. Here the Uros had built huge islands of reeds—ten-foot-thick reed mats on which they would build villages. When threatened by their enemies, they would sail the whole island away to safety.

We learned that the Uros had lived with each other a while before marriage. If it didn't work, they could try someone else—up to three partners—till a marriage took. Despite all our progress, perhaps civilized society could learn something from a more natural way of life.

Local superstition said black blood had coursed through the Uros' veins, allowing them to survive the frigid nights on the lake. The last full-blooded Uro died in 1959, but the island's current inhabitants—a mix of Uro, Aymara, and Quechua peoples—still followed the Uro ways. They fished, hunted birds, and lived off lake plants, including the all-important reeds used to make their homes, build their boats, and form the base of their islands.

On a bleak plateau nearly thirteen thousand feet high stand the remains of the brilliant, long-forgotten Stone Age civilization Tiahuanaco, which we now know predates the Spanish discovery of the Americas by several hundred years.

Its stones are square and rigid, its vistas blocky and rectangular. Who were these pre-Columbian people? What was their fate? Unlike other ancient South American civilizations, they left no written records, only their buildings.

One of the city's largest structures, Puma Puncu, is now only a jumble of stones, some of them twenty-six feet long and sixteen-feet wide, hurled about as if by a natural catastrophe. No one knows whether this had once been a palace or a temple; it's now a mystery.

Excavations have proved that over the thousand years of its existence this was as many as five separate cities, one built on top of another. A thousand years of sophisticated civilization in the depths of the Bolivian jungle!

More amazing, the quarries for the city's stones lay sixty to two hundred miles away. Blocks of stones weighing up to one hundred tons, a few even more, were carried across the jungle floor by men without the wheel, metal, or horses. Yet even without metal blades, the blocks were as regular as if a die had cut them.

What struck me was the universal genius of man. I was reared to think that the glories of the Hebrews, the Greeks, and the Romans were the heights of ancient man's accomplishments. But this trip was opening my eyes. In Carthage, in Zimbabwe, in Xi'an, in the Sahara, and in Siberia—here in Tiahuanaco, Lake Titicaca, Suzdal, Istanbul, and Samarkand—I found ancient glory after ancient glory.

To build a mammoth stone city like this, miles square and several stories high, took more than a strong king who wanted to be well buried. A people first had to rise above the subsistence level, after which such huge structures took dozens, scores of generations of social development and organization. Their leaders had to remain focused on their goals over generations and not succumb to the burning consumption fever that later infected the Spaniards in colonial Lima. Housing, food, and labor had to be arranged; some form of capital had to be assembled; plans had to be laid and executed; and a way of motivating workers and middle management had to be found. All this by societies we deign to call primitive. To me they represented everything that makes man great. I realized again that mankind would take care of itself and survive.

And here stood one of their cities, Tiahuanaco. A succession of rulers had had the vision to plan and build this colossal city, this monument to man's genius.

In 1911, Hiram Bingham, an American explorer searching for the Lost City of the Incas, was led along the same route into the Andes used by the Inca chief Manco in eluding the Spanish conquistador Pizarro.

After a strenuous climb to seven thousand feet, he was taken by his guide to a great flight of beautifully constructed stone-faced terraces, perhaps a hundred of them, each hundreds of feet long and ten feet high. Bingham had seen similar flights before, and he was unexcited.

"Suddenly," he later recalled, "I found myself confronted with the walls of ruined houses built of the finest quality of Inca stonework. It was hard to see them for they were partly covered with trees and moss, the growth of centuries, but in the dense shadow, hiding in bamboo thickets and tangled vines, appeared here and there walls of white granite ashlars [square-hewn stones] carefully cut and exquisitely fitted together."

Following on, he found a semicircular building "whose outer wall followed the natural curvature of the rock and was keyed to it by one of the finest examples of masonry I had ever seen. Furthermore, it was tied into another beautiful wall, made of very carefully matched ashlars of pure white granite, especially selected for its fine grain. Clearly, it was the work of a master artist."

He continued to hack away jungle and to explore. "Dimly, I began to realize that this wall and its adjoining semicircular temple over the cave were as fine as the finest stonework in the world. . . . It fairly took my breath away. What could this place be?"

Bingham had been led to Machu Picchu, which because of its emerald-like mountain setting is arguably the most famous and spectacular archaeological site in the Americas. Certainly today it is the most visited site in South America. Since farmers were living and farming there when he arrived, it is hard to say that he "discovered" Machu Picchu. The correct way to phrase it, we were told, was that his was a "scientific discovery."

We rode in by train along the silvery Urubamba, legendary river of the sun. The mountains rising around us were a deep, deep green, their tops shrouded in evermoving mists.

The ancient city, perched on a steep green slope, is still largely intact, as only the original peaked thatch roofs have disappeared. The city straddles the narrow saddle of a mountain high above a U-bend of the Urubamba. A backdrop of snowcapped peaks rise to eighteen thousand feet. The sight that greeted us as we passed through the portals of Intipunku was magical. What an incredible place this must once have been!

The Tower of the Sun was built over the royal mausoleum with such perfect precision that no mortar was required. The Spanish found this stonework without mortar throughout the Americas but could never duplicate it.

The Temple of Three Windows opened onto the glory of the Andes. The city was the terminus of a 625-mile road through the mountains, which like all Inca roads had been paved and had post houses at intervals. I was agog at all this, also built by men without horses, the wheel, or metal. We think of Stone Age man as benighted and primitive, but here as in many other places, he had erected an elaborate civilization, obviously employing hierarchical social structures, elaborate planning, and sophisticated technical know-how.

For those with a little nerve there was the pièce de résistance—climbing up the hair-raising stone steps to the top of Huayna Picchu, which overlooked the fabled city. At its summit stood the Temple of the Moon.

Since Hiram Bingham's day a tremendous amount of clearing and restoration had been done, which included thatching some of the buildings and setting the original watercourses to work again. It was a romantic, otherworldly site—a place for dreaming.

Much like Pachacamac and other less important temples in the Inca empire, Machu Picchu had been home to priests, high functionaries, craftsmen, and servants, and most important, to the *mamacunas,* the virgins chosen to dedicate their lives to the sun god. It seemed to have been a city without poor, a mountain fortress of liturgical fountains and glorious walkways.

No one knew what had happened to these people. The Incas had left no written record, and the Spanish chronicles didn't mention the city. They might have been killed by an epidemic, or the occupants might have been swept away by the bloody political disputes raging throughout the Inca empire before and after its fall.

Here at Machu Picchu excavations only added to the mystery of what had happened to its inhabitants. In all, the skeletons of 173 people were found; 150 were women, many buried with valuables, which led to the conclusion that Machu Picchu was a sanctuary of the Virgins of the Sun to protect them from the conquistadors' lust. At the tomb of the high priestess, as Bingham called it, the remains of a woman and a small dog were found, along with some ceramic objects, two broaches, and woolen clothing. The woman had suffered from syphilis.

At Cuzco, we dined on guinea pig, a local delicacy, which tasted like good crisp pork barbecue. We ate the head and all. The local *chicha,* or corn moonshine, was horrible, like wine that had gone bad and then rotted.

The main painting of the Last Supper in the local cathedral showed guinea pig being served as well as local cheeses and green peppers stuffed with meat. An Andean artist three hundred years ago would naturally have assumed that was what was served at the Last Supper.

32

ON DARWIN'S TRAIL

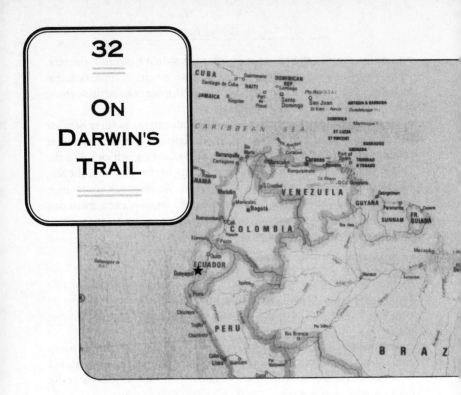

THE BORDER CROSSING from Peru to Ecuador was unique. The Pan-American suddenly turned into a mass of people milling about countless stalls, a bazaar, all as crowded as those in China. As we inched our way through the mob, I wondered what was going on, where the border guards were. Six or eight guys suddenly rushed at us, yelling and gesturing. They said we had to stop, as we had driven right by the border post. They turned out to be money changers. The government employees didn't pay much attention to who came and went here, but the money changers weren't about to miss a pair of potential customers. I was worried that we would be searched at the post, but getting through turned out to be a breeze.

On the other side of the border we found scores of money changers on chairs by the road, each with a calculator and a briefcase on his lap. I went from one to the other, checking the rate. It was like shopping for a stock on NASDAQ, as this was a competitive, liquid market. They all had basically the same rate. I couldn't figure out how they made a living, as this border, due to all the problems to the south, wasn't busy with travelers.

For the past two thousand miles we had been traveling on the Pan-American Highway through desert. After crossing the river into Ecuador, however, the landscape dramatically changed into lush rain forest. Spanish moss grew on phone lines, along with what I took to be air plants. Although the road was not bad, driving was difficult as there were no signs on the roads or in the towns. Not only did we feel constantly lost, but a couple of times we entered a major traffic circle and came out the other side, only to discover we were headed the wrong way on a one-way street.

Ecuador was prosperous, with much more traffic and economic activity than in Peru. We were in the south, the least prosperous portion of the country; the northeast was where oil had been found.

I'd seen an efficient free-market money system, and now I saw prosperity and great roads, along with lots of trucks, cars, and buses. That the border was so easy meant the country was open and fluid. If I could find a stock exchange, I decided I'd look into investing here.

Along this part of the route, the Pan-Am was a continuous fiesta, open day and night.

Shops on both roadsides displayed bananas, pineapples, oranges, lemons, limes, guavas, tomatoes—every kind of fruit and vegetable. Whole pigs hung in front of restaurants, few of which had more than fifteen tables. We could pick out our pork chop, which we'd have along with a salad, beans, rice, and a beer, and they'd grill it on the spot. Other stalls sold clothes, shoes, plumbing items, whatever was needed for daily life.

We drove into Guayaquil, Ecuador's largest city, on a good road over great bridges. The town had a glittering skyline. We found the best hotel, parked our motorcycles, and set out to find how to get to the Galápagos, which we knew were restricted for conservation reasons.

We were able to arrange a flight. From the island's airport we boarded a boat called the *Daphne* for five days of exploration.

With all the wildlife here—seals, turtles, lizards, and birds—it was easy to see why Darwin had found these islands a natural laboratory for evolution. As an example, a certain starling, all its numbers come from one great-granddaddy starling, had evolved differently on two separate islands, giving Darwin a clear vision of evolution.

On one of the shorelines, we stumbled onto a seal who had just given birth. Her blood was drying on the rock on which she lay. She was completely exhausted, but her new baby was bouncing around beside her. All about us turtles, seals, and birds were mating or giving birth. Baby somethings were everywhere. This was certainly a fecund place.

Darwin's days were long gone. As recently as thirty years before, the Galápagos might still have been a laboratory of evolution; now, with all of us traipsing around, it was over. Tourists were everywhere, ninety thousand a year, along with twelve thousand inhabitants recently arrived to service the visitors. Some of the nearby ocean fish had turned poisonous from eating garbage and sewage tossed overboard by the boats transporting tourists.

Goats had been here for generations; they were tame when introduced but had long since become wild. Now they were being killed to restore some centuries-old balance that the environmental authorities believed in. Not only was this a travesty in itself, but it was all the more appalling since some of the goats had evolved so that they could thrive on salt water.

The locals had used some of the money brought in by tourism to build a pathetic football stadium. So much for nature.

In Guayaquil we stayed in the town's best hotel, the Oro Verde, or "green gold," so named after the country's chief export, bananas, which accounted for 25 percent of its foreign-exchange earnings.

Banana trees were so plentiful here that we frequently had to brush their leaves and branches out of our path. It was easy to see how Ecuador, Costa Rica, Colombia, Honduras, Panama, and Guatemala had gotten the name "banana republics."

Together these countries accounted for three quarters of the world's exports of bananas, half of which went to Europe, 2.7 million tons of green gold a year. Apparently the Germans and Belgians were their best customers, their purchases having tripled during the eighties.

I continued to have a good feeling about Ecuador. The currency was convertible, the country prosperous. Following my usual custom, after several attempts to find someone who understood what I wanted, I went to the largest local bank that was a member of the stock exchange and had a branch in the United States.

I am not sexist, but every Latin American country is macho. I was immediately encouraged because everybody in the bank's stock department was a woman. If these jobs were so unimportant that they were filled by women, it meant the stock market was still on the ground floor. It meant I was in time.

I asked to see the head person, and to my joy another woman came out. Here I was in a black leather jacket and chaps, wanting to buy stocks. The chief, Irene Inez, immediately figured me for a drug runner. Luckily a friend of mine from the investment world had coincidentally connected with us in Guayaquil and happened to bring along John Train's book, *The New Money Masters,* the first chapter of which is about my investment methods. It took an entire day, but this book and a couple of faxed magazine articles convinced Señora Inez I was legit; otherwise she'd still be checking to see if I was a drug peddler. She took pictures of my passport, and I signed my name a thousand times. I began to consider myself lucky she didn't fingerprint me—all so I could give her my money.

Finally we opened an account. "When you arrive in Quito, the capital," Señora Inez said, "go by our legal department to sign some more forms."

I wrote her a dollar check and gave her instructions on what I wanted to buy, my usual mix, seven of the bluest chips on this very depressed exchange, such companies as a bank, a newspaper, and a brewery.

No problem, she told me.

In Quito I called the bank's legal department, but the lawyer didn't return my calls. I went by to see him twice, but both times he wasn't there. Figuring that seeing him was a formality, I let it go. After we looked around the city, we made our way north.

To jump ahead, long after I returned to New York, all I had for my dollar investment was a canceled check. I repeatedly wrote Señora Inez in Guayaquil asking for confirmation slips, records, an account statement, something.

After seven or eight months of this I wrote the ambassador in New York. He called the head of this department at the bank, and I finally received a letter from her.

"Señor Rogers," Señora Inez wrote, "it is not legal for foreigners to own shares in our country, so I will send you your money back. You must understand that the rate of exchange of our currency has gone down a bit since you deposited money here. You probably will not receive the entire amount you left."

I was beside myself. I had spent an entire day confirming this very point, the first one I make sure of when I invest in a country. Now I was glad one of my rules about these investments was to start small, so when problems like this cropped up, they were small problems. Another rule was that the foreign banks I dealt with have a branch in the States. First, if you want to straighten something out, it is easier if they are here, and second, they are a lot easier to sue if you have to—which I haven't.

Naturally, its United States branch was in Miami, which today is a South American money center. Americans in the Northeast think everything of consequence must be in New York, but to many people from Latin America the United States is Miami—it's Spanish-speaking, it's all they know of the States, and it's all they want to know. From their point of view it's a Latin American Hong Kong, Singapore, or Bangkok, an international city hospitable to their business.

So, I called up the Miami branch, got a Colombian who worked for them, and wanted to know what was going on, if he could help me.

"If the bank is only now telling me this is illegal," I said, holding my outrage in check, "then I shouldn't get my money back at a depreciated rate, because you took the money with a promise to buy me shares. I don't mind taking the currency risk in the stock market, but the bank shouldn't come back now, nine months later, and say, 'Hey, it wasn't legal in the first place.'"

"I don't understand this," said Señor Lopez. "I'm a foreigner. I own Ecuadorean shares."

"You own shares?"

"Yes. This sounds like a runaround. I'll see what I can do."

Letters passed back and forth, each exchange taking a month or so. At last my new friend in Miami told me, "We've got it taken care of. You can own shares if you sign certain papers. The legal department is going to translate the proper documents into English."

"Send them in Spanish," I said, knowing that translating them would take another two months.

Finally, I got the documents, in both Spanish and English. The cover letter told me to go to the Ecuadorean embassy in New York and have it certify my signature. It's no wonder there weren't more foreign investors in Ecuador if they each had to go through all this, but at least for once something in this mess was straightforward and clear.

At the embassy I gave the papers to the document consul, who asked what I was buying.

"Shares," I said.

"No," she said, "I can't sign that."

"Miss, please, just read the letter."

"No, I'm not going to read the letter. This isn't how these things are done. You have to obtain . . ." She rattled off a jumble of what sounded like intricate procedures.

"Wait a minute, Miss," I said, my exasperation rising. "Please, just read the letter. It's from the largest bank in Ecuador. It's written by their legal department, and they say I'm supposed to bring it here to you."

"They don't know what they're talking about."

Bureaucracy! I insisted on seeing the ambassador, or whatever the head guy was called here in New York.

Consul-General Ramos came out, listened to me, and murmured to the document clerk, but she was adamant. She wasn't going to do anything.

Señor Ramos started in on me, too, telling me all the steps I had to take, repeating her refusals.

"Would you simply read this?" I asked.

He glanced at it and began to shake his head, no.

"Look," I said, my voice rising in frustration, "I'm trying to invest money in your country. Why are you making this difficult? The legal department in the largest bank in your country says it's okay, I say it's okay—I want to give your country money, and all I've gotten is a huge runaround."

He kept shaking his head, and I was growing dizzy with disbelief. What century were these guys living in? I said I wanted to go over his head, to talk to his boss. Well, in the entire northern hemisphere there was nobody over his head; he *was* the boss.

Señor Ramos and I went back and forth a while longer, and finally something clicked with him. He had been thinking I was there to buy Ecuadorean alpaca or wool or some other cash crop, and that I needed contracts that had been approved by a million different departments back home. Obviously nobody had ever been in here to buy shares before, a fact that usually lights me up but that right then did not seem such an advantage. I'm almost always too early in these things. Maybe this was like Nepal, where I'd had the God-given sense to recognize that the country was too primitive and too much at risk of social disturbance to invest in and stayed out on my original trip there.

"Come back in three hours," he said, "and we'll have something typed up and you can sign it."

He gave me a beatific smile. All this for a signature guarantee.

He did it, I did it, and fifteen months after I gave them my dollar check I received the confirmations that I had bought shares. Cocky now, I bought some more—or rather sent another dollar check. Then I again had trouble getting confirmations of these new trades. I would call down there and one of Señora Inez's clerks would tell me they had bought the shares, but they would never quite manage to get me the confirmation slips.

International investing has its risks, and they're not all those of declining currencies and share prices.

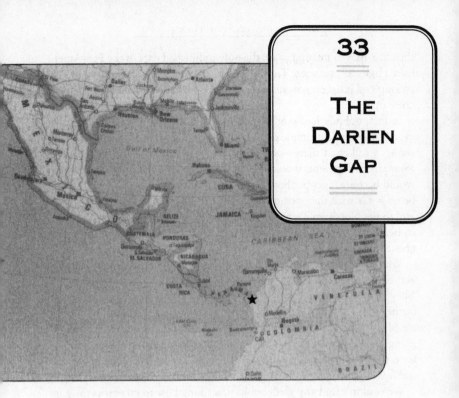

WITHIN AN HOUR OR SO of crossing the Colombian border we rode again through the glories of the Andes. In a forty-five-minute period we went from blazing summer at low levels into freezing winter at the misty tops of mountains, where we rode into clouds and then came out above them. We plunged into the desert, then across fields and up, down, and around hills. For people who love to drive, this was one of the world's great roads. These would be the last real mountains we would see until we hit the Canadian Rockies on our way to Alaska. What a glorious ride—but not many people vacationed here because of the guerrillas, the drug wars, and the cholera epidemic.

Everybody had heard of the Shining Path, but the Colombian guerrillas were just as dangerous and we were as worried here as we'd been in Peru. These guerrillas didn't have the PR geniuses on staff that the Shining Path had, or the cadres it sent to Europe to sell other left-wing movements on how terrific it was, how much it needed support, and how it was the "fourth wave."

We also began to worry seriously about the Darien Gap. Stretching from Colombia to Panama, it was a little more than a hundred miles as the crow flies of missing road, the only unfinished part of the Pan-American Highway between Tierra del Fuego and Alaska. Because of the swamp and jungle it covered, no ground traveler ever went over it as the crow flies.

In fact, nobody had ever figured out how to pave a way across it, or even how to build a simple path. If an entrepreneur could, and if he could set up a toll road there—and keep the local authorities from taking it away from him—he would become fabulously wealthy, for tourism would become gigantic through the region. Opening such a road would be on a par with the opening of the Silk Roads and routes to California and to the Northern Territory in Australia: boom-time, big-time. To do it, he would have to fight raging rivers, jungle, swamps, and the rabid greed of politicians.

Who would use it? Drive to Alaska in the summer and count the number of American RVs on the roads. Americans have an itchy foot. They're now beginning to tour Mexico, and before long they will push farther into Panama. There they will look longingly south and wish they could go yet farther, but they will have run out of road. Americans aren't going to load their RVs on a boat and tour Europe or Asia. South America is the obvious frontier for American travelers. A road to South America! It will produce one of the great travel booms of all time.

We couldn't find any guidebooks describing how to go across the gap from south to north. They all assumed you were headed south only, and nobody expected you to drive. We had to figure out how to cross it, a hundred-odd miles of swamp and jungle.

On many roads we continued to get astonished looks as Tabitha's bike swung into view.

Heads turned to follow her. Smooth brown faces registered shock as they realized, "It's a girl!" from the blond braid hanging out of the back of her helmet. Then they turned and said, "There's another one!" as I passed by their astonished gapes.

As tall, blond Tabitha strode down these streets in jeans and a black leather jacket, heads turned, especially those of women.

Driving into Pasto felt and looked like driving into a typical American city. Colombia was more prosperous than Ecuador, with shopping centers, American cars, stores, the whole modern works. I wondered if drug money had come this far south in Colombia and made this into a boomtown. Despite condos that reminded us of Wichita, guerrillas were active here, too. Seven government officials were assassinated the same day we passed through, but we saw nothing. We continued on toward Bogotá, still on an extraordinary road.

An investor had to be here to discover the prosperity, because it wasn't in the balance-of-trade figures. Drug trade statistics don't show up there. A lot of the money probably got stashed in Switzerland or Panama, so that it wasn't recorded by the central bank.

The road from Pasto to Cali was wonderful, but we had to be on the lookout for rock slides. The roadsides were full of *vulcanizadoreos,* places that patched and changed tires, symbolized by a used tire sticking up by the edge of the road. We had found this to be a symbol for these shops around the world. Tires here weren't made as well as in the States, yet the locals rode on them forever and needed a place to have them repaired. Here there were many more roadside repair shops than back in Africa, Siberia, and China, as there was lots more traffic, lots more people riding.

We encountered more blacks and people of mixed Native South American blood here than down south. The road life on the Pan-Am continued to be alive with cafés, hotels, fruit stands, and butchers.

As we had in Guayaquil and Quito, in Pasto we made inquiries about crossing the Darien Gap at airlines and boat companies.

In Cali we found out that a boat would take us around the missing leg of the Pan-American Highway. Boats left erratically from Buenaventura, although one travel agent here was certain they would not take motorcycles. The road to Buenaventura was bad, and we would have to cross a mountain. Another agent thought the boat would take the motorcycles but not us.

Then we were told about an airline that would take us, motorcycles and all, and surprisingly, the airfare was cheaper than that for the boat. Cheaper and faster appealed to me. A couple of hours and we'd go from Bogotá to Panama City.

That was the story, yet we had learned never to believe any of this stuff till we got to the point of departure and were actually on board.

In Bogotá the airline agent said he had a load ready to go. He would put us on the plane if we would go the next day. It meant we wouldn't spend as much time in Bogotá as we would like, but it also meant we wouldn't have to take a chance on not getting a flight at all. Transportation between countries was never simple. Next week somebody might want to know who had authorized us, if we were transporting drugs, were we smugglers, who had allowed the bikes to come, and had we been vaccinated. Besides, it might take them two weeks to load another plane, and then it might not have room for us.

At the airport we found that it was a cargo plane going north. As back in Beijing, they had never taken a motorcycle this way before, thus they didn't have any regulations and were easy about it. They didn't even want us to unhook the batteries and drain the gas tanks.

Getting aboard turned out to be such a snap, taking only two or three hours to process us through instead of an entire day, that we were early for the flight by several hours. We hot-footed it back into Bogotá by taxi to the Gold Museum, which had more and better gold work than any place in South America, and for my money, in the world. The tragedy was that the Spanish had melted down tons of gold artifacts for coins and sent them back to the motherland, all in a futile effort to prop up the sagging Spanish empire.

The plane turned out to be as long and empty as a truck. A hydraulic lift hoisted the pallet on which the bikes were strapped and shoved it inside. The plane was then loaded right up to the pilot's aluminum door. I sat on a padded bench outside, next to the toilet. Tabitha spent the hour flight in the cockpit looking at the countryside and oohing and aahing, letting the pilots show her what was going on. Doubting they'd have the same enthusiasm for me, I read the *International Herald-Tribune*.

I left South America even more bullish on the continent than when I'd arrived.

The old dictators and exchange controls were mostly gone, and the people were no longer in a mood to tolerate dictatorships by the military or left-wing professors of philosophy. Chile's economic miracle was a beacon to every other South American society: If Chile could better the lot of rich and poor alike, why couldn't their country?

South America didn't have the potential border problems of Central Europe and Africa, which lent it stability. The Spanish had given it two great gifts: a common language for a good portion of the continent and a common religion, Roman Catholicism. A third great cause of border strife, tribal differences, was minimal, partly because Chile and Argentina had solved their tribal problem by killing off everyone not of European descent in the nineteenth century. Only a stalled dispute between Peru and Ecuador over their border remained.

The South Americans were developing real stock exchanges, and in many cases, sound money. What else did an investor need to know? Using my formula of buying nearly every stock on the exchange, I'd bought shares in Ecuador, Peru, Bolivia, and Uruguay, as well as shares in Argentina. As exciting as Chile's prosperity was, its market wasn't for me at the time.

I was eager to see if the same economic revolution had visited Central America, where because of the strategic importance of the Panama Canal, Americans had meddled for more than a century.

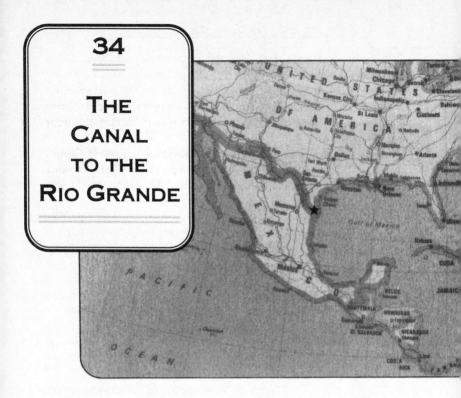

34

THE CANAL TO THE RIO GRANDE

FOR ALL MY SANGFROID about Judd, we were rushing by the time we reached Panama. Compared with the places we had crossed, Central America was small, about the size of France. Its 29 million people were about half France's population.

I suspected that Panama was a great short. While there might be a boomlet over the next several years in tourism, over the long term, as the military and canal employees leave, the economy will contract. Someday the world will come to its senses and legalize drugs, which will cause the money laundering and banking frenzy in this Switzerland of Central America to collapse.

The U.S. dollar is Panama's official currency although the Panamanians call it the balboa. After we leave, the Panamanians will literally have to print their own currency, since I can't see where else they will get more. When it comes to printing money, Latin Americans have a long and rich tradition of overdoing it. For a while they will make enough dollars off the canal to keep the country looking prosperous, especially if they allow the canal's maintenance to run down.

Panama City is essentially an American outpost, an American colony. It made us think we were back in America—a Marriott hotel, a Kentucky Fried Chicken, and a McDonald's. The supermarkets looked like those in the States. We didn't even need a carnet to enter the country, which almost made me dizzy, like a deepwater fish suddenly come to the surface. We were told we wouldn't need one between here and the States, which is one of the reasons recreational vehicles eventually will be able to come this far south.

We found a BMW dealer. In addition to the regular ten-thousand-kilometer servicing, the luggage racks had to be welded again and one of my rear shocks had to be replaced. God knew when we would see another dealer. We had a book listing them, but it might be out of date or the dealers might have gone broke.

Panama was peaceful because of the American military presence, but we were about to head into three or four more war zones. As usual, we gathered information about what was ahead. We would have to go through at least six of the seven Central American countries, although we still weren't sure what to do about El Salvador, which was said to have a good road but was in an all-out, shoot-'em-up war. Costa Rica was at peace, but in Nicaragua, where theoretically the war had ended, the Sandinistas and the contras were going at it again because they weren't happy with the peace settlement. Not only was the road through Honduras bad, but bandits and smugglers would come at you, and sometimes the guerrillas in Nicaragua and El Salvador spilled across its borders. In Guatemala, a major civil war raged. There were two ways to go through Guatemala, and we kept trying to find someone who knew which was safer.

We set out to see the canal, which was extraordinary. I was prepared for an operation run with the efficiency of the U.S. post office, but I was surprised. As they did with the early days of the space program, our people ran the canal successfully, with military precision and dispatch.

The canal itself is one of the wonders of the modern age. It took seventy-five thousand men ten years to construct it at a cost of $400 million, real money back in 1903. The builders of the canal faced huge problems: tropical disease; the unusual geology of the isthmus, which made landslides a constant hazard; the enormous size of the locks and the volume of the excavation needed; and the need to establish entire new communities, to import every last nail, and to organize work on a scale to rival that at the pyramids and Machu Picchu.

Through an intricate series of locks, the canal raised a ship eighty-five feet to Gatun Lake, which at the time of construction had been the world's largest manmade lake. Ships then crossed its 23.5 miles and were lowered a second eighty-five feet to the other ocean.

The Canal doesn't operate on a first-come, first-served basis. Ships make appointments long in advance. A screw-up, forcing the canal to be down for a few days, ties up shipping all over the hemisphere.

Unfortunately, the canal had been built almost a hundred years before. By now ships had grown to the point where many were too large to pass through. Even when they fit, it took eight to ten hours to travel the fifty miles from deep water in the Atlantic to deep water in the Pacific.

The Panama Canal is technically obsolete now—too narrow, and it takes too long for ships to go through. For years builders had had to design ships so they could pass through the canal by making them narrower and smaller than was ideal. With advances in engines and fuel efficiency, however, which enabled ships to round the Horn in days instead of months, they could build super sizes and bypass the canal for the Horn.

Supply and demand was working hard once again. For a long time our government had had a monopoly on this Atlantic-Pacific passage and it had kept raising prices. When it had cost say $100,000 to go through the canal and $97,000 to go around, owners had sent their ships through the canal, figuring the risk of rounding the Horn wasn't worth it. When it had become twice as expensive to go through the canal, they went around.

In the history of the world there has never been a monopoly that has lasted forever. The canal was one you'd have thought was perfect; but the world changed, as it always does. Most monopolies price themselves too high or become inefficient and lax and provide bad service. Our post office is a good example, a monopoly imposed by law. No one but the U.S. postal service is even allowed to put an envelope into your mailbox. Still, United Parcel captured the package business because its customers couldn't afford to send their packages through the monopoly.

It was a marvel to watch huge boats go through the canal, no more than a foot of margin on either side of a hundred-foot-wide hull. The need for such military precision in all operations of the canal made me pessimistic about the future of the canal and Panama. What most heads of state do in a place like Panama with a prize like the canal is use it as a job source for cronies and hacks.

In 1990 the canal took in $355 million dollars on thirteen thousand transits. During the prior ten years the U.S. government had spent $100 million a year streamlining and improving canal facilities and operations. Had it made a profit? Did anyone know?

For the first year or even several years after the U.S. leaves in 1999, the canal will be well run by the old employees, who have been running it properly, but then some politician will decide his nephew can do a better job. (Remember, every nephew down here needs a job.) Taking a look at the books, this smart nephew will say, "Hmmm, our profit is going down. Why do we have to spend so much money oiling the gates?" or, "Why patch that crack where the tanker banged the wall? Why paint continuously? Why run the air conditioners night and day to keep out a little mold?" The easiest way to raise profits will be to defer maintenance.

Eventually Panama will put itself out of the canal business, partly because all the money brought in by American support personnel will be gone, and partly because it will make a mess of the maintenance. The Panamanians have misjudged the canal as a big moneymaker. Nobody has any idea whether it's profitable or not. If anything has ever been abundantly clear, it's that the U.S. government does not know how to keep a proper set of books, and our government becomes especially hopeless whenever the money spent is listed for national defense.

Central America, to a far greater extent than South America, has been heavily influenced by North America. Someday lots of Americans will drive down to Panama and back. I see the day when Avis will rent you a car you can drop off in Panama City, or you will be able to rent one there and drive to Tulsa. We were even able to find a road map in a filling station, something almost unheard of over the past four continents.

The United States has had a 150-year-long history of basically owning these Central American countries. When they have strayed too far afield, when they've gotten too uppity, we've come in and thrown our weight around. Just in my lifetime, this has happened in El Salvador, Nicaragua, Costa Rica, and Panama.

Costa Rica had a huge national or civil guard, to whom American advisors were teaching map reading and other military techniques. Map reading? After all these years, you'd think their instructors would have got the hang of it, but no, our advisors were still there, still a buffer between Nicaragua and our interests in Panama. With the airplane and today's instant communications, the canal was not as important as it had been in the First World War, but generals often lack the vision to look ahead and continue to be stuck fighting the last war, if not the one before. Once Panama had become important, the domino theory took hold. Every country next to one next to Panama had become important to keep in line.

Costa Rica periodically was pushed in the States as a place to invest because of its beautiful beaches, mountains, jungles, etc. Many American retirees had moved there. Costa Rica had been bankrupt three or four times in the past one hundred and fifty years, but the hucksters always left that out. It had an extremely high debt per capita, a huge fiscal deficit, and high inflation. We heard talk of increasing taxes on retirees going to Costa Rica to live. Talk about killing the goose that laid the golden egg! Nobody ever accused governments of being wise. The smart retirees would move to Nicaragua, Panama, and Mexico.

Still, I invested in Costa Rica because the government had decided to develop a stock market. I went down to the stock market and saw the president of the exchange, a woman. She was getting ready to join the International Association of Stock Exchanges. Exchange officials had a mandate to develop a stock exchange and it wanted to see what other people in the world were doing, how it was done.

Once she told me she was joining IASE I could have walked out right then and said, "This is all I need to know. Buy. It's this simple." But I talked to her some more, found a solid broker, and opened an account. Tourism through here will be gigantic in the future. Costa Rica's principal economic industries are in sugar, cocoa, coffee, and tourism. Cocoa, sugar, and coffee have been in long-term bear markets, but when and if these agricultural markets revive, the Costa Rican economy will go through the roof just because of them. Nothing like a bull market to make an investor look smart.

I bought what I always buy: the largest, soundest companies on the exchange—the largest newspaper, the biggest brewery, a bank, an agricultural company, pretty much everything it had to sell. I left word to let me know if more came on the market, and went back on the road.

As we were heading for the border of Costa Rica, we were stopped by a speed trap.

"You were doing eighty kilometers in a fifty-kilometer zone," the sergeant said in Spanish.

"No," I argued in Spanglish, "it says right here on your own government maps the speed limit is eighty unless posted otherwise."

"No, it's fifty here in the town," said Sergeant Mendoza.

"What! This is all rain forest. There hasn't been a town for thirty kilometers."

"Back there is a sign saying fifty kilometers," he insisted. "You have to pay a fine."

"Let's go back," I said. "Show me."

So, like a caravan, we went back twenty-five kilometers, fifteen miles. He proudly showed us a sign facing opposite to our direction saying the limit was fifty kilometers.

"This is going the other way," I said in English. "Into the town we were coming out of, you stupid son of a bitch."

Sergeant Mendoza knew one phrase in English, and "son of a bitch" was it.

"You have insulted an officer of the law, Señor," he said, "and you were doing eighty-eight. Follow us."

We all drove to headquarters, where a captain came out and each side gave his story. While we were talking Tabitha noticed one of the soldiers edging toward the bikes.

Immediately suspecting that he would plant drugs, I walked over and said, "Hey, what do you want? If you want to look at something we'll show it to you." We had been warned about this throughout Africa, South America, and Central America, a favorite cop trick to deal with people they wanted to gouge or put in jail, and we looked like prime targets.

I paid our fine, acting properly humble. I said I was sorry I'd called Sergeant Mendoza a son—*if* I called him a son of a bitch, I was sorry.

In fact, it was the only speeding ticket we got in going around the world.

After the border crossing into Nicaragua, we hit a checkpoint a few miles farther on. Then another several miles later, and then yet another.

Sometimes the soldiers were so occupied with backed-up cars, we'd sail by without their flagging us. More often, however, we were the event of a boring week for the soldiers. In addition to scrutinizing our papers, they wanted to flirt with Tabitha and ogle the bikes. If we were lucky, this took fifteen minutes; if unlucky, forty-five. Nearly always we persuaded them not to search everything.

After the tenth checkpoint, I was boiling over even though I knew it didn't do any good to get angry. After so many tens of thousands of miles of delays, I kept trying to reconcile myself to these inevitable snags of travel, but two hundred forty miles across this country and what, twenty checkpoints? One every twelve miles? Rationally, I understood everything. The Sandinistas and the contras had been integrated into the armed forces, and the country had to do something with them.

I asked, "Why do you need to look at these passports? How do you think we got here if we haven't been through one checkpoint after another? Here we are in the middle of this country—do you think we fell from the sky?"

We were moving through Central America in the rainy season. Fortunately when it rained, it didn't last long in any one spot.

As we rode along, sometimes we saw a sheet of rain ahead that looked like a waterfall splashing from the sky. We would stop, put on our rain suits, and creep forward. Unlike the States, where rain sprinkles first, here we would enter a wall of water. After a few minutes we would exit the ministorm, which was like driving out from under a waterfall.

Managua, Nicaragua's capital, was a beaten-up city with seedy buildings and bullet holes. No glitz here, no glamour, nothing. The war had worn out everybody and everything—people, buildings, environment.

Here was a country with 3.9 million people that had been superpowered to death, and for no decent reason. One machine gunner's pillbox around a curve had written on it, "All will be better," somebody's pathetic hope.

After Roosevelt withdrew the marines from Nicaragua back in the thirties, we left the Somozas in power. Various family members ruled until President Carter withdrew his support, enabling the Sandinistas, the Communist-socialist-left-wing crowd, to take over.

There was an election and the Sandinistas won. The CIA and the State Department realized what had happened here—Oh, my God, the Communists! The first domino had fallen.

Around the world the socialists were shouting, "Praise, socialism triumphant!" The Swedes sent money and volunteers. The *Nation* magazine sent its readers on special tours. The Russians sent rubles. Daniel

Ortega, leader of the Sandinistas, sent himself to Moscow. Here was another foothold for the benighted peoples of the world in the western hemisphere. Naturally, the Sandinistas were great friends with Castro. Naturally, we started financing the contras, which eventually led to Colonel North and Irangate.

The world went berserk over this tiny country, ruining what wealth it had, because its government might have been Commies in disguise, and another domino was falling.

Then the contras won the next election. To the contras' consternation, before turning over the reins of power, the Sandinistas had handed over land, jobs, and payoffs to their supporters, just as politicians do everywhere.

The whole thing would have been comic if so many people's lives hadn't been destroyed by these passing ideological wars.

In Costa Rica we decided to drive through El Salvador rather than try to go around it. It worried me that we were getting blasé about war zones, particularly when we still had three through which to drive.

We couldn't find high-octane gas here, nor was I optimistic about getting any when we reached El Salvador.

It took time even to leave these countries, an hour to clear Costa Rica, an hour and a half for Nicaragua.

Entering Honduras was rough. At its border we were more thoroughly searched than we had been for months, and we had to pay little bribes at every step of the absurd process.

We found a decent hotel, and at night we went to the American International Circus, which was in town. Sitting in the front row, Tabitha was referred to as the "gringa."

Showers didn't work at the hotel so we again used the bucket method. I couldn't find postcards here since not many travelers come this way— too many wars in neighboring countries.

From the border of El Salvador to its capital, San Salvador, we constantly encountered soldiers. Here was the first bridge I'd seen destroyed by war, a majestic span sprawled in the river and replaced by a pontoon bridge, over which we drove. It was painful to see. God knew how many years it had taken these people to build this bridge, how important it had been to them, how much it had cost, and some self-proclaimed savior had blown it up.

· · ·

San Salvador, even in the middle of an awful civil war, was vibrant and dynamic. We drove in on a Sunday, right into a traffic jam, cars everywhere. On every side was street life—outdoor cafés, stalls, and people strolling about. We tried iguana, which tasted like fish, and roast armadillo, which had the flavor of a hefty steak carved out of a thick, gamy slab of chicken.

In stark contrast to Managua, San Salvador looked like Los Angeles. For the same reason that New York was more exciting and vibrant than Salt Lake City—the population was denser—San Salvador was exciting because it contained so many people.

In El Salvador the government had set up a special project to establish a stock market, which might open in a year.

Much to my own surprise, I decided to invest here, figuring the worst was over. The country's most important industry was textiles, but it also produced shoes, furniture, chemicals, fertilizers, pharmaceuticals, cosmetics—the list went on and on. Exports of manufactured goods, mostly to other Central American countries, accounted for 24 percent of its foreign-exchange earnings. And all this even though a war had raged here over the past twelve years between the right and the left, the capitalists and the socialists, a typical conflict of the late twentieth century that will make our great-grandchildren shake their heads in wonder as we shake our heads today over religious wars of the Middle Ages.

Everybody here was sick of the war. Billboards pictured a mutilated kid with the caption WHY ARE WE DOING THIS? The impression I had was of a people saying, "Enough is enough. Let's get this damn thing over with." The Communists didn't have more money to pour in here, and we Americans were fed up with the entire thing because every time we opened up a newspaper our allies had killed six nuns or blown up something or done something else that made us sick. Posters from both sides proclaimed, "We don't want to do this anymore."

Looking for a means to invest, I finally wound up with the guy whose job it was to develop the stock market. In his thirties, he'd been to Northeastern University. I was a year or so early, here before the market had officially opened, so I'd have to do something unorthodox if I wanted to buy now, right at what I thought was the bottom.

So, I did something I almost never do: I bought shares in a large private project, the newly developing free-trade industrial park. I saw the end of the war staring me in the face, and I figured coffee and sugar prices were certain to rise someday. I was certain El Salvador had to be a winner. The U.S. had spent billions blowing the place up, so I knew we would pour billions in after the war ended. We couldn't very well let El Salvador fail after all that.

Investing a bit in El Salvador and Costa Rica wasn't quite as promising as investing in Japan or Germany in 1945, but no one could deny these countries had hit bottom.

We stopped in on Tikal in northern Guatemala to see what we'd been told were the best Mayan ruins.

Tikal had been an extensive city of 50,000 at its peak, from 500 A.D. to 1000 A.D. When they arrived in Yucatan in the sixteenth century, the Spaniards found only primitive descendants of the Mayans, poor *indígenas* who had but legends of the race of giants who had spawned them.

Vast buildings rose over several square miles, primitive skyscrapers thrusting up through the lush jungle. This civilization had endured for thirty-four centuries, rivaling those of the Egyptians and Chinese for longevity and complexity. The Mayan civilization had spread over an area the size of France, encompassing present-day Guatemala, Belize, parts of Mexico, Honduras, and El Salvador. Tikal alone had three thousand buildings, temples, palaces, shrines, ceremonial platforms, ordinary residences, ball courts, terraces, causeways, and burial vaults, the result of eleven hundred years of ceaseless construction. None of this might ever have been discovered if some ambitious entrepreneur in the nineteenth century hadn't been beating his way through the jungle looking for chicle, the resin needed for chewing gum, and stumbled on these gigantic stone structures. When he spotted Tikal, only the tops of its tallest buildings stuck out, a couple of feet above the earthen mounds encompassing them. In some mysterious fashion the omnivorous jungle had raised earth to cover over these giant buildings. Ten years later and this entrepreneur might well have missed this discovery, and the glory of Tikal would have been lost for all time. This story, that of Easter Island, and those of many other sites we'd seen made me wonder how many civilizations, lasting how many hundreds if not thousands of years, had never been discovered by modern man.

Stories of the sacred Mayan ball games, after which the winning team's captain was sacrificed to honor his victory, bewildered us. Human sacrifice, like war, was an aspect of man I couldn't understand any more than I could understand or condone capital punishment, in which we trust the state to decide who is to live or die. In eighteenth-century France starving men were put to death for stealing bread. Think of the millions throughout history who have been executed for "crimes" we now do not even punish—being a Christian, trading in currencies, not wearing a veil, not joining a collective, not supporting an evil dictator—whatever. Today in our country drug "criminals" are executed on the word of a single snitch, himself subject to immense pressure by heavy-handed threats from the state. Prosecutors gunning for governor aren't too particular who they convict; a death-penalty case adds another trophy for their campaign. Today among the "civilized" nations, only Russia, China, the United States, and South Africa still execute criminals. Are we in the company we want to keep?

Throughout history thousands of innocent men have been executed. How many stories have we read in which murderers were hanged and yet later the murder victim was found alive and well? I shudder at what it must be like to go to your own execution knowing it is all a mistake—that you are in fact innocent.

In the ruins of Tikal, archaeologists had found more than one hundred thousand tools and implements, as well as more than a million potsherds, useful in carbon dating. They estimated that what they had uncovered was only the tip of the iceberg, that they needed another century of digging and evaluation to understand these ancient people fully. The North Acropolis took one thousand years to build, and it had within it layers of older buildings, giving archaeologists a means of unraveling this civilization's development. The Mayans had implemented the use of zeros and positional digits in their numbering system a thousand years before such sophistication reached Europe from India via the Arabs.

This was the highest flowering of Stone Age civilization archaeologists had yet uncovered. Man's adaptability allowed him, with whatever he had, to develop to extraordinary heights, to create great art and architecture. If he had stone only, he could still create quite a civilization, sometimes more elaborate than many others using iron and the wheel.

On viewing this site with its thousands of buildings, I was struck by mankind's propensity for social organization and hierarchy. The highest authority appeared to have been a combination of the religious and the civil, as if the ruler were both high priest and commander-in-chief. Like the pharaohs, he was half man and half god. He and his class devoted themselves to civic purposes, as well as to the scientific and artistic pursuits of the high Stone Age.

And what pursuits these were! In Petén, temple-pyramids rose as high as 225 feet. At Uxmal, a single building was composed of 450,000 cubic yards of material, a million tons of cut stone, mortar, and building blocks. The Acropolis at Copán covered twelve acres, rose 125 feet, and was composed of more than 2.5 million cubic yards and 5 million tons of material. None of these buildings was thrown up over a weekend; all were evidence of a successful and prosperous society, a powerful hierarchy, and a centralized administration.

Throughout this trip we encountered many societies with varying social structures that had accomplished amazing feats. We stood now in the ruins of a theocracy, but we'd traveled through socialist, Communist, fascist, and democratic systems, with every gradation in between, along with any number of monarchic ancient civilizations, from the Carthaginians to the Aztecs. What struck me was that in every one a hierarchical structure had prevailed. Whether the system was organized by priests, party bosses, barons, kings, capitalist owners, or ward heelers, somebody was on top and somebody else was on bottom. Even if we could magically start out on the proverbial level playing field, no matter what the system, it wouldn't take more than a day for those who were ambitious and those who were smart to figure out a plan for getting a bigger grass hut or even two grass huts. The fellow who was both ambitious and smart would shortly have himself a dozen grass huts, and the next thing you knew, he'd crown himself king and have his sons and daughters called princes and princesses.

It looked to me like a law of social dynamics.

In Mexico I bought some grasshoppers cooked in thick hot sauce. Tabitha wouldn't eat them, but I thought they were even better than the grilled termites back in Africa.

Predictably, the government-owned Pemex gas-station monopoly gave poor service and an awful selection.

The people here were mestizo, a change from the *indígenas* we had seen since Costa Rica. Mexicans seemed more sophisticated than the people we'd encountered for a while. They seemed even sleek and prosperous. Here we found outdoor cafés and public concerts. Like Argentina, Mexico was selling off its state-owned banks, TV stations, and other companies, invigorating them. The stock market was on the front pages of the newspapers, so that boom had to be nearing a top—at least temporarily.

We skipped Mexico City, forgoing its pollution for a drive along a wonderful road through the Sierra Madres to Puebla. The country's fourth largest city, Puebla was a real charmer, with street after street of old colonial buildings, balconies, tiles, filigree, towers, and churches. It brought home all over again how glorious and rich Mexico and Peru had been in the sixteenth, seventeenth, and eighteenth centuries, during a time when the United States had been little more than a scrub tract. Here had risen centers of civilization with their own art, culture, and religion. Unfortunately, money had come to the citizens so easily that they hadn't had to invest, become productive, and plan for the future. Their problem had been how to spend it fast enough, and spend they had, on monuments, carriages, houses, and churches instead of on factories, canals, and roads. Consumption rather than investing for the future—it's no wonder their grandeur was so short-lived.

This trip had been the most enormous event of my life, and now that we were nearing its end, several emotions surged through me. I was having a hard time wrestling with the grim reality that the trip was nearly over. I ached for it to last longer, and at the same time I was pleased that it looked as if it would be successful.

On a broader plane, I was saddened for my country. Everywhere we'd been, every society was untying the statist knots that had strangled it for decades, centuries in some cases. Everyone was throwing off all sorts of social and economic shackles, but the United States was heading in the other direction, relentlessly putting on controls, regulations, rules, and laws to control centrally its citizens, businesses, schools, and charities, one of the prime methods the Soviets, Latin Americans, and Africans had used to strangle themselves.

We found that the rest of the world was trying to be like what they thought we were—and indeed were at one time.

Today many businesses in Europe and Japan are loath to sell to us because we sue at the first glitch and our myriad regulations eliminate all profit. As an example dear to motorcyclists' hearts, BMW won't sell its excellent motorcycle helmets here. The regulations, insurance, potential liabilities, possible boycotts, and lawsuits eliminate all incentive. The manufacturers of the French morning-after birth-control pill, RU-486, have been extremely reluctant to market their pill here. Today even though an ex-husband pays alimony and child-support promptly, his ex-wife can garnishee his salary, creating more paperwork for corporations, who must hire employees to administer these rules. Our doctors are drowning in paperwork and federal procedures, often spending twenty hours a week on them.

Our statist nightmare goes on and on. Under the Clean Air Act employers must actively help their employees develop alternatives to driving to work. Under the Disabilities Act an employer has to keep employees who have had nervous breakdowns on the job, and must find work they can do. As much as we need export earnings, even in 1994 many U.S. cities and states wouldn't do business with companies that trade with South Africa, even though virtually every other country, including black African nations, have been doing so for years. In both South Africa and Vietnam, where enormous positive changes have taken place for some time, there's a feast to which every country in the world was invited. We Americans didn't get there till after dessert, in time to dine on the scraps.

The United States can't compete with others who don't have such requirements, so how beneficial to us are they in the long run? These may be worthwhile, but someone has to pay for them. And you know who that is, you and me—and eventually the entire country's prosperity.

The North American Free Trade Agreement should be good for the United States, Canada, and Mexico.

If it's good for California and Mississippi to trade duty-free with each other, why not the United States with Mexico and Canada? We forget free trade was one of the great secrets of the British Empire's success. The British brought capital, markets, and administrative and technical know-how to the colonies, which in turn provided labor, natural resources, and markets, a perfect recipe for commercial success.

Many well-intentioned Americans don't see it this way. Along the *maquiladora,* the industrial zone in northern Mexico where five hundred thousand Mexicans work for United States companies, Zenith pays a dollar an hour, Ford $1.25, and General Motors and General Electric pay hundreds of workers only thirty dollars to forty dollars a week.

These low wages put up the backs of many United States' unions and workers. How can we possibly compete? they ask. Surely the U.S. should protect its citizens' jobs.

I don't see it that way. In fact, G.E. sells more goods to Mexico, $750 million worth, than all G.E.'s Mexican-based operations sell to the U.S., $500 million worth. This surplus contributes to our overall favorable balance of trade with Mexico of some $5 billion a year. Working off the Commerce Department's assumption that every $1 billion in U.S. exports supports twenty thousand jobs, G.E.'s $750 million in exports to Mexico supports fifteen thousand jobs. Our positive balance of trade means that we have one hundred thousand extra jobs in this country because of our trade with Mexico.

With Mexico's coming growth and elimination of protectionism, we'll sell the country a lot more, too, particularly high-tech products like cars, computers, medical equipment, and machine tools. Only one out of sixteen Mexicans has a car, compared with one out of two Americans. What an opportunity for us instead of the Japanese with the advantage of NAFTA.

Freed at last of its statist restrictions, Mexico will grow. As it continues to expand, it will need to develop its infrastructure. The U.S. Agency for International Development has estimated that power demand in Mexico will grow as much as 7 percent annually between 1989 and 1999. In this expansionary boom it will spend tens of billions of dollars. The chairman of General Electric de Mexico estimates that a recent order his company received to help construct the Samalayuca II power plant is worth $200 million to G.E. and that it will generate more than seven hundred employee-years of work in Schenectady, New York, and Greenville, South Carolina. Is this *bad* for the United States?

From a long-term perspective, NAFTA ties together three natural trading partners. We have some capital and markets, the Canadians have the natural resources, and Mexico has abundant labor and growing markets.

Yes, there will be some worker dislocations here, but should we preserve several thousand steelworkers' jobs and deprive 260 million Americans of the benefits of cheaper steel?

Yes, we might even lose large numbers of jobs, maybe 250,000 over the next several years, but we will gain another 500,000. The political problem is that those 250,000 who think they'll lose their jobs are highly vocal, whereas Joe Smith, twenty-three, who in two years will go to work making air conditioners to be shipped to Mexico, doesn't yet know about his new job, isn't organized along with the other lucky Americans to clamor for it, and isn't lobbying his congressman.

What worries me is something entirely different. The marriages of our individual states into the United States, and of the Common Market countries, each contains a mix of the rich and poor, the well-financed and the nearly bankrupt. However, NAFTA brings together the United States, Mexico, and Canada, three of the largest debtor nations in the world, all three nearly bankrupt. It is a good plan with benefits for all three countries, but no one has ever put together three such large bankrupt entities. In the end it could turn out to be three drunks leaning on one another in what might be a vain lurch to find home, but on balance it should benefit everyone.

The risk is that the three deadbeats might try to go it alone in their new union and build barriers to trade against the outside world. As with the Common Market, this would be the worst possible outcome, containing within it the seeds of our own destruction, as we would give up learning how to compete successfully with the rest of the world.

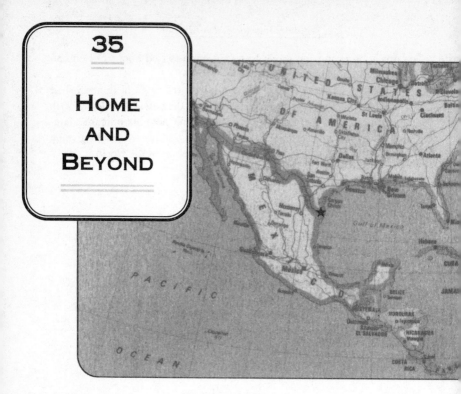

35

HOME
AND
BEYOND

WE CROSSED THE U.S. border at Brownsville, Texas, and celebrated with a dinner of Church's fried chicken and Pabst Blue
Ribbon beer. We had to sit outside in the parking lot because of the beer,
but who cared. We'd made it!

It astonished me how Hispanic southern Texas is. Brownsville is 80
percent Hispanic. Even the Brownsville newspaper, in existence since
sometime in the nineteenth century, was now being published in Spanish.

The second night in the States we wound up in the Houston home of a
friend, George Stark. This was the first time we'd been with Americans
for almost two years. I was under so much culture shock, I was almost
dizzy.

My friend's wife, Lois, was taken by our voyage and kept asking us,
"How has it changed you?"

We scarcely realized we were back. We were still worrying about
crossing borders and finding gas, wondering if our tires were okay and if
the road ahead was paved and where we could find a decent room for the
night. She asked a lot of perceptive questions, but all I could mutter was
"I hope next time we meet I'll have better answers to your questions."

Something was different within me, but I couldn't say what. As we drove east I began to muse on the question.

I knew that for a long time I had wanted to scrap completely my old life and start a new one. I had yearned to find a new road that was right for me. If I could just find the right road, I'd know it and follow it to its culmination. If I could just find the right road . . . Would this trip lead to the epiphany I'd been seeking?

We went on to New Orleans and to Alabama, where my cousins Pettus and Cathy Randall gave us a celebratory barbecue.

Everybody else was in dress-up clothes, but all I had still were my jeans and leather jacket. I tacked our multicolored map of the world on the wall, traced out our route, and answered questions.

After that was over, a latecomer cornered me. "How was the trip?"

"Well, it's not over yet," I said. "We plan to head on up to New York in a couple of days."

"My God!" he said. "Don't tell me you're going to drive all the way from Alabama to New York on a motorcycle!"

We had parties all along the coast, looking up people and eating dinner with friends in Montgomery, Birmingham, Atlanta, Charlotte, Washington, and Philadelphia. We'd seen so much and had been gone so long that I understood the difficulties Marco Polo must have experienced trying to communicate the glory and vastness of China to thirteenth-century Italians.

I kept warning Tabitha not to get overconfident just because we were close to home, but I was the one who fell off the bike. It happened in Tennessee. Again, I was pushing too hard in the evening, trying to make more mileage than I should. Ironically, having been around the world without mishap, I finally had an accident. I banged a rib, chipped two bones in my hand, and cut my chin.

We drove into Philadelphia and got caught in a huge rush-hour traffic jam.

Gosh, I thought, traffic jams are the same all over the world.

Finally we drove into New York on a fabulous November day accompanied by the bright, dancing strains of Chopin on WQXR.

We'd now been gone twenty months. My odometer said we'd covered

57,020 miles, and we hadn't yet gone to Alaska. We'd been on boats and in the air another forty-odd thousand for a total of nearly one hundred thousand miles.

Arriving home we felt weak, overwhelmed, and tearful. As I entered my house, I wished the trip wasn't over, but I also wanted to know if everything was all right. What had happened to my life over the past two years? Box after box of mail rose on the kitchen floor, and I had all the problems Judd had engineered to sort out.

I went through the entire house, basement to roof, to satisfy myself that everything was as I'd left it. Even though it was the seventeenth of November, on the roof garden two yellow roses had blossomed, which I took to be a sign of good luck.

We opened a bottle of Dom Pérignon and had black-eyed peas, rice, and collard greens for the first time in two years.

The next morning I went to a board meeting at nine o'clock.

"I haven't seen you in a while," a guy asked. "What have you been up to?"

"I've just been around the world on a motorcycle."

He smiled and said that was nice.

It takes a lot to impress a New Yorker.

AFTERWORD

In December I gave Tabitha the gold necklace I'd bought in Buenos Aires, and she was surprised and delighted.

After a rest, we hit the road again, this time to Alaska, bringing our trip total to 65,067 miles.

When we got there, we realized how different people in the Yukon and Alaska are from those in Ottawa and Washington, D.C. As in so many places we passed through around the world, these people aren't the joiners and backslappers of the capitals, they are loners and mavericks, a hardier breed produced by the rugged nature of their habitat. Thousands of miles and several time zones from Washington, Alaska has only a half-million people in a space a sixth the size of the lower forty-eight states.

How can Alaskans allow Washington to run their lives? What do the moles of the Beltway know of their lovely, stark country? Alaskans have only a single congressman and two senators in Washington, which means the capital largely ignores the wishes of its inhabitants.

In fact, Alaskans have more in common with their neighbors in the Yukon and in Siberia than they have with bureaucrats in Washington, Ottawa, or Moscow. If the three of them, fabulously rich in mineral resources, aligned themselves into an independent frontier nation, they could attract enormous development capital.

Her eyes opened to several things by her nearly two years of traveling, Tabitha's off to graduate school now, studying international relations, although she might be better equipped to teach it than someone who's only read about it in books.

To show you how fast the world changes, I have traded in several additional countries outside the United States, including Austria, Italy, Turkey, and Ireland, countries that when we passed through them didn't seem like good buys. Not only did the market in Turkey drop 85 percent, but the government took many steps to make the environment better for investment, providing me with an excellent opportunity. As the African National Congress became more moderate, at least for negotiating and electorial purposes, I invested in the South African stock market for awhile. I've even started putting small amounts of money into other African countries, as the continent has evolved as I expected it would.

There's a warrant out for Judd's arrest, but the police tell me that even though he admitted forging my signature several times, it's not worth their while to extradite him. It's a sad state of affairs when the criminal-justice system is too busy with other crimes to chase down an admitted felon.

I fulfilled my dream. I now know the world in the way I'd hoped to, and it has not only helped me understand investing better, it has given me a better sense of who we are as a species. We're certainly a lot more robust than statist politicians, seeking to solve every problem conceivable—real and imagined—would have us believe.

Now that I'm back, having seen a good part of the world close to the ground, people ask how the United States looks to me. I hate to say it, because this is my home, but I see America as an obvious short sale.

It's painful to see how hopelessly provincial and isolated we still are in this country. It's frightening that neither political party has been or is willing to address our economic problems.

Around the world we saw firsthand what statist shackles had done to so very many countries, and I can see clearly that here in the States it will have to become far worse before it gets better.

I am convinced that Clinton will be the last president of his party. In 1918, Lloyd George, head of the Liberal Party, was Prime Minister of England. To the Brits, he and his party won World War I. He was as popular as any post-war hero in history.

However, the British economy, the system, the society, the currency—
you name it—was a mess underneath, just as ours is today. Even though
Lloyd George was a world-renowned leader of his party, which had
dominated U.K. politics for decades, there has never been a prime minister from his party since because of that mess, just as Clinton will be the
last leader his party ever elects. The Democrats controlled both the exec-
utive and the legislative branches of government during the pivotal
1992–1994 period, so they will get a lot of the blame. The Democrats also
have serious demographic problems. Their strength for decades has been
(1) converts during the Depression who are now decreasing in numbers,
(2) unions that continue to lose power, (3) white Southerners who are
abandoning the party in droves, and (4) blacks from whom they cannot
hope for more than the 80% support they get now. The Democrats will
not just disappear any more than did the British Liberal Party. In fact, the
Liberal Party still exists as a rump all these decades later. No, the
Democrats will just wither away.

Don't get me wrong, the Republicans deserve a lot of the blame; their
split and/or demise will come later if they do not do something quickly
about the problems we face. I worry when I hear Republicans saying
they want to balance the budget by 2002. That says to me they do not
understand the problem. Our situation is so severe that it needs to be corrected *now*. By 2002 it will be too late. Even assuming that the current
politicians actually mean it, we have heard the same solemn resolve half
a dozen times since 1979. We have even had laws passed requiring balanced budgets. If they ever report a "balanced budget" we should all
insist on an independent audit to flush out the smoke and mirrors of Beltway accounting.

Republican talk, regulations, and requirements may be better than
Democratic ones, but we need a lot more fast.

Let's look at the big picture again if this seems shocking. Seemingly
permanent politcal structures around the world are fracturing. Who
could have conceived of a non-Liberal Democrat running Japan—much
less a Socialist? The parties that dominated Italy since World War II have
all been supplanted and/or disappeared. Look at what's happening in
Canada, Belgium, Sweden, and Mexico. During the Cold War, voters
around the world accepted a lot of nonsense as they were afraid to ask
too many questions. Serious changes in the status quo could lead to who
knew where.

The Cold War is over so people worldwide feel free to question old
assumptions.

Our system is so rotten, so corrupted and bloated with debt, obvious and disguised, that no matter what any politician does, it will become the focus of an immense crisis before the decade is over.

Our politicians, both Democrats and Republicans, have followed a policy of debasing and devaluing the dollar for years. It took the Romans four hundred years, the Spanish two hundred years, and the British seventy-five years to debase their currencies as much as we are debasing ours in a couple of decades. The people running the government don't care, and the Federal Reserve would rather save the politicians than save the currency. I don't see much hope for the dollar. Given what we'd seen as the consequences of weak currencies around the world, I expect a continued deterioration of our situation. We are going to hear the term "currency crisis" a lot more. The world won't end; after all Britain is still around, as is Spain, but they are now only shadows of their former selves. Britain was the richest, most powerful country in the world in 1920, but coined the term "brain drain" as early as the 1950s, when people began leaving.

We're now the largest debtor nation in the world. That would be okay if we were investing the money in productive assets, as we did in the nineteenth century, but it's all going into entitlements, welfare, agricultural subsidies for such crops as mohair and sugar, interest payments, tanks, and intercontinental missiles, none of which builds future productivity. Our troops still occupy Europe and Japan, over fifty years after the end of the Second World War, at a cost of $150 billion a year. Despite massive publicity about the foolishness of it, we still pay huge subsidies to our farmers when we should fly them to Siberia or Zaire instead. They'd all get rich!

Why, thirty years after the Pentagon has told Congress it doesn't want any more mohair, are we still spending $50 million a year on the stuff?

There are five thousand sugar growers in the United States. We spend approximately $5 billion annually to support sugar prices, which works out to roughly $1 million per sugar grower. We could save a fortune by going to each of those producers and saying, "Here's one hundred thousand dollars a year for life, a condominium at the beach, and a Porsche. The only thing we ask in return is that you never raise sugar again." A further irony is that, waste aside, the massive spending for the sugar-support program actually has a detrimental impact on our economy. Because of sugar price supports, 270 million consumers in the United States end up paying two to three times the world price for sugar. We're also ruining the economies of our Latin American allies because they can't sell us their natural product, sugar.

Why is this? Because there is a constituency for each of these programs—the sugar producers, the mohair producers, the defense industry, the military itself—walking up and down the halls of Congress to make sure the money keeps rolling in.

There are such an extraordinary number of cases like these that raising taxes to pay for such misguided, wasteful programs is lunacy. Eighteen-year-olds should be in the streets over these issues, for they are the ones who have the most to lose, who will suffer the most. We have guaranteed them a bankrupt future.

The chief concern of our government at this moment ought to be to cut needless spending in order to put our budget on a sound fiscal basis. The measures Chile has taken to put its economy in order ought to be lesson enough. If a country that was far more of a basket case than ours can pull itself up by its bootstraps in fifteen years, we ought to be able to do the same in less time—if we have the leadership and stamina to pull it off.

Should taxes then be cut? Yes, but the essential issue is not the level of taxes but the tax system itself. We need to completely change our tax structure, which penalizes savings and investment. If you're lucky enough to have a job, you pay taxes on the money you earn. If you then put some money in a bank or a mutual fund and earn interest or dividends, you pay taxes again. If you earn any capital gains on that investment, you pay taxes a third time.

The rest of the world doesn't do it that way. All the economies running circles around us—Japan, Germany, Singapore, and others—encourage savings and investment; they don't tax them. They tax consumption. We do just the opposite: We encourage consumption and we tax savings.

Our savings rate is 4 percent; the Japanese rate is five times this. More savings means more money for investment. More money for investment means more productivity. More productivity means an increasing standard of living—precisely what we've lacked for the past twenty-odd years.

Here's another dead-simple, easy-to-understand, natural law of economics: what you tax you get less of.

We need to change things in the United States. We must eliminate all taxes on savings and investments. We should junk the present tax code, which is several thousand pages long, and replace it with a flat tax. Huge money and energy in this country are devoted to wrestling with the tax code and avoiding taxes—at least 1 percent of our gross domestic product at a time when we're struggling to achieve a 2 percent rate of growth. We could have a five-page tax code and file our income taxes on a postcard. We should supplement the flat tax with a consumption tax, making it more expensive for people to spend than to save.

Then we should eliminate a host of wasteful government programs. Washington is spending enormous sums on tanks and missiles, which do absolutely nothing for future productivity, and on transfer payments, which also do nothing for productivity or the future of the country. Why aren't the eighteen-year-olds in the streets?

More radically, why allow congressmen to go to Washington, where as a group it's easy to lobby them? Let's make them stay in their home districts, conduct their meetings through video conferencing, and vote electronically. If lobbyists in this country had to go to 535 districts, our laws would be quite different. Wouldn't we be better off having the local banker, teacher, and plumber watch our congressman vote from our high-school gym rather than have lobbyists watch them in Washington? Plus we could eliminate the travel and staff waste built up around Congress in DC.

While we're at it, let's change the date of the elections to April fifteenth. It's no accident that November was chosen, the date six months before and six months after we pay our taxes. Let's select our politicians at the same time we're paying them—as we do everything else in life. We would all vote better if we realized how much our votes cost us.

A main tenet of my philosophy is that when you have a leak in your roof, you'd better fix it, as it's sure to cost you more later. Unfortunately, another lesson history teaches us is that little reform happens until it's forced on people. The air now is full of talk that fiscal reform isn't "politically feasible."

Given all this, what does the future actually hold for the United States? Given the real political, economic, and social world, what will happen?

Twenty years ago we could have afforded the luxury of "politically feasible" measures. However, our debt now is $5 trillion and rising by several hundred billion dollars a year. It's too late for moderate measures. We're coming to a time when only strong measures will stop the hemorrhaging. Even if we somehow balance the budget tomorrow, there's still the debt of trillions of dollars for someone to pay. It will kill the economy to cut spending further, so the sensible way to pay this down and put ourselves on a sound basis is through privatization, through selling off government assets such as our public lands, airports, seaports, and the post office. As an example, most of Nevada is owned by the government and could be sold. The list of assets we could sell is endless. The rest of the world is doing it; why not us? Wouldn't it be glorious to live in a debt-free country with a balanced budget?

If this sounds radical, all I can say is wait until everything collapses around us—that's really going to be radical. Eventually even the politicians are going to have to discuss these ideas because the country is sliding toward bankruptcy. As happens to all societies that keep their heads in the sand, the markets will force the issue upon us. Then it will be a lot more painful.

Simplistically, we'll encounter either an inflationary collapse or a deflationary collapse. Under the inflationary scenario, our government will print more money than it has assets to back it. Nobody will want the dollar. A dollar then won't buy 1.7 deutsche marks; it will buy half a mark.

Or, if the government doesn't overprint money, because of the enormous public debt there won't be enough money to fund building houses, businesses, and factories. We'll have deflation, some of which was felt in the early nineties in the U.S. with the collapse of residential and commercial real estate values. In a deflationary collapse, as in the Great Depression, asset values will fall because there won't be enough money to fund anything.

When Americans ask me to suggest solid currencies in which to invest, I mention the deutsche mark, the Dutch guilder, the Swiss franc, the Austrian schilling, the New Zealand dollar, and the Singapore dollar. Central banks' policies are tremendously important. The European currencies are tied to the German Bundesbank, whose mandate is to keep the mark hard. Our own Federal Reserve seems more interested in maintaining a short-term even keel than pulling into dock and overhauling our bloated, out-of-control monetary system.

Will our country survive? Sure. The Italians and the British haven't had their fiscal houses in order for decades, yet life there has gone on even if there hasn't been much *dolce* in their *vita*. In 1910, Argentina was the richest country in the Americas and yet by the Depression it had collapsed into poverty. Life was hard, but, yes, it has continued for sixty years.

If there's one thing I've learned in going around the world, it's that societies become rich, swagger around for a few years, decades, or centuries, and then their hour is done. The other thing I've learned is that even when all the wealth is gone, life goes on.

More important, I've also learned that if you've got a dream, you have to try it; you must get it out of your system. You will never get another chance.

If you want to change your life, do it.

APPENDIX I

*How We Packed for Our
Twenty-two-Month Motorcycle Trip*

CLOTHES

Jim:
> 5 shirts (2 business)
> 3 pairs underwear
> 3 pairs socks
> 2 bow ties
> 1 running shirt
> 1 pair of running shorts
> 1 jogger's watch

Tabitha:
> 4 cotton turtlenecks
> 3 washable silk blouses
> 3 pairs socks
> 4 pairs underwear
> 2 pairs tights
> 1 pair high heels
> 1 washable black silk dress
> 1 silk scarf to cover head in Muslim countries
> 1 sun hat

Each of us:
>3 pairs jeans*
>3 wool sweaters
>Motorcycle boots*
>Running shoes
>Foul weather gear
>Leather jacket* and chaps
>Helmet, goggles, and gloves
>Silk long underwear and a silk ski mask

EQUIPMENT AND SUPPLIES

>2 BMW motorcycles (an R100RT and an R80)
>Spare parts (tires, plugs, gaskets, etc.)
>Repair manuals and tools
>1 hand-cranked winch
>Small jerry cans for gasoline and water
>Shovel, bucket, bungee cords, ropes, and chains
>Shortwave radio (God bless the BBC!)
>3M super tape to repair everything from carburetors to windshields
>Camping, water-purification, and cooking gear
>Extra pair prescription eyeglasses
>Toiletries and sunscreen
>First-aid kits, anti-malaria pills, and antibiotics
>Sterile syringes, needles, and sutures
>Birth control pills and tampons, three-month supply
>Sewing kit for leather as well as cloth
>Guidebooks and maps (rarely available where you need them)
>Lots of passport photos for visa applications
>Stamp kit for forging entries in documents, I regret to say
>4 cassette tapes—*Eine kleine Nachtmusik,* Beethoven's Ninth Symphony, Mozart's Thirty-ninth and Forty-first symphonies, Willie Nelson's "On the Road Again," and the Fine Young Cannibals' "She Drives Me Crazy"
>Polaroid camera and film, to win friends in the wild
>200 $1 bills, useful for small purchases and as gifts
>50 Susan B. Anthony dollars as commemorative gifts
>Cigarettes and liquor with which to bribe border guards or whomever
>1 top-of-the-line Swiss army knife, used every day
>Tube of Loctite

*Doubled as Jim's dress-up wear for fancy hotels, restaurants, and business meetings

Appendix II

Daily Log

The way to read this log is a little complicated. We wrote it every morning as we were taking off. So the date is the date of *departure* from that place. For example, on April 5, 1990, we were in London, having left Oxford on the second.

COUNTRY	DATE	MILES	LOCAL REFERENCE
Ireland	28-Mar-90	0	Shannon Airport
	31-Mar-90	123	Aghadoe Heights Hotel, Killarney
	31-Mar-90	183	Dunquin post office
	01-Apr-90	320	Youghal, Avonmore House
	01-Apr-90	418	Ferry at Rosslare
United Kingdom	02-Apr-90	631	The Randolph Hotel, Oxford
	07-Apr-90	731	Cumberland Hotel, London
France	08-Apr-90	995	Paris Hilton
Germany	09-Apr-90	1,522	Arabella Hotel, Munich
Austria	11-Apr-90	1,696	Hotel Trend, Linz
Hungary	12-Apr-90	1,982	Forum Hotel, Budapest
Yugoslavia	13-Apr-90	2,238	Hotel Yugoslavia, Belgrade
	14-Apr-90	2,278	Hotel Yugoslavia, Belgrade

COUNTRY	DATE	MILES	LOCAL REFERENCE
Turkey	16-Apr-90	2,835	Klassis Hotel, Silivri
	17-Apr-90	3,178	Ankara Dedeman, Ankara
	19-Apr-90	3,357	Hotel Nevsehir Dedeman, Nevsehir
	20-Apr-90	3,669	Hotel Turban, Samsun
	21-Apr-90	3,890	Hotel Ozgur, Trabzon
	21-Apr-90	3,999	Turkish/Soviet border
Georgia	22-Apr-90	4,011	Intourist hotel, Batumi
	24-Apr-90	4,254	Hotel Iveria, Tbilisi
Azerbaijan	26-Apr-90	4,621	Hotel Azerbaijan, Baku
Turkmeniya	28-Apr-90	4,979	Hotel Ashkhabad, Ashkhabad
	30-Apr-90	5,203	Hotel Mary, Mary
Uzbekistan	02-May-90	5,451	Hotel Bukhara, Bukhara
	04-May-90	5,617	Hotel Samarkand, Samarkand
	06-May-90	5,803	Hotel Uzbekistan, Tashkent
Kazakhstan	07-May-90	5,995	Hotel Taraz, Dzhambul
Kyrgyzstan	08-May-90	6,166	Hotel Alatoo, Frunze
Kazakhstan	10-May-90	6,315	Hotel Otrar, Alma-Ata
	10-May-90	6,537	Soviet/China border
China	12-May-90	6,600	Friendship Hotel, Yining
	13-May-90	6,936	Shihezi Guest House, Shihezi
	15-May-90	7,151	Oasis Hotel, Turpan
	16-May-90	7,409	Hami Guest House, Hami
	18-May-90	7,670	Dunhuang Hotel, Dunhuang
	19-May-90	7,923	Jiuquan Hotel, Jiuquan
	20-May-90	8,210	Flying Horse Hotel, Wuwei
	22-May-90	8,390	Friendship Hotel, Lanzhou
	23-May-90	8,641	Pingliang Hotel, Pingliang
	26-May-90	8,835	Golden Flower Hotel, Xi'an
	27-May-90	9,081	Friendship Guest House, Luoyang
	28-May-90	9,196	International Hotel Henen, Zhengzhou
	29-May-90	9,452	Hebei Guest House, Shijiazhuang
	29-May-90	9,634	Arrived at Capitol Hotel, Beijing
Japan	06-Jun-90	9,691	Fukuda Motors, Shinjuku, Tokyo
	07-Jun-90	9,892	Okura Hotel, Niigata
	08-Jun-90	10,135	Fukuda Motors, Shinjuku, Tokyo
	08-Jun-90	10,166	Osambashi Pier, Yokohama
Siberia	12-Jun-90	10,169	Arrived in Nakhodka
	17-Jun-90	10,210	Hotel Nakhodka, Nakhodka
	18-Jun-90	10,364	Hotel Ussuriysk, Ussuriysk
	19-Jun-90	10,524	Hotel Spassk-Dal'niy, Spassk-Dal'niy
	23-Jun-90	10,807	Intourist Hotel, Khabarovsk
	25-Jun-90	10,929	Hotel Vostok, Birobidzhan
	26-Jun-90	11,037	Hotel Berioska, Obluch'ye
	28-Jun-90	11,289	Hotel Drusba, Blagoveshchensk
	29-Jun-90	11,387	Hotel Zeja, Svobodny

COUNTRY	DATE	MILES	LOCAL REFERENCE
	30-Jun-90	11,550	Hotel Tayoznyay, Shimanovsk
	02-Jul-90	11,551	Flatcar, Chernyshevsk
	05-Jul-90	11,808	Hotel Zabalkalye, Chita
	06-Jul-90	12,106	Hotel Siberia, Petrovsk-Zabaykalskiy
	07-Jul-90	12,246	Hotel Oktybryaskya, Ulan-Ude
	10-Jul-90	12,314	Hotel Oktybryaskya, Ulan-Ude
	11-Jul-90	12,531	Hotel Baikal, Baykal'sk
	14-Jul-90	12,649	Hotel Emnteka, Irkutsk
	15-Jul-90	12,763	Hotel Cedar, Ceremkhovo
	17-Jul-90	12,860	Sports complex, Zima
	18-Jul-90	13,021	Hotel Taiga, Nizhneudinsk
	19-Jul-90	13,227	Hotel Siberia, Kansk
	20-Jul-90	13,484	Ceramic Company Hostel, Achinsk
	21-Jul-90	13,709	Hotel Kuzbass, Kemerovo
	24-Jul-90	13,872	Hotel Central, Novosibirsk
	27-Jul-90	13,909	Hotel Novosibirsk, Novosibirsk
	28-Jul-90	14,183	Village Theatre, Novokarasuk
	29-Jul-90	14,418	Campsite south of Omsk
Kazakhstan	30-Jul-90	14,628	Hotel Kaziljar, Petropavlovsk
Siberia	31-Jul-90	14,960	Campsite on Petrovski State Farm, e. of Chelyabinsk
European Russia	31-Jul-90	15,069	Crossed the Europe/Asia boundary
	04-Aug-90	15,265	Hotel Rossia, Ufa
	10-Aug-90	15,545	Hotel Orenburg, Orenburg
	12-Aug-90	15,768	Hotel Buzuluk, Buzuluk
	14-Aug-90	15,992	Hotel Volga, Tol'yatti
	16-Aug-90	16,232	Hotel Penza, Penza
	17-Aug-90	16,528	Hotel Lovech, Ryazan
	26-Aug-90	16,691	Sport Hotel, Moscow
	27-Aug-90	16,953	Hotel Rossia, Smolensk
Belorussia	29-Aug-90	17,179	Hotel Tourist, Minsk
	31-Aug-90	17,436	Hotel Druzba, Zadvortsi (Brest)
Poland	31-Aug-90	17,446	Crossed Soviet/Polish border
	02-Sep-90	17,570	Marriot, Warsaw
	03-Sep-90	17,572	Holiday Inn, Warsaw
	04-Sep-90	17,759	Hotel Poznan, Poznan
	04-Sep-90	17,878	Crossed Polish/German border
Germany	10-Sep-90	17,949	Hotel California, Berlin
	16-Sep-90	18,204	Toni Frank's house, Neustadt an der Waldnaab
	19-Sep-90	18,337	Marriott Hotel, Munich
	20-Sep-90	18,597	Home of H. and K. Krahmer, Glashütten
	21-Sep-90	18,690	Hyatt Hotel, Cologne
France	23-Sep-90	19,100	Hotel du Park, Chantilly
	24-Sep-90	19,138	Hotel de Longchamps, Paris

COUNTRY	DATE	MILES	LOCAL REFERENCE
United Kingdom	26-Sep-90	19,402	28 Ovington Square (Oxbridge Apts., London)
	27-Sep-90	19,590	Hyatt Regency, Birmingham
Ireland	29-Sep-90	19,767	Berkeley Court Hotel, Dublin
	29-Sep-90	19,994	Arrived again at post office in Dunquin
	30-Sep-90	20,007	Benners Hotel, Dingle
	01-Oct-90	20,241	Cedars Hotel, Rosslare
United Kingdom	14-Oct-90	20,505	John and Linda Hammerbeck's, London
Germany	15-Oct-90	20,800	Hotel Drees, Dortmund
	16-Oct-90	20,811	WUDO BMW, Dortmund
Netherlands	18-Oct-90	20,965	Holiday Inn, Amsterdam
Germany	19-Oct-90	21,311	Pension Ikarus, Düsseldorf
	20-Oct-90	21,529	National Hotel, Frankfurt
Switzerland	22-Oct-90	21,800	Hans and Jill Aebi's, Küssnacht am Rigi
	23-Oct-90	21,836	Nova Park Hotel, Zurich
	24-Oct-90	21,905	Steinengraben Hotel, Basel
France	25-Oct-90	22,335	Hotel Mercure, Marseille
	26-Oct-90	22,339	Napoleon Ferry, across Mediterranean
Tunisia	01-Nov-90	22,364	Hotel Africa Meridien, Tunis
	06-Nov-90	22,377	Hotel Abou Nawas, Gammarth
Algeria	07-Nov-90	22,568	Aigle Hotel, Tébessa
	11-Nov-90	22,950	Hotel El Aurassi, Algiers
	12-Nov-90	23,135	Hotel Senalba, Djelfa
	15-Nov-90	23,323	Hotel Rostimedes, Ghardaia
	16-Nov-90	23,743	Hotel Tidikelt, In Salah
	17-Nov-90	23,919	Palmieri camp ground, Arak
	05-Dec-90	24,284	Hotel Tahat, Tamanrasset
	06-Dec-90	24,359	Camp in Sahara
	07-Dec-90	24,467	Camp in Sahara at 125-km post
	08-Dec-90	24,543	Camp at In Guezzam
Niger	09-Dec-90	24,562	Camp at Assamakka
	11-Dec-90	24,770	Auberge Caravane, Arlit
	12-Dec-90	25,036	House in Aderbissinat
	14-Dec-90	25,273	Hotel Amadou Kourandaga, Zinder
Nigeria	16-Dec-90	25,484	Hotel Central, Kano
	17-Dec-90	25,860	Hotel Deribe, Maiduguri
	18-Dec-90	26,066	Border post, Kerawa (Nigeria-Cameroon)
Cameroon	19-Dec-90	26,080	Customs House in Kolofata (Nigeria-Cameroon)
	28-Dec-90	26,505	Maroua Palace Hotel, Maroua
	29-Dec-90	26,649	Hotel La Benoue, Garoua
	30-Dec-90	26,932	Jeunnesse Hotel, Meiganga

COUNTRY	DATE	MILES	LOCAL REFERENCE
C.A.R.	31-Dec-90	27,004	Camp at Central African Rep border, Béloka
	23-Jan-91	27,710	Novotel, Bangui
	04-Feb-91	27,710	The Sangha and the Fleuve Congo (rivers)
	18-Feb-91	27,990	Meridien, M'Bamou Palace, and Hotel Cosmos, Brazzaville
Zaire	23-Feb-91	28,152	Intercontinental Hotel, Kinshasa
	24-Feb-91	28,493	U.S. Services' Guest House, Kikwit
	25-Feb-91	28,592	Catholic mission, Idiofa
	26-Feb-91	28,631	Uncompleted maternity clinic, Mukoko
	27-Feb-91	28,712	Catholic mission, Mapangu
	07-Mar-91	28,779	Hotel du Palme, Ilebo
	15-Mar-91	28,779	Flatcar 16535-3, Tenke
	16-Mar-91	28,940	Sheraton Karavia, Lubumbashi
Zambia	17-Mar-91	29,058	Hotel Edinburgh, Kitwe
	20-Mar-91	29,290	Hotel Intercontinental, Lusaka
	22-Mar-91	29,594	Musi-O-Tunya Intercontinental, Livingstone
Zimbabwe	23-Mar-91	29,596	Victoria Falls Hotel, Victoria Falls
	25-Mar-91	29,718	Ivory Lodge, Hwange National Park
	26-Mar-91	30,066	Kadoma Ranch Motel, Kadoma
	29-Mar-91	30,156	Sheraton Hotel, Harare
	30-Mar-91	30,356	Great Zimbabwe Hotel, Masvingo
Botswana	31-Mar-91	30,670	Thapama Lodge, Francistown
	02-Apr-91	30,947	Sheraton, Gabarone
South Africa	06-Apr-91	31,193	Humphry Mullard's house, Johannesburg
	07-Apr-91	31,498	Hotel Kimberlite, Kimberley
	11-Apr-91	32,129	Cape Sun Hotel, Cape Town
	12-Apr-91	32,822	Home of Tony and Sue Sparg, Knysna
	13-Apr-91	32,844	Home of Martin and Caroline Kennard, Grahamstown
	15-Apr-91	33,473	Home of Humphry and Serenity Mullard, Johannesburg, (then to Nairobi, Mauritius, and Singapore)
Australia	29-Apr-91	33,479	Perth Airport
	29-Apr-91	33,511	Perth Hilton, Perth
	30-Apr-91	33,780	Ocean Centre Hotel, Geraldton
	02-May-91	34,124	Fascine Lodge, Carnarvon
	03-May-91	34,749	Pardoo Road House, Pardoo
	04-May-91	35,038	Cable Beach Club, Broome
	06-May-91	35,694	Hotel Kununurra, Kununurra
	08-May-91	36,216	Hotel Beaufort, Darwin
	09-May-91	36,413	Katherine Hotel, Katherine

COUNTRY	DATE	MILES	LOCAL REFERENCE
	10-May-91	36,910	Wycliffe Roadhouse, Wycliffe Well
	11-May-91	37,443	Sheraton Ayers Rock, Yulara
	12-May-91	37,720	Sheraton Alice Springs, Alice Springs
	13-May-91	38,049	Three Ways Road House, Three Ways
	14-May-91	38,601	Gannon's Motel, Julia Creek
	17-May-91	38,862	Sheraton Casino, Townsville
	20-May-91	39,119	Hilton International Hotel, Cairns
	21-May-91	39,395	Relax Motel, Home Hill
	22-May-91	40,058	Great Eastern Motor Inn, Gympie
	23-May-91	40,486	Canute and Sally Meyers', Nambucca Heads
	25-May-91	40,819	Sheraton Wentworth, Sydney
	26-May-91	41,133	Halfway Motor Inn, Tarcutta
	27-May-91	41,458	Erik and Sue Val Meyers', Corio
	28-May-91	41,524	On board the Abel Tasman Ferry, Devonport
	29-May-91	41,793	Sheraton Hobart Hotel, Hobart
	30-May-91	41,918	International Hotel, Launceston
	31-May-91	41,985	On board the Abel Tasman Ferry, Melbourne
	01-Jun-91	42,011	Patrick and Cathy Moore's, Hawthorn
	02-Jun-91	42,315	Hotel Genoa, Genoa
	03-Jun-91	42,652	Sheraton Wentworth, Sydney
New Zealand	06-Jun-91	42,656	Auckland International Airport, Auckland
	07-Jun-91	42,781	Takapura International Motorlodge, Auckland
	08-Jun-91	43,031	Waiouru Welcome Inn, Waiouru
	09-Jun-91	43,201	Aldan Lodge Motel, Picton
	10-Jun-91	43,439	Mana Hotel, Wellington
	11-Jun-91	43,865	Holeshot BMW (Auckland Sheraton), Auckland
Argentina	25-Jun-91	43,865	Río Gallegos Airport, Río Gallegos
	03-Jul-91	43,871	Río Costa Apart Hotel, Río Gallegos
	04-Jul-91	44,092	Residencial Sada, San Julián
	05-Jul-91	44,354	Comodoro Hotel, Comodoro Rivadavia
	07-Jul-91	44,629	Hotel Peninsula Valdes, Puerto Madryn
	08-Jul-91	45,042	Hotel Austral, Bahía Blanca
	09-Jul-91	45,297	Gran Hotel Azul, Azul
	03-Aug-91	45,491	Sheraton and Embassy Apart Hotel, Buenos Aires
Uruguay	04-Aug-91	45,496	Hotel El Mirador, Colonia del Sacramento

COUNTRY	DATE	MILES	LOCAL REFERENCE
	06-Aug-91	45,615	Victoria Plaza Hotel, Montevideo
	10-Aug-91	45,703	Zelmira Pena's Condo, Punta del Este
	11-Aug-91	45,911	Gran Hotel Flores, Trinidad
Argentina	12-Aug-91	46,058	Nuevo Hotel Plaza, Colón
	13-Aug-91	46,319	Hotel Comedor, San Francisco
	15-Aug-91	46,451	Crillon Hotel, Córdoba
	17-Aug-91	46,465	Sanatorio Diquecito, La Calera
	18-Aug-91	46,633	Hosteria Quines, Quines
	21-Aug-91	46,885	Hotel Plaza, Mendoza
	22-Aug-91	46,993	Hosteria Puente del Inca, Puente del Inca
Chile	31-Aug-91	47,103	Holiday Inn Crowne Plaza, Santiago
	01-Sep-91	47,269	Hotel Cesar, Zapallar
	02-Sep-91	47,599	Hosteria Vallenar, Vallenar
	03-Sep-91	48,047	Hotel Antofagasta, Antofagasta
	05-Sep-91	48,495	Hotel St. Gregory, Arica
Peru	06-Sep-91	48,636	Hostal de Turistas, Moquegua
	07-Sep-91	48,964	Hostal de La Union, Atico
	08-Sep-91	49,216	Las Dumas, Içá (then to Lima, for a side trip to: La Paz, Lake Titicaca, Cuzco, Machu Picchu, Cuzco, and back to Lima)
	17-Sep-91	49,408	Sheraton, Lima
	18-Sep-91	49,587	Hotel de Turistas, Huarmey
	19-Sep-91	50,024	Hotel de Turistas, Piura
Ecuador	20-Sep-91	50,315	Residencial el Oro, Naranjal (then to Guayaquil, side trip to the Galápagos)
	27-Sep-91	50,373	Hotel Oro Verde, Guayaquil
	30-Sep-91	50,632	Alameda Real, Quito
Colombia	01-Oct-91	50,852	Hotel Morasurco, Pasto
	02-Oct-91	51,087	Intercontinental, Cali
	03-Oct-91	51,258	Hotel Ambala, Ibagué
	04-Oct-91	51,397	Hotel Tequendama, Bogotá
Panama	07-Oct-91	51,423	Marriott, Panama City
	08-Oct-91	51,695	Hotel Fiesta, David
Costa Rica	10-Oct-91	51,945	Aurola Holiday Inn, San José
	11-Oct-91	52,140	Cabinas Santa Rita, La Cruz
Nicaragua	12-Oct-91	52,240	Hotel Intercontinental, Managua
Honduras	13-Oct-91	52,421	Hotel Miramar, San Lorenzo
El Salvador	15-Oct-91	52,574	Camino Real, San Salvador
Guatemala	17-Oct-91	52,732	El Conquistador Hotel, Guatemala City
	18-Oct-91	52,757	Hotel Antigua, Antigua
Mexico	19-Oct-91	53,104	Hotel Ik Lumaal, Arriaga
	20-Oct-91	53,373	Hotel Victoria, Oaxaca

COUNTRY	DATE	MILES	LOCAL REFERENCE
	22-Oct-91	53,594	Hotel Aristos, Puebla
	23-Oct-91	53,880	Hotel Tancachil, Ozuluama
	24-Oct-91	54,233	Hotel Del Prado, Matamoros
USA	25-Oct-91	54,493	Edna Inn Motel, Edna, Texas
	29-Oct-91	54,723	Wyndham Warwick Hotel, Houston
	31-Oct-91	55,075	Royal Orleans, New Orleans
	02-Nov-91	55,367	Holiday Inn, Tuscaloosa, Alabama
	07-Nov-91	55,470	Parents' home, Demopolis, Alabama
	08-Nov-91	55,577	Radisson Inn, Montgomery
	09-Nov-91	55,683	Hampton Inn, Birmingham
	10-Nov-91	55,864	University Inn, Atlanta
	11-Nov-91	56,094	Holiday Inn, Charlotte
	12-Nov-91	56,306	Holiday Inn, Johnson City, Tennessee
	13-Nov-91	56,591	Cavalier at the University, Charlottesville, Virginia
	15-Nov-91	56,714	Steve Rogers' guest apartment, Fairfax, Virginia
	17-Nov-91	56,899	Wayne Hotel, Wayne, Pennsylvania
	17-Nov-91	57,020	Back home, New York
	31-Jul-92	57,020	Leaving home, New York
	01-Aug-92	57,327	Millers Motel, DuBois, Pennsylvania
	02-Aug-92	57,848	Marriott O'Hare, Chicago
	03-Aug-92	58,318	Prairie Winds Motel, Jackson, Minnesota
	04-Aug-92	58,796	Quality Inn, Rapid City, South Dakota
	05-Aug-92	58,846	Home of Spencer Paulson, Sturgis, South Dakota
	06-Aug-92	59,204	Comfort Inn, Cody, Wyoming
	07-Aug-92	59,431	Yellowstone Motor Inn, Livingston, Montana
	08-Aug-92	59,804	Desert Mountain Guest Ranch, Hungry Horse, Montana
Canada	09-Aug-92	60,146	Mountaineer Lodge, Lake Louise, Alberta
	10-Aug-92	60,541	Coast Inn of the North, Prince George, British Columbia
	11-Aug-92	60,931	Pink Mountain Motor Inn, Pink Mountain, British Columbia
	12-Aug-92	61,230	Muncho Lake Lodge, Muncho Lake, British Columbia
	13-Aug-92	61,566	Hilstead's Lake Resort and Shell, Teslin, Yukon
	14-Aug-92	61,872	Talbot Arms Motel, Destruction Bay, Yukon
USA	15-Aug-92	62,190	Chistochina Trading Post, Chistochina, Alaska

COUNTRY	DATE	MILES	LOCAL REFERENCE
	16-Aug-92	62,430	Captain Cook Hotel, Anchorage
	20-Aug-92	62,661	Chistochina Trading Post, Chistochina, Alaska
Canada	22-Aug-92	63,198	M.V. Matanueka, Prince Rupert
	23-Aug-92	63,202	Highline Hotel, Prince Rupert
	24-Aug-92	63,208	Pioneer Inn, Port Hardy
	25-Aug-92	63,467	Le Meridian, Vancouver
USA	26-Aug-92	63,513	Olympic Lodge, Port Angeles, Washington
	27-Aug-92	63,895	Embarcadero, Newport, Oregon
	28-Aug-92	64,076	Best Western Medford Inn, Medford, Oregon
	29-Aug-92	64,222	Sandy Bar Ranch, Orleans, California
	30-Aug-92	64,620	Alfa Inn, San Francisco
	31-Aug-92	64,971	Len & Marianne Baker, Palo Alto, California
	31-Aug-92	65,067	Shipping Depot, San Francisco, for shipment to Barber Motorcycle Museum, Birmingham, Alabama

INDEX

ABOUT THE TYPE

This book was set in Sabon, a typeface designed by the well-known German typographer Jan Tschichold (1902-74). Sabon's design is based on the original letterforms of Claude Garamond and was created specifically to be used for three sources: foundry type for hand composition, Linotype, and Monotype. Tschichold named his typeface for the famous Frankfurt typefounder Jacques Sabon, who died in 1580.